W9-DEX-541

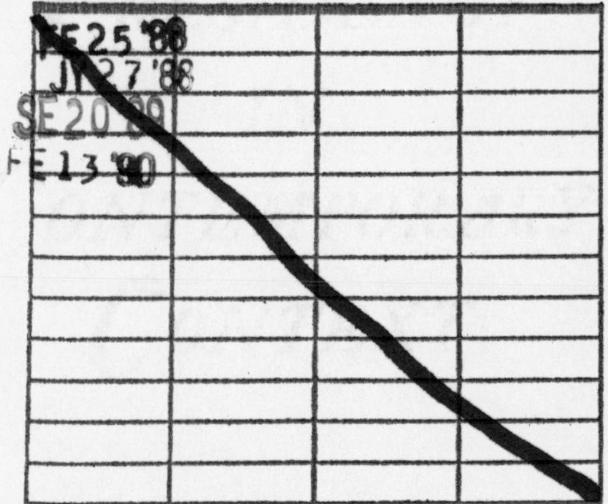
DATE DUE
SE 25 '88
JY 27 '88
SE 20 '89
FE 13 '90

LIBRARY OF CONGRESS CATALOG CARD NUMBER: 74-26166
ISBN: 0-396-07105-8

PRINTED IN THE UNITED STATES OF AMERICA
DESIGNED BY LIBRA GRAPHICS, INC.

THE PRESIDENCY IN CONTEMPORARY CONTEXT

EDITED BY

NORMAN C. THOMAS
University of Cincinnati

DODD, MEAD & COMPANY
New York 1975

Contents

Preface

Newly developed perspectives and approaches to the study of the presidency—approaches developed since 1960—when added to the vast body of existing studies and the continuation of traditional lines of inquiry, have produced an expanded capacity of scholars to explain and evaluate presidential performance, developments in the presidency, and the interaction between the man and the office. Nevertheless, from the great number of biographies, accounts of former participant-observers of the workings of the presidency, scholarly articles, essays by journalists, political actors, and academics, textbooks, treatises, and anthologies there emerge only a limited number of options for the instructor organizing a course on the presidency. Much of the material is either so outdated as to be of little use or of primarily historical significance. Recent changes in the structure and functioning of the presidential office (e.g., Reorganization Plan No. 2 of 1970, issues concerning the president's power vis-à-vis Congress, the president's relations with the press, the current political and leadership context in which the president must operate) are not analyzed, or they are treated from the perspectives of the early 1960s and before. Even such incisive and stimulating discussions as are found in Richard E. Neustadt's *Presidential Power* (1960) and in James M. Burns's *Presidential Government* (1965) require supplementation with more recent illustrations and analyses. Furthermore, with only a few notable exceptions, much of what is available is heavily historical-descriptive in approach and devoid of the theoretical concerns of empirical political science.

In preparing this book, I have sought to close this gap. Its distinguishing feature is its contemporary content, combined with a variety of methodological approaches. It excludes all of the classic scholarly articles and historic documents, none of the selections having been published prior to 1969. It is an attempt to examine through contemporary materials some of the most pressing questions about presidential power and leadership arising in the continuous development of the office. Even so, the rapid pace of events involving and affecting the presidency since the uncovering of the Watergate affair in April, 1973, has overtaken many of the selections. Indeed, so much has happened so quickly that my objective, as editor, to impart a highly topical tone to the book has suffered greatly. I will attempt to extrapolate from the themes articulated and the illustrations employed in the selections to the most recent developments, but the reader will undoubtedly have to proceed a considerable distance on his own.

The organization of the book is quite straightforward. Part I presents two overviews of the presidency, one from the standpoint of constitutional provisions regarding it and the other in terms of contemporary scholarly analysis and evaluation. These selections should provide a clear picture of recent and prospective changes in the formal constitutional status of the presidency and of the sharp shift in recent academic thought and consideration of the office. Part II provides a set of perspectives on the president as the nation's leading political figure. Part III focuses on the operational dynamics of the presidency. Part IV examines the president's policy-making activities.

I would like to give special recognition to my colleague and sometime collaborator, Thomas E. Cronin, for his valuable suggestions and assistance in developing the project. I am also grateful to Mr. William Oman, Vice President of Dodd, Mead and Company for his confidence in the idea behind the book and his support and encouragement.

Norman C. Thomas

THE PRESIDENCY IN CONTEMPORARY CONTEXT

Introduction

In the course of studying and teaching about the American presidency, I have been impressed with the disparity between the great quantity of published works that treat the subject and the limited availability of materials suitable for classroom purposes. This gap appears to be due, to a considerable degree, to three factors: the numerous changes and developments in American society during the years since 1960 and accompanying related changes in the presidential office; the recent academic and public reappraisals of the office, its powers, and the political roles of the president; and a shift in the perspectives and the methodological orientation of political scientists who study presidents and the presidency. A brief examination of these factors will provide an indication of the considerations that guided me in preparing this volume.

Since the inauguration of President John F. Kennedy in January, 1961, four major developments in American society and politics have profoundly affected the ways in which scholars and journalists view presidents and the presidency. To a lesser degree, the perspectives of the mass public also appear to have been altered. The developments to which I refer—each a series of events extending over time—are the Vietnam war, the increased incidence of political violence and nonconventional forms of protest, the modified agenda of domestic politics that has emerged following the legislative triumphs of the mid-1960s, and the Watergate affair and its aftermath. To a considerable degree, these developments appear to have been interrelated.

The Vietnam war had its origins in the closing days of World War II and still loomed large on the political landscape at the second inaugural of President Richard Nixon. However, it did not become a center-stage factor in American politics until 1964, when President Lyndon B. Johnson obtained congressional authority in the Gulf of Tonkin Resolution to engage in all military operations necessary "to repel any armed attack against the forces of the United States and to prevent further aggression." The subsequent escalation of American involvement into a ground war in Southeast Asia, and heavy and protracted air and naval bombardment over all of Vietnam, Laos, and Cambodia, led to the longest, most frustrating, and least successful war in American history. The war was accompanied by the most vigorous and violent protests ever lodged against an American military operation. It occupied much of the attention and energy of Presidents Johnson and Nixon, and embroiled each of them in protracted controversy with powerful members of Congress. The presidential-congressional conflict over the war resulted in a sustained debate concerning the respective constitutional roles of the two branches of government in making foreign policy. Furthermore, the prolonged effort to bring the war to a satisfactory settlement called into question both the efficacy of the processes for formulating national security policy and the goals of that policy.

The war also had an extensive effect on the economy and on funding for federal domestic programs. The persistent inflation that has plagued the economy since 1966 owes its origins in large part to excess demand generated by war-related spending. The balance of payments deficit, a serious and nagging economic problem, was greatly aggravated by the flow of money to Southeast Asia. These economic difficulties in turn reduced the public sector resources available for domestic programs, thus limiting the ability of the federal government to deal with serious social and economic problems.

Already it is apparent that this discussion has moved away from the war itself and is ranging over major problems that confront the nation and its political leaders. This is not to argue that all of the nation's troubles stem from the Vietnam war, but rather to demonstrate that the war profoundly affected social, economic, and political life in the United States. Much of what the president must deal with in the 1970s is either directly or indirectly, at least in part, a consequence of the war.

The sharp rise in the incidence of political violence and nonconventional forms of protest is the second development since 1960 that has changed our thinking about the presidency. In part, the violence and protest were directed at and spurred by the war; but they have also been a reaction to intractable social and economic problems and an outburst against injustices, and they have resulted, additionally, from the irrational actions of psychologically disturbed individuals. Assassinations, anomic urban riots, bombings, physical combat between demonstrators and police have contributed to and become part of a climate in which the politics of bargaining and negotiation has given ground to the politics of confrontation and demands. The ability to induce people to reason together toward a consensus has been joined by an iron will as essential elements of effective political leadership. The alteration in the political climate and in modes of political actions has also had a nonviolent side. Civil disobedience and nonviolent protests (e.g., sit-ins) expanded as certain groups found the traditional channels of political action to be ineffective or, in some instances, closed to them. Even though there has been a perceptible cooling of the new politics in the last few years, the political climate has been permanently modified by the events of the 1960s. The expectation of violence is manifestly higher, and the willingness of individuals and groups to resort to it or to nonelectoral forms of political action has increased sharply. For example, in December, 1973, several hundred truck drivers blocked key interstate highways to protest reduced speed limits, shortages of diesel fuel, and price gouging resulting from the energy crisis. In spite of periods of relative tranquility, American politics promises to be more volatile and unstable in the future.

The third major development since 1960 has been the transformation of the domestic political scene that followed the legislative successes of President Johnson in the period 1964–66. The passage of the Civil Rights Act of 1964, the Voting Rights Act of 1965, and the statutes that authorized the programs of the Great Society * brought to a conclusion simultaneously two of the principal continuing concerns of domestic politics in the post-World War II period: the struggle of black Americans for legal and political equality, and the uncompleted agenda of reform inherited from the New and Fair Deals. The legal-political phase of the civil rights movement ended with congressional affirmation of the racial equality guaranteed by the Constitution and previously adjudicated in the federal courts. The completion of the major reform items left from the Roosevelt and Truman eras terminated over a quarter-century of liberal frustration at the hands of congressional conservatives. Many liberals sincerely believed the legislation would provide the basis for positive governmental action that would quickly lead to social and economic equality for blacks, the elimination of poverty and dependency, and the rejuvenation of America's blighted and decaying cities.

The transformation in domestic politics began as the federal government moved to implement the Great Society legislation. Black Americans and federal officials quickly learned that full legal and political rights were no guarantee of social and economic democracy. The white majority that had sympathized with the drive to desegregate schools and public accommodations and to open up polling places has proved to be either hostile toward or uninterested in such administratively determined goals as racially balanced schools, integrated neighborhoods, and affirmative action to secure employment for minorities. Appeals to antiblack, antiwelfare sentiments and fears of the "silent majority" have become a powerful weapon in the hands of politicians seeking office. In the meantime, congressional and academic liberals have discovered that poverty, economic dependency, and urban decay are problems that will not yield to the infusion of several billion federal dollars a year into the estab-

---

* The Economic Opportunity Act of 1964, the Elementary and Secondary Education Act of 1965, the Medicare Act of 1965, and the Model Cities Act of 1966 constituted the major legislation.

lished educational and welfare systems and into local and state governmental agencies. Not only has the amount of money appropriated by Congress been insufficient to accomplish these objectives, but the ability of government to do so without a radical restructuring of society and the economy has been questioned with increasing frequency by liberal spokesmen. Still, the scope and intensity of demands for federal funds has been increasing. Under these circumstances, domestic politics is characterized by the absence of any strong, identifiable sense of basic purpose and by multiple cleavages along racial, religious, occupational, and class lines. The politics of conflict calls for different leadership skills from the politics of consensus, and public expectations of presidential performance are more demanding. Yet the ability of individual presidents and the presidency to meet these challenges is by no means assured, in part because of the changes that monumental secular developments have wrought in the presidency and the political system.

One of the most notable of these changes, the loss of credibility suffered by recent presidents and the reduction of public trust in government, is also associated with the fourth major development—the Watergate affair and its aftermath. The 1972 Democratic presidential nominee, Senator George McGovern, was unable to convert the bugging of the Democratic party's national headquarters in the Watergate apartment complex by operatives of the Committee to Reelect the President into a vote-getting issue. Throughout the 1972 campaign, journalists repeatedly quoted voters as saying that they expected such behavior in politics and that they assumed that the Democrats were engaged in it also, the only difference being that they had not been caught. Whether this reflected increased sophistication or expanded cynicism on the part of the public is a matter of question, but probably both explanations are partly valid.

The significant consequences of the Watergate break-in did not develop until the spring and summer of 1973, when two *Washington Post* reporters, a federal grand jury, and a select Senate committee uncovered a wide pattern of improper and illegal activities by members of the White House staff, other government officials, and political supporters of the president. Charges of President Nixon's involvement in the affair and a bizarre series of attempts to establish his innocence resulted in a precipitous drop in his popularity (as measured in public opinion polls), demands for his resignation by members of Congress and influential news organs, and the initiation of formal impeachment proceedings in the House of Representatives.

Congressional and judicial proceedings involving President Nixon reached their climax in the summer of 1974. On July 24, the Supreme Court ruled unanimously against the president's claim of an unqualified executive privilege as grounds for withholding evidence (tapes of presidential conversations and various documents) relevant to the criminal trial of some of his former aides on charges arising from the Watergate affair. On July 27, 29, and 30, the House Judiciary Committee adopted, with bipartisan majorities, three articles of impeachment charging the president with obstruction of justice, abuse of presidential powers, and contempt of Congress.

As the House of Representatives prepared for debate on the articles, the passage of which by substantial majorities seemed certain, President Nixon released additional transcripts of conversations with his former aide, H. R. Haldeman, which clearly implicated him in the cover-up of the Watergate break-in. In an accompanying statement, the president acknowledged that he had withheld the evidence from his staff, his counsel, and the House Judiciary Committee. This startling development led to the dissolution of most of his support in Congress and a sharp increase in public demands for his removal from office. Under mounting pressure from his staff and Republican congressional leaders, Richard M. Nixon resigned the presidency on August 9 and Vice-President Gerald R. Ford became the nation's thirty-eighth president.

As Nixon became the nation's first chief executive to resign from office, so Ford became the first person to succeed to the office without having been elected. (Ford had been chosen as vice-president under the provisions of the Twenty-fifth Amendment, following the resignation of Spiro T. Agnew in October, 1973.) The impact of these events and of the Watergate affair on the presidency and on American politics is not yet fully apparent.

The altered political climate since 1960 has been marked by a change in the character of presidential leadership. Charismatic figures such as Roosevelt, Eisenhower, and Kennedy have given way to less heroic men such as Johnson, Humphrey, Nixon, and Ford, all of whom have been successful party functionaries. Whether the shift from charismatic to more technocratic leaders has been caused by public preferences or because none of the former have emerged and presented themselves is not clear, but it has been accompanied, quite expectedly, by lowered presidential popularity. It has also been marked, in the cases of Johnson and Nixon, by increased physical isolation of the president from the public and from other participants in the national policy-making process. The isolation of these two presidents assumed different forms and had multiple causes, but in each instance it led commentators to compare the presidency to a medieval English court with the president as an elected monarch.

Although presidential popularity has waned, presidential power has expanded. Presidents Johnson and Nixon both successfully challenged Congress through the assertion of the doctrine of executive privilege, the impoundment of appropriated funds, and use of the pocket veto.* The paramountcy of the president in national security policy has been maintained, indeed enhanced, in spite of the efforts of congressional doves to force a conclusion of the Vietnam war. (The enactment over President Nixon's veto in late 1973 of legislation restricting the president's powers as commander in chief and the Budget Reform Act of 1974 may have signaled a reversal to these trends. However, some commentators have questioned whether the new statutes will constitute effective limitations of presidential authority.) The seeming paradox of expanding power and declining popularity indicates that presidential power lies in the office rather than in the individual who occupies it. But it is up to the president to tap the power and utilize it. Increasingly in recent years, this has been done through staffing, management, and bureaucratization instead of through the application of charm, persuasion, and manipulative interpersonal relations, although President Johnson employed both approaches.

Certainly the years since 1960 have seen the presidency grow in size and in the scope of its operations. Scholars and politicians have become aware of the distinction between the man and the office, and presidents have discovered new uses they can make of the institution that they head. There has been, then, an expansion of institutional functions and powers that has paralleled the diminution of the public personage (in terms of popularity) of the president. It may well be, however, that this is only a temporary phenomenon and not a long-range trend.

Whatever the causes, the growth in the presidential office and its powers has been accompanied by changes in the relative importance of several of the roles that the president has traditionally performed in national politics. The president's responsibilities as chief administrator, commander in chief, and chief diplomat have grown in importance with the Vietnam war and the growth of federal domestic programs. The reduced importance of his roles as party chief and as public leader has been compensated for by the addition to the White House staff of special operatives who act as political surrogates for the president and of specialists in mass communications who manage his relations with the press and are responsible for shaping and maintaining his image. The only two major roles that appear unchanged in importance, chief of state and

---

* President Nixon sustained his challenges to Congress in these areas until the last months of his administration. However, in June, 1974, Congress passed a Budget Reform Act that limited presidential authority to impound money appropriated by Congress. Also, as noted above, in July, 1974, the Supreme Court rejected Nixon's claims of an unqualified doctrine of executive privilege. Finally, on August 14, 1974, five days after Nixon's resignation, the U.S. Court of Appeals for the District of Columbia placed specific restrictions on the pocket veto by ruling that it could not be applied to an "intrasession adjournment."

chief legislator, have not recently produced comparable growth in the presidency.

Along with the shift in desired leadership skills, the diminished role of the president as a public figure, and the burgeoning of the presidency there has been a sharp rise in the intensity and frequency of presidential conflict with other elements of the political system. In recent years attacks on the media by members of the presidential establishment have been commonplace as the president's staffers and associates have sought to secure "objective" (i.e., favorable) coverage of their chief. The White House has employed news management, threats, and petty retaliation (as in President Kennedy's summary cancellation of his subscription to the *New York Herald Tribune* in 1962 and in the exclusion in December, 1972, of the *Washington Post's* society reporter from a White House party) to achieve this end. The press has responded with charges of censorship and heightened, often carping, criticism of presidential policies and actions. There has also been an escalation in congressional-presidential conflict as Congress has attempted to assert itself in the formulation of national security policy and to establish a measure of control over economic policy, the federal budget, and domestic programs. And there have been continuing struggles with the bureaucracy as presidents have sought to coordinate and rationalize the vast activities of the executive branch in accordance with their overall objectives. President Johnson's most notable attempt to achieve this end was the imposition of the Program, Planning, and Budgeting System, a form of cost-benefit analysis developed in the Department of Defense, on all government agencies. President Nixon sought to accomplish it by reorganization of the bureaucracy, by strengthening the managerial capabilities of the presidency, and by placing direct authority over the line operations of federal agencies in the hands of presidential staff aides and in the Office of Management and Budget.

The original rationale for the legislation formally establishing the Executive Office of the President in 1939—to give the president assistance—has been lost sight of in the exponential growth of the office. Instead of acting as a functional staff that helps the president control the bureaucracy and effectively perform his other leadership roles, the presidency has become a bureaucracy in its own right that defies control within itself. With presidents isolated within their own establishment by well-meaning but subservient staffers, and with presidential assistants superseding cabinet members in importance as policy makers, it is no wonder that controversy and antagonism with the bureaucracy has intensified, and presidential control of the operating units of the executive branch has appeared more elusive than ever.

Conflicts with Congress and the press also appear to have stemmed, at least partially, from the isolation of the president within the enlarged presidency. Until the events of 1973–74 this has prevented the traditional constitutional and political checks and balances from operating to insure the accountability of the president and his closest associates. The powers of the presidency have been exercised in an anonymous fashion that is often shrouded in secrecy. Under these circumstances, explanations of momentous decisions have been vague or not offered at all; surprise has become a tactic in itself; and the critical scrutiny and appraisals of congressmen and the press have been limited to speculative prognostications or post hoc complaints, neither of which could contribute much to insuring democratically responsible performance. Significantly, President Ford began his administration with a pledge to cooperate fully with Congress, and he quickly established a pattern of open accessibility to the press.

Congressional-presidential conflict has always been latent in the American constitutional system, and it has manifested itself on several occasions in the past. It is only in the years since 1965, however, that such conflict has become a permanent feature of national politics. It can be argued that tension is a healthy phenomenon which keeps politicians honest and has a therapeutic impact on democratic processes. A more somber interpretation is that the conflict is symptomatic of serious, if not basic, weaknesses in the political system (e.g., an imbalance of economic and social power, and a maldistribution of resources) and that it indicates that democratic processes are not functioning properly. No doubt a moderate degree of presidential conflict with other political institutions is beneficial, but the desirable amount appears to have been substantially exceeded over the last decade.

These transformations in the presidency and in presidential roles have generated renewed interest in the office and the behavior of its occupant. Serious analysts have shifted their perspective and orientations also. Journalists and academicians have turned away from the heavy reliance that most of them had placed since the days of Franklin D. Roosevelt on presidential power as the key to solving the nation's major problems. Rather than advocating proposals that would strengthen presidential leadership, they have begun to question the wisdom of doing so and have suggested that there exists an imbalance in the national government that threatens the constitutional system itself. They argue that overcommitment to presidential leadership has led to a blurring of the political and constitutional limits to presidential power, with negative consequences for the goal of democratic responsibility. The strong presidency still has its advocates, however, and popular expectations of omnipotent and omnicompetent presidential performance do not appear to be nearly as diminished as those of scholars and journalists who closely watch the White House and its tenant.

Among political scientists particularly, the primary source of academic students of the presidency, there has been since 1970 a renewed interest in the subject of the presidency and a shift in the approach to it. A methodological transformation has occurred that involves reduced emphasis on descriptive scholarship and an attempt to develop theories that help to explain and predict institutional growth and individual behavior. This development, however, occurred later among students of the presidency than it did for students of most other areas of American politics. The explanation for the later development lies primarily in the "data problem," the difficulty in obtaining hard data concerning the presidency. The growth of scientific political analysis, or behaviorism, took place initially in the study of phenomena that yielded readily to quantification. Once hard data could be obtained, hypotheses could be tested using statistical techniques, and a cumulative body of knowledge could be acquired that would lead to the development of predictive and explanatory theories. The "scientific study of politics" thus advanced rapidly in such areas as voting behavior, public opinion, and legislative roll call voting.

Following the publication of Richard E. Neustadt's *Presidential Power* in 1960 there was a notable lapse in the study of the presidency. In this seminal work, Neustadt drew upon empirical information derived from the analysis of three crucial presidential decisions, from his own experience on the White House staff during the Truman administration, and from biographical studies of Franklin D. Roosevelt to fashion a theory of presidential leadership. Neustadt's theory stressed the need for persuasive skills, an effective intelligence (i.e., information gathering and analysis) operation, and flexibility. It was prescriptive rather than predictive, and it added little explanatory power to the extant literature. The theory was enthusiastically received, however, perhaps because of its consonance with the conventional wisdom and the normative expectations of most political scientists, which called for a stronger presidency, and because it satisfied their desire for any kind of a theory of presidential leadership. Neustadt's work remained the last word on the subject for most of the 1960s as Democratic presidents seemingly tried to implement its prescriptions.

The difficulty of obtaining hard data for scientific analysis and the high regard accorded Neustadt help to explain scholarly neglect of the presidency during much of the 1960s, but there were during the decade numerous careful studies of the mass public, including its attitudes toward presidents and its behavior in presidential elections. The use of survey research and the theory developed in the study of mass political behavior contributed to the understanding of the environment in which presidents must function. As important as this research is, it bears only indirectly on the presidency and presidential behavior, and has not contributed to the development of analytical theories regarding those phenomena.

In the 1960s there was a movement from biographical studies of presidents to psycho-biography and theories of presidential leadership derived from psychology. The most ambitious and significant of these psychological studies is James David Barber's study of presidential character (1972), which provides a basis for predicting the broad outlines of a prospective president's behavior. Barber's thesis, which is well documented with evidence drawn from biographies, is that the roots of presidential behavior are to be found in the individual's character, which is shaped in childhood. The significance of Barber's work is not that it reveals all that a president will do, but that it offers a theoretical framework for explaining presidential actions and forecasting the probable dimensions of a president's conduct under certain circumstances. This is a major addition to the prescriptive theory of Neustadt.

The study of the presidential office has also been advanced. Until the early 1970s, scholars were content with the facile assertion that the presidency had become "institutionalized" and with a theory of institutional development no more refined than the late Edward S. Corwin's observation that the modern presidency is the product of two discontinuous factors, "crisis and personality." But the study of the presidency has now moved from legalistic analyses of constitutional interpretations by the courts, statutory grants of power, and executive orders, to theoretical analyses based on empirical evidence of organizational development, functioning, and conflict.

Of particular significance in this latter vein are the works of Richard E. Neustadt, Graham T. Allison, and Thomas E. Cronin. Neustadt, particularly in *Presidential Power,* developed a theory of presidential leadership that is both analytical and prescriptive, and related it to the institutional development of the office. Allison, in *The Essence of Decision* (1971), examined President Kennedy's handling of the Cuban missile crisis employing three levels of analysis, devoting particular attention to "bureaucratic politics." Cronin, in *The State of the Presidency* (1975), systematically surveyed the efforts of recent presidents to maintain policy control within the executive branch. All three of these scholars rely heavily on empirical information obtained through interviews with participants in presidential policy making, and they all proceed far beyond mere description in their analyses.

The selections that comprise this anthology reflect these and other recent developments in the constitutional, political, governmental, and policy contexts of the presidency. They also illustrate changing patterns in the study of the presidency. Through them should emerge a better understanding of the contemporary presidency and an appreciation of the many unresolved (and as yet unanticipated) questions about the future of the office and the leadership role of its incumbents.

PART ONE

The Constitutional Context

Two factors that receive consideration in most serious attempts to analyze the current state of the presidency are its constitutional status and the perspectives of scholars who study it. It is necessary to recall that the Constitution established the office and that the president acts either directly on its authority or on the basis of statutes enacted pursuant to it. Challenges to the president's actions (or inactions), his relations with the legislative and judicial branches of the government, his role in making and implementing national security policy, and the process by which he is elected all rest on the Constitution or interpretations of it. Consequently, efforts to place the office in a contemporary context necessarily examine the constitutional situation. Much work of this sort has been done by scholars, but it by no means represents the full ambit of their inquiry. Moving outward from constitutional theory, either explicitly defined or implicitly assumed, they take account of political and other factors.

In his review of analyses of the presidency and its relationships with Congress, William G. Andrews reveals that scholars also undergo changes in their appraisals and evaluations of the office. His paper furnishes a good summary of current thinking. It is of particular interest because it calls attention to the impact that the personal values and experiences of various scholars have had on their conclusions. This is not to imply that students of the presidency have been heavily biased, but it is well to keep in mind that they do not write with complete objectivity, nor should we expect them to do so. Of particular relevance is the aphorism known as Miles's Law, named after Rufus Miles, a former career official in the Department of Health, Education, and Welfare: "where you stand depends on where you sit."

In the second selection, Joseph E. Kallenbach discusses the significance of recent constitutional amendments affecting the presidency. He points out, however, that some of the most important constitutional issues relating to the presidency and presidential power (e.g., the impoundment of funds) involve matters of interpretation. Even the adoption of an amendment leaves many unresolved questions, as is revealed in Kallenbach's examination of the provisions of the Twenty-fifth Amendment for filling a vacancy in the vice-presidency. The viability of that aspect of the amendment was not demonstrated until late 1973 when Representative Gerald R. Ford, a Michigan Republican, was nominated by President Nixon to succeed Vice-President Spiro T. Agnew and was confirmed by a Democratic Congress. The amendment was further tested in late 1974 when Congress acted on President Ford's nomination of Nelson A. Rockefeller to serve as vice-president. Readers may wish to consider the issues raised following the Agnew and Nixon resignations and during the confirmation of, first, Ford and, later, Rockefeller in the context of Kallenbach's discussion.

Kallenbach's discussion of proposals to modify the presidential election system emphasizes the fact that the president's constitutional role as official governmental leader and his party leadership role are inextricably intermingled. The issue of electoral reform may appear to have receded from view during the national preoccupation with the Watergate affair, but it remains very much alive. The Senate Judiciary Subcommittee on Constitutional Amendments concluded hearings in late 1973 on a direct election amendment and plans to recommend action in the near future. Direct election has had substantial majority support in both houses of Congress for some time, the principal obstacle to the reform being the refusal of slightly more than one-third of the senators to accept the concept of a runoff election in the event no candidate receives a plurality of over 40 percent. Kallenbach argues that it is impractical to attempt to convert Congress into a potential electoral college in any fashion and that the runoff device is sound. Electoral reform may well gather additional support as the next presidential election approaches.

The two selections in this part illustrate the continuing and changing nature of scholarly thinking about the presidency. They also demonstrate the dynamic character of the presidency as an institution. The powers and structure of the office and its constitutional position vary with events, the actions of presidents and other political figures, and the attitudes of the people.

1.

THE PRESIDENCY, CONGRESS, AND CONSTITUTIONAL THEORY

William G. Andrews

I. INTRODUCTION

In close neighborhood to 1960, the political science profession burst forth with a veritable barrage of elaborate encomiums to the American Presidency. Some of the most distinguished members of the profession virtually tied themselves in knots to explain why that institution was superior to Congress and should, therefore, wield commensurately greater power. Ten years later, that school of thought was in wild disarray, under furious assault from an army of outspoken critics of presidential power. This paper reviews these developments, seeks to explain them, and proposes a constitutional theory approach to avoid such problems in the future.

II. HALLOWED BE THE PRESIDENCY

Probably no other period of our history has produced a richer harvest of books on the Presidency than the bumper crop of the 1960 era. At least eleven serious studies of the Presidency as an institution appeared within three or four years of that magic moment.[1] They reflected remark-

---

An earlier version of this paper was presented to the annual meeting of the American Political Science Association, Chicago, Illinois, September, 1971. Reprinted with the permission of the author and the American Political Science Association.

[1] The principal works to be treated here are: Edward S. Corwin, *The President: Office and Powers,* New York U.P., New York, 4th ed., 1957, 517 pp.; Clinton Rossiter, *The American Presidency,* Harcourt Brace, New York, revised ed., 1960, 281 pp.; Corwin and Louis W. Koenig, *The Presidency Today,* New York U.P., New York, 1956, 138 pp.; Koenig, *The Chief Executive,* Harcourt Brace, New York, 1964, 431 pp.; Richard E. Neustadt, *Presidential Power: The Politics of Leadership,* Wiley, New York, 1960, 224 pp.; Rexford G. Tugwell, *The Enlargement of the Presidency,* Doubleday, Garden City, 1960, 508 pp.; Francis H. Heller, *The Presidency: A Modern Perspective,* Random House, New York, 1960, 114 pp.; Herman Finer, *The Presidency: Crisis and Regeneration,* U. of Chicago Press, Chicago, 1960, 374 pp.; Walter Johnson, *1600 Pennsylvania Avenue,* Little, Brown, Boston, 1960, 390 pp.; Wilfred E. Binkley, *The Man in the White House,* Johns Hopkins U.P., Baltimore, 1959, 310 pp.; and Binkley, *President and Congress,* Knopf, New York, 3rd ed., 1962, 403 pp.

ably concordant views. All agreed that the Presidency was the seat of virtue and the principal seat of power in our governmental system. Because of its virtue, they contended, its power almost inevitably would be wielded for the welfare of the nation. Because of its virtual monopoly on virtue, almost nothing constructive could be accomplished without its leadership. Unfortunately, they said, its power was exceeded by the requirements of our national problems. Therefore, they urged that its authority be increased and suggested ways to do so.

Virtue. The 1960 consensus preached that the Presidency derived its extraordinary virtue from its lofty height. Being the sole office in the land that is filled through election by the entire nation and that has general responsibility for the nation's welfare, it rises high above the petty, particularistic concerns of congressmen, each elected by a tiny fragment of the Presidency's constituency. From that eminence, it shines like a beacon, guiding Congress and the nation along the paths of righteousness. Alone among our institutions, they believed, the Presidency has a truly national perspective.

The virtue of the Presidency derives from more than perspective, however, according to the 1960 school. Also, unlike Congress, it lacks the taint of such undemocratic fetters as the seniority system and the dispersal of leadership in a rickety system of committees. They saw the Presidency, in contrast to Congress, as a kind of governmental Mr. Clean—tall, straight, vigorous, unencumbered by a bad conscience or defects of character or constitution—ready to ride forth with dispatch and decisiveness to do battle with the enemy at a moment's notice. Herman Finer summed up this attitude well when he called the Presidency, in a burst of lyrical rhetoric, "the incarnation of the American people in a sacrament resembling that in which the wafer and the wine are seen to be the body and blood of Christ."

Burden. Quite naturally for the 1960 writers, the great virtue of the Presidency attracted great responsibilities to it. In 1956, Rossiter called the burden of the Presidency "colossal" (p. 26). By 1960, it had become "monstrous" (p. 42). Corwin called the office a "killing job"; Finer wrote about "the torturing responsibilities of the President"; and Koenig described the "horrendous challenge" that faces him. The other writers agreed. None suggested that Presidents are underemployed.

The burdens of the Presidency were believed to be so great that the job could be understood only if sliced up into chewable portions, each being "chief" of something. Rossiter's categories are classic: chief of state, chief administrator, chief diplomat, commander in chief, chief legislator, chief of party, voice of the people, manager of prosperity, and leader of a coalition of free nations. He compared the President to Gilbert and

Sullivan's Pooh-Bah, the "particularly haughty and exclusive person" in *The Mikado*. Other writers used similar labels. Finer included chief executive of the laws, chief executive of policy, chief legislator, chief economist, "sole representative of the 'nation as a whole,'" sole "enforcer of national sovereignty in establishing the rights and obligations of the nation," "sole maker of war and peace," chief of a party, etc. Corwin, Koenig, and Binkley compiled similar—if less colorful—lists. Heller summarized these burdens, calling them "popular expectation," in words that are reflected by all the writers of the 1960 consensus group:

> They expect him to be a chief of state . . . to see to it that policies once arrived at are carried through with maximum effectiveness. They expect him to assume responsibility for the stature of the United States in the world, both as he speaks and meets with the heads of other great powers and as he provides the means and devices, and approves and carries on the plans that will assure the nation's safety. They expect him to move forward the legislative program of the government by affirmative proposals to the Congress and by equally affirmative actions to seek to move the Congress along with him. And last, but not least, they expect him to be not only the chief political leader of his party, but the master politician of the nation.

The 1960 writers allowed for no other national political or governmental leadership than the President's. He was called upon to be absolute No. 1 in each area of activity of the national government. He could not do everything personally, of course, but he was expected to provide the top leadership in everything.

So far as Congress entered the picture at all, it followed. The President was alone in the driver's seat. At best, Congress was a loyal helpmate, encouraging, offering support, obeying; at worst, it was an aggressive backseat driver, grabbing at the steering wheel, fighting to put on the brakes, threatening to overturn and destroy the whole vehicle. "One of the few political truths about the American system of government," wrote Walter Johnson, "is that the President alone can give the nation an effective lead."

Glory. The 1960 writers saw, not only virtue and responsibility, but also great power in the Presidency. Corwin wrote that "the history of the presidency has been a history of aggrandizement" and that its growth in power had reached the point of "presidential domination." Rossiter concurred on the matter of aggrandizement. Tugwell called the Presidency's power a "vast accumulation" and wrote of the "enormous" enlargement of the office in recent decades. The other writers agreed on the existence of "great" or "substantial" power in the Presidency.

* * *

Gaps. Most of the 1960 consensus writers felt that the Presidency's power, however great, was not adequate to give full effect to the virtue of the office in fulfilling its responsibilities. Despite his general satisfaction over the Presidency, Rossiter felt that it suffered from a "gap between responsibility and authority." Koenig saw a "chasm" between the amount of power the Presidency needs and is believed to have and what it really has. In each chapter of his magisterial study, he examines how that chasm affects a given aspect of the office. Tugwell expressed concern that "even though the enlargement" of the Presidency "has been enormous, it may possibly not have been enough." Finer argued that the effective power of the office was inadequate, because no one person was capable of wielding enough to meet its responsibilities.

Remedies. Much of the writing of the consensus school searched for ways to close the gaps. Each of Koenig's chapters concluded with a list of suggestions for political and institutional reforms to make the Presidency stronger and more capable of meeting its responsibilities. Finer proposed the creation of eleven elective vice-presidencies to share executive power, much in the manner of the British cabinet. Tugwell suggested a similar plural executive.

Others prescribed personal, rather than institutional nostrums. Johnson charged Hoover and Eisenhower with failing to use fully the power at their command. He called for Presidents with the wisdom and skill to emulate such "strong" Presidents as Franklin Roosevelt and Truman. Heller agreed on the personalist solution. His thesis was that "the need for adequate instruments for the exercise of power is so 'great' that the adequacy of executive power under democratic conditions *per se* deserves to be carefully examined and thoroughly pondered." After examining carefully and pondering thoroughly, he concludes that, although some institutional reforms should be made in order to strengthen the Presidency, the real solution lies in choosing for the job men who will use fully the power it has already.

The most eloquent exponent of the personalist solution, however, was Neustadt. His *Presidential Power* is virtually a latter-day version of Machiavelli's *Prince,* a manual to instruct the President on how to make the most of the power of his office. The book is replete with such maxims as: "The more determinedly a President seeks power, the more he will bring vigor to his clerkship. As he does so he contributes to the energy of government." Obviously, power in the Presidency and energy in government were cardinal virtues for Neustadt.

Prerogative. Although the 1960 writers advocated presidential strength generally, they were especially emphatic in asserting the need for presidential domination in foreign and military affairs. Eisenhower's deference to Congress in asking for resolutions authorizing American intervention in the Formosan Straits in 1955 and in the Middle East in 1957 was attacked as an abdication of responsibility and a dangerous precedent for the erosion of presidential authority in what should be a reserved domain for executive prerogative. Rossiter called it "a brake on his progress toward the stature of a great President" and blamed it on his "modest conception of the Presidency." Koenig quoted with approval Senator J. William Fulbright's remark that "for the existing requirements of American foreign policy we have hobbled the President by too niggardly a grant of power." Finer contended that the President's power to dispose of "the armed forces abroad . . . is not limited by the Constitution" and worried that Presidents, in using that power, may be "overcareful, timid, in an age of swift decisions." On the other hand, congressional power in this area was dangerous, for "it can use its legislative powers . . . to debate his measures in such ways as to shake the confidence of allies and other nations in America's reliability and to arouse the distrust and/or aggressiveness of enemies by the exhibition of a divided and confused national will."

In summary then, the 1960 writers glorified the Presidency, especially in foreign and defense affairs. That institution incarnated governmental virtue. If only it could be made virtually omnipotent through institutional reforms and by electing men with enough will power and skill, the Presidency could solve as many of our problems as is humanly possible.

III. DELIVER US FROM PRESIDENTS

Quite a different picture of the Presidency emerges from the literature of the 1968–71 period. Although a few holdouts remained on the Glory Heights, consensus had retreated into the Valley of Disillusion. Glorification of the Presidency had fallen into disrepute by the 1968–71 period.

Members of the 1960 group were far less prominent on the 1968–71 scene. Corwin and Binkley were dead by 1968. Finer died in 1969 and Rossiter in 1970. No books or articles in national periodicals by them or by Heller or Johnson on the Presidency as an institution were published in 1968–71. Only Koenig, Neustadt, and Tugwell published on that topic during that period. Their views had shifted somewhat and they were joined by a number of other writers with views sharply different from the 1960 consensus.

Alumni Contributions. Tugwell was the most active of the 1960 group in the later period. His 1960 biography, *Grover Cleveland,* falls squarely in the "strong Presidency" camp. In a proposal for a new American constitution, moreover, he sought to strengthen the Presidency in various ways in order that it may be "head of . . . government, shaper of its commitments, expositor of its policies, and supreme commander of its protective forces." On the other hand, Tugwell's constitution would forbid the President to carry out "the deployment of forces in far waters, or in other nations without their consent" over the objections of the Senate, except in emergencies that could be declared by the President only if the Senate were recessed.

Another article by Tugwell suggested that his faith in a strong Presidency had been shaken still further.[2] The President, he wrote, "has too much power; and he has not enough power. He can send the armed forces into any part of the world, risking war on any scale," virtually unchecked. Yet he has too little power as "chief legislator and maker of foreign policy" and "no longer has time or energy for . . . the carrying into effect of laws."

A similar change had occurred in Koenig's views. The 1968 edition of *The Chief Executive* retained the thesis of the 1964 edition and is consistent with it generally. However, in his new edition he departed from the earlier edition by distinguishing "two Presidencies in foreign affairs. . . . One possesses maximum autonomy . . . and . . . has grown by leaps and bounds in the nuclear age. . . . The other . . . is marked by its dependence upon Congress and upon public opinion." In 1968, he applied only to the "dependent" President his 1964 proposals for strengthening the institution, and he worried whether the "independent Presidency [can] be held sufficiently accountable to enable it to reflect the popular will, the nation's historic purposes and values, and . . . can be linked to institutions and practices upon which democracy depends."

Neustadt gave up ground even more grudgingly. The text of the second edition (1968) of *Presidential Power* had no significant changes from the 1960 edition. In his "Afterword on JFK" to the 1968 edition and in an "Afterword" which he co-authored for Robert F. Kennedy's *Thirteen Days,* moreover, he reaffirmed his belief in the President as "our system's Great Initiator" and "when what we once called 'war' impends . . . our system's Final Arbiter." However, in the RFK "Afterword" he hedged a bit, saying, "Whether Presidents should now be . . . constrained" by Congress in exercising the war powers "are matters of judgment" about which he provided no fresh opinions. In *Alliance Politics,*[3] he was much more cautious in his claims for presidential power than he had been a decade earlier, although the two studies are not strictly comparable

[2] "The Historian and the Presidency: An Essay Review," *Political Science Quarterly,* June, 1971, pp. 183–204.

[3] Columbia U.P., New York, 1970, 167 pp.

because of the later book's exclusive concern with foreign relations and its division of attention between American and British governments. His caution seemed to be dictated by a new realization of the internal political and administrative constraints that operate on other countries and of the difficulties that our decision makers in the White House have in gaining an adequate understanding of those constraints. In any case, the whole tone and thrust of *Alliance Politics* marks a clear retreat from *Presidential Power*, whatever may be its basis.

Critics. The 1960 survivors were reluctant to sound retreat. Most of the other contributors to the 1970 discussion were not. They seemed quite content to send the Presidency glorifiers into full rout. The 1970 writers who had not written books on the Presidency in the 1960 period overwhelmingly regarded the Presidency with much less awe.

Only three new books on the Presidency as an institution appeared in 1968–71, one by journalist–presidential aide George E. Reedy, one by British historian Marcus Cunliffe,[4] and one by political scientist Dorothy Buckton James. The Cunliffe book reiterates the 1960 thesis, but even before its American edition had been published, he noted in print that "Americans who were once sure that strong leadership was necessarily wholesome leadership, no longer take the belief as axiomatic.[5] Apparently, James was one of those Americans. In her introduction, she identifies herself with American "organic liberals" who "tend to approve of the contemporary development of presidential power." Yet she sets out to expose "weaknesses in liberal analysis of the Presidency which need correction," and argues that "the consequence of increased power for any President is increased power in the hands of a bureaucracy over which he can exercise only marginal control." [6]

In a 1969 book, Arthur Schlesinger, Jr., acknowledged doubts "growing for some time . . . regarding . . . the thesis of the strong Presidency," [7] and Hans J. Morgenthau confessed that he "used to implore a succession of Presidents to assert their constitutional powers against Congress": but now urges the Senate to "restore its historic function as an independent

[4] *The American Heritage History of the Presidency*, American Heritage Publishing Co., n. p., 1968, 384 pp.

[5] "A Defective Institution?" *Commentary*, February, 1968, p. 28. Cunliffe had reinforced those doubts by the time the English edition of his book went to press: *American Presidents and the Presidency*, Eyre and Spottiswoode, London, 1969, 343 pp. The epilogue to this edition is dated March, 1969. In the preface Cunliffe says that he finished writing the American edition in September, 1967, p. 11.

[6] *The Contemporary Presidency*, Pegasus, New York, 1969, pp. 187, at pp. xii–xiii.

[7] *The Crisis of Confidence: Ideas, Power, and Violence in America*, Houghton Mifflin, Boston, 1969, 313 pp., at p. 288. See a similar remark in Laurin J. Henry, "A Symposium: The American Presidency," *Public Administration Review*, September/October, 1969, p. 441.

political factor." Perhaps the most sweeping criticism of the 1960 school of interpretation has been made by Thomas E. Cronin.[8] Although he addressed his comments especially to the authors of several then recent textbooks, he included Rossiter and Neustadt. He accused them of making "inflated and unrealistic interpretations of presidential competence and beneficence" and of exaggerating "past and future presidential performance."

This new view of the power relationship between Congress and the Presidency reversed the 1960 consensus almost completely. Some of the new plaints were as sweeping as the old—though opposite. They called the Presidency a "Frankenstein monster" and warned that "a dangerous institutional imbalance" had given the Presidency so much power as to contradict "the principles of democratic government" because the Presidency "is not, as compared with Congress, an institution of participatory democracy." Dwight MacDonald argued that "the President has too much prestige and too much freedom of action," and George E. Reedy felt that the Presidency had become dangerous because "what was little more than managerial authority" in the Presidency had grown into "power over the life of the nation itself." [9]

Some assaults on the Presidency were more selective. Schlesinger refused to "renounce the idea of an affirmative Presidency or surround the President with hampering restrictions" of a general sort, but agreed that the office required additional checks in the area of foreign affairs. Reedy and the *New Republic* also believed that the most grievous problem lay "in the field of foreign affairs and defense," but neither thought it ended there. Merlo J. Pusey drew a still finer distinction, seeing the Presidency's authority to wage war as excessive, but not its "control of foreign policy short of making war and . . . its essential right to repel sudden attacks." [10] Saul K. Padover called the President "for all practical purposes . . . a dictator in international affairs," [11] and Francis O. Wilcox viewed the balance of power between President and Congress in foreign affairs as having tipped too far toward the former.[12] A lengthy legal treatise on the war powers concluded that presidential prerogative had become excessive, a view shared by Eric F. Goldman in a more popular medium.[13]

---

[8] "The Textbook Presidency and Political Science," paper presented to the 1970 annual meeting of the American Political Science Association and reprinted in the *Congressional Record,* October 5, 1970.

[9] *The Twilight of the Presidency,* World, New York, 1970, 205 pp., at p. 47.

[10] "The President and the Power to Make War," *Atlantic,* July, 1969, p. 67.

[11] "The Power of the President," *Commonwealth,* August 9, 1969, pp. 571, 575.

[12] "President Nixon, The Congress, and Foreign Policy," *Michigan Law Quarterly,* Winter, 1970, pp. 41, 42.

[13] "Congress, the President, and the Power to Commit Forces to Combat," *Harvard Law Review,* June, 1968, pp. 1771–1805; Goldman, "The President, the People, and the Power to Make War," *American Heritage,* April, 1970, p. 35.

Most of the 1970 critics believed that the solution to the problem lay in strengthening congressional control. The 1960 writers had urged Congress to restrain itself, especially in foreign and defense affairs. The 1970 writers urged Congress to assert itself, especially in foreign and defense affairs. MacDonald proposed that the President be replaced by a "Chairman," whose power would be limited "by integrating the Executive more closely with the Legislative branch." Pusey would have Congress assert its "authority to decide the issue of war or peace." Padover pleaded for "manageable restraints upon [the Presidency's] power in foreign affairs" through "a number of steps . . . to strengthen Congress." Schlesinger, Wilcox, and the *Harvard Law Review* writer agreed. Perhaps Goldman said it most eloquently in asking for "a congressional stance that will give the American people some degree of responsible surveillance over the disposition abroad of their lives, their fortunes, and their sacred honor."

Other 1970 writers who agreed on the diagnosis disagreed on the treatment. Reedy considered proposing that the Presidency be brought under close congressional control by introducing a form of parliamentarism, but dismissed this idea as unlikely to come about. Instead, he argued for a return "of the operating authority of the presidency to a managerial status" and for greater willingness by Presidents to "plunge into the world of reality." Cronin suggested that the exaggerated notions of presidential power be counterbalanced by recognition of the validity of an "ebb and flow" of power between President and Congress, as well as with other "policy actors" such as the bureaucracy and interest groups. For Henry Steele Commager, the solution lay in national reeducation to overcome our "national paranoia . . . with communism and other ideological threats" which, he believed, led to abuse of a proper "imperative of a strong President in the realm of foreign affairs.[14] Finally, Norton E. Long contended that inability to mobilize popular support is adequate restraint on the inclinations of Presidents to engage in foreign military adventures.[15]

The 1970 group spoke with scarcely less concordance and, certainly, no less emphasis than the 1960 group. Yet, they preached an almost completely contradictory doctrine. The Glorified Presidency, erected and exalted by the 1960 group was being destroyed—at least abstractly—by the 1970 group. The following section will consider reasons for this abrupt reversal.

---

[14] "Can We Limit Presidential Power?" *New Republic*, April 6, 1968, pp. 15, 17.

[15] "Reflections on Presidential Power," *Public Administration Review*, September/October, 1969, p. 447.

IV. EMPIRICAL APPLICATION: THE PRESIDENCIES OF THE 1960s

A Litmus Test. The 1960 writers made a fetish of presidential activism. The more active, assertive, and energetic the President, the better. Never mind the quality of the activity. Quantity counts for all. They justified this, in part, on the grounds that if the President were not active, nothing would be accomplished in the national government. In particular, they had no confidence in the ability of Congress to take the initiative. If Congress accomplished anything, it could be traced in some way or another to the White House. They made two implicit assumptions, therefore: whatever the President does is good and the President deserves the credit for whatever Congress does.

Using those two assumptions, we can make an empirical test of the 1960 thesis on its own terms. We can rank the Presidents who have served from 1960 on (Eisenhower, Kennedy, Johnson, Nixon) on the criteria of that thesis, and we can compare that ranking with the preferences, so far as they are known, of the 1960 writers. In that manner, we can discern whether the test they proposed before the fact produces, after the fact, the results they wish. A more demanding test would be the extent to which that ranking would fit the ratings given by the American people through public opinion surveys at the ends of the respective administrations. We need not concern ourselves with that test, for the 1960 thesis fails even the less exacting test. If the baby is so ugly that even her mother can't love her, no confirmation is needed from entering her in a beauty contest.

The methodological problems of evaluating the impact of Presidents on congressional policy are enormous. I do not pretend that I have solved them all satisfactorily. One problem is to control for external variables. What effects on a President's performance result from such factors as the partisan control of Congress, the general international situation, the legacy of assets and liabilities bequeathed by his predecessor, etc., over which he has no or little support? I see no way to reduce these factors to any kind of measure of comparability. A second problem is to discover and measure presidential involvement. Active, open public support is easy to observe. But what about private moves? May not a President support a measure publicly, but send word privately that he wants it killed—or vice versa? Alternatively, may he not believe that the best way to ensure passage of some other measure that he wants is to remain discreetly silent? This is true, not only of support or opposition, but of initiative as well. A case in point is the Kennedy administration's Alliance for Progress. Its founder, former Secretary of State Dean Rusk, announced recently that it "was started by Milton Eisenhower in the closing days of the Eisenhower administration." Most important policies gestate too long and are influenced by too many people for one man—even a President—to claim exclusive credit. Too many cooks boil the broth. To try to sort out and measure those influences on legislation over an eighteen-year span would be impossible and won't be attempted here. Finally, legislative acts are not all equal in value. Some are good; some are bad. Some are important; some are not. They fall all along the spectrum on both those axes. However, the task of gaining general agreement on categorizing and measuring them would be impossible. Also, many bills contain more than one measure, but often these cannot be identified clearly. To reach independent conclusions on these matters (external variables, presidential involvement, relative merit of legislation) would be to plunge into a quagmire of conjecture, uncertainty, and subjective judgment.

Fortunately, the meat-axe approach of the 1960 school relieves me of that task. Those writers were interested in raw, undifferentiated accomplishment. They assumed that all accomplishments were good if the President approved. Also, they assumed that nothing could be accomplished without presidential involvement. Therefore, to test their criteria in the area of legislation we need ask only how many laws and how many "important" laws were enacted with presidential approval in each administration and make comparisons.

To identify accomplishments, we shall compare *total* legislative output by administration first. Then we shall compare *important* legislative output. To reduce subjective bias as much as possible, I used an authoritative, neutral source (*Congressional Quarterly Almanacs*) to identify the important bills. I accepted as "important" all bills discussed in the *Almanacs*' "Major Legislation" or "Major Congressional Action" sections, except certain classes. First, I included no bills that only extended, expanded incrementally, or renewed previous or existing programs. Second, I included no appropriations bills. Third, I included no bills authorizing special projects such as reclamation, irrigation, or recreation facilities that were parts of general programs. In short, I included all enacted bills that established policy, rather than merely continued or reiterated it. To identify presidential approval, I relied entirely on his signature. If a law bore his signature, I included it. If his veto had been overridden or he had allowed a bill to become law without signing or vetoing it, I excluded it. In all other walks of life, signature comports responsibility. Consistency and logic bring Presidents under the same principle.

Total Legislative Output. A President has three options upon passage of a bill by Congress. He can sign it, veto it, or permit it to become law with neither his veto nor his signature. Almost all enacted laws bear presidential signatures. From 1953 through 1971, Congress passed

7,538 public bills. The Presidents signed 7,410 of these bills and vetoed 127. Only one bill became law during that time without veto or signature. Four bills were passed over presidential vetoes. Therefore, the Presidents bore responsibility for almost all legislation enacted during the period in question.

The overridden vetoes and unsigned bills had relatively little significance. Two were Eisenhower vetoes, a Civil Functions Appropriations bill in 1959 and a Federal Employees Pay Increase bill in 1960, and two were Nixon vetoes, a hospital construction bill and the Office of Education appropriations, both in 1970. The unsigned bill was a 1970 amendment to the Child Nutrition Act of 1966. No legislation of great significance, then, lacked presidential approval.

Taking the raw figures for public bills enacted, without making any attempt to control for importance, the Eisenhower administration was the most productive of the four. An average of 430 public bills per year were enacted and signed by the President during Eisenhower's eight years in office. Kennedy and Johnson had records nearly identical to each other. Under the Kennedy administration an average of 373 public bills per year became law with presidential signature. The corresponding figure for the Johnson administration was 366. During the first two years of the Nixon administration, the average was 343. Using only the first three years of each administration, because the Kennedy administration lasted only that long, the total numbers for each administration were: Eisenhower 781, Kennedy 885, Johnson 757, and Nixon 695.

Important Policy Output. Everyone agrees, of course, that policy enactments vary in importance. Using the method described above, I have compiled lists of important legislation for the four administrations. The records look like this:

Major Bills Enacted In

Administration	*1st year*	*2nd year*	*3rd year*	*Total*
Eisenhower	26	44	16	86
Kennedy	19	40	12	71
Johnson	34	50	86	170
Nixon	18	70	46	134

Analysis. The implications of these data are surprising and a bit confusing. Ranking the administrations by average annual total output or by total output during their first three years we get: Johnson, Eisenhower, Kennedy, Nixon. Ranking them by important output during their first three years we get: Johnson, Nixon, Eisenhower, Kennedy.

I have the impression that most writers on the Presidency, including the 1960 school, would rank the four in the order Johnson, Nixon, Kennedy, Eisenhower on a spectrum from "active" to "passive," although such an impression cannot be reduced to very concrete form. On the other hand, in overall popularity, they would run something like Kennedy, Eisenhower, Johnson, Nixon. During his first two years, Johnson got under way many of Kennedy's programs that had been stalled for two or three years. Whatever one may say of Nixon, few would argue that he has not been active. Yet neither Johnson nor Nixon are as popular among such writers as Kennedy and probably not as popular as Eisenhower either.

The problem probably arises from the fact that during the Johnson administration the Vietnam war became a major American political issue and that both Johnson and Nixon came out of the wrong partisan political traditions to meet with much favor among most writers on the Presidency. The one was a southern Democrat, the other a Republican, whereas the 1960 consensus was built by northern Democrats. Neither of these factors was built into the 1960 criteria of evaluation as an independent variable. In fact, under Binkley's thesis in *President and Congress,* a Republican activist President was almost a contradiction in terms. However, the explicit criteria—which all turned on activism—was overridden by unwritten criteria arising, as had the explicit ones originally, from partisan and policy preferences, except that some shoes were on different feet now.

Thus, the slide from popularity of the activist Presidency cannot really be accounted for within the framework of the 1960 consensus theory. However, those partisan and policy preferences recur persistently. Perhaps a more detailed examination of them will help explain the fragility of the 1960 consensus and lead the way to the discovery of a sounder basis for constitutional theory in this area.

V. THE ELEVATION OF PERSONAL POLITICAL BIAS INTO CONSTITUTIONAL THEORY

Something must be wrong with a constitutional concept that dominates political science so completely for a time, yet fails so dismally the tests of reputational survival and empirical application. One handy explanation that deserves consideration is that the constitutional theory consensus of the 1960 writers sprang from their partisan political consensus. Their previous personal experiences and political commitments were remarkably similar in pertinent respects and relate logically to the theories they expostulated. They were all deeply touched by and, in most cases, deeply involved in the New Deal of the 1930s. They elevated that experience into a general constitutional theory without really considering, with reference to fundamental principles, the extent to which it was generalizable. They were, in a very real sense, victims and perpetrators of what Cronin has called the "Franklin Roosevelt halo-effect." This resulted partly from national experiences in which they shared, but, even more, from their very special involvement in those experiences.

The national experience that most influenced the 1960 writers led from the intensity of American involvement in World War I through the relatively calm 1920s to the trauma of the Great Depression, the accumulating national excitement of economic recovery, World War II, cold war, and the Korean War, and back into the relative calm of the eight-year interval between the Korean and Vietnam wars. All members of the 1960 group had lived through that entire period. Quite naturally, like most Americans, they identified the various phases of that experience with the Presidents whose terms coincided remarkably closely with the various phases: intensity with Wilson(D); calm and trauma with Harding (R), Coolidge (R) and Hoover (R); excitement of recovery and war with Roosevelt (D) and Truman (D); calm again with Eisenhower (R). The Ds and Rs sorted themselves out into two categories all too nicely. So, too, did the correlations between each category of President and one type of presidential activity. The Ds all came out looking intense and exciting. The Rs all came out looking calm and passive. The one trauma in our collective memory has marked the end of an eight-year period of R calm. As 1960 approached we were nearing the end of another eight-year period of R calm. Small wonder that political scientists might form a chorus to sing the praises of exciting D Presidents and warning of calm R Presidents! Our recent national experience led them in that direction naturally. Their own personal experiences, however, moved them that way even more powerfully.

Most of the presidency glorifiers had in common the experience of service in the executive branch of the national government during the administrations of Roosevelt (D) and Truman (D), but not under any of the Republican Presidents.* Several of them also had personal or political associations with Democratic Presidents. None of the 1960 writers had ever worked for Congress. Every member of the 1960 group (but one) had some personal commitment to Democratic Presidents Roosevelt or Truman or to Democratic presidential candidate Stevenson. Roosevelt had selected Truman as his successor and Truman had selected Stevenson as his. All three were articulately assertive about the powers of the Presidency. The writings of the 1960 period raised that assertion to the level of a general virtue, dissolving constitutional theory in partisan political preference.

* Details on these generalizations are presented in the version of this paper given to the American Political Science Association meeting of 1971.

The career and constitutional concepts of Corwin provide an especially instructive illustration of how that process worked. Corwin had been hired by Princeton President Woodrow Wilson personally as one of the original "preceptors" in 1905, was a departmental colleague of his, received faculty tenure from him, succeeded to his faculty chair, and brought one of his books up-to-date for a new edition. During this time, while Wilson was President or en route, Corwin was an exponent of a strong Presidency. In 1909, he described the Presidency as "the natural and responsible, because sole, representative of that citizenship" which is independent in its affiliations of either labor or capital." In 1917, he argued that it could not "be reasonably doubted that these results [or presidential dominance in foreign affairs] have proved beneficial." I have found no published trace of concern by Corwin with the constitutional theory of presidential-congressional relations nor of personal political involvement by him in the years between the Wilson and FDR administrations.

Between 1933 and 1938, he supported Roosevelt actively. He held two short-term appointments advising Roosevelt's attorney general on constitutional matters, apparently involved in the "court packing" affair. He wrote articles, statements, and letters for newspapers advocating support for Roosevelt's policies, especially the court plan. He testified before a congressional committee on behalf of that project.

During that period he published two scholarly books in which he expounded constitutional theory relevant to the questions of presidential power.[16] In both books, he argued that the Supreme Court should "give over attempting to supervise national legislative policies on the basis of a super-constitution which in the name of the Constitution, repeals and destroys that historic document." Obviously, in the circumstances of the time such abdication would have facilitated the growth of presidential power.

Reportedly, Corwin had aspirations to be appointed to the Court during this period, but was disappointed, despite his standing as the leading constitutional law scholar in the country, because he lacked a law degree and was not a member of the bar.[17] Roosevelt appointed five justices in 1937 through 1940, but he did not appoint Corwin. In 1940, Corwin publicly supported Wendell Willkie for President against Roosevelt.

Once again, his constitutional theory followed his politics. In 1934, he had proposed a joint legislative-executive presidential cabinet in order

---

[16] *Twilight of the Supreme Court,* Yale U.P., New Haven, 1934, 237 pp.; and *Court over Constitution,* Princeton U.P., Princeton, 1938, 273 pp.

[17] This information was supplied to the writer by Professor Clinton Rossiter in 1957.

to provide Presidents with the means to influence Congress more directly and effectively. After his break with Roosevelt, he gave his proposed cabinet a new purpose: to "bring presidential whim under an independent scrutiny which today is lacking" and to avoid "two dangers: antagonism between President and Congress and autocracy." By 1948, Roosevelt had been dead three years; Corwin was retired and mellowing. A new edition of *The President* moved back toward his 1934 position. The first passage quoted above was revised as follows (italicized words added):

> bring presidential whim under an independent scrutiny which today is lacking *and yet who, by putting their stamp of approval upon his proposals would be able to facilitate their enactment into law.*

The second passage cited above became:

> two dangers: *the slowing down of the legislative process to an extent that unfits it for a crisis-ridden world in which time is often of the essence, and—in consequence*—autocracy.

By 1957, Corwin had moved still further into the presidential camp politically. In 1954, for instance, he headed a national committee to defeat the Bricker amendment. His constitutional doctrine followed. A passage in *The President* that read in the 1948 edition:

> As matters stand today, presidential power is dangerously personalized.

became in the 1957 edition:

> As matters *stood till the other day presidential power has been at times* dangerously personalized.

Corwin's constitutional theory, then, closely followed his political preferences. While a protégé of "strong" President Wilson and a supporter of "strong" President Roosevelt, he argued the theoretical virtues of a strong Presidency. When he broke with Roosevelt, he discarded that view, returning to it only after Roosevelt was cold in his grave.

Corwin's case may be clearest, but the close connection between political preference and constitutional theory in the 1960 group as a whole is obvious. The genesis of the 1960 consensus, then, lay in the presidential style of Roosevelt and Truman elevated to the level of constitutional theory by partisan supporters of those Presidents and contrasted with the style of the man who, despite their opposition, defeated Truman's chosen successor.

The first half of my thesis, then, is that the constitutional theory of the 1960 consensus school rested on the partisan political bias of the members of that school and that events showed their bias to be a fragile foundation. Note that I am not making an ad hominem argument. I am not calling their theory into question on the grounds that they had had certain personal experiences that biased them. Rather, I showed that their theory had fallen into disrepute and had failed the test of empirical application. Then I showed how this failure might be understood by examining the partisan political biases and commitments of the writers. To paraphrase the turn-of-the-century American imperialists, one might say that "the constitutional theory followed the party flag."

Unfortunately, because a pendulum has swung does not necessarily mean that it has progressed. This pendulum has not. Most of the present detractors of the Presidency rest their theories on no more solid ground than did the glorifiers. They, too, tend to dissolve constitutional theory in their personal political biases. The acid of hatred for the Vietnam war may have replaced the nectar of affection for the New Deal, but the solvent effect remains.

Since 1960, writers on the Presidency have been learning to their chagrin that the Presidency can thwart their purposes as well as serve them. The power that they urged upon the Presidency has been used to support policies of which they disapprove. Power per se is neutral. Power wielders may not be. Some power wielders are "good guys"; others are "bad guys," depending on the viewer's perspective. That lesson has been surprisingly hard for constitutional theorists to learn. Even today, the most common response of critics of the Presidency is to urge that power be shifted from it to Congress. Yet by the time that transfer is accomplished, the "good guys" may be back in the White House and the "bad guys'" back in Congress.

Constitutional theory cannot depend upon this "report card" approach. It is very thin indeed if it evaluates an institution on the basis of the constitutional theorists' agreement with its incumbents or its policies of the moment and adjudges it, thereby, to be worthy of more or less power for the indefinite future. Such constitutional theory has been dissolved in the policy and partisan preferences of the theorists. If those preferences leak out of the institution, the constitutional theory goes with them. Note that I am not impugning motives nor questioning the propriety of the biases or of their expression, even as constitutional theory. I am saying, simply, that theory generated that way is unlikely to be very good or very durable. Unless the theorist is extraordinarily lucky, he won't explain things very well very long.

Constitutional theory should have more substance than that. The Glorified Presidency of the 1960 consensus was like the Biblical house builded on sand. During the late 1960s a lot of rain fell on it and floods came and it fell. But instead of following the example of the wise man in the Bible, the new constitutional theory of the 1970s is being builded on another strip of sand, doomed to last no longer than the next stormy blast. Durable constitutional theory requires a firmer foundation. Without that, our understanding of our governmental institutions will remain as fragile as the 1960 consensus on the Presidency. This brings me to the second half of my thesis, a proposal for means to avoid that fragility.

VI. LAYING A FIRM FOUNDATION

The task of rebuilding American constitutional theory so as to avoid the shoals on which the 1960 writers ran aground is not to be undertaken lightly, but a start must be made. The remaining paragraphs of this essay shall sketch out briefly some elements of theory aimed in that direction. I suggest that our understanding of the constitutional power relationships of the Presidency and Congress must rest on an understanding of the nature of the American polity, the nature of the institutions themselves, and the character of the problems with which they are dealing at a given moment and over a period of time. Because of their natures, all institutions perform some political tasks better than others. Because of their natures, all polities require the performance of some political tasks more urgently than they require others. Because of its character, each problem is dealt with better by one institution than by another. To understand the proper power relationship between President and Congress, then, one must look at the polity, the institutions, and the problems of the United States.

The American polity, the political aspect of our national community, may be described as having a great deal of superficial diversity resting on a fundamental common character. At least, this is how it appears, viewed over 200 years of history, compared to such other modern polities as England, France, Germany, and Italy. We lack the deep political-ideological cleavages that have marked the histories of the latter three countries, but, also, we lack the pervasive homogeneity that has been so characteristic of the English polity. The American polity is an amalgam of diversity at one level and unity at another.

The Presidency and Congress have very different natures. Presidents are elective by a single national constituency. All participating voters throughout the nation choose between the same candidates at the same time. This makes the Presidency the representative of the entire nation and the defender of the general national interest. Upon election, the President stands alone at the apex of a vertical authority structure. We have only one President. No one in the executive branch of the national government has equal or greater authority than he. No one has the legal authority to countermand or resist his orders. Of course, in practice bureaucratic interia may make his exertion of that authority difficult, but, in fact, the authority still is his alone. "Unity" is the key word to describe the nature of the Presidency: unity of constituency, unity of representation, unity of membership, and unity of authority.

In contrast to the Presidency, Congress is elective by 485 different constituencies. In each of 435 of them, voters choose from a different set of candidates for the House of Representatives. In the other fifty constituencies (the states), not only does each set of voters have a different set of candidates, but also, only a third of the representatives (senators) are chosen in each election. Each of the 435 representatives and each of the 50 pairs of senators represents a different constituency and a different set of interests. Therefore, each represents only a small part of the nation. No part is larger than about 9 percent of the nation, and most parts are only about 0.2 percent of the nation each. Upon election, the members of Congress form a horizontal authority structure. No member has any real authority over any other. They are all chiefs; none are Indians. Unity of command is absent completely. Diversity is the keyword to describe the nature of Congress: diversity of constituencies, diversity of representation, diversity of membership, diversity of authority.

Political problems, also, differ in their natures. The basic differences that concern the power relationship of Presidency and Congress arise from whether the problem is to accommodate interests or to serve an interest. Some problems spring from the conflicting interests of significant groups in the polity as represented in the machinery of the national government's decision-making process. For instance, economic difficulties in the sugar-producing industry might lead some congressional representatives to propose a tariff that other congressional representatives might regard as antithetical to their constituents' interests. Resolution of the problem may require give-and-take, negotiation, accommodation among the various interests. In other cases, national consensus agrees on a single interest, and the problem lies in finding the most effective way to serve that interest and in giving effect to that national consensus. For instance, an attack by a foreign power may produce instant consensus on the need to repulse the attack without any significant conflict of opinion on the overriding importance of serving that single national will and that single national interest.

Resolution of the former kind of problem in a democratic polity requires negotiation and accommodation among the groups with conflicting interests. Without give-and-take and an earnest search for a generally satisfactory solution, disagreements deepen into social cleavages. Congress is the institution best suited to resolve such problems in the American system, because it contains the designated representatives of most significant interest communities in the United States and is structured in such a way as to provide maximum opportunities for those representatives to seek together solutions to those problems. On the other hand, the second kind of problem requires action, not accommodation, or the national will and national interest will not be served effectively. This requires a different kind of institution, one like the Presidency which has the capacity for command because of its vertical authority structure and the legitimacy to do so because its incumbent is the single designated representative of the nation as a whole. Its unity enables the Presidency to act with greater dispatch, greater secrecy, and therefore, usually greater effectiveness in serving the national interest than can Congress in dealing with that kind of problem.

The nature of the polity affects the basic character of the relationship between the legislature and the political executive over a period of time. If the polity is characterized by deep, fundamental cleavages that manifest themselves politically, the problems facing the governmental system will tend to be the kind that requires group accommodation and, hence, resolution within the legislature. In such cases, of which France before de Gaulle is a prime example, the legislature will tend to dominate the governmental system to a certain extent regardless of the character of the specific problem being handled at any particular moment.

On the other hand, if the polity is characterized by basic harmony, the attention of the governmental system will tend to be directed outward, and its problems will tend to be the kind on which national consensus exists and which require positive action rather than group accommodation. This makes the executive the dominant branch of government. Great Britain during the first half of this century is a leading example of that kind of polity.

Finally, if a polity has the nature of the United States, underlying unity overlaid by significant diversity, neither kind of problem dominates the political scene for long periods of time and neither branch of government is able to establish permanent dominance. They remain coordinate in power and authority. Power moves back and forth between them fairly easily in response to the differing needs of the society in solving the leading problems of the moment. That has been the case with the United States.

Application of this analytical framework to the issue of presidential power in the 1960s should help resolve the contradictions of that debate. First, though, we must discard such notions as too much power now and too little power then. Also, we must put aside personal policy and party preferences. Instead, we must consider whether power flowed to and from the Presidency depending on whether the problem at issue required consensual action or accommodation. If the American political system was working well, power flowed to the Presidency in the former case and to Congress in the latter. For instance: if Congress followed the President more or less blindly when consensus supported the Vietnam operation and if Congress turned on him when that consensus evaporated, the system was working well.

Theory grounded on the kind of analysis I propose offers no magic formula. A lot of independent judgment still must be fed into it. Reasonable and perceptive scholars may disagree on the nature of a polity or of a problem or on the existence of consensus. No framework of analysis can determine precisely its content. However, it should keep the attention of the analysts directed more clearly and steadfastly toward its intended object. If it does, it should, at least, produce better and more durable constitutional theory than emerged from the Presidency studies of 1960.

2.

THE PRESIDENCY AND THE CONSTITUTION: A LOOK AHEAD

Joseph E. Kallenbach

Current fashion in scholarly discussions of the presidency is to focus upon its internal organizational arrangements and operational methods, the "style" and the "public image" of the occupant of the moment. This emphasis is by no means misplaced. The dimensions of the presidency are determined in large measure by the occupant's capacity and skill in converting his post into a center for policy-initiation and leadership in the political process. Without question, it has become a highly *personalized* office. Yet it is well to remind ourselves from time to time that with reference to this great office, the Constitution still "does matter." Underlying all that it has come to be is the constitutional framework which gives it form and substance.

I. THE CONSTITUTIONAL FOUNDATION

In formulating the constitutional phraseology creating this office the framers of the Constitution wrote on a clean slate. They were in the rather enviable position of being able to give concrete form to what was in their collective judgment a "model" plan of executive organization. Blending theory with practical wisdom derived from the British model and from American experience with various types of "republican" executive organization, they set down as their contribution on this subject the language of Article II of the Constitution.

Viewing these original constitutional provisions in the perspective afforded by time, one is impressed first of all by the extraordinary viability and durability of the terminology hit upon in defining the President's powers, functions, and relations with the other elements making up the governmental scheme. It remains to this date without alteration. One notes further, however, that the formal amending procedure has been resorted to with unusual frequency to tinker with certain structural features of the original plan—chiefly those concerned with the mode of selection.

Since 1791, when the perfecting Bill of Rights amendments were incorporated into the Constitution, there have been fifteen amendments engrafted upon the handiwork of the framers. No less than five of these—the twelfth (1804), twentieth (1933), twenty-second (1951), twenty-third (1961), and the twenty-fifth (1967)—have dealt with what may very properly be described as structural aspects of the office of President. To these might well be added three others—the fifteenth (1870), nineteenth (1920), and twenty-fourth (1963) amendments. These revisions of the original document, to be sure, were directed generally toward broadening the popular electoral base upon which government in the United States rests. But these amendments were adopted after developments through state legislation and party usage had already occurred that had converted the original plan of presidential selection into a system of indirect popular choice. These franchise-extending amendments therefore contributed very materially toward democratizing in greater measure the office of President.

Formal amendments adopted to date have been essentially responses to change in conception of the functions assigned to this office. As has been noted, the original phraseology detailing its formal powers and defining its relationships to the other organs of government remains unchanged. But it is precisely *because* new conceptions of the President's role in the governmental process have become institutionalized that it has been deemed necessary to introduce structural modifications by resort to the amendment procedure.

Constitutional revisions effected to date have been, essentially, accommodations dictated by the President's having assumed a more open,

---

Reprinted with permission from a symposium on the institutionalized presidency appearing in *Law and Contemporary Problems,* Vol. 35, No. 3 (Summer, 1970), pp. 445–460, published by the Duke University School of Law, Durham, North Carolina. Abridged; footnotes have been renumbered for this volume.

active leadership role in government affairs. This has resulted from the new interpretations read into his original grants of constitutional authority. Supplemented further by congressional enactments, these grants have become a vast reservoir of power and influence. The President's "headship" of the government has become far more than symbolic. The primacy of the *presidency,* if not of the *President,* as an element in the governing process, has become apparent to all. Simultaneously developments have occurred that have placed in his hands also a national party leadership role, supplementing his official governmental "headship" powers at almost every point.

II. THE ROLES OF THE PRESIDENT

Implicit in these developments there is discernible a certain ambivalence, even a contradiction, of purpose and result. This ambivalence arises from a duality in the roles that have come to be associated with this office. On the one hand, providing a direct popular base on which the office rests, coupled with a broadened conception of his official powers and authority, has given the President a new source of support for vigorous assertion and use of his constitutional powers vis-à-vis Congress, the courts, and the states. He speaks and acts as the *people's* agent. He lays claim to a mandate from them for his acts. Authority *descends* upon him from the nation, not from the other organs of government. *Vox populi legati suprema lex est* becomes his credo.

Thus when Franklin D. Roosevelt addressed Congress in 1942 in his role as President, requesting that it pass a more effective price and wage control bill, he underscored his request with a threat to act on his own authority if Congress failed to respond promptly. He concluded his remarkable statement with these significant words:

> When the war is won, the powers under which I act [will] automatically revert *to the people—to whom they belong.*

Essentially what FDR was enunciating was a kind of fuhrership principle of executive authority. As National Leader and Head of Government he was laying claim to a right to act in the name of the people for the public good, independent of congressional sanctioning of his action. Granted, he may well have been bluffing, knowing that the Congress would respond to his request, given the state of public opinion at the time; but this statement is a clear illustration of the ultimate reach of executive prerogative in an "emergency."

Added to this latitudinarian conception of the powers of the office is the idea that the President should exercise a "moral leadership" role in the affairs of the American people generally. Again it was FDR, echoing views earlier expressed by Theodore Roosevelt and Woodrow Wilson, who can be cited as voicing most emphatically this view. Shortly before his assumption of office, he characterized it as "pre-eminently a place of moral leadership." This responsibility, he went on to say, far outweighs the purely administrative functions of the office. The range of this responsibility extends to every matter of vital concern to the people and their welfare. The presidency thus becomes an office of spiritual as well as political leadership. It combines the functions of a Caesar and a Pope.

But when the "people" invest the President with his powers of office, they do so through a partisan electoral contest. He speaks through and for the political party whose acknowledged champion and spokesman he has become by virtue of his emerging as its nominee. Of course, his objective as a leader of a partisan faction is only to prevail over a Loyal Opposition party (or parties) with regard to certain policies he believes the government should pursue. His objective is not to utterly destroy them. His mandate as party leader is limited by the democratic dogma of toleration for opposing views—a concept that supplies the key to successful operation of democratic systems of government generally. In view of the non-ideological, quite decentralized character of the two major parties in the United States, moreover, this partisanship of toleration extends in great degree into the area of intra-party politics as well. Over neither his "congressional party" wing nor the state and local party cadres upon whose shoulders he has ridden into power can the President realistically expect to exercise a discipline and control that unites them into a solid phalanx under his leadership.

Joining in his hands these two kinds of leadership roles places the President in a somewhat awkward position. He becomes at once the surrogate of a united people and at the same time, the leader and spokesman of a faction of the people. In his first capacity he wields broad "moral leadership" and none-too-closely defined official powers as Head of State. In his latter capacity, by contrast, he speaks and acts for a segment of the people aligned in opposition to other important elements in American political society. As such, he must expect to encounter, and be obliged to tolerate, a great amount of sniping, criticism, and mulish obstructionism, if not downright sabotage, of his undertakings. Those in and out of government who speak and act for an organized, constantly evolving partisan opposition will see to that. Intent upon scoring points that will enhance their chances of taking over control of this power center at the next election, his partisan opponents are naturally loath to act in ways that might make the President and the partisan element he represents "look good" in the eyes of the national electorate; for his partisan opposition is committed to an attempt to oust him and his party when the contest for preferment is staged anew.

Because of this duality of roles, the presidency necessarily presents to the nation and the world a kind of schizophrenic aspect. As influences and pressure play upon the President from the two poles of his sometimes inconsistent roles, he performs his functions in a state of continual tension. Let him address the Congress—and his national constituency as well—in discharge of his constitutional responsibility to "give to the Congress information on the state of the Union, and recommend to their consideration such measures as he shall deem necessary and expedient," and the cry arises immediately for "equal time" on the communications media for his Loyal Opposition to reply. His engagement in active congressional campaigning to further election of partisan colleagues pledged to support of his policies immediately sparks charges of "slicksterism" and misuse of the prestige of his office for partisan ends. Searching and sometimes embarrassing questions are raised on exactly how and by whom the expenses entailed by his campaign tours and speeches are being met. On the other hand, his failure to include an active, effective party leadership role in his conception of his official responsibilities exposes him to criticism from other directions for ineptness and unwillingness to exploit to the fullest extent the potential of his office for advancing the public welfare.

The "moral leadership" aspect of the President's modern role in governmental affairs serves further to magnify the tensions arising from his having assumed a party leadership function in addition to a greatly broadened conception of an official authority derived from the constitutional sources. One commentator recently began a short discussion of this problem in its current context in this fashion:

> Around the White House they worry quite sincerely that a lot of Americans are confusing the President with God. Their concern, of course, stems from the fear that if the populace approaches the Oval Office with spiritual expectations and then finds only a human in there, the result will be general despair and a tendency to blame everything from riots and race hatred to dope and divorce on Richard Nixon.[1]

In the eyes of the populace—with some assistance from Presidents themselves as well as from none-too-discerning learned commentators—the President is elevated to the status of the Great Wizard, the Healer of All the Nation's Woes. Let him fail to express his views and concern about one of the great problems of the day, and he is assailed for failure to exert appropriate "moral leadership." All would be well, it is said, if he would only sound the tocsin to battle against this or that evil in American life. It is his function to inspire the people and point the way to realization

---

[1] Sidey, "The Presidency: Demand for 'Moral Leadership.'" *Life*, Oct. 23, 1970, at 2.

of every man's conception of the American Dream. Yet if he announces a position and issues a call for action on some burning social or economic issue—with the inevitable result of offending some elements in society who do not agree with his point of view—his critics will be quick to charge him with "creating divisiveness," "alienating" important elements of society, or "polarizing" the American Public.

III. THE PROSPECTS FOR CHANGE

It is within the context of these built-in conflicts between the roles the modern presidency has assumed that one must approach the question of the possibility and desirability of change in the Constitution as it relates to this office. Given the history of failure of past efforts, both from within Congress and from outside it, to effect fundamental changes of this kind (except as to the mode of filling the office and keeping it filled), the prospects appear to be practically nil. The method by which the popular choice of the nation is determined in the selection of the President and Vice President will probably soon be brought into closer focus with political realities by formal amendment of the Constitution. Beyond that, however, the prospects for change appear slim indeed. Change in a fundamental sense is likely to occur only if some great catastrophe in the nation's life—such as, God forbid! an all-out nuclear war, or an internal upheaval of the sort apparently sought by some of our young revolutionary nihilists—should befall us.

It should never be forgotten that the modern Presidency is the product of a continual struggle for power and influence deliberately invited by the nature of the original constitutional plan. So far as concerns the constitutional ground rules setting up the arena and allocating weapons of political warfare as among the three branches of the national government, they have to date resisted all efforts to alter them by the formal amendment route. There is no good reason to believe they will not continue to do so.

Note, for example, the controversies that have arisen over the question of alteration of the original veto arrangements in the Constitution. An unusually vigorous use of this authority by Andrew Jackson produced in reaction a series of serious but unsuccessful attempts by the Whigs to cut back the veto power by constitutional amendment during the 1840's. Enactment by a run-away Congress of 15 of 21 measures vetoed by President Andrew Johnson in the 1860's ultimately demonstrated that the veto was not an absolute weapon in the hands of the President. It could be blunted by a determined congressional majority.

Later the pendulum swung the other way again. Every President from Grant to Eisenhower has expressed dissatisfaction with the original veto arrangements and pleaded for a constitutional amendment granting them the item veto over appropriation bills. Numerous pundits have endorsed the idea as a sound one. When no favorable response came from Congress, the Presidents eventually turned increasingly to the device of "impoundment" of appropriated funds which in their judgment were improvidently authorized by Congress.[2] Still more recently, enactment by Congress of a major appropriation bill over President Nixon's veto has demonstrated anew that the "pull and haul" system set up by the framers as between Congress and the President in the enactment of money bills is by no means outmoded. It still works both ways.

All this is not to say, of course, that changes in the constitutionally ordained equilibrium of power as between the President, the Congress, and the courts, and as between him and state authorities has not occurred, or will not continue to occur. The role of the President in the constitutional scheme will doubtless be altered as the future unfolds; but alteration will come about through the more subtle, informal methods of constitutional change rather than by constitutional amendment. Changes in the balance of powers between Congress and the Executive that will be effected cannot be expected to eliminate the state of tension that exists between them. They may well cause it to become even more acute from time to time as the President appears in his various roles before the Congress and the American public.

For the moment it would appear that the mood in Congress and in the nation is one of seeking and exploiting new, and refurbishing old, ways of redressing the balance more explicitly on the side of congressional power and influence. This would appear to have been a more or less inevitable result, given the fact that in four of the last eight Congresses (five out of nine if the new 92nd Congress chosen in November, 1970, is included) both Houses have been under the control of the President's political opposition.

It can be predicted that among the strategies Congress may be expected to pursue in the future in its never-ending tug-of-war with the President will be the following:

1. Further efforts to exploit more effectively its inquisitorial and other types of authority to command production of information relevant to public policy in the hands of the President or his agents.

2. More frequent use of a built-in concurrent resolution "cut-off"

---

[2] For a discussion of this development, see Goostree, "The Power of the President to Impound Appropriated Funds: With Special Reference to Grants-in-Aid to Segregated Activities," and Kranz, "A Twentieth Century Emancipation Proclamation: Presidential Power Permits Withholding of Federal Funds from Segregated Institutions," in *The Presidency* 727 (A. Wildavsky ed. 1969); Church, "Impoundment of Appropriated Funds; The Decline of Congressional Control Over Executive Discretion," 22 *Stan. L. Rev.* 1240 (1970).

device, whereby grants of authority to the President by legislative act may be cancelled without running the risk of a veto.

3. Wider employment of the committee-clearance-in-advance procedure for supervising administration of particular statutes.

4. Increased resort to House and/or Senate resolutions declarative of attitudes, intent, and understandings of the respective bodies on questions of public policy, as illustrated by the Senate's passage of the National Commitments Resolution in 1969.[3]

5. Freer use by the Senate of its power to reject nominations to major posts by the President. Illustrative of the point was the Senate's breaking a precedent of some forty years standing by refusing to confirm two presidential nominations to the Supreme Court within the past two years. This followed soon after a resignation of an incumbent Justice was induced by a Senate inquiry into his qualifications while he was being considered as the President's nominee for the post of Chief Justice.

6. Fuller exploitations by Congress of its "power of the purse" to limit presidential discretion in various policy-initiating and policy-executing areas. The ultimate reach of this potent weapon remains unexplored, at least in the minds of some members of Congress. As indicated in the Senate debates on the Cooper-Church Amendment to the Military Procurement Act of 1970, it might conceivably be used in such a way as to substitute Congressional judgment for that of the President in the exercise of his commander-in-chief functions with respect to matters of military strategy and tactics in an area of actual combat. It might be observed, in passing, that when Congress in 1942 sought to use the "power of the purse" to usurp the President's constitutionally based power of removal over subordinate executive officials, it was rebuked by the Supreme Court. But the Court's ruling in that instance turned on a point of constitutional construction that carefully evaded the basic question of implied limits on the power of the purse growing out of the Constitution's allocation of executive powers to the President.

The long-range impact of these and other devices Congress may be expected to experiment with in the next decade on the constitutional balance of power between the two branches cannot be fully appraised at this point. They may well prove to be futile and ineffective. The pressures

---

[3] *S. Res.* 85, 91st Cong., 1st Sess. (1969). The resolution, which was passed by a 70–16 vote, reads as follows:

Resolved, That (1) a national commitment for the purpose of this resolution means the use of armed forces of the United States on Foreign territory, or a promise to assist a foreign country, government, or people by the use of armed forces or financial resources of the United States, either immediately or upon the happening of certain events, and (2) it is the sense of the Senate that a national commitment by the United States results only from affirmative action taken by the executive and legislative branches of the United States by means of a treaty, statute, or concurrent resolution of both Houses of Congress specifically providing for such commitment.

that exist both in the foreign and domestic policy-making areas appear to make aggrandizement of the executive side of government an imperative. Efforts in Congress to retrieve for itself a wider decision-making authority may simply prove to be impractical.

IV. CONSTITUTIONAL AMENDMENTS

Meanwhile, the impact of both recent and anticipated constitutional revisions pertaining to the office of President can be evaluated. These changes by amendment, it has been pointed out above, have reference to the mode of election and perfecting the arrangements for succession, rather than to the powers of the office per se. Nevertheless they have a significance with respect to the extra-constitutional role of the President as party leader in ways that have not been widely appreciated.

The twenty-second amendment, which became a part of the constitutional plan in 1951, has usually been conceived of as an instrument for enforcing a rule of rotation with respect to the holding of the *official* powers of the office. And so it is. But it may be suggested that the amendment was understood by its more perceptive advocates as significant primarily as an instrument for regulating *party* government. Its immediate impact was to enforce a rule of limited tenure on a national party head by arbitrarily displacing him after an interval as the dominant force in his party nationally.

After all, as had been demonstrated by the Taft and Hoover candidacies in 1912 and 1932, respectively, an incumbent President seeking reelection could be turned out of office after one term if the people were so inclined. But no incumbent President since 1900 who had sought renomination by his party had been rejected as its *nominee*. It was the domination of the national party convention by an incumbent President so as to compel his own renomination that was the primary target of the amendment. Rather than tinker with the constitutional arrangements relating to the official powers and duties of his office (on the terms of which probably no agreement could have been achieved in Congress), this indirect bi-partisan approach to the end desired—a freeing of the *party* from one-man rule—was adopted.

Again, one may discern a connection between the twentieth amendment and the twenty-fifth amendment in their bearing on the question of succession in the party leadership aspect of the presidency. The main object of the twentieth amendment, of course, was to effect a closer coordination between the beginning of an in-coming President's term of office and the functioning of the newly-chosen Congress under his leadership. An infrequently noted provision of the amendment, however, was the language of its third section. This section makes clear that in the contingency of an inconclusive presidential election and an ensuing deadlock in the House of Representatives, the new Vice President-elect must temporarily assume the post of *Acting* President until the deadlock is resolved. His doing so, it is made clear, does not permanently displace the President-to-be.

This language went part way, at least, toward resolving the question whether a Vice President might legitimately *act* as President without *becoming* President—an unresolved issue that had been a serious barrier to implementation of the original constitutional arrangements regarding succession in the event of the President's disability. Beyond that, however, it implied that the President and the Vice President, rather than being regarded as candidates for two separate offices, should be looked upon as a "team." The Vice President, as the potential deputy party leader, should therefore be politically compatible with and enjoy the confidence of the President in that capacity.

In addition to legitimizing either a temporary or permanent Head of State role for the Vice President—an important criterion for any arrangement relative to the presidential succession—this provision led almost immediately to introduction of the usage of the national party convention's deferring to the presidential nominee's wishes in the selection of a vice presidential running mate. In other words, the national party leader was accorded the privilege of naming the deputy leader. This practice manifested itself in the Democratic Party's convention in 1940 when F.D.R. imposed upon a rather reluctant body of delegates his choice of running mate. The precedent of consulting the presidential nominee and deferring to his wishes in the matter of the vice presidential nomination has been followed in every national major party convention, with one exception, since then.[4]

This usage, in its turn, led directly to inclusion of the language of section 2 in the twenty-fifth amendment. That section, which follows immediately upon language in the amendment declaring that the Vice President shall "become" President in case of the removal of the President, or his death or resignation, reads as follows:

> Whenever there is a vacancy in the office of the Vice President, the President shall nominate a Vice President who shall take office upon confirmation by a majority vote of both Houses of Congress.

Potentially this provision of the amendment is of far greater signifi-

---

[4] Adlai Stevenson, the Democratic Party's nominee in 1956, permitted the party convention to exercise a free choice in the matter of the vice presidential nomination. His endorsement of Senator Sparkman, of Alabama, as his running mate in the 1952 election had given rise to considerable criticism in certain "liberal" circles of the party, who maintained that it had weakened the ticket.

cance than the other sections concerning succession to the powers and duties of the office of President by the Vice President in the event of the President's disability. It has as its objective keeping the line of succession filled by a President-in-waiting, thus obviating the necessity, for all practical purposes, of going beyond the vice presidency in providing a successor. In view of the increasing importance that has come to attach to the vice presidential post so far as the party leadership aspect of the office of President is concerned, it is remarkable that this provision in the amendment received comparatively little attention in the congressional debates. It deserved far more attention than it was given. Of all the provisions in the amendment, it is the one that may well prove to be either unworkable in practice or, if it works, of profound significance in its impact upon the office of President in its party leadership aspect.

Since World War II, the vice presidency has become the most frequently used stepping stone to the presidency, or at least to preferment as the nominee for that post by the President's party. Two presidentially designated deputy party leaders, Harry S. Truman and L. B. Johnson, have succeeded to the office of President upon the death of incumbents and have gone on to win election in their own right for full terms. Two other incumbent Vice Presidents, Richard Nixon in 1960 and Hubert Humphrey in 1968, were nominated with the blessing of the incumbent President of their respective parties, but were defeated in their runs for the big prize. Nixon, of course, was successful in a second try after an intervening election. Increasing reliance of Presidents from F.D.R. to Nixon on their Vice Presidents to carry a major share of the party campaigning burden in off-year congressional elections demonstrates the point that the Vice President's *ex officio* role as deputy party leader is something more than an empty title.

It is this dimension of the President's position in relation to his party that raises doubts about the feasibility of this provision of the amendment. Placing the responsibility in his hands to nominate a person to fill a vice presidential vacancy, insofar as that officer becomes an *ex officio* deputy party leader, is of course, in line with the practice that has come to prevail at the national party convention in selecting the vice presidential nominee. Presumably a President will consult other party leaders in and out of Congress in settling on his choice, in case the post becomes vacant, as he does at a national party convention. But his filling a vacancy in the *office* is not merely that of selecting a candidate for election, subject to the suffrage of the people. It is to fill an office with prescribed constitutional and statutory powers and duties plus other important partisan political functions.

The twenty-fifth amendment proposes to give legitimacy to a new incumbent in the vice presidency as an *officer* by requiring that his appointment be confirmed by a majority vote in both Houses of Congress.

This is likely to be forthcoming if the President's party has a majority in both Houses. But what if the President's party does not have majority control in Congress?

This is no idle speculation. In no less than six of the last thirteen Congresses, the President's party has been in the minority in both Houses of Congress. May it be readily assumed in this kind of situation that as a matter of partisan "courtesy" the majority party in the two Houses will readily go along with the President's selection of a person who will become his "heir apparent" as party leader? Would the temptation not be too strong for the President's loyal opposition to simply "sit" on the nomination, keep the vice presidency vacant, and thereby, under arrangements regarding the presidential succession presently set forth in the Presidential Succession Act of 1947, retain the opposition party's House Speaker in the position of being only "one heartbeat away" from the presidency itself?

Other features of the twenty-fifth amendment are less open to criticism on the ground that they fail to take into account the fact that the presidency has become a party leadership post as well as a powerful Headship of State office. The arrangements of section 3 of the amendment providing for temporary assumption of the powers and duties of the office of President by the Vice President upon due notice and request by a temporarily disabled President are in line with understandings reached on an informal basis by President Eisenhower and his Vice President, as well as by Presidents Kennedy and Johnson and their "Deputy Presidents." These "understandings," it should be noted, had followed upon resolution of the point in the twentieth amendment that a Vice President might "act" as President without "becoming" President.

The rather complex procedure provided for effecting a temporary succession by a Vice President when the President is unable to declare his disability commendably takes into account the partisan political aspects of the succession problem as well as the official duty aspects. On the partisan side, associating the heads of the principal departments (or of "such other body as Congress may by law provide") with the decision of the Vice President to assume the powers of the presidency in this kind of contingency affords protection against a rash challenge of the party head by an ambitious Vice President, or perchance, may spur him to take necessary action.

A similar procedure must be invoked by a Vice President to resist a President he deems still disabled who seeks to resume the powers of office. But the support of a two-thirds majority in both branches of Congress must be secured by a Vice President within a specified time limit if he is to be permitted to retain the official powers of the presidency in the face of a claim by the incumbent President that his disability has been eliminated.

In simpler terms, the amendment provides a rational procedure by which a President regarded as unable to exercise his official powers as head of state, and his unofficial functions as party chief as well, may be *suspended* though not permanently *removed.* The procedure adopted seeks to provide a check upon the Vice President's action in such a case both as to its impact on the party leadership role as well as upon the head of state role of the President. A contingency of the sort that might involve Congress as the ultimate judge of the merits of the claims of rival contenders for the office is very unlikely to occur; but if it does, requiring a substantial bi-partisan majority in each House of Congress to suspend the regularly elected President from office is appropriate insurance that this step will be taken only in the event a crisis of major proportions has arisen—one transcending ordinary considerations of partisan advantage.

V. PRESIDENTIAL ELECTORAL REFORM REVISITED: CONGRESS AS AN ELECTORAL BODY

A final point of consideration concerns the impact upon the President's dual roles of head of state and party head that might flow from a revision of the current constitutional language regarding the mode of his election. It may be predicted with some degree of confidence that a constitutional amendment will be adopted in the near future abolishing the present electoral college machinery for registering the will of the voters of the nation in the selection of the President and Vice President and making a direct vote of the people at large determinative of the outcome. But certain nagging problems have appeared with regard to the details of such an amendment.

One of the problems that loomed large in the past in debates on a proposal of this kind has all but disappeared. The logical implication that such a plan should include provisions for uniform national suffrage standards in presidential elections has been eliminated for all practical purposes by adoption of the twenty-fourth amendment and passage of the Voting Rights Extension Act of 1970. Taxpaying and literacy tests as state requirements for voting in presidential elections have been abolished, 18 years has been prescribed as a minimum age requirement, and a minimum period of 30 days residence in the state has been set. Another problem—how to assure that the President and Vice President chosen will always be of the same party—can be easily disposed of by requiring that they be presented by their respective parties before the electorate as inseparable pairs, to be voted upon jointly by the electorate.[5] This device would, of course, be wholly in keeping with the spirit of the provisions of the twenty-fifth amendment designed to keep the vice presidency filled at all times by a politically compatible person through appointment by the incumbent President.

The most difficult question presented by a direct presidential electoral reform amendment, however, is whether to rest the outcome simply upon a plurality vote in a "one-shot" final electoral confrontation, as is done in all final elections to Congress and, with only a very few exceptions, in elections to statewide offices; or to set a minimum plurality standard that must be obtained to make the popular election determinative, with some sort of contingent method of choice if the first trial of strength is not conclusive. In the version of the direct election amendment proposal passed by the House by a 339–70 majority in September, 1969, this problem was dealt with by a provision that if no pair of party candidates receives a plurality of 40 percent or more of the total national vote, a "run-off" popular election must be held within a matter of weeks between the two leading pairs of candidates. In Senate debate in 1970 on this proposal, opponents, although they were distinctly in the minority, were able to prevent a definitive Senate vote on the House-passed version. Two efforts to invoke closure on debate on the issue fell short by narrow margins. Opponents centered their fire heavily on the 40 percent clause and the "run-off" election features of the House plan.

Alternative plans advanced by them looked generally toward preserving the present electoral vote arrangements for weighting state voting for the President and Vice President. Most of these alternative proposals also embraced the idea of continuing to require a majority of the electoral votes from the nation to produce a winner at the initial stage. Some of the alternative plans included the present "winner-take-all" statewide vote system, with an automatic casting of all of a state's electoral votes for the candidate receiving a statewide plurality. Others looked toward the splitting up of a state's electoral votes. There was some support among the opponents to direct popular election for the idea of awarding a state's electoral votes in accordance with the proportion of popular votes each candidate receives. Others favored awarding them to the candidates on the basis of the popular pluralities received by them in the respective congressional districts, with two to be awarded in each state on the basis of the statewide plurality result. Some of the alternative plans would have left unchanged present constitutional provisions requiring a national electoral vote majority for a definitive result, with an inconclusive presidential

---

[5] A rapidly growing number of states have followed the example set by New York in 1953 of "tieing in" the election of the governor and the lieutenant-governor in this fashion.

electoral vote contest to be resolved by the House, voting by state units, and in the case of the vice presidential contest, by the Senate. More commonly, however, the alternative electoral reform proposals provided for reference of inconclusive contests for both offices to a joint session of the two Houses, with each member having an equal and independent vote in determining the final result.

It would appear that the dominant feeling in Congress is that a direct election reform amendment embracing the plurality vote principle, with no "floor" as to the proportion of the total popular vote the winner's plurality must represent to be definitive, would be unwise and potentially dangerous to the political stability of the nation. The fear is expressed repeatedly in the debates that a simple plurality vote requirement, with nothing more, would be an open invitation to party schismatics to flex their muscles, splinter the popular vote, destroy the major two-party structures, and bring about as a regular matter installation in the presidential chair of sectionally- or class-based minority choices with little general nationwide appeal and support. Whether this is a correct assessment of the results that would follow upon adoption of a simple, national, popular plurality vote requirement for determining the outcome is highly questionable. Nevertheless, the existence of such strongly held fears among members of Congress on the point appears to dictate that a direct election reform amendment, to be acceptable to a two-thirds majority in each House, must contain a minimum plurality standard as being necessary for a conclusive result at the initial stage. A figure of a minimum plurality of 40 percent of the total vote has been found to be generally acceptable for this purpose among supporters of the direct election concept.

This, in turn, presents a question concerning the nature of the contingent mode of resolution of the election if no pair of candidates receives the requisite national popular plurality. In opposing the idea of a second "run-off" election as the appropriate means for resolving this kind of impasse and preferring instead to refer such an election to Congress for resolution, it would appear that some members of Congress have not given as much thought as is warranted to the prospect of their having to perform this kind of contingent electoral function. In part their lack of concern about this feature of a presidential election system is attributable to the fact that within recent memory Congress has not been called upon to act as an electoral body. Since adoption of the twelfth amendment in 1803, only one presidential election—that of 1824—has had to be resolved by the House and only one vice presidential election—in 1836—has had to be referred to the Senate. But so long as the Constitution contains a provision that contemplates resort to voting by members of Congress to resolve an inconclusive contest in the selection of the President and/or the Vice President, the possibility exists that that machinery may have to be called into play. If it ever is, the impact such a development would have on presidential-congressional political relations, on party institutions and structures, and on the political security and independence of congressional candidates from national party control, would doubtless be far-reaching.

It should never be forgotten that even the present system of choosing electors on a statewide plurality vote basis, rests, after all, merely upon state legislation which can be altered by state action at any time.[6] Moreover, during the present century, as anyone knowledgeable about American presidential elections is aware, there have been four presidential elections—in 1912, 1924, 1948, and 1968—which, despite the "winner-take-all" method of choosing a state's electoral slate, produced three-way splits in the national electoral vote totals. In addition to these elections, the 1960 election produced a similar result when "unpledged" electors chosen in Alabama and Mississippi cast their electoral votes for presidential and vice presidential candidates other than those nominated by one of the two major parties. In each of the 1948, 1956, 1960, and 1968 elections, furthermore, there was one "disloyal" party elector who chose to demonstrate that he was a free agent by casting his electoral vote for candidates other than the ones on his party's slate.

Each of these threatened malfunctionings in the electoral vote system has generated interest in Congress in presidential electoral reform. The 1948 and 1968 elections, in particular, produced reaction in Congress to the point of inducing one of the two Houses to pass soon afterwards a reform amendment proposal. The action of the House in passing such an amendment proposal by an overwhelming margin in 1969 can be understood as largely a reaction by its members to their narrow escape from having to function as presidential electors following the 1968 November election.

As the 1968 presidential campaign developed, the very real possibility that the presence in the field of a third party candidate with strong sectional appeal would result in a three-way split in the electoral vote sufficiently broad to prevent any candidate from achieving a national electoral majority was recognized by many pre-election analysts and party leaders. In anticipation of such an outcome, Representative Morris Udall, Democrat, of Arizona and Representative Charles E. Goodell, Republican, of New York launched a movement to induce their respective national party heads to issue a joint statement pledging that their respective party memberships in the House, if the choice should devolve upon them, would cast their votes for the candidate, irrespective of party, who re-

---

[6] It should be noted that in 1969 the state legislature in Maine adopted legislation putting into operation in that state the "district system" of choosing two of its electors. Cf. *Public Laws of Maine*, 1969, ch. 131.

ceived a popular plurality in the national popular vote. The movement "died a-bornin'," however, when the national party leaders evinced no interest in such a plan.[7]

Whether the House would actually have been required to resolve an inconclusive electoral vote outcome in the 1968 election is problematical, even if the electors chosen had been so distributed as to assure no candidate of a nationwide electoral vote majority. Governor Wallace had announced prior to the general election that if he won a sufficient number of electoral votes to give his electors a "balance of power" position as between the two major party candidates, he stood ready to "dicker" with either of the two major party candidates on how his electors' votes would actually be cast. He had extracted pledges from his elector candidates that they would cast their votes for him, or for "whomsoever he might direct." Both major party candidates issued pre-election statements disavowing their willingness to "bargain" with him on the disposition of his electors' votes. But the prospect of a presidential contest resolved either by a post-election "bartering" of electoral votes or by employment of the antiquated, politically indefensible system of "state unit" votes in the House evidently left an indelible impression on the minds of a good many members of Congress.

The 1968 election results were extremely close. Nixon, with 43.4 percent of the popular vote, obtained 301 electoral votes (with one North Carolina elector defecting to Wallace); Humphrey, with 42.7 percent of the popular vote, received 191 electoral votes; and Wallace, who obtained 13.5 percent of the popular vote, received 46 electoral votes. But the narrowness of Nixon's electoral victory is revealed when it is noted that if the California electorate, which gave him a popular margin of 1.6 percent over Humphrey, had registered a plurality preference for Humphrey instead, no candidate would have had a national electoral vote majority. The same result would have followed if the party results in Ohio and either Missouri or New Jersey, all of which Nixon carried by very narrow pluralities of less than 1 percent, had been reversed.

This invites consideration of what the House and Senate membership would have faced if the election of the President and Vice President, respectively, had devolved upon them. In the House the state delegations in the ensuing 91st Congress were composed as follows (Table 1):[8]

---

[7] Cf. *Congressional Quarterly Weekly Report*, July 19, 1968, pp. 1817–1823; and for October 25, 1968, pp. 2955–2956. Movements were also launched to induce congressional candidates to pledge themselves to vote for the presidential candidate who was favored by the voters of their districts; but the idea failed to gather much support except in some of the Southern state contests.

[8] The vote figures used in deriving this and the following tables are those found in the *Congressional Quarterly 1968 Election Supplement* (1969).

TABLE 1

Distribution of House Unit Votes for President, 1968

State Carried in Popular Vote	*Total*	*House Delegation Rep.*	*House Delegation Dem.*	*House Delegation A.I.P.*	*Evenly Divided*
By Nixon	32	17	11	—	4
By Humphrey	13	2	10	—	1
By Wallace	5	—	5	—	—
Totals	50	19	26	—	5

Democrats thus controlled 26 of the House delegations, the minimum number of state unit votes necessary to elect Humphrey. (The District of Columbia, which had chosen three Humphrey electors, would have had no voice at this stage in the election process—an anomaly which the drafters of the twenty-third amendment evidently failed to foresee.) But would the Democratic majorities in the eleven states carried by Nixon in the popular voting for President have had the political fortitude to stand fast for their popularly rejected candidate, and cast their state votes for Humphrey rather than follow the clearly expressed will of their states' voters?[9] Furthermore, there were five Democratically controlled House delegations[10] whose voters had registered a choice for Wallace. In addition, there were four states[11] whose voters had expressed a preference for Nixon, but whose House delegations were evenly divided as between Republicans and Democrats. If the Democratic party members in these delegations persisted in casting their votes for their party's candidate in their House delegation caucuses, they would thereby be denying to their respective state electorates voting power altogether in the choice of the President. Republican members of the House would have also been exposed to a similar "cross-pressure" in reverse in two state delegations—Michigan and Minnesota—where the state's electorate had registered a preference for Humphrey; and in one instance in an evenly divided state delegation—Maryland—where the state's voters had registered a plurality for Humphrey. There were also six Republican members of the House from states whose voters had indicated a preference for Wallace; but they were in the minority and could not, by themselves, have determined how their state unit vote should be cast.

---

[9] The Democratically controlled House delegations caught in this "cross-pressure" situation were those of California, Colorado, Florida, Kentucky, Missouri, Nevada, New Jersey, North Carolina, Oklahoma, South Carolina, and Tennessee.

[10] Alabama, Arkansas, Georgia, Louisiana, and Mississippi.

[11] Illinois, Montana, Oregon, and Virginia.

Altogether, a total of 126 Democratic and 21 Republican House members would have been placed in a political "squeeze play" type of situation, in which they could cause their state unit vote to be cast for a candidate other than their state's popular vote winner or prevent its being cast at all by reason of there being an evenly split House delegation. The choice they would have had to make would have been politically unpalatable in either case. They could behave like "loyal" partisans and subvert the will of their state's voters; or they could function as "representatives" of the people and desert their party's candidate. A total of 147 members, or more than one-third of the entire House membership, would have had to face this kind of "Hobson's choice."

If the Senate had been required to function as an electoral body in the choice of a Vice President, it would appear at first glance that Senator Muskie would have had no difficulty in being chosen over Governor Agnew. The Senate, after the 1968 election, was composed of 57 Democrats and 43 Republicans. But again, this result could have come about only if 31 of the Democratic senators had chosen to follow the "party loyalty" line, rather than to register the vote of their respective states in accordance with the revealed popular preference for the Republican candidate. The partisan make-up of the Senate, in relation to the state-by-state presidential popular vote, would have been as follows (Table 2):

TABLE 2

Senate Seats Compared with Presidential Election Results, 1968

	Rep. Senators (Elected & Holdovers)	*Dem. Senators (Elected)*	*Dem. Senators (Holdovers)*	*Total*
State for Nixon:	33	11	20	64
	Dem. Senators (Elected & Holdovers)	*Rep. Senators (Elected)*	*Rep. Senators (Holdovers)*	
State for Humphrey:	16	3	7	26
		Dem. Senators (Elected)	*Dem. Senators (Holdovers)*	
State for Wallace:	—	4	6	10

Ten Republican Senators would have been under a similar "cross-pressure"; but the 10 Democratic senators from the five Wallace states would have been spared embarrassment in that only the Republican and Democratic candidates for Vice President were eligible to be voted for.

As already noted, most of the Senate drafts of alternatives to the House-passed direct election amendment resolution in 1969 seemed to recognize the obvious political inequities in the current constitutional provisions for making final decisions in presidential and vice presidential contests. In both the House and the Senate, voting under present arrangements is based on the principle of equal state voting power. Most of them, therefore, included provisions in their alternative plans that would have referred an inconclusive electoral vote result to a *joint* session of the two Houses, with each member entitled to an individual, independent vote, and with a majority being necessary to a choice. In other words the Congress, sitting as an electoral body with a membership paralleling the electoral vote strength of the respective states, would become the functioning body of electors with an opportunity to cast a series of ballots until the issue is resolved.

If the backers of such a plan were of the opinion that this change in voting procedure would give individual members of Congress relief from the political "cross-pressure" influences analyzed above, they were in error. While freeing House members from the necessity of voting as a state unit, sometimes at cross-purposes with the statewide vote as recorded by the electorate, the joint voting procedure would merely change the focus of the "cross-pressure" as to the House members affected. The number of them affected would be approximately the same.

So far as Senate members of the joint group are concerned, the number exposed to this dilemma under the 1968 election results would have been the same as that shown in Table 2. The House picture in terms of the partisan make-up as compared with the popular vote for President in the respective congressional districts would have been as follows (Table 3):

TABLE 3

House Seats Compared with Presidential Election Results, 1968

	Rep. Elected	*Dem. Elected*	*AIP Elected*	*Total*
District for Nixon	160	66	—	226
District for Humphrey	28	133	—	161
District for Wallace	4	44	—	48
Total	192	243	—	435

There were 66 House districts carried by Nixon that elected Democrats; Humphrey carried 28 districts that elected Republicans; and 44 Democrats and 4 Republicans were elected in districts that voted for Wallace. A total of 142 House seats were held by partisans "out of line" with the presidential election results of their respective districts. Thus under a joint voting basis in Congress a total of 193 Republican and Democratic party members would have had to make the difficult choice between supporting their party's candidate or simply recording by their votes the revealed wishes of their constituents for another party's candidate. Caught in this kind of "bind" would have been 110 Democratic and 32 Republican House members, and 41 Democratic and 10 Republican senators. Together these groups would have constituted 44 percent of the membership of the joint electoral body. How they would have actually resolved their dilemma one can only speculate.

VI. CONCLUSION

Viewed in its long-range aspect, retention of language in a presidential election reform amendment that reserves to Congress power to resolve in one way or another an inconclusive first step in the election of the President, whatever the nature of that first and presumably "normal" step may be, might well prove to have very far-reaching consequences. If the first step procedures are defined in terms that create a definite possibility that Congress may be called upon to make the final disposition of a presidential election contest, partisan candidates for Congress might well have to accept the role of *de facto* or stand-by presidential elector candidates in their respective constituencies. Only an electoral reform plan that excludes congressional action altogether as a part of the election scheme will serve to give them complete protection against this eventuality. If the plan eventually adopted should prove to be one that increases the likelihood of resort to a contingent mode of election, the national party organizations can logically be expected to develop means of exerting pressure on their state and local organizations, as they have already been forced to do to deal with the problem of potentially "disloyal" presidential elector candidates, to insure that only candidates for congressional seats whose loyalty to the national party leadership is beyond question are nominated. A "fence-straddling" or "uncommitted" congressional candidate on the matter of his choice for President would, in all likelihood, be opposed in the final election by a party "regular" whose loyalty is secure. Candidates for Congress would necessarily have to tie themselves more closely to the national party leadership, and rise or fall with the fortunes of the national party in their respective constituencies. The relationship of the President to his congressional party element would become closer, and party discipline in Congress would doubtless approach more closely to that found in a parliamentary democracy.

Use of some other method than referral to Congress of an inconclusive popular election for President, such as a run-off election device, on the other hand, would tend to keep the constituency bases of members of

Congress and of the President more distinct and separate. While it might strengthen him in his role as head of government by giving him a political base different from that of the local and state party hierarchy, his party's members in Congress would by the same token remain in a stronger position to challenge his leadership, if so inclined. In fashioning a presidential election reform amendment, it would be well, therefore, for the members of Congress to recognize that the mechanics of the system they devise can have profound implications with respect to their relationship to their presidential candidate and the national party organizational leadership generally. It may further continuance of a viable system of checks and balances, or it may promote movement toward subordinating the congressional party of the President to a much greater degree of executive leadership than is now the case.

PART TWO

The Political Context

It is axiomatic that the president is the most important participant in the American political system; consequently, a knowledge of the political setting in which he must operate and of his behavior as a political actor is essential in appraising the man and the office. The selections in Part II examine key aspects of the political environment and the president's behavior in it. Although the picture derived from these rather diverse pieces is far from complete, it should furnish the basis of an understanding of the president as a politician and of the presidency as a political office.

In the first selection, James David Barber gives careful theoretical treatment to the behavior of presidents as political leaders. He argues that the key to explaining and predicting presidential performance is to be found in a president's character, in terms of two dichotomous variables: activity-passivity in office and positive-negative affect toward the office. In Barber's view, active-positive presidents are most desirable. The other types all manifest potentially dangerous behavior. Barber's typology enables us to understand past presidential actions and to predict in general terms how an individual president will behave in various circumstances. For example, an active-positive president like Franklin D. Roosevelt or John F. Kennedy will adopt a flexible and rational approach to difficult problems, while an active-negative like Lyndon B. Johnson or Richard M. Nixon will react forcefully but inflexibly to challenges. The typology may also suggest something about how he will organize and use the presidential office, as in the case of President Nixon. What Barber's theory does not do is to reveal how a president will organize his policy-making activities or what his substantive policy goals are likely to be. Barber's theory and the resulting typology may not be wholly satisfactory, but they stand as a challenge to critics to develop a more useful and valid alternative.

The actions and inactions of a president affect and are affected by the political environment in which they occur. The president's most important political involvement occurs in the process of securing his party's nomination and winning the approval of the electorate. The quest for the nomination establishes the presidential nominee's relationships with important interest groups and with other leaders in his own party. To a considerable degree his success in the election campaign and his ability to govern effectively and to translate his and the party's goals into policies and programs depend on those relationships. The election results are equally if not more important in this latter regard, however, as they provide an indication of public support for the president and his proposals. The meaning and extent of election mandates is often debated, but their symbolic significance is generally recognized by both scholars and politicians.

The behavior of the electorate in presidential elections is therefore a subject of great interest and importance. For several decades students of voting have examined American presidential elections through the use of sample surveys and the analysis of election returns. The general substance of their findings has been that approximately 60 percent of the eligible voters participate in each presidential contest and that a long-term psychological factor, partisan identification, is the best single predictor of voting choice although two factors of a less permanent and more transitory nature, issue orientation and candidate orientation, can and do intervene to offset the advantage that the Democrats enjoy over the Republicans in party preference. Studies of recent elections have demonstrated, however, that there has been a sharp increase in issue voting, and some analysts have suggested that the attachment of voters to both major parties is waning and that a major party realignment may be in progress.

Seymour Martin Lipset and Earl Raab analyze the 1972 contest for the presidency. They attribute Senator George McGovern's resounding defeat to his failure to judge correctly the attitudes, expectations, and values of a vast majority of voters. In their view, McGovern won the nomination as the head of an ideological faction within the Democratic party and then proceeded to conduct his campaign as a factional leader. This interpretation is partly confirmed in a survey study of the election conducted by the Center for Political Studies at the University of Michigan and published in 1975. The Michigan group found a sharp issue cleavage within the ranks of Democratic party identifiers.

In spite of President Nixon's overwhelming election victory, Lipset and Raab do not find any evidence in his reelection of a partisan triumph or an electoral realignment favoring the Republicans. The Democrats did manage to retain substantial majorities in both houses of Congress, and they fared quite well in state and local elections. This suggests that what may be happening is either the separation of presidential elections from the normal pattern of partisanship that dominates contests for all lesser offices or that the linkage between the parties and voters is becoming "disaggregated," to use Walter Dean Burnham's terminology.

Lipset and Raab are the first of many academic students of voting behavior to analyze the 1972 election. Some readers will doubtless disagree with their conclusions, and they may find other analyses based on more extensive data or studies incorporating a more dispassionate view of Senator McGovern more satisfying. Certainly the meaning of President Nixon's mandate and the significance of the outcome can only be assayed from the perspectives of several studies and after the consequences of the Watergate affair and Nixon's resignation have become more apparent. The 1972 election stands as one of the monumental landslides of American political history, but the mandate won was rapidly dissipated before its significance for and impact on presidential policy leadership could be felt. Lipset and Raab provide an informative and provocative interpretation of the election, which goes well beyond mere speculation.

The president's relationship with the mass public is not limited to election campaigns, however. Rather, it is continuous and dependent on several factors. John E. Mueller has examined one major manifestation of that relationship, the president's popularity. Using data from the Roper Public Opinion Research Center and the Gallup organization, Mueller traces the trend of presidential popularity from the beginning of the Truman administration in 1945 to the end of the Johnson administration in 1969. He examines the effects of four independent variables—the time that has elapsed since inauguration, international crises, economic conditions, and war—on popularity. His analysis does not, however, reveal how presidential popularity affects presidential decisions. It is probably safe to assume that presidents are aware of their popularity ratings and that they are cognizant of the effects of international crises, declining employment, and limited wars on their standing with the public. Therefore, we can further assume that they act on the basis of such knowledge at least part of the time. In fact president watchers expect them to do so. For example, when President Nixon placed the armed forces on alert in response to a Soviet threat to intervene in the Arab-Israeli war of October, 1973, and when he traveled to the Middle East and the Soviet Union in June, 1974, some newsmen suggested that he was attempting to revive his Watergate-damaged popularity ratings. We can also assume that other participants in the policy-making process are not unaware of the president's popularity with the public and that this knowledge affects their calculations in dealing with him. Congressmen, interest groups, and even government officials will be less willing to resist or to impose conditional demands on a highly popular president than on one whose ratings are down. It should be remembered that although Mueller uses sophisticated quantitative techniques, he is studying the attitudes of the public and the results of presidential behavior rather than that behavior itself.

The final selections in Part II are concerned with one of the most important means of presidential interaction with the public, relations with the press. Much of the president's impact on the public is shaped by information transmitted by the media. How the president and his staff regard the press and the uses that the president makes of the press are always matters of considerable consequence. Whatever a president does or fails to do with respect to the media and whatever his attitude is toward the press will ultimately affect his relationship with the public.

A perceptive presidential view of the press is forcefully stated by Daniel P. Moynihan, a former counselor to President Nixon and now ambassador to India. Moynihan argues that the national press, specifically the *New York Times* and the *Washington Post,* have placed the government "at an operating disadvantage" through hypercritical reporting and that this is bad for the nation. His complaints against leaks to the news media are pertinent to certain aspects of the events leading to the resignation of Vice-President Spiro Agnew in October, 1973, and to the Watergate trials and the impeachment proceedings before the House Judiciary Committee in 1974.

Moynihan's criticism of the press draws a sharp response from Max Frankel of the *New York Times.* He charges that Moynihan misunderstands the function of the press and unfairly attributes malevolent motives to it. Moynihan and Frankel are, of course, debating a complex and subtle phenomenon in the context of specific events and actions. The problems in the relationship involve such questions as the responsibility of the press fully to inform the public, a vital aspect of any free society, and the responsibility of the press to withhold or delay reporting information on grounds that it would be harmful to national security. The conflict between freedom and security is not susceptible to a final solution. Each president and his administration must face it anew. The result is never likely to be more than an uneasy and shifting balance which, in spite of the tension inherent in the situation, is quite functional for the realization and enhancement of both values.

It is important to recognize that the press and the presidency have different roles to play in national politics. The task of the former is to help insure responsible performance by public officials including the president, while that of the latter is to identify and pursue policy goals on behalf of the public. The press and the presidency also have a different attitude toward information. For the press, news has economic value: the press is in the *business* of gathering and disseminating news. For the presidency, information can be highly useful or highly threatening. The presidency's objective, then, is to obtain as favorable a presentation of news as possible in order to build and maintain public support. Conflict is inherent in this situation, but if kept within limits it can contribute to the health of the democratic process. It is when the press becomes subservient to the presidency or any other component of the regime, or when governmental institutions lose the capacity to act independently and function largely in response to the press or the private power blocks that often support and control the media through direct ownership or leverage gained by advertising, that democracy is in jeopardy.

Sharp conflict between the presidency and the press, particularly the broadcasting network news organizations and the national newspapers and newsmagazines, was a prominent feature of the Nixon administration. Until his resignation, Vice-President Agnew served as the spearhead of administration criticism. The principal charges included unbalanced, biased reporting and deliberate distortion of the news in order to portray President Nixon and the administration in an unfavorable light. The antagonism increased during the Pentagon Papers case in 1971. In this case the government sought to prevent publication, in the *New York Times* and the *Washington Post,* of the contents of a classified official study of American involvement in Vietnam. The documents had been copied by Daniel Ellsberg, a former Defense Department official, while he was working for the Rand Corporation (a government-funded private research organization) in 1969. The U.S. Supreme Court ultimately ruled in favor of the newspapers, but its opinion did not resolve the question of the extent to which freedom of the press would be allowed to prevail over the claims of national security.

The Nixon administration's hostilities with the press continued at a high level throughout the Watergate and Agnew affairs in 1973, and during the Watergate trials and the House Judiciary Committee's impeachment inquiry in 1974. The official position was that the press, through unrestrained reporting and disclosures, had prevented persons accused of wrongdoing from exercising their constitutional rights to due process of law. Defenders of the press argued that without such vigilance the affairs of state would have continued to be conducted and be vitally influenced by persons who had either engaged in or had been accused of criminal activity. The administration's claims of grossly unfair treatment at the hands of network news organizations brought strong denials and the countercharge that the president had repeatedly used the free and unlimited access given to him by the networks to advance his own interests. Presidential use of television is an important aspect of relations with the press that neither Moynihan nor Frankel considers.

Nor does either author address such questions as: How does the president influence the press and vice versa? What devices can the president use to rally public opinion? Does he use the press as a scapegoat? How do internal constraints on the press (e.g., norms of professionalism and organizational imperatives) affect its treatment of the president? The Moynihan-Frankel debate should be evaluated in light of the broader problem. The reader will have to judge who has the better of the argument.

3.

PRESIDENTIAL CHARACTER AND HOW TO FORESEE IT

James David Barber

. . . crucial differences can be anticipated by an understanding of a potential President's character, his world view, and his style. This kind of prediction is not easy; well-informed observers often have guessed wrong as they watched a man step toward the White House. One thinks of Woodrow Wilson, the scholar who would bring reason to politics; of Herbert Hoover, the Great Engineer who would organize chaos into progress; of Franklin D. Roosevelt, that champion of the balanced budget; of Harry Truman, whom the office would surely overwhelm; of Dwight D. Eisenhower, militant crusader; of John F. Kennedy, who would lead beyond moralisms to achievements; of Lyndon B. Johnson, the Southern conservative; and of Richard M. Nixon, conciliator. Spotting the errors is easy. Predicting with even approximate accuracy is going to require some sharp tools and close attention in their use. But the experiment is worth it because the question is critical and because it lends itself to correction by evidence.

My argument comes in layers.

Reprinted from the book *The Presidential Character: Predicting Performance in the White House* by James David Barber, pp. 6–13. Published by Prentice-Hall, Inc., Englewood Cliffs, New Jersey, and reprinted with permission of the publisher. Footnote omitted.

First, a President's personality is an important shaper of his Presidential behavior on nontrivial matters.

Second, Presidential personality is patterned. His character, world view, and style fit together in a dynamic package understandable in psychological terms.

Third, a President's personality interacts with the power situation he faces and the national "climate of expectations" dominant at the time he serves. The tuning, the resonance—or lack of it—between these external factors and his personality sets in motion the dynamic of his Presidency.

Fourth, the best way to predict a President's character, world view, and style is to see how they were put together in the first place. That happened in his early life, culminating in his first independent political success.

But the core of the argument . . . is that Presidential character—the basic stance a man takes toward his Presidential experience—come in four varieties. The most important thing to know about a President or candidate is where he fits among these types, defined according to (a) how active he is and (b) whether or not he gives the impression he enjoys his political life.

Let me spell out these concepts briefly before getting down to cases.

PERSONALITY SHAPES PERFORMANCE

I am not about to argue that once you know a President's personality you know everything. But as the cases will demonstrate, the degree and quality of a President's emotional involvement in an issue are powerful influences on how he defines the issue itself, how much attention he pays to it, which facts and persons he sees as relevant to its resolution, and, finally, what principles and purposes he associates with the issue. Every story of Presidential decision-making is really two stories: an outer one in which a rational man calculates and an inner one in which an emotional man feels. The two are forever connected. Any real President is one whole man and his deeds reflect his wholeness.

As for personality, it is a matter of tendencies. It is not that one President "has" some basic characteristic that another President does not "have." That old way of treating a trait as a possession, like a rock in a basket, ignores the universality of aggressiveness, compliancy, detachment, and other human drives. We all have all of them, but in different amounts and in different combinations.

THE PATTERN OF CHARACTER, WORLD VIEW, AND STYLE

The most visible part of the pattern is style. *Style is the President's habitual way of performing his three political roles: rhetoric, personal relations, and homework.* Not to be confused with "stylishness," charisma, or appearance, style is how the President goes about doing what the office requires him to do—to speak, directly or through media, to large audiences; to deal face to face with other politicians, individually and in small, relatively private groups; and to read, write, and calculate by himself in order to manage the endless flow of details that stream onto his desk. No President can escape doing at least some of each. But there are marked differences in stylistic emphasis from President to President. The *balance* among the three style elements varies; one President may put most of himself into rhetoric, another may stress close, informal dealing, while still another may devote his energies mainly to study and cogitation. Beyond the balance, we want to see each President's peculiar habits of style, his mode of coping with and adapting to these Presidential demands. For example, I think both Calvin Coolidge and John F. Kennedy were primarily rhetoricians, but they went about it in contrasting ways.

A President's world view consists of his primary, politically relevant beliefs, particularly his conceptions of social causality, human nature, and the central moral conflicts of the time. This is how he sees the world and his lasting opinions about what he sees. Style is his way of acting; world view is his way of seeing. Like the rest of us, a President develops over a lifetime certain conceptions of reality—how things work in politics, what people are like, what the main purposes are. These assumptions or conceptions help him make sense of his world, give some semblance of order to chaos of existence. Perhaps most important: a man's world view affects what he pays attention to, and a great deal of politics is about paying attention. The name of the game for many politicians is not so much "Do this, do that" as it is "Look here!"

"Character" comes from the Greek word for engraving; in one sense it is what life has marked into a man's being. As used here, *character is the way the President orients himself toward life*—not for the moment, but enduringly. Character is the person's stance as he confronts experience. And at the core of character, a man confronts himself. The President's fundamental self-esteem is his prime personal resource; to defend and advance that, he will sacrifice much else he values. Down there in the privacy of his heart, does he find himself superb, or ordinary, or debased, or in some intermediate range? No President has been utterly paralyzed by self-doubt and none has been utterly free of midnight self-mockery. In between, the real Presidents move out on life from positions of relative strength or weakness. Equally important are the criteria by which they judge themselves. A President who rates himself by the standard of achievement, for instance, may be little affected by losses of affection.

Character, world view, and style are abstractions from the reality of the whole individual. In every case they form an integrated pattern: the man develops a combination which makes psychological sense for him, a dynamic arrangement of motives, beliefs, and habits in the service of his need for self-esteem.

THE POWER SITUATION AND "CLIMATE OF EXPECTATIONS"

Presidential character resonates with the political situation the President faces. It adapts him as he tries to adapt it. The support he has from the public and interest groups, the party balance in Congress, the thrust of Supreme Court opinion together set the basic power situation he must deal with. An activist President may run smack into a brick wall of resistance, then pull back and wait for a better moment. On the other hand, a President who sees himself as a quiet caretaker may not try to exploit even the most favorable power situation. So it is the relationship between President and the political configuration that makes the system tick.

Even before public opinion polls, the President's real or supposed popularity was a large factor in his performance. Besides the power mix in Washington, the President has to deal with a national climate of expectations, the predominant needs thrust up to him by the people. There are at least three recurrent themes around which these needs are focused.

People look to the President for *reassurance,* a feeling that things will be all right, that the President will take care of his people. The psychological request is for a surcease of anxiety. Obviously, modern life in America involves considerable doses of fear, tension, anxiety, worry; from time to time, the public mood calls for a rest, a time of peace, a breathing space, a "return to normalcy."

Another theme is the demand for a *sense of progress and action.* The President ought to do something to direct the nation's course—or at least be in there pitching for the people. The President is looked to as a take-charge man, a doer, a turner of the wheels, a producer of progress—even if that means some sacrifice of serenity.

A third type of climate of expectations is the public need for a sense of *legitimacy* from, and in, the Presidency. The President should be a master politician who is above politics. He should have a right to his place and a rightful way of acting in it. The respectability—even religiosity—of the office has to be protected by a man who presents himself as defender of the faith. There is more to this than dignity, more than propriety. The President is expected to personify our betterness in an inspiring way, to express in what he does and is (not just in what he says) a moral idealism which, in much of the public mind, is the very opposite of "politics."

Over time the climate of expectations shifts and changes. Wars, depressions, and other national events contribute to that change, but there also is a rough cycle, from an emphasis on action (which begins to look too "political") to an emphasis on legitimacy (the moral uplift of which creates its own strains) to an emphasis on reassurance and rest (which comes to seem like drift) and back to action again. One need not be astrological about it. The point is that the climate of expectations at any given time is the political air the President has to breathe. Relating to this climate is a large part of his task.

PREDICTING PRESIDENTS

The best way to predict a President's character, world view, and style is to see how he constructed them in the first place. Especially in the early stages, life is experimental; consciously or not, a person tries out various ways of defining and maintaining and raising self-esteem. He looks to his environment for clues as to who he is and how well he is doing. These lessons of life slowly sink in: certain self-images and evaluations, certain ways of looking at the world, certain styles of action get confirmed by his experience and he gradually adopts them as his own. If we can see that process of development, we can understand the product. The features to note are those bearing on Presidential performance.

Experimental development continues all the way to death; we will not blind ourselves to midlife changes, particularly in the full-scale prediction case, that of Richard Nixon. But it is often much easier to see the basic patterns in early life histories. Later on a whole host of distractions—especially the image-making all politicians learn to practice—clouds the picture.

In general, character has its *main* development in childhood, world view in adolescence, style in early adulthood. The stance toward life I call character grows out of the child's experiments in relating to parents, brothers and sisters, and peers at play and in school, as well as to his own body and the objects around it. Slowly the child defines an orientation toward experience; once established, that tends to last despite much subsequent contradiction. By adolescence, the child has been hearing and seeing how people make their worlds meaningful, and now he is moved to relate himself—his own meanings—to those around him. His focus of attention shifts toward the future; he senses that decisions about his fate are coming and he looks into the premises for those decisions. Thoughts about the way the world works and how one might work in it, about what people are like and how one might be like them or not, and about the values people share and how one might share in them too—these are typical concerns for the post-child, pre-adult mind of the adolescent.

These themes come together strongly in early adulthood, when the person moves from contemplation to responsible action and adopts a style. In most biographical accounts this period stands out in stark clarity—the time of emergence, the time the young man found himself. I call it his first independent political success. It was then he moved beyond the detailed guidance of his family; then his self-esteem was dramatically boosted; then he came forth as a person to be reckoned with by other people. The *way* he did that is profoundly important to him. Typically he grasps that style and hangs onto it. Much later, coming into the Presidency, something in him remembers this earlier victory and re-emphasizes the style that made it happen.

Character provides the main thrust and broad direction—but it does not *determine,* in any fixed sense, world view and style. The story of development does not end with the end of childhood. Thereafter, the culture one grows in and the ways that culture is translated by parents and peers shapes the meaning one makes of his character. The going world view gets learned and that learning helps channel character forces. Thus it will not necessarily be true that compulsive characters have reactionary beliefs, or that compliant characters believe in compromise. Similarly for style: historical accidents play a large part in furnishing special opportunities for action—and in blocking off alternatives. For example, however much anger a young man may feel, that anger will not be expressed in rhetoric unless and until his life situation provides a platform and an audience. Style thus has a stature and independence of its own. Those who would reduce all explanation to character neglect these highly significant later channelings. For beyond the root is the branch, above the foundation the superstructure, and starts do not prescribe finishes.

FOUR TYPES OF PRESIDENTIAL CHARACTER

The five concepts—character, world view, style, power situation, and climate of expectations—run through the accounts of Presidents in the chapters to follow, which cluster the Presidents since Theodore Roosevelt into four types. This is the fundamental scheme of the study. It offers a way to move past the complexities to the main contrasts and comparisons.

The first baseline in defining Presidential types is *activity-passivity.*

How much energy does the man invest in his Presidency? Lyndon Johnson went at his day like a human cyclone, coming to rest long after the sun went down. Calvin Coolidge often slept eleven hours a night and still needed a nap in the middle of the day. In between the Presidents array themselves on the high or low side of the activity line.

The second baseline is *positive-negative affect* toward one's activity—that is, how he feels about what he does. Relatively speaking, does he seem to experience his political life as happy or sad, enjoyable or discouraging, positive or negative in its main effect. The feeling I am after here is not grim satisfaction in a job well done, not some philosophical conclusion. The idea is this: is he someone who, on the surfaces we can see, gives forth the feeling that he has *fun* in political life? Franklin Roosevelt's Secretary of War, Henry L. Stimson wrote that the Roosevelts "not only understood the *use* of power, they knew the *enjoyment* of power, too. . . . Whether a man is burdened by power or enjoys power; whether he is trapped by responsibility or made free by it; whether he is moved by other people and outer forces or moves them—that is the essence of leadership."

The positive-negative baseline, then, is a general symptom of the fit between the man and his experience, a kind of register of *felt* satisfaction.

Why might we expect these two simple dimensions to outline the main character types? Because they stand for two central features of anyone's orientation toward life. In nearly every study of personality, some form of the active-passive contrast is critical; the general tendency to act or be acted upon is evident in such concepts as dominance-submission, extraversion-introversion, aggression-timidity, attack-defense, fight-flight, engagement-withdrawal, approach-avoidance. In everyday life we sense quickly the general energy output of the people we deal with. Similarly we catch on fairly quickly to the affect dimension—whether the person seems to be optimistic or pessimistic, hopeful or skeptical, happy or sad. The two baselines are clear and they are also independent of one another: all of us know people who are very active but seem discouraged, others who are quite passive but seem happy, and so forth. The activity baseline refers to what one does, the affect baseline to how one feels about what he does.

Both are crude clues to character. They are leads into four basic character patterns long familiar in psychological research. In summary form, these are the main configurations:

Active-positive. There is a congruence, a consistency, between much activity and the enjoyment of it, indicating relatively high self-esteem and relative success in relating to the environment. The man shows an orientation toward productiveness as a value and an ability to use his styles flexibly, adaptively, suiting the dance to the music. He sees himself as developing over time toward relatively well defined personal goals—growing toward his image of himself as he might yet be. There is an emphasis on rational mastery, on using the brain to move the feet. This may get him into trouble; he may fail to take account of the irrational in politics. Not everyone he deals with sees things his way and he may find it hard to understand why.

Active-negative. The contradiction here is between relatively intense effort and relatively low emotional reward for that effort. The activity has a compulsive quality, as if the man were trying to make up for something or to escape from anxiety into hard work. He seems ambitious, striving upward, power-seeking. His stance toward the environment is aggressive and he has a persistent problem in managing his aggressive feelings. His self-image is vague and discontinuous. Life is a hard struggle to achieve and hold power, hampered by the condemnations of a perfectionistic conscience. Active-negative types pour energy into the political system, but it is an energy distorted from within.

Passive-positive. This is the receptive, compliant, other-directed character whose life is a search for affection as a reward for being agreeable and cooperative rather than personally assertive. The contradiction is between low self-esteem (on grounds of being unlovable, unattractive) and a superficial optimism. A hopeful attitude helps dispel doubt and elicits encouragement from others. Passive-positive types help soften the harsh edges of politics. But their dependence and the fragility of their hopes and enjoyments make disappointment in politics likely.

Passive-negative. The factors are consistent—but how are we to account for the man's *political* role-taking? Why is someone who does little in politics and enjoys it less there at all? The answer lies in the passive-negative's character-rooted orientation toward doing dutiful service; this compensates for low self-esteem based on a sense of usefulness. Passive-negative types are in politics because they think they ought to be. They may be well adapted to certain nonpolitical roles, but they lack the experience and flexibility to perform effectively as political leaders. Their tendency is to withdraw, to escape from the conflict and uncertainty of politics by emphasizing vague principles (especially prohibitions) and procedural arrangements. They become guardians of the right and proper way, above the sordid politicking of lesser men.

Active-positive Presidents want most to achieve results. Active-negatives aim to get and keep power. Passive-positives are after love. Passive-negatives emphasize their civic virtue. The relation of activity to enjoyment in a President thus tends to outline a cluster of characteristics, to set apart the adapted from the compulsive, compliant, and withdrawn types.

4.

THE ELECTION AND THE NATIONAL MOOD

Seymour Martin Lipset and Earl Raab

The reasons underlying Senator McGovern's defeat in the 1972 elections had been thoroughly analyzed long before the polls opened on November 7. There was, indeed, no great trick to predicting the likely drift of the vote, since the nation was wearing its motivations on its sleeve, and no polltaker or political analyst could fail to take notice. But apart from the specific issues and candidates, and apart from the idiosyncrasies of this particular election year, the results of the balloting afford an opportunity to relearn some important lessons about the continuing character of the American electorate.

I

In this election there was no real gap, on political issues, separating the body of McGovern voters and the body of Nixon voters. As the various polls indicated, getting out of the war was foremost in the minds of Americans, along with reducing the high cost of living. But on neither of these issues were the voters split along partisan lines. In a late Gallup poll, more than 7 out of 10 Nixon voters and 9 out of 10 McGovern voters said that getting out of Vietnam was a prime motivation for the way they were voting; pare away the ideological edges, and the figures would coincide.

Similarly with the general issue of economy. Not surprisingly, over 90 per cent of both Nixon and McGovern voters felt that checking the rise in the cost of living was of major importance to them. But (again allowing for the ideological edges) about an equal percentage of Nixon

---

Reprinted from *Commentary*, Vol. 55 (January, 1973), pp. 43–50, by permission of the author and publisher.

and McGovern voters were also strongly against the lifting of wage and price controls (58 and 48 per cent), and both sets of voters were overwhelmingly in favor of the government's guaranteeing a job to everyone (74 and 90 per cent). On the matter of crime, the third most pressing item on the minds of the voters, about the same percentage of Nixon and McGovern supporters were anxious for "tougher sentences for lawbreakers" (87 and 72 per cent). The voters, in fact, were on the same side of *all* political issues, including national health insurance. Haynes Johnson of the Washington *Post* recapitulated the typical experience of interviewers when he reported that with respect to *issues*, "the voters we met say they don't see all that much difference between what the two Presidential candidates stand for."

It would be wholly mistaken, then, to conclude that the results of the 1972 election represented a conservative backlash on political or economic matters. Nor, in addition, did evidence emerge of a racial backlash. About the same percentage of white Nixon and white McGovern voters said that they would be more likely to vote for a candidate who would improve opportunities for blacks; in each case, these voters constituted a majority of more than 2-1. The same pattern, but in reverse, applied to the issue of school busing. Both white Nixon and white McGovern supporters were overwhelmingly opposed to "busing schoolchildren to achieve racial balance." Yet, according to the polls, less than 10 per cent of the people thought that busing was a major Presidential issue. It is highly questionable in any case whether opposition to busing can legitimately be seen as evidence of racial backlash, and it does not become less questionable when one considers the fact that only about half of the black people polled indicated they would support a candidate because he *favored* busing. About a third of the blacks said that they would be *less* inclined to support a candidate if he favored busing.

If political and racial issues were not the determinants of this election, neither was the personal attractiveness, or "charisma," of the candidates. Americans were asked in October whether they thought Nixon or McGovern had a "more attractive personality." The kindly polltakers provided a third alternative, "Neither," who won handily. Barely half of each of the candidate's *own* committed supporters were willing to say that he had an attractive personality. Of course, one does not have to like a person to vote for him, if one thinks he can do an effective job; on the contrary, Americans do not normally expect effective politicians to be likable. But the factor of "trust, credibility, and effectiveness" was apparently equally unrevealing as an index of voter sentiment. On the one hand there was a clear-cut public reaction of mistrust to the McGovern "1,000-per-cent" syndrome, but on the other hand a plurality of Americans in one Harris poll felt that Nixon was also "uncertain and wishy-washy in what he stands for."

Nevertheless, the American voter obviously did find a great difference between the two candidates, something not accounted for by divergencies in economic or political philosophy, or by varying appraisals of personal competency. Approximately where that difference lay was suggested by one typical Harris poll, which reported that the American people by a 2-1 margin found that McGovern had "too extreme liberal views." On the eve of the vote they felt, again by a 2-1 margin, that he wanted to "change things too much." This same thread ran through all the man-in-the-street interviews: "He's too extreme . . . he's too far ahead of his time. . . . He wants to turn things upside down." To be sure, when it came to what McGovern was too "extreme" about, or what he wanted to "change too much," clarity dissolved. Certainly, as we have pointed out, most voters were not disturbed by his desire to get out of Vietnam, or his support of national health insurance, or his proposal of a guaranteed job program. Even most Nixon supporters agreed with him on these basic issues. What disturbed people was the *way* they felt he would pursue these objectives. Thus, union members told pollsters that McGovern's social program was more for "the little man" than was Nixon's, but they also said that Nixon would treat unions "more fairly," and gave him a voting edge on that account. Champ Clark of *Time* found that "Nixonians are not against change. I have yet to meet one who wants the U.S. to stay exactly the way it is. But they have in kindred spirit a sense of orderliness, of tidiness."

"Orderliness" is the key word. It is tempting to say that whereas the 1972 election did not represent a backlash of political conservatism, or of racism, it did represent a cultural backlash. But to say that the election represented a cultural backlash, although true, would also be something of a confusion of cause and effect. It is a fact, for example, that cultural issues like the decriminalization of marijuana tended to be the *only* kinds of issues on which there was a wide disparity between McGovern and Nixon supporters. Thus, there was a 43-point spread between those Nixon supporters who opposed reducing penalties for marijuana use, and those who favored it, while only an 11-point spread separated McGovern supporters who opposed reducing penalties and those who favored it. And marijuana, like abortion and amnesty, was also an age-connected issue; there was a 45-point difference between those aged 18-24 and those 50 and over on the marijuana question. While McGovern did not end up with many more youth votes than did Nixon, young voters constituted over a fifth of those who voted for him altogether—twice the Nixon proportion—and thus showed up heavily on age-connected cultural issues like marijuana. *But these issues did not in themselves determine the election.*

More often than not in America's social and political history, specific cultural issues have served as the symbolic expression of larger and deeper concerns. Americans are not typically opposed to economic and social change. Indeed, progressive change is an American tradition, part of the American creed. Moreover, large sectors of the electorate usually find their self-interest meshing with one or another movement for change. What they resist is change that takes place in a non-traditional manner. One would not, of course, wish to deny the threat of status deprivation which drastic change poses, but the basic threat perceived by the electorate in the McGovern candidacy was not so much to existing social arrangements as to the social order itself, and especially to due process. *That* is the "extremism" which the voters finally rejected, not any liberal social or economic policy *per se.*

II

McGovern's Presidential campaign formally began and practically ended with the Democratic party convention. With very few exceptions (the disastrous 1968 Chicago convention is one), nominees customarily make great gains in the polls immediately after a national convention; for a week or so, a party has been given a monopoly by the media, and the electorate has heard repeated attacks on the opposition and has witnessed a demonstration of party unity at the end of the convention. But in the 1972 campaign, virtually no change was registered in public support for McGovern after the convention that nominated him—a phenomenon which has occurred only once before in modern election history, in the case of Barry Goldwater. Richard Nixon, on the other hand, increased his support in the polls twice, the first time *immediately* after the Democratic convention, when support for him jumped from 53 to 56 per cent, and then again after the Republican convention, when it went from 57 to 64 per cent.

In the case of McGovern, even more than in that of Senator Goldwater in 1964, the negative image that helped destroy his campaign was fixed by the convention itself. And as also with the subsequent campaign, what created the image was not the political issues which emerged from the convention, but the way in which the McGovern forces appeared to be disregarding traditional due process. Senator Abraham Ribicoff exclaimed during the convention: "Just look at what's happening: Averell Harriman being beaten by a 19-year-old girl for a place on the New York delegation! That's why I think McGovern is going to win. . . ." But that is exactly why McGovern had so little chance of winning. People may not have cared one way or another about Averell Harriman, but they were suspicious of the arbitrary manner in which he and so many others were being displaced. When Senator Eagleton requested that his nomination be seconded by his friend, Governor Warren Hearns of Missouri, millions of television viewers saw him being turned down in this request in favor of a seconding speech by an undergraduate coed. There was a consistent pattern being followed here. Adult white males were being symbolically ignored or even, as in the case of the duly-elected Daley delegation from Illinois, expelled from the convention. Party regulars, representatives of labor and of traditionally Democratic ethnic blocs, were being systematically passed over and displaced, in an apparently high-handed manner, by a faction identified with the "new" constituencies: the young, the poor, women, homosexuals. At the head of this faction stood George McGovern.*

McGovern himself seemed aware that he was an outsider in the traditional party, and not only from the point of view of the older politicians. At the post-convention Al Smith dinner in New York, he commented, "I feel a little like Al Smith addressing the Baptist League of Eastern Texas." This was an amazing statement to come from the Presidential nominee of the Democratic party. The Al Smith dinner, after all, is not only a Catholic commemoration, it is *de facto* a significant Democratic party festival; Protestants and Jews like Herbert Lehman, Harry Truman, and Lyndon Johnson have addressed it in their time, men who were not and could not be ill at ease among the core constituency of New York's Catholic Democrats. But the real irony of the moment lay in McGovern's comparison: for the hard-necked Southern Baptists before whom Al Smith spoke during his campaign ended up voting for Herbert Hoover!

But if the new McGovernite politicians were factionalists, they also had qualities generally associated with extremism: they were ideological, moralistic, and evangelistic. These are characteristics which a coalition party, containing sharply diverse factions, cannot afford to harbor or encourage. In a system based on two competing coalition parties, there has to be a much greater capacity for fudging issues, for hedging, for ideological compromise and impurity, than in multi-party systems in which each party appeals during elections to limited sectors of the nation. Only thus can a coalition-party system reflect the needs of a highly diversified society. But the McGovern convention, like McGovern himself, shunned political compromise, and embraced instead a fundamentally religious notion of purity, suitable more to a third-party movement than to the standard-bearers of a coalition party. In the course of an interview McGovern remarked: "All my life I've grown up in a religious climate where I was taught that life is a struggle between good and evil, and that's what it's all about." But this kind of political moralism makes the electorate uneasy. When McGovern told an interviewer, William Greider of the Washington *Post*, that he felt very strongly that the 1972 election should

* See "The New Politics & the Democrats," by Penn Kemble and Josh Muravchik in the December 1972 issue.—Ed. [of *Commentary*]

be seen in moral terms, Greider, startled, commented: "Well, the good-and-the-evil—Washington would say certainly, wow, that's an arrogant black-and-white description of the choice." Unfazed, the candidate replied, "That's the way I feel."

In this, McGovern clearly resembled another Democratic nominee of three-quarters of a century ago, William Jennings Bryan, who also lost heavily among traditional Democratic voters, particularly Catholics and Jews. Both combined an evangelical Protestant outlook and style with an effort to push the country to the Left. McGovern, like Bryan, moved through his campaign with the "deep inner certitude of godly men." As Peter Goldman and Richard Stout noted, he engaged basically in "the politics of the revival tent." A critical section of the American electorate has a highly developed distaste for political moralism of this kind, and the combined experience of 1964 and 1972 shows that this distaste extends in both directions, to the Left as well as to the Right.

Where McGovern was concerned the paradox was that many of those who were repelled by the moralistic tone of his campaign saw that campaign, and even the candidate himself, as representing or embodying an *im*moral force. For McGovern's campaign repeatedly associated itself with the more permissive position in the area of personal morals, and, thanks in part to astute political maneuvering on the part of President Nixon, also came to be linked with an anti-work, "welfare-ethic" view of society. The issue of "quotas" and "proportional representation" fell partly within this rubric, as did the question of whether the candidate favored the principle of equal results over the principle of equal opportunity as the basis of social and economic policy. The general populace perceived this cluster of issues as a single whole. It regarded marijuana abuse, sexual excess, the subversion of the work and performance principle, as signals of a total attack on the American social order, and it identified them all with the McGovern candidacy.

This perception of McGovern as an "immoral" political moralist colored public reaction in turn to the issues of corruption and hypocrisy. The charge of hypocrisy is a constant potential hazard to any politician who establishes himself as a factional leader and then attempts to make the delicate transition to coalition leader. Hubert Humphrey offers the example of a one-time factional leader who began this process of transition while serving in the Senate, and accomplished it successfully, but not without the image-trace of hypocrisy dogging him in certain quarters. Richard Nixon, similarly, was a factional leader in the 1950's; he managed to make the transition to coalition leader, within his party, partly because of his association with President Eisenhower, partly because of being set off in contrast to Barry Goldwater, whose arch-factionalist slogan in 1964 was "A choice, not an echo." But like Humphrey, Nixon has never been free of the charge of hypocrisy. (It remains to be seen now whether Vice

President Agnew, the factional leader *par excellence*, will make the necessary transition by 1976.)

Senator McGovern, however, never really moved beyond being a factional leader, despite his few efforts in that direction after the convention—efforts which opened *him* to charges of hypocrisy. Thus, when the Senator began to abandon a number of the more left-wing or extreme moralistic positions which he had taken during the primary campaign—especially with respect to welfare policy, the maintenance of military forces in Southeast Asia, tax reform, and the question of support for Israel in the Middle East—he found, to his amazement and fury, that such actions were regarded by many as hypocritical, and that in consequence a substantial majority of those polled saw him as less "moral" than Richard Nixon. He blamed this, in large part, on the press, which emphasized his shifts rather than what he regarded as the essential consistency of his position But in fact the public's impression was a reaction to the image he himself had created.

McGovern had presented himself as a new type of candidate who was above the petty compromises of politics, who was *totally* different in this respect from Richard Nixon. The standard image of Nixon, going back to the 1950's, was above all that of a "politician," that is, a man with relatively few principles, prepared to adjust his policies and tactics to fit the slightest shifts in the public mood. Nixon's enemies called him an unprincipled opportunist, while his friends stressed his flexibility, his capacity to change with the times, his undoctrinaire conception of politics. Both descriptions referred basically to the same behavior, and it was the kind of behavior to which McGovern had defined himself as being absolutely opposed. Small wonder, then, that public reaction took the form it did when George McGovern, who had led the two-year-long pre-convention battle against the "corrupt politicians" and labor bosses, turned around in the course of his campaign and said of President Lyndon Johnson that he had "sacrificed himself to gain peace"; endorsed Boston's Louise Day Hicks against a liberal New-Politics opponent; went out of his way to praise Richard Daley (Hubert Humphrey stayed away from Daley during the 1968 campaign); dumped Senator Eagleton after giving him "1,000 per cent support." The "politics of the revival tent" simply did not mix with those of Tammany Hall.

As with the issue of hypocrisy, so with the issue of corruption in government. The polls consistently showed a majority of the electorate believing that Nixon would be able to handle corruption better than McGovern. In the light of the Watergate scandal, this especially confused and infuriated McGovern and many of his supporters. But the relatively mild reaction to the Watergate affair must be seen in the context, not only of McGovern's perceived hypocrisy, but of his perceived extremism: that is, his association with cultural radicalism. Under ordinary circumstances, with a more conventional coalition candidate, a scandal like Watergate would probably have cut seriously into Republican Presidential support (in fact it may have played a role in Congressional voting). It is likely that its impact was as small as it was not simply or even primarily because of public apathy about corruption, but because large segments of the public saw a bigger, more threatening, and ultimately more corrupting attack on the social order coming from the other side. Anarchic process and anarchic morals, pursued with evangelical fury, were evidently felt to be more ominous than political espionage.

III

In the spring of 1972, the Survey Research Center of the University of Michigan asked the American people: "All things considered, how satisfied are you with life in the United States today?" More than three-quarters of those asked said that they were satisfied or very satisfied. Only 9 per cent indicated that they were dissatisfied. Surprisingly, those at the lower rungs of the socioeconomic ladder indicated *more* satisfaction with American life than those higher up. For example, 42 per cent of those in the lowest economic rank said that they were "very satisfied," as compared with 31 per cent of those in the highest. As to the black population, although in general it expressed less satisfaction than the white, only a total of 17 per cent expressed actual dissatisfaction. This overwhelmingly favorable response did not mean that the American people were without severe gripes. They had specific complaints: about income (a third), about housing (a quarter), about the schools (a third), and so forth. According to Gallup such complaints increased (except among blacks) in the two years preceding the election, while Harris reported an increase in "feelings of alienation" (that is, feelings of political powerlessness) among Americans from 1966 through 1972.

From other evidence, however, it became apparent that neither the specific complaints nor the feelings of alienation were directed against the nature of the traditional social order itself. Thus, more of the alienated people, according to Harris, were Nixon supporters than McGovern supporters. A similar perspective was offered by Teresa E. Levitin and Warren Miller of the Michigan Center, who built a portrait of two divergent streams in America which they called the Silent Minority and the Liberal Coalition. There were no specific "issues" involved in constructing this model, only "style," related to a basic stance toward the American social order. The Liberal Coalition was comprised of those who favored protest and the counter-culture, and opposed law-and-order and the established agents of social control. Levitin and Miller calculated that only about 12 per cent of the public fell into this category. Conversely, only about

16 per cent fell into the category of the Silent Minority—that is, those who held reverse positions on all of the four criteria. The vast majority were in the middle.

It is relevant to note in this connection that not even the ideological edges—the Liberal Coalition and the Silent Minority as isolated by Levitin and Miller—were fixed in their place by social class. It was not just the affluent American who was found to feel a stake in the social order. There was, of course, an affluent-class bias toward the Republican party, but on the other hand there was also a tendency for some of the affluent to be attracted to the anti-order style of the Liberal Coalition. But their disaffection was of a different quality altogether from those who had specific gripes about housing, employment, and the working of the system. This was subsequently illustrated in the one major effort made by the McGovern convention leadership to accommodate an "opposition" faction, that of George Wallace. The McGovernites worked hard to prevent Wallace from losing the votes of delegates in states in which he had won the preferential primaries. Wallace delegates were offered every opportunity to present their case, both in committees and at the convention. Wallace himself was allowed to address the convention at length during the platform debate, a courtesy never before shown to an announced Presidential candidate. Orders were given, and carried out, not to boo or heckle this representative of the most powerful racist element in American politics.

All this was done by the McGovernites on the assumption that the name of the game was not "issues" but root alienation. It was hoped that the mass base of "alienated" and "populist" sentiment represented by Wallace could be attracted to the form of anti-establishment politics found in the McGovern movement. Yet, in the first place, any analysis of the opinions of Wallace supporters would have clearly suggested that their frustration had little in common with those associated with McGovern supporters. It should also have been clear that if the Wallaceites and McGovernites were both extremist, Wallace extremism leaned toward violating due process in order to *maintain* the social order, not in order to overturn it. Thus the Wallaceites ended up voting 2-1 for Nixon.*

---

* Despite what McGovern said after the election, the Wallace vote was not a determining factor in the final result. If Wallace had run on his own ticket and secured around 15 per cent of the vote, the election would have wound up with 50 per cent for Nixon, 35 for McGovern.

There are other aspects of the final voting which will deserve greater study on this score as well. Over 90 per cent of the black vote in the ghettos was for McGovern, but he won only about 80 per cent of the black vote in non-ghetto areas. And only 67 per cent of the one out of 16 blacks who live in the suburbs voted for McGovern. Tangled in this pattern are a social-class pull, plus a new feeling of stake in the American society, plus a highly developed sense of the liberal political and economic agenda.

In evaluating the response of the electorate to the strains of recent years, however, it is important to note the abundant evidence that the large majority of Americans have not only indicated their continuing commitment to the traditional social order; they have also indicated a continuing commitment to the traditional economic and class issues and values associated with the image of the New Deal-Fair Deal-Great Society policies pressed by Democratic leaders from Roosevelt to Humphrey. Opinion surveys show two seemingly contradictory findings. The proportion of Americans describing themselves as "conservatives" rather than "liberals" reached a point in the 60's where the once-convincing liberal lead had been replaced by a conservative one on the order of 2-1 (although a recent Harris poll has indicated a very slight liberal upswing to 19 per cent once again). But while many more people now call themselves conservatives rather than liberals, the Democratic advantage over the GOP in party registration and in party identification in the polls is still extremely large. This seeming conflict appears to reflect a change in the meaning attached to the terms "liberal" and "conservative." Where they once were seen primarily in economic terms, e.g., attitude toward social-security policy, governmental economic planning, trade-union rights, progressive tax policy, and the like, they now appear to apply more to feelings and attitudes on cultural and moral issues. Conversely, however, the variations between the two major parties are still seen in economic and class terms: most voters still identify the Republicans as the party of "big business," and the Democrats as the party of the "people." The Democrats continue to be seen as the best party for helping the poor, the trade unions, the workers, and for handling unemployment and other economic issues, including tax policy.

The various referenda in 1972 testify to the validity of this new set of findings. In California for example, the electorate voted by close to 2-1 against legalizing possession of marijuana and in favor of restoring the death penalty, but it also voted by an overwhelming majority against a proposition which had been defined as an effort to prevent the farm labor union led by Cesar Chavez from operating effectively. California gave Richard Nixon a substantial majority, but the GOP strength in the State Assembly fell from 35 seats to 29, while the Democrats jumped from 45 to 51. And the Republican Assembly leader, Robert Monagan, publicly

---

Analyses of Jewish voting are also instructive. On its face the Jewish vote represented a sharp departure from the recent past, 2-1 for the Democratic nominee as against 4-1 last time around. But actually the Jews were roughly at the same distance from the rest of the population in 1972 as they were in 1968. The unique aspect of the Jewish vote, the fact that Jews do not tend to vote more heavily Republican as their incomes rise, continued to show. The interesting fact is that preliminary precinct analyses indicate that lower-income Jews defected more sharply to the Republicans, on the Presidential vote, than did upper-income Jews. (This was, of course, true of lower-income ethnics in general, but arose from a different initial pattern.)

expressed doubt that the Republicans would be able to retain the governorship in the 1974 elections.

The American electorate is thus caught in a crosscurrent between political liberalism and cultural conservatism. Its conservatism comes to the fore when the nature of cultural change seems to signify a basic threat to the social order. The McGovern campaign, starting with the convention, appeared to be doing that in 1972, and the population opted for the traditional social order. But few were happy with the choice they had to make. For the other side of the coin was that President Nixon had done nothing to convince the electorate that he possessed the kind of social sense which boded well for liberal domestic economic programs. In consequence, there was no Rooseveltian exultation among the populace about the election or its results. As a matter of fact, ambivalence at the polls was demonstrably deep. "Which candidate are you most apathetic about?" asked one cartoon pollster. And, even after voting, many people felt that they had not yet quite made up their minds. The abstention rate was high—an expression not so much of apathy as of liberal-conservative ambivalence.*

IV

The principal issue which gave rise to the New-Politics campaigns of Eugene McCarthy and Robert F. Kennedy in 1968, and which underlay much of the ardor of the McGovern pre-nomination battle, was the Vietnam war. In spite of the poll data indicating that economic and class concerns were more likely to find support among traditionally Democratic groups, whose backing he desperately needed, McGovern returned time and again to the issue of the war, reserving his most extreme language for this topic.

Yet the record seems clear that McGovern misread the mood of the country on the war too, even though he had been personally involved in the publication of the most comprehensive and sophisticated book-length analysis of that mood, *Vietnam and the Silent Majority: The Dove's Guide* (1970), written by three major academic authorities on public opinion, Milton Rosenberg, Sidney Verba, and Philip Converse. McGovern contributed the Foreword to this detailed analysis of the many opinion surveys on attitudes toward the war. Among other things, the book revealed that since 1969 a majority of Americans had been convinced that our involvement in the war in Vietnam was a mistake. On the other hand, the authors documented and stressed the fact that most Americans tended

* In the Jewish precincts analyzed, the abstention rates in lower- and middle-income areas were staggering; in one case the percentage registered and not voting increased from 8 to 25 per cent between 1968 and 1972.

"to be patriotic, to be proud of the fact that we have 'never lost a war,' and to be moved by the symbols of patriotism such as the flag." Moreover, the bulk of the public wished to end our commitment in Vietnam under conditions that would avoid a Communist takeover of South Vietnam. Most Americans (this continued to be the case well into the polls taken in 1972) favored giving support to the anti-Communist forces in South Vietnam after an American withdrawal.

Concurrent with a strong desire for peace on the part of the large majority was strong disapproval of the militant confrontationist tactics of sections of the anti-war movement. Even young people under 30—and by overwhelming majorities—condemned student strikes against the war. These negative attitudes toward anti-war and student protest were not limited to those with mild feelings about the war. As the authors pointed out about the results of a study completed in 1968:

> Respondents were asked to evaluate a wide range of political leaders and groups on a "feeling" scale, ranging from extremely negative to highly positive. Reactions toward "Vietnam war protesters" were by a substantial amount the most negative half of the scale, and more than 33 per cent placed them at the extreme negative point, which was not otherwise much employed. But one can go further. Sixty-three per cent of those believing the war was a mistake viewed protesters negatively, and *even of the group favoring complete withdrawal from Vietnam 53 per cent put the protesters on the negative side of the scale.* Plainly, opposition to the war and opposition to active protest against it go together for a significant part of the population. [Emphasis in original.]

As of 1970, George McGovern seemed to understand the implications of these facts. In his Foreword to *Vietnam and the Silent Majority* he acknowledged that many Americans who opposed the war did so for the "wrong" reasons. As a result, he said:

> Long-time apostles against our intervention in Vietnamese affairs must therefore face the disquieting choice between ending the war sooner for what we see as many of the wrong reasons—"it is costing too much," "the general policy is sound, but it has not worked here," and the like—or waiting and debating until a decisive majority of the American people accept our notion of an appropriate U.S. foreign policy and is thus ready to demand, for the right reasons, that the fighting be stopped.
>
> The former approach is more compelling if we consider only the young men who must die and be maimed, the opportunities which will be lost, and the more complete physical and human destruction of a tiny nation which will be inflicted if we are to wait for the latter. Indeed, if it has been immoral for us to bring the battlefield of our

> misguided war with Communism to the innocent people of Vietnam and to sacrifice their country in pursuit of our "larger" interests, then it is just as immoral for advocates of peace to allow the annihilation to continue until we complete the ambitious task of putting America's conscience in order.

By 1972 Senator McGovern had evidently forgotten these words. During his campaign for the Presidency he constantly issued statements which could only have outraged many Americans who opposed the war for the "wrong" reasons. His moralistic strictures against Richard Nixon, his comparing of the consequences of the President's actions with those of Adolf Hitler, his seemingly unabashed assumption that his own election would probably be followed immediately by the fall of the Saigon government and its replacement by a Communist regime, his praise of draft-evaders who had fled the country, simply alienated many of these Americans.

The surveys summarized in *Vietnam and the Silent Majority* also pointed up, two years before the election, another basic weakness of the subsequent McGovern strategy, namely, its assumption that the enlarged youth vote would provide the margin for electoral victory. McGovern strategist Fred Dutton, in a pre-primary campaign memorandum which McGovern personally found credible, had anticipated a considerable majority for McGovern among the twenty-five million new voters between 18 and 24. Dutton estimated that three-quarters of them would actually vote, and that three-quarters of those who balloted would vote for a New-Politics Democratic nominee. This advantage would presumably be sufficient to offset any defections among the older segments of the electorate.

Yet a variety of opinion surveys, many of them reported in the volume introduced by Senator McGovern, indicated that these were ridiculously optimistic forecasts, and that in fact youth as such possessed no special anti-war or movement-oriented characteristics. The authors pointed out that strong anti-war sentiment was limited largely to students attending the minority of leading schools and to their parents. Otherwise, "there is no sign whatever of a younger generation—say those under 30—that makes consistently dovish responses, thereby putting it in sharp opposition to a hawkish older generation." Just the reverse was true: "whites under 30, particularly males have been in the aggregate quite hawkish in terms of desires to solve the Vietnam problem through escalation." In effect, the authors concluded, as had many other analysts of youth and student behavior, there was no "generation gap" on this issue but rather "a profound cleavage on Vietnam among the young themselves."

This, of course, was precisely what showed up in the pre-election surveys and in the voting returns. According to the findings of a CBS survey of 17,405 respondents taken as they were leaving the polls on election day, the 18-24 group divided 46 per cent for Nixon and 52 for McGovern; while among the 25-29-year-old group, Nixon led 54-44. McGovern did only slightly better among students, 54-45, than he did among first-time voters as a whole. And in conformity with all previous studies of the electoral participation of first-time voters, only 47 per cent of those under 24 actually bothered to go to the polls. Thus the generation of Consciousness III (McGovern also wrote a blurb for Charles Reich's *The Greening of America*) turned out never to have existed, never to have been "out there," available, and waiting for the call of a moralistic New Politics.

And if young voters—McGovern's much-vaunted "sure" constituency—were split among themselves on Vietnam, it should hardly have come as a surprise to anyone that the country as a whole was similarly divided on this issue, nor that McGovern should have proved unable even to summon a majority among those favoring an end to the war. Indeed, survey after survey showed most people who favored peace in Vietnam believing that the reelection of Richard Nixon would be the best way to accomplish that goal. For Richard Nixon's proclaimed policy was to describe American withdrawal as "peace with honor"—i.e., avoiding a Communist takeover—while Senator McGovern, in another display of his evangelical moralism, presented withdrawal as a deserved defeat—that is, the morally superior course of action.

V

In sum, George McGovern and his strategists totally misjudged the character of the American electorate. The convention and the campaign were conducted as though the American public consisted of two large factions: one basically alienated from the American order, the other evilly dedicated to turning the clock back. There undoubtedly are such factions in the country, but they are hardly large ones, and they do not represent the greater majority of the American electorate. Throughout the 60's, and especially since 1965, many Americans felt that they were experiencing an enormous amount of cultural change, and the last man they wanted for President in 1972 was one who was identified with those who proposed to carry cultural change further, when the social order was already a-tremble. This does not mean that these same Americans were prepared to reject programs for social reform in areas such as health, educational opportunity, equal rights, or the economy. The opinion surveys indicated clear and continuing majorities in favor of extending opportunity to the underprivileged, to those facing discrimination, to the handicapped, while at the same time restoring a sense of personal security to those who live in the urban areas.

Furthermore, all other things being equal, the majority of Americans would still prefer the "party of compassion" to the party they associate with the business elite; nothing attests to this fact more strikingly than President Nixon's failure in the election to carry Republican Congressional or local candidates on his coattails. The GOP decline in governorships over a four-year period from 31 in 1968 to 19 in 1972 was a prolonged landslide in reverse. Indeed, in many ways the President was a tellingly weak candidate. In each of his previous national races, 1960 and 1968, as well as in the California gubernatorial contest in 1962, his Democratic rivals had started considerably back in the polls and had managed to close the gap: Hubert Humphrey, for example, came from 16 points behind to an almost dead heat in 1968. In 1970, when the President campaigned vigorously for Republican Congressional candidates, he failed utterly to sway the electorate. From this point of view the Nixon electoral victory was an amazing phenomenon; it occurred in spite of the fact that his campaign style and personality clearly had a negative effect on the public, and in spite of the fact that a majority of Americans still prefers the Democratic to the Republican party.

Through a peculiar accident of history, the Democratic party in 1972 was divided among a number of candidates. The representative of the smallest faction of a major party ever to secure the Presidential nomination won out within the party—and then continued to act like a factional leader (only 30 per cent of Democrats polled by Gallup just before the Miami convention favored McGovern). The result was a landslide for a Republican candidate who has never possessed widespread charismatic appeal, and who clearly polled more "reluctant" votes than any candidate in recent political history. There are lessons to be drawn from this event. The Republicans learned theirs after 1964; whether the Democrats will do likewise remains an open question.

5.

PRESIDENTIAL POPULARITY FROM TRUMAN TO JOHNSON

John E. Mueller

> I think [my grandchildren] will be proud of two things. What I did for the Negro and seeing it through in Vietnam for all of Asia. The Negro cost me 15 points in the polls and Vietnam cost me 20.
>
> Lyndon B. Johnson [1]

With tenacious regularity over the last two and a half decades the Gallup Poll has posed to its cross-section samples of the American public the following query, "Do you approve or disapprove of the way (the incumbent) is handling his job as President?" The responses to this curious question form an index known as "Presidential popularity." According to Richard Neustadt, the index is "widely taken to approximate reality" in Washington and reports about its behavior are "very widely read" [2] there, including, the quotation above would suggest, the highest circles.

Plotted over time, the index forms probably the longest continuous trend line in polling history. This study seeks to analyze the polling history. This study seeks to analyze the behavior of this line for the period from the beginning of the Truman administration in 1945 to the end of the Johnson administration in January 1969 during which time the popularity question was asked some 300 times.

Four variables are used as predictors of a President's popularity. These include a measure of the length of time the incumbent has been in office as well as variables which attempt to estimate the influence on his rating of major international events, economic slump and war. To assess the independent impact of each of these variables as they interact in as-

---

[1] Quoted, David Wise, "The Twilight of a President," *New York Times Magazine*, November 3, 1968, p. 131.

[2] Richard E. Neustadt, *Presidential Power: The Politics of Leadership* (New York: Wiley, 1960), p. 205n.

Reprinted from the *American Political Science Review*, Vol. 64 (March, 1970), pp. 18–34. Edited for inclusion in this volume and used with the permission of the author and publisher. For a fuller report of this research, see J. E. Mueller, *War, Presidents and Public Opinion* (New York: John Wiley, 1973).

sociation with Presidential popularity, multiple regression analysis is used as the basic analytic technique.

I. THE DEPENDENT VARIABLE: PRESIDENTIAL POPULARITY

The Presidential popularity question taps a general impression about the way the incumbent seems to be handling his job at the present moment. As Neustadt notes, the response, like the question, is "unfocused," unrelated to specific issues or electoral outcomes. The respondent is asked to "approve" or "disapprove" and if he has "no opinion," he must volunteer that response himself. He has infrequently been asked *why* he feels that way—and many respondents when asked are able only vaguely to rationalize their position. And only at times has he been asked to register how strongly he approves or disapproves.

A disapproving response might be considered a non-constructive vote of no-confidence: the respondent registers his discontent, but he does not need to state who he would prefer in the Presidency. Thus the index is likely to be a very imperfect indicator of success or failure for a President seeking re-election. While approvers are doubtless more likely than disapprovers to endorse his re-election, on considering the opposition some approvers may be attracted into voting against the incumbent just as some disapprovers may be led grudgingly to vote for him.

Whatever peculiarities there are in the question itself, they are at least constant. Unlike many questions asked by the polling organizations, wording has not varied from time to time by whim or fashion. The stimulus has therefore been essentially fixed; only the response has varied.

And the variation has been considerable. Harry Truman was our most popular President in this period—for a few weeks in 1945 when more than 85 percent of the public expressed approval—and our least popular—from early 1951 until March 1952 when less than 30 percent were usually found to be favorably inclined. Other Presidents have stayed within these limits with Lyndon Johnson most nearly approaching the Truman extremes. President Eisenhower's popularity was never higher than 79 percent, but it never dropped below 49 percent either. President Kennedy also maintained a rather high level of popularity but was in noticeable decline at the time of his death.

The proportion of respondents selecting the "no opinion" option, averaging 14 percent, remained strikingly constant throughout the period. This is a little surprising since it might be expected that when opinion changes, say, from approval to disapproval of a President, the move would be seen first in a decrease in the support figure with an increase in the no opinion percentage, followed in a later survey by an increase in the disapproval column with a decrease in the opinion portion. There are a few occasions in which the no opinion percentage seems to rise and fall in this manner, one occurring in the early weeks of the Korean War, but by and large it would appear that if movements into the no opinion column do occur they are compensated for by movements out of it.

This means therefore that the trend in approval is largely a mirror image of the trend in disapproval; the correlation between the two is –.98. And, most conveniently, this almost means that the President's popularity at a given moment can be rendered by a single number: the percentage approving his handling of the job. The no opinion percentage is almost always close to 14 percent and the percentage disapproving is, of course, the remainder.

Since one of the propositions to be tested in this study proposes that there exists a general downward trend in each President's popularity, this initial rating situation causes something of a problem. If the disapproval score is used as the dependent variable there will be a slight bias in favor of the proposition. It seems preferable to load things against the proposition; hence for the purposes of this study *the dependent variable is the percentage approving the way the incumbent is handling his job as President.* The average approval rating for the entire twenty-four year period is 58 percent.

II. THE INDEPENDENT VARIABLES

If one stares at Presidential popularity trend lines long enough, one soon comes to imagine one is seeing things. If the things imagined seem also to be mentioned in the literature about the way Presidential popularity should or does behave, one begins to take the visions seriously and to move to test them.

In this manner were formulated four basic "independent" variables, predictor variables of Presidential popularity. They are: 1) a "coalition of minorities" variable that suggests the overall trend in a President's popularity will be downward; 2) a "rally round the flag" variable which anticipates that international crises and similar phenomena will give a President a short-term boost in popularity; 3) an "economic slump" variable associating recessions with decreased popularity; and 4) a "war" variable predicting a decrease in popularity under the conditions of the Korean and Vietnam wars.

1. *The "Coalition of Minorities" Variable.* In a somewhat different context Anthony Downs has suggested the possibility that an administration, even if it always acts with majority support on each issue, can gradually alienate enough minorities to be defeated. This could occur

when the minority on each issue feels so intensely about its loss that it is unable to be placated by administration support on other policies it favors. A clever opposition, under appropriate circumstances, could therefore forge a coalition of these intense minorities until it had enough votes to overthrow the incumbent.[3]

Transposed to Presidential popularity, this concept might inspire the expectation that a President's popularity would show a general downward trend as he is forced on a variety of issues to act and thus create intense, unforgiving opponents of former supporters. It is quite easy to point to cases where this may have occurred. President Kennedy's rather dramatic efforts to force back a steel price rise in 1962, while supported by most Americans, tended to alienate many in the business community. Administration enforcement of the Supreme Court's school desegregation order tended to create intense opposition among white Southerners even if the Presidential moves had passive majority support in most of the country.

Realistically, the concept can be extended somewhat. From time to time there arise exquisite dilemmas in which the President must act and in which he will tend to alienate *both* sides no matter what he does, a phenomenon related to what Aaron Wildavsky has called a "minus sum" game. President Truman's seizure of the steel mills in 1952 made neither labor nor management (nor the Supreme Court, for that matter) happy. For the mayor of New York, situations like this seem to arise weekly.

There are other, only vaguely related, reasons to expect an overall decline in popularity. One would be disillusionment. In the process of being elected, the President invariably says or implies he will do more than he can do and some disaffection of once bemused supporters is all but inevitable. A most notable example would be the case of those who supported President Johnson in 1964 because he seemed opposed to escalation in Vietnam. Furthermore initial popularity ratings are puffed up by a variety of weak followers. These might include leering opposition partisans looking for the first excuse to join the aggrieved, excitable types who soon became bored by the humdrum of post-election existence, and bandwagon riders whose fair weather support dissolves with the first sprinkle. As Burns Roper notes, "In a sense, Presidential elections are quadriennial myth builders which every four years make voters believe some man is better than he is. The President takes office with most of the nation on his side, but this artificial 'unity' soon begins to evaporate." [4]

For these reasons the coalition of minorities variable, as it is dubbed here, predicts decline. "Love," said Machiavelli, "is held by a chain of

---

[3] *An Economic Theory of Democracy* (New York: Harper and Row, 1957), pp. 55–60.

[4] Burns Roper, "The Public Looks at Presidents," *The Public Pulse,* January 1969.

obligation which, men being selfish, is broken whenever it serves their purpose."[5]

The coalition of minorities variable is measured simply by the length of time, in years, since the incumbent was inaugurated (for first terms) or re-elected (for second terms). It varies then from zero to about four and should be negatively correlated with popularity: the longer the man has been in office, the lower his popularity. It is; the simple r is −.47. The decline is assumed to start over again for second terms because the President is expected to have spent the campaign rebuilding his popular coalition by soothing the disaffected, re-deluding the disillusioned, and putting on a show for the bored. If he is unable to do this, he will not be re-elected, something which has not happened in the post-war era although twice Presidents have declined to make the effort.

The analysis will assume a *linear* decline in popularity. That is, a President's popularity is assumed to decline at an even rate for all four years of his term: if a decline of 6 percentage points per year is indicated, he will be down 6 points at the end of his first year, 12 at the end of the second, 18 at the end of the third, and 24 after four years. There is nothing in the justification for the coalition of minorities variable which demands that the decline must occur with such tedious regularity but, when curvilinear variants were experimented with, little or no improvement was found. Hence the reliance in this study on the linear version which has the advantage of simplicity and ease of communication.

2. *The "Rally Round the Flag" Variable.* This variable seeks to bring into the analysis a phenomenon often noted by students of the Presidency and of public opinion: certain intense international events generate a "rally round the flag" effect which tends to give a boost to the President's popularity rating. As Kenneth Waltz has observed, "In the face of such an event, the people rally behind their chief executive."[6] Tom Wicker: "Simply being President through a great crisis or a big event . . . draws Americans together in his support."[7] Richard Neustadt notes "the correspondence between popularity and happenings," Burns Roper finds "approval has usually risen during international crises," and Nelson Polsby observes, "Invariably, the popular response to a President during international crisis is favorable, regardless of the wisdom of the policies he pursues."[8]

---

[5] *The Prince,* ch. XVII.

[6] Kenneth N. Waltz, "Electoral Punishment and Foreign Policy Crisis" in James N. Rosenau, *Domestic Sources of Foreign Policy* (New York: Free Press, 1967), p. 272.

[7] Tom Wicker, "In the Nation: Peace, It's Wonderful," *New York Times,* July 4, 1967, p. 18.

[8] *Congress and the Presidency* (Englewood Cliffs, N. J.: Prentice-Hall, 1964), p. 25.

The difficulty with this concept is in operationalizing it. There is a terrible temptation to find a bump on a popularity plot, then to scurry to historical records to find an international "rally point" to associate with it. This process all but guarantees that the variable will prove significant.

The strategy adopted here to identify rally points was somewhat different and hopefully more objective. A definition of what a rally point should look like was created largely on *a priori* grounds and then a search of historical records was made to find events which fit the definition. Most of the points so identified *are* associated with bumps on the plot—that after all was how the concept was thought of in the first place—but quite a few are not and the bumps associated with some are considerably more obvious than others.

In general, a rally point must be associated with an event which 1) is international and 2) involves the United States and particularly the President directly; and it must be 3) specific, dramatic, and sharply focused.

It must be international because only developments confronting the nation as a whole are likely to generate a rally round the flag effect. Major domestic events—riots, scandals, strikes—are at least as likely to exacerbate internal divisions as they are to soothe them.

To qualify as a rally point an international event is required to involve the United States and the President directly because major conflicts between other powers are likely to engender split loyalties and are less likely to seem relevant to the average American.

Finally the event must be specific, dramatic and sharply focused in order to assure public attention and interest. As part of this, events which transpire gradually, no matter how important, are excluded from consideration because their impact on public attitudes is likely to be diffused. Thus sudden changes in the bombing levels in Vietnam are expected to create a reaction while the gradual increase of American troops is not.

Errors in this process could occur by including events whose importance is only obvious in retrospect or by ignoring events like the Geneva summit of 1955 which may seem minor in historical perspective but were held significant at the time. For this reason more reliance has been put on indexes of newspaper content than on broad, historical accounts of the period. In general if there has been a bias in selecting rally points it has been in the direction of excluding border-line cases. This was done in profound respect for the lack of public interest and knowledge on most items of international affairs.

At that, some 34 rally points were designated. In general they can be said to fall into six categories. First, there are the four instances of sudden American military intervention: Korea, Lebanon, the Bay of Pigs, and the Dominican Republic. A second closely related category encompasses major military developments in ongoing wars: in Korea, the Inchon landing and the Chinese intervention; in Vietnam, the Tonkin Bay episode, the beginning of bombing of North Vietnam, the major extension of this bombing, and the Tet offensive. Third are the major diplomatic developments of the period: crises over Cuban missiles, the U-2 and atomic testing, the enunciation of the "Truman doctrine" with its offer of aid to Greece and Turkey, the beginning of, and major changes in, the peace talks in Korea and Vietnam, and the several crises in Berlin. Fourth are the two dramatic technological developments: Sputnik and the announcement of the first Soviet atomic test. The fifth category includes the meetings between the President and the head of the Soviet Union at Potsdam in 1945, Geneva in 1955, Camp David in 1959, Paris in 1960, Vienna in 1961, and Glassboro in 1967. While these events are rarely spectacular they, like crisis, do generate a let's-get-behind-the-President effect. Because they are far less dramatic—even if sometimes more important—Presidential conferences with other powers (e.g., the British at Nassau) are excluded as are American meetings with the Soviet Union at the foreign minister level.

Sixth and finally, as an analytic convenience the start of each Presidential term is rather arbitrarily designated as a rally point. Presidents Truman and Johnson came in under circumstances which could justifiably be classified under the "rally round the flag" rubric although the crisis was a domestic one. The other points all involve elections or re-elections which perhaps might also be viewed as a somewhat unifying and cathartic experience.

These then are the events chosen to be associated with the rally round the flag variable. No listing will satisfy everyone's perspective about what has or has not been important to Americans in this 24 year period. However, in the analysis the variable has proven to be a rather hardy one. Experimentation with it suggests the addition or subtraction of a few rally points is likely to make little difference.

The rally round the flag variable is measured by the length of time, in years, since the last rally point. It varies then from zero to a theoretical maximum of about four or an empirical one of 1.9. Like the coalition of minorities variable, it should be negatively correlated with popularity: the longer it has been since the last rally round the flag event, the lower the popularity of the incumbent. It is; the simple r is −.11. Some experiments with curvilinear transformations of the variable were attempted but, since improvement again was marginal at best, the variable has been left in linear form.

Each rally point is given the same weighting in the analysis. One effort to soften this rather crude policy was made. The rally points were separated into two groups: "good" rally points (e.g., the Cuban missile crisis) in which the lasting effect on opinion was likely to be favorable to the President and "bad" ones (e.g., the U-2 crisis, the Bay of Pigs) in which the initial favorable surge could be expected to be rather transitory. Two separate rally round the flag variables were then created with the anticipation that they would generate somewhat different regression coefficients. The differences however were small and inconsistent. The public seems to react to "good" and "bad" international events in about the same way. Thus, to this limited extent, the equal weighting of rally points seems justified.

In tandem, the concepts underlying the coalition of minorities and rally round the flag variables predict that the President's popularity will continually decline over time and that international crises and similar events will explain short term bumps and wiggles in this otherwise inexorable descent.

3. *The "Economic Slump" Variable.* There is a goodly amount of evidence, and an even goodlier amount of speculation, suggesting a relationship between economic conditions and electoral behavior. The extension of such thinking to Presidential popularity is both natural and precedented. Neustadt, for example, concludes the recession in 1958 caused a drop in President Eisenhower's popularity.

The economic indicator used here will be the unemployment rate. The statistic recommends itself because it is available for the entire period and is reported on a monthly basis. It is used as a general indicator of economic health or malaise and is not taken simply as a comment about the employed. It is assumed that the individual respondent, in allowing economic perceptions to influence him, essentially does so by comparing how things are *now* with how they were when the incumbent began his present term of office. If conditions are worse, he is inclined to disapprove the President's handling of his job, if things are better he is inclined to approve. The economic variable therefore becomes the unemployment rate at the time the incumbent's term began subtracted from the rate at the time of the poll. It is positive when things are worse and negative when things are better. It should be negatively correlated with popularity. But it isn't.

Unemployment reached some of its highest points during the recessions under the Eisenhower administration. The problem, to be examined more fully in Section VI below, is that Eisenhower was a *generally* popular President. Thus even though his popularity seemed to dip during the recessions, high unemployment comes to be associated with a relatively popular President. This problem can be handled rather easily within regression analysis by assigning to each of the Presidential administrations a "dummy" variable, the care and feeding of which will be discussed more fully in Section III below.

However, even when this circumstance is taken into account, the correlation coefficient and the regression coefficient for the economic variable remain positive. This seems to be largely due to the fact that *both* unemployment and the popularity of the incumbent President were in general decline between 1961 and 1968. The correlation for the period is .77.

Therefore a final alteration administered to the economic variable was to set it equal to zero whenever the unemployment rate was lower at the time of the survey than it had been at the start of the incumbent's present term. This alteration is a substantive one and is executed as the only way the data can be made to come out "right." In essence it suggests that *an economy in slump harms a President's popularity, but an economy which is improving does not seem to help his rating.* Bust is bad for him but boom is not particularly good. There is punishment but never reward.

Perhaps this can be seen in a comparison of the 1960 and the 1968 campaigns. In 1960, as Harvey Segal notes, "What was important was the vague but pervasive feeling of dissatisfaction with the performance of the economy, the pain that made the public receptive to JFK's appeals." In 1968, representing administrations that had presided over an unprecedented period of boom, Vice President Humphrey never seemed able to turn this fact to his advantage.

It is important to note that in practice this variable, which will be called the "economic slump" variable because of its inability to credit boom, takes on a non-zero value only during the Eisenhower administration and during the unemployment rise of 1949–50.

4. *The "War" Variable.* It is widely held that the unpopular, puzzling, indecisive wars in Korea and Vietnam severely hurt the popularity of Presidents Truman and Johnson. As noted in the quotation that heads this report, President Johnson himself apportions 20 percentage points of his drop in popularity to the Vietnam War.

This notion seems highly plausible. The popularity of Presidents Truman and Johnson was in steady decline as the wars progressed with record lows occurring during each President's last year in office at points when the wars seemed most hopeless and meaningless. The wars unquestionably contributed in a major way to their decisions not to seek third terms and then, when they had stepped aside, the wars proved to be major liabilities for their party's candidates in the next elections. Overall, the correlation between Presidential popularity and the presence of war is −.66.

There are problems with this analysis, however. The coalition of minorities concept argues that decline is a natural phenomenon and, indeed, a glance at a plot of Presidential popularity clearly shows Truman and Johnson in decline *before* the wars started. Furthermore, as will be seen, both men experienced noticeable declines during their *first* terms when they had no war to contend with. The real question is, then, did the war somehow add to the decline of popularity beyond that which might be expected to occur on other grounds?

An answer can be approached through multiple regression analysis. After allowing for a general pattern of decline under the coalition of minorities variable, the additional impact of a variable chosen to represent war can be assessed. It is also possible in this manner to compare the two wars to see if their association with Presidential popularity differed.

The presence of war is incorporated in the analysis simply by a dummy variable that takes on a value of one when a war is on and remains zero otherwise. The beginning of the Vietnam War was taken to be June 1965 with the beginnings of the major US troop involvement. At that point it became an American war for the public; before that ignorance of the war was considerable: as late as mid-1964, 25 percent of the public admitted it had never heard of the fighting in Vietnam.

Other war measures of a more complex nature were experimented with. They increase in magnitude as the war progresses and thus should be able to tap a wearying effect as the years go by and should be negatively associated with popularity. These measures, however, are very highly correlated with the coalition of minorities variable for the two relevant Presidential terms and thus are all but useless in the analysis. The simple dummy variable suffers this defect in lesser measure, although it is far from immune, and thus, despite its crudities, has been used.

5. *Other Variables.* The analysis of Presidential popularity will apply in various ways only the four variables discussed above—a rather austere representation of a presumably complex process. As will be seen, it is quite possible to get a sound fit with these four variables, but at various stages in the investigation—which involved the examination of hundreds of regression equations—a search was made for other variables which could profitably be added to the predictor set.

International developments are reasonably well incorporated into the analysis with a specific variable included for war and another for major crisis-like activities. Domestically, however, there is only the half-time variable for economic slump and the important but very unspecific coalition of minorities variable.

Accordingly it would be valuable to generate some sort of domestic equivalent to the rally round the flag variable to assess more precisely how major domestic events affect Presidential popularity. Operationally, however, this is a difficult task. First, while it is a justifiable assertion that international crises will redound in the short term to a President's benefit it is by no means clear how a domestic crisis, whether riot, strike, or scandal, should affect his popularity. Furthermore major domestic concerns have varied quite widely not only in intensity and duration, but also in nature. Labor relations, which rarely made big news in the mid-1960s, were of profound concern in the middle and late 1940s as a multitude of major strikes threatened to cripple the nation and the adventures of John L. Lewis and the Taft-Hartley bill dominated the headlines. In the 1950s, however, labor broke into the news only with an occasional steel or auto strike or with the labor racketeering scandals in the last years of the decade. On the other hand, race relations, of extreme importance in the 1960s, made, except for the Little Rock crisis of 1957 and an occasional election-time outburst, little claim to public attention before that time. From the late 1940s into the mid-1950s sundry spy and Communist hunts were of concern, but the issue fairly well fizzled after that. Other issues which might be mentioned had even briefer or more erratic days in the sun: the food shortage of 1947, the MacArthur hearing of 1951, various space flights. Similarly, personal crisis for the Presidents such as heart attacks and major surgery for Presidents Eisenhower and Johnson and the attempted assassination of President Truman could not readily be fashioned into a predictor variable. In any event, these events seem to have far more impact on the stock market than on popularity ratings.

Scandal is a recurring feature of public awareness and thus is more promising as a potential variable in the analysis. Besides the scandals associated with alleged spies and Communists in the government during the McCarthy era and those associated with labor in the late 1950s, Americans, with greatly varying degrees of pain, have suffered through the five percenter scandal of 1949–50; charges of corruption in the RFC in 1951, in the Justice Department in 1952, and in the FHA in 1954; and scandals over Sherman Adams in 1958, over television quiz shows in 1959, over industry "payola" in the late 1950s, over Billie Sol Estes in 1962, and over Bobby Baker in 1963. While scandal is never worked into the regression analysis some preliminary suggestions as to its relevance to a "moral crisis" phenomenon which may in turn affect Presidential popularity are developed in Section VI below.

Some thought was given to including a "lame duck" variable when it was observed that the popularity of Presidents Truman and Johnson rose noticeably after they decided not to seek third terms. The trouble is, however, that President Eisenhower was a lame duck for his entire second term and it was found easier to ignore the whole idea than to decide what to do about this uncomfortable fact.

One domestic variable which did show some very minor promise was a dummy variable for the presence of a major strike. The variable takes on a zero value almost everywhere except in parts of President Truman's first term. After that time major strikes were rather unusual and, when they did occur, usually lasted for such a short time that there was barely time to have a public opinion survey conducted to test their effects.

Despite these peculiarities, the variable did show statistical significance, though only after the Korean War dummy had been incorporated in the equation to allow for a major peculiarity of President Truman's *second* term. Substantively the variable suggests a popularity drop of less than three percentage points when a major strike is on and, as such a minor contributor, it is not included in the discussion below. Its small success, however, may suggest that further experimentation with the effects of specific domestic events could prove profitable.

III. RESULTS WITHOUT THE WAR VARIABLE

In summary the expected behavior of Presidential popularity is as follows. It is anticipated 1) that each President will experience in each term a general decline of popularity; 2) that this decline will be interrupted from time to time with temporary upsurges associated with international crises and similar events; 3) that the decline will be accelerated in direct relation to increases in unemployment rates over those prevailing when the President began his term, but that improvement *in unemployment rates will not affect his popularity one way or the other; and 4) that the President will experience an additional loss of popularity if a war is on.*

In this section the relation of the first three variables to Presidential popularity will be assessed. In the next section the war variable will be added to the analysis.

The association between the first three variables and Presidential popularity is given in its baldest form in equation 1 in Table 1.[9] The equation explains a respectable, if not sensational, 22 percent of the variance. The coalition of minorities variable shows, in conformity with the speculation above, a significant negative relationship. The equation suggests that, in general, a President's popularity rating starts at 69 percent and declines at a rate of about six percentage points per year.

However, while the coefficients for the rally round the flag and economic slump variables are in the expected direction, they are not significant either in a statistical or a substantive sense. The trouble with the economic slump variable was anticipated in the discussion about it in

[9] Each equation is displayed vertically. The dependent variable, the percentage approving the way the President is handling his job, has a mean of 57.5 and a standard deviation of 14.8. The number of cases is 292. The figures in parentheses are the standard errors for the respective partial regression coefficients. To be regarded statistically significant a regression coefficient should be, conventionally, at least twice its standard error. All equations reported in this study are significant (F test) at well beyond the .01 level. The Durbin-Watson d is an indicator of serial correlation which suggests decreasing positive serial correlation as the statistic approaches the value of 2.0. All equations in this study exhibit a statistically significant amount of positive serial correlation.

Section II: the economic decline occurred during the relatively popular reign of President Eisenhower; while the slump seems to have hurt his popularity, even with the decline he remained popular compared to other Presidents; hence what is needed is a variable to take into account this peculiar "Eisenhower effect."

To account for this phenomenon, equation 2 mixes into the analysis a dummy variable for each of the Presidents. This formulation insists that all Presidents must decline (or increase) in popularity at the same rate but, unlike equation 1, it allows each President to begin at his own particular level. Thus peculiar effects of personality, style, and party and of differences in the conditions under which the President came into office can be taken into account.

The addition improves things considerably. The fit is much better and the rally round the flag and economic slump variables attain respectable magnitudes in the predicted direction, although the rally round the flag variable does not quite reach statistical significance.

The equation suggests that the Presidents have declined at an overall rate of over five percentage points per year but that each has done so at his own particular level. President Truman's decline is measured from a starting point of 54.51 percent (when the dummy variables for the Eisenhower, Kennedy, and Johnson administrations are all zero). President Eisenhower declines from a much higher level, about 79 percent (54.51 + 24.08), President Kennedy from 78 percent, and President Johnson from 65 percent.

The importance of these dummy variables clearly demonstrates that *an analysis of Presidential popularity cannot rely entirely on the variables discussed in Section II, but must also incorporate parameters designed to allow for the special character of each administration.* To an extent this is unfortunate. The beauty of equation 1 is that it affords a prediction of a President's popular rating simply by measuring how long he has been in office, how long it has been since the last rally point, and how many people are unemployed. Such predictions, however, would be quite inaccurate because the fit of the equation is rather poor. Instead one must include the administration variables, the magnitudes of which cannot be known until the President's term is over. So much for beauty.

In equation 3 administration effects are incorporated in a different manner, greatly improving fit and reducing serial correlation. In this formulation each President is allowed to begin at his own level of popularity as in equation 2, but in addition each may decline (or increase) at his own rate: for each administration there is a different coefficient for the coalition of minorities variable. Three of the four values so generated are strongly significant while the magnitudes of the administration dummies drop greatly. When the administration dummies are dropped entirely from consideration, as in equation 4, the regression coefficients

TABLE 1

Regression Results Including Administration Effects

	Equations			
	(1)	(2)	(3)	(4)
Intercept	69.37	54.51	68.15	71.52
Independent variables				
Coalitions of minorities (in years)	−6.14 (0.71)	−5.12 (0.48)		
Rally round the flag (in years)	−0.31 (1.95)	−2.15 (1.35)	−1.87 (1.07)	−2.63 (1.07)
Economic slump (in % unemployed)	−0.09 (0.96)	−3.18 (0.75)	−5.30 (0.60)	−5.86 (0.60)
Dummy variables for administrations				
Eisenhower		24.08 (1.42)	0.51 (2.29)	
Kennedy		23.87 (1.82)	11.33 (2.96)	
Johnson		10.46 (1.54)	4.26 (2.48)	
Coalition of minorities variable for administrations (in years)				
Truman			−11.44 (0.84)	−12.54 (0.50)
Eisenhower			0.83 (0.57)	0.13 (0.47)
Kennedy			−5.96 (1.36)	−1.58 (0.82)
Johnson			−9.12 (0.67)	−8.68 (0.50)
Standard error of estimate	13.16	8.88	6.86	7.06
R^2	.22	.65	.79	.78

mostly remain firm and the fit of the equation is scarcely weakened. It is clear that *the important differences between administrations do not lie so much in different overall levels of popularity, but rather in the widely differing rates at which the coalition of minorities variable takes effect.*

The popular decline of Presidents Truman and Johnson has been almost precipitous. President Truman's rating fell off at some 11 or 12 percentage points per year while President Johnson declined at a rate of around 9 points a year. President Kennedy was noticeably more successful at holding on to his supporters. Then there is the Eisenhower phenomenon: in spite of all the rationalizations for the coalitions of minorities concept tediously arrayed in Section II, President Eisenhower's rating uncooperatively refuses to decline at all.

In equation 3, Presidents who served two terms were required to begin each term at the same level and their rate of decline or increase also had to be the same in each term. Liberation from these restrictions is gained in the rather cluttered equation 5 of Table 2 which is like equation 3 except that it affords a term by term, rather than simply an administration by administration comparison. As can be seen President Eisenhower managed a statistically significant *increase* of popularity of some two and a half percentage points per year in his first term. His second term ratings showed a more human, but very minor and statistically non-significant decline.

No important differences emerge in the Eisenhower phenomenon when the economic slump variable, which functions mainly during the Eisenhower years, is dropped from the equation.

No matter how the data are looked at then the conclusion remains the same. *President Eisenhower's ability to maintain his popularity, especially during his first term, is striking and unparallelled among the postwar Presidents.* An examination of some of the possible reasons for this phenomenon is conducted in Section VI below.

The rally round the flag and the economic slump variables emerge alive and well in equations 3, 4, and 5 (and 6). Both are usually statistically significant but their substantive importance varies as one moves from an administration by administration formulation of the coalition of minorities variable (equations 3 and 4) to the term by term formulation in Table 2. Specifically, the rally round the flag variable gets stronger while the economic slump variable weakens.

The rally round the flag variable is very much a parasite—it is designed to explain bumps and wiggles on a pattern measured mainly by the other variables. Consequently the rally round the flag variable does very poorly on its own and only begins to shine when the overall trends become well determined by the rest of the equation. In the end, *the rally round the flag variable suggests a popularity decline of around five or six percentage points for every year since the last rally point*—about the same magnitude as the coalition of minorities variable in its general state as in equations 1 and 2.

The declining fortunes of the economic slump variable suggest that the variable in equations 3 and 4 was partly covering for the differences between the two Eisenhower terms: the first term was associated with increasing popularity and a smaller recession, the second with somewhat declining popularity and a larger recession. With the Eisenhower terms more thoroughly differentiated in equation 5, the variable is reduced to a more purely economic function. The magnitude of the coefficient of the

TABLE 2
Regression Results Including Term Effects and the War Variables

	Equations (5)	Equations (6)
Intercept	72.00	72.38
Independent variables		
Rally round the flag (in years)	–4.88	–6.15
	(1.04)	(1.05)
Economic slump (in % unemployed)	–2.67	–3.72
	(0.65)	(0.65)
Dummy variables for terms		
Truman—second	–15.25	–12.41
	(3.69)	(3.57)
Eisenhower—first	–3.17	–2.41
	(3.15)	(3.02)
Eisenhower—second	–5.30	–4.35
	(3.07)	(2.94)
Kennedy	7.53	7.18
	(3.29)	(3.14)
Johnson—first	7.14	6.77
	(5.50)	(5.26)
Johnson—second	–1.15	–0.79
	(3.06)	(3.25)
Coalition of minorities variable for terms (in years)		
Truman—first	–9.21	–8.93
	(1.41)	(1.35)
Truman—second	–7.98	–2.83
	(1.00)	(1.37)
Eisenhower—first	2.45	2.58
	(0.85)	(0.82)
Eisenhower—second	–0.07	0.22
	(0.65)	(0.62)
Kennedy	–5.11	–4.76
	(1.21)	(1.16)
Johnson—first	–4.98	–3.71
	(14.01)	(13.39)
Johnson—second	–8.15	–8.13
	(0.66)	(0.80)
Dummy variables for wars		
Korea		–18.19
		(3.43)
Vietnam		–0.28
		(2.79)
Standard error of estimate	6.07	5.80
R^2	.84	.86

economic slump variable in this equation *suggests a decline of popularity of about three percentage points for every percentage point rise in the unemployment rate over the level holding when the President began his present term.* Since the unemployment rate has varied in the postwar period only from about 3 to 7 percent, the substantive impact of the economic slump variable on Presidential popularity is somewhat limited.

IV. RESULTS WITH THE WAR VARIABLE ADDED

The variable designed to tap the impact on Presidential popularity of the wars in Korea and Vietnam was applied with no great confidence that it would prove to have an independent, added effect when the coalition of minorities had already been incorporated into the equation especially given the problem of multicollinearity. It is obvious from a perusal of a plot that, as noted in Section II and as demonstrated in equation 5, Presidents Truman and Johnson were in popular decline during their warless first terms. Furthermore each was in clear decline in the first part of his second term before the wars started and it is not at all obvious that this trend altered when the wars began.

The equations suggest otherwise, however. When a war dummy was appended to the equations already discussed, it emerged significant and suggested that the presence of war depressed the popularity of Presidents Truman and Johnson by over seven percentage points.

The next step, obviously, was to set up a separate dummy variable for each war. This brought forth the incredible result documented in equation 6: *the Korean War had a large, significant, independent negative impact on President Truman's popularity of some 18 percentage points, but the Vietnam War had no independent impact on President Johnson's popularity at all.*

Confronted with a result like this, one's first impulse is to do something to make it go away. This impulse was fully indulged. Variables were transformed and transmuted, sections of the analysis were reformed or removed, potentially biassing data were sectioned out. But nothing seemed to work. The relationship persisted. In fact under some manipulations the relationship became stronger.

One's second impulse, then, is to attempt to explain the result. One speculates.

The wars in Korea and Vietnam differed from each other in many respects, of course, but it seems unlikely that these differences can be used in any simple manner to explain the curious regression finding. This is the case because, as one study has indicated, public response to the wars themselves was much the same. Support for each war, high at first, declined as a logarithmic function of American casualties—quickly at first, then more slowly. The functions for each of the wars for comparable periods were quite similar. Furthermore both wars inspired support and opposition from much the same segments of the population.

Therefore it is probably a sounder approach in seeking to explain the regression finding to look specifically at popular attitudes toward *the President's relation to the war,* rather than to perceptions of the war itself. A comment by Richard Neustadt seems strikingly relevant in this respect. "Truman," he observes, "seems to have run afoul of the twin notions that a wartime Chief Executive ought to be 'above politics' and that he ought to help the generals 'win.'"

President Johnson seems to have run considerably less afoul. In seeking to keep the war "above politics," he assiduously cultivated bipartisan support for the war and repeatedly sought to demonstrate that the war effort was simply an extension of the policies and actions of previous Presidents. He was especially successful at generating public expressions of approval from the most popular Republican of them all: General Eisenhower. Vocal opposition to the war in Vietnam came either from groups largely unassociated with either party or from members of the President's own party. Then, when the latter opposition began to move from expressions of misgivings at congressional hearings to explicit challenges in the primaries, President Johnson removed himself from the battle precisely, he said, to keep the war "above politics." And, while there were occasional complaints from the right during Vietnam that President Johnson had adopted a "no win" policy there, these were continually being undercut by public statements from General William Westmoreland—a man highly respected by the right—insisting that he was receiving all the support he needed from the President and was getting it as fast as he needed it.

If these observations are sound, the single event which best differentiates the impact of the Korean and Vietnam wars on Presidential popularity was President Truman's dismissal of General Douglas MacArthur. That move was a major factor in the politicization of the war as Republicans took the General's side and echoed his complaints that it was the President's meddling in policy that was keeping the war from being won.

The differing impact of the wars on Presidential popularity therefore may be due to the fact that Korea became "Truman's war" while Vietnam never in the same sense really became "Johnson's war."

One other item of speculation might be put forth. Domestically, the war in Vietnam was accompanied by a profoundly important crisis as America confronted its long-ignored racial dilemma head on. There seems to have been nothing comparable during the Korean War. The clamor associated with McCarthyism comes to mind but many analysts feel that, however important to politicians, intellectuals, and journalists, McCarthyism was of rather less than major concern to public opinion. Furthermore its dramatic climax, the Army-McCarthy hearings, took place months after the Korean War had ended and over a year after President Truman left office.

It may be, then, that the discontent associated with the racial crisis was enough by itself to cause much of President Johnson's popular decline and thus that the unhappiness over the Vietnam War could make little additional inroad. In the Truman case, there was no profound independent domestic source of discontent: his second term coalition of minorities decline is usually found as in equation 5 to have been less than his first term decline and when, as in equation 6, a variable has already accounted for the war effect, his decline is quite moderate. Thus in a sense there was "room" for the war to have an independent impact.

It would be wise in concluding this section to emphasize what has and what has not been said. It has *not* been argued that the war in Vietnam had nothing to do with President Johnson's decline in popularity and thus the analysis cannot really be used to refute the President's own estimation of the impact of Vietnam as indicated in the quotation that heads this study. However it is argued that whatever impact the war had was tapped by the other variables in the equation, especially the coalition of minorities variable which is specifically designed to account for general overall decline. When the same sort of analysis is applied in the Korean period it is found that a variable associated with the Korean War does show significance even after other variables have been taken into account. What the regression analysis shows therefore is that, while the Korean War does seem to have had an *independent, additional* impact on President Truman's decline in popularity, the Vietnam War shows no such relation to President Johnson's decline.

V. THE RESIDUALS

An analysis of the residuals finds that equation 6 predicts worst in President Truman's first term. The President's extremely high initial ratings are not well predicted suggesting that the equation does not adequately account for the trauma of President Roosevelt's death combined as it was with the ending of World War II and with important peace conferences. It was almost as if Americans were afraid to disapprove of President Truman.

From these spectacular highs, President Truman plunged to great lows during the labor turmoil of 1946. These ratings are also badly specified by the equation. The Truman popularity rose in early 1947, as the labor situation eased, and then declined for the rest of the term. Thus while President Truman's first term, like the other Democratic terms, shows an overall decline of popularity, that decline was considerably more erratic than the others. The dummy variable for strikes, discussed briefly in Section II, improved matters only slightly.

Beyond this, the residuals are reasonably well behaved. There are small but noticeable effects from the lame duck phenomenon at the end of the Truman and Johnson administrations and from the "no opinion" peculiarity of the initial weeks of the Eisenhower and Kennedy administrations. And here and there are data points whose magnitudes have somehow managed to escape specification by the variables in the regression equation. One can of course generate a unique explanation for each of these but this procedure clutters the analysis more than it is worth. Besides, the laws of sampling insist that Gallup must have made *some* mistakes.

VI. THE EISENHOWER PHENOMENON

Great noise was made in Section II about the coalition of minorities variable with its stern prediction that a President's popularity would decline inexorably over his four year term. The noise was not entirely unjustified since the variable proved to be a hardy and tenacious predictor for the postwar Democratic administrations.

The variable fails for the Eisenhower administration, however, especially for the General's first term. The analysis suggests then that if a President wants to leave office a popular man he should either 1) be Dwight David Eisenhower, or 2) resign the day after inauguration.

The Eisenhower phenomenon, noted but left dangling without explanation or rationalization in Section III, deserves special examination. Why didn't President Eisenhower decline in popularity like everybody else? A number of suggestions can be proffered.

1. To begin with, credit must be given to President Eisenhower's *personal appeal:* he was extremely likeable—a quality very beneficial in a popularity contest and one lacked in abundance by, say, Lyndon Johnson. As Fillmore Sanford has observed, "The American people, in reacting to a national leader, put great emphasis on his personal warmth"—a quality projected to an unusual degree by President Eisenhower. As part of this, he was able to project an image of integrity and sincerity which many found to be enormously attractive.

2. Early in his first term President Eisenhower was able to present to the public one sensational achievement: he *ended the Korean War*—or, at any rate, presided over its end. This accomplishment was seen by the public as he left office to be a great one and was used with profit by the Republicans in a Presidential campaign a full 15 years after it happened. From the standpoint of public opinion it may well have been the most favorable achievement turned in by any postwar President. As

such it may have tended to overwhelm the negative impact of anything else the President did, at least for the first years of his administration. Some credit for this is given in the regression analysis since the signing of the truce is counted as a rally point, but this may be a totally inadequate recognition.

There is another aspect of President Eisenhower's first term which may not be sufficiently accounted for in the rally round the flag variable: the euphoria of the "spirit of Geneva" period toward the end of the term when the President's popularity should have been at its lowest ebb.

3. President Eisenhower's *amateur status* may also have worked to his benefit, at least for a while. The public may have been more willing to grant him the benefit of a doubt, to extend the "honeymoon" period, than it would for a President who is a political professional. It is also easier under these circumstances for the President to appear "above the battle" and thus to be blamed only belatedly and indirectly for political mishaps, thereby softening their impact.

4. President Eisenhower may have been curiously benefited by the fact that, especially on the domestic front, *he didn't do anything.* Indeed analysts of the Eisenhower administration often argue that its contribution lies in what it *didn't* do. The times called for consolidation, they argue, and President Eisenhower's achievement was that he neither innovated nor repealed, but was content to preside over a period of placidity in which he tacitly gave Republican respectability to major Democratic innovations of earlier years: the programs of the New Deal domestically and the policies of the Truman Doctrine internationally.

In terms of the justification for the coalition of minorities variable as discussed in Section II, such behavior could have a peculiar result. It was assumed in part that the President would enact programs which, while approved by the majority, would alienate intense minorities which would gradually cumulate to his disadvantage. But suppose the President doesn't do anything. Those who want no change are happy while, if things are sufficiently ambiguous, those who support change have not really been denied by an explicit decision and can still patiently wait and hope. At some point of course those who want change begin to see that they are never going to get their desires and may become alienated, but this will be a delayed process. At least in moderate, placid times, a conservative policy may dissipate some of the power of the coalition of minorities phenomenon. Were polls available, one might find that President Warren Harding maintained his popularity as strikingly as President Eisenhower.

5. Although it might be difficult to sort out cause and effect, it is worth noting that President Eisenhower's first term (and most of his second) coincided with a *period of national goodness.* In a brilliant article Meg Greenfield has noted that "moral crises" as appraised and bemoaned by intellectuals seem to follow a cyclic pattern: we go through a period

in which the popular journals are filled with articles telling us how bad we are after which there is a period of respite.[10]

Miss Greenfield's main indicator of these ethical cycles is exquisite: the number of items under the heading, "US: Moral Conditions," in the *Readers' Guide to Periodical Literature*. The pattern, elaborated and duly pedantified, is given in Table 3. As she notes, our first moral crisis in the

TABLE 3

The Greenfield Index

Number of Items under the Heading, "US: Moral Conditions" in Readers' Guide to Periodical Literature, *1945–1968, by year*

1945	1	1957	7
1946	0	1958	0
1947	8	1959	9
1948	1	1960	32
1949	1	1961	23
1950	3	1962	10
1951	35	1963	11
1952	17	1964	5
1953	1	1965	6
1954	4	1966	7
1955	2	1967	18
1956	0	1968	10

postwar period arose in the early 1950s and was associated with "'five percenters,' deep freezes, mink coats, the Kefauver hearings, and a series of basketball fixes," while "the symbols of our present [1961] decline are Charles Van Doren, payola, cheating in school, and the decision of Frances Gary Powers not to kill himself." We never recovered as thoroughly from that crisis as we did from the earlier one for, as the crisis showed signs of waning (the success of the Peace Corps began to show how good we were at heart), new elements—Billie Sol Estes, Bobby Baker, President Kennedy's assassination, campus revolts, the hippies, and the city riots—proved once again that we have a "sick society." Our moral crises are regenerated every eight years and seem to coincide with the end of Presidential administrations.

Of course objective indicators of public morality have not been careening in this manner. Much of the fluctuation in the Greenfield index is no doubt due to journalistic fad. A sensational fraud, scandal or disruption causes theologians, journalists, and other intellectuals to sociologize: society is sick. Others pick up the idea and it blossoms into a full moral crisis. In a year or two the theme no longer sells magazines and the space

[10] Meg Greenfield, "The Great American Morality Play," *The Reporter*, June 8, 1961, pp. 13–18.

is filled with other profundities. Fraud, scandal, and disruption continue, but the moral crisis eases.

But—and this is a logical and empirical leap of some magnitude—to the extent that these patterns reflect and influence public attitudes, they may be relevant to Presidential popularity. The early Eisenhower years are notable for their absence of moral anguish and they differ from other between-crisis periods in an important respect: not only were we not demonstrably bad, we were positively good for we were undergoing a religious revival. Miss Greenfield looked at the items under the heading, "US: Religious Institutions." She finds only six items in the 1951–53 period, but 25 in 1953–55 while "in the 1955–57 volume, at the height of our virtue . . . the religious listings reached thirty-four with twenty-eight 'sees alsos.'"

If we were so good ourselves, how could we possibly find fault in our leader?

VIII. SUMMARY

This investigation has applied multiple regression analysis to the behavior of the responses to the Gallup Poll's Presidential popularity question in the 24 years period from the beginning of the Truman administration to the end of the Johnson administration. Predictor variables include a measure of the length of time the incumbent has been in office as well as variables which attempt to assess the influence on his rating of major international events, economic slump, and war. Depite the austerity of this representation of a presumably complex process, the fit of the resulting equation was very good: it explained 86 percent of the variance in Presidential popularity.

This degree of fit could only be attained, however, by allowing the special character of each Presidential administration to be expressed in the equation. Thus it does not seem possible to predict a given President's popularity well simply by taking into account such general phenomena as the state of the economy or of international affairs.

The first variable, dubbed the "coalition of minorities" variable, found, as expected, the popularity of most Presidents to be in decline during each term. The important differences between administrations do not lie so much in different overall levels of popularity, but rather in the widely differing rates at which this coalition of minorities variable takes effect. Specifically, the popular decline of Presidents Truman and Johnson was quite steep while President Kennedy seems to have been somewhat better at maintaining his popularity. President Eisenhower's popularity did not significantly decline at all during his second term and actually increased during his first term.

In considering this Eisenhower phenomenon it is suggested that a combination of several causes may be relevant: the President's personal appeal, his ending of the Korean War, his amateur status, his domestic conservatism at a time when such a policy was acceptable, and his fortune in coming to office at a time of national goodness.

The second variable, the "rally round the flag" variable, predicts short term boosts in a President's popularity whenever there occurs an international crisis or a similar event. The variable proves to be a sturdy one and suggests a popular decline of about five or six percentage points for every year since the last "rally point."

Economic effects were estimated in the third variable. The variable could only be made to function if it was assumed that an economy in slump harms a President's popularity, but an economy in boom does not help his rating. A decline of popularity of about three percentage points is suggested for every percentage point rise in the unemployment rate over the level holding when the President began his present term.

The fourth variable attempted to take into account the influence of war on Presidential popularity. It was found that the Korean War had a large, significant independent negative impact on President Truman's popularity of some 18 percentage points, but that the Vietnam War had no independent impact on President Johnson's popularity at all. It is suggested that this difference may be due to the relationship between the Presidents and the wars: President Truman was less able than President Johnson to keep the war "above" partisan politics and he seemed to the public to be interfering and restraining the generals. The absence in the Truman case of a domestic crisis comparable to the racial turmoil of the Johnson era may also be relevant.

6.

THE PRESIDENCY AND THE PRESS

Daniel P. Moynihan

As his years in Washington came to an end, Harry S. Truman wrote a friend:

> I really look with commiseration over the great body of my fellow citizens, who, reading newspapers, live and die in the belief that they have known something of what has been passing in the world in their time.

A familiar Presidential plaint, sounded often in the early years of the Republic and rarely unheard thereafter. Of late, however, a change has developed in the perception of what is at issue. In the past what was thought to be involved was the reputation of a particular President. In the present what is seen to be at stake, and by the Presidents themselves, is the reputation of government—especially, of course, Presidential government. These are different matters, and summon a different order of concern.

There are two points anyone would wish to make at the outset of an effort to explore this problem. First, it is to be acknowledged that in most essential encounters between the Presidency and the press, the advantage is with the former. The President has a near limitless capacity to "make" news which must be reported, if only by reason of competition between one journal, or one medium, and another. (If anything, radio and television news is more readily subject to such dominance. Their format permits of many fewer "stories." The President-in-action almost always takes precedence.) The President also has considerable capacity to reward friends and punish enemies in the press corps, whether they be individual journalists or the papers, television networks, news weeklies, or whatever these individuals work for. And for quite a long while, finally, a President who wishes can carry off formidable deceptions. (One need only recall the barefaced lying that went with the formal opinion of Roosevelt's Attorney General that the destroyer-naval-base deal of 1940 was legal.)

With more than sufficient reason, then, publishers and reporters alike have sustained over the generations a lively sense of their vulnerability to governmental coercion or control. For the most part, their worries have been exaggerated. But, like certain virtues, there are some worries that are best carried to excess.

The second point is that American journalism is almost certainly the best in the world. This judgment will be disputed by some. There are good newspapers in other countries. The *best* European journalists are more intellectual than their American counterparts, and some will think this a decisive consideration. But there is no enterprise anywhere the like of the New York *Times*. Few capitals are covered with the insight and access of the Washington *Post* or the Washington *Evening Star*. As with so many American institutions, American newspapers tend to be older and more stable than their counterparts abroad. The Hartford *Courant* was born in 1764, twenty-one years before the *Times* of London. The New York *Post* began publication in 1801, twenty years before the *Guardian* of Manchester. What in most other countries is known as the

---

Reprinted from *Commentary*, Vol. 51 (March, 1971), pp. 43–50, by permission of the author and publisher.

"provincial" press—that is to say journals published elsewhere than in the capital—in America is made up of a wealth of comprehensive and dependable daily newspapers of unusually high quality.

The journalists are in some ways more important than their journals—at least to anyone who has lived much in government. A relationship grows up with the reporters covering one's particular sector that has no counterpart in other professions or activities. The relationship is one of simultaneous trust and distrust, friendship and enmity, dependence and independence. But it is the men of government, especially in Washington, who are the more dependent. The journalists are their benefactors, their conscience, at times almost their reason for being. For the journalists are above all others their audience, again especially in Washington, which has neither an intellectual community nor an electorate, and where there is no force outside government able to judge events, much less to help shape them, save the press.

That there is something wondrous and terrible in the intensities of this relationship between the press and the government is perhaps best seen at the annual theatricals put on by such groups of journalists as the Legislative Correspondents Association in Albany or the Gridiron in Washington. To my knowledge nothing comparable takes place anywhere else in the world. These gatherings are a kind of ritual truth telling, of which the closest psychological approximation would be the Calabrian insult ritual described by Roger Vailland in his novel *The Law*, or possibly the group-therapy practices of more recent origin. The politicians come as guests of the journalists. The occasion is first of all a feast: the best of everything. Then as dinner progresses the songs begin. The quality varies, of course, but at moments startling levels of deadly accurate commentary of great cruelty are achieved. The politicians sit and smile and applaud. Then some of them speak. Each one wins or loses to the degree that he can respond in kind; stay funny and be brutal. (At the Gridiron John F. Kennedy was a master of the style, but the piano duet performed by Nixon and Agnew in 1970 was thought by many to have surpassed anything yet done.) A few lyrics appear in the next day's papers, but what the newspapermen really said to the politicians remains privileged—as does so much of what the politicians say to them. The relationship is special.

How is it then that this relationship has lately grown so troubled? The immediate answer is, of course, the war in Vietnam. An undeclared war, unwanted, misunderstood, or not understood at all, it entailed a massive deception of the American people by their government. Surely a large area of the experience of the 1960's is best evoked in the story of the man who says: "They told me that if I voted for Goldwater there would be 500,000 troops in Vietnam within a year. I voted for him, and, by God, they were right." The story has many versions. If he voted for Goldwater we would be defoliating the countryside of Vietnam; the army would be sending spies to the 1968 party conventions; Dr. Spock would be indicted on conspiracy charges; and so on. By 1968 Richard Rovere described the capital as "awash" with lies.

The essential fact was that of deceit. How else to carry out a full-scale war that became steadily more unpopular with none of the legally-sanctioned constraints on the free flow of information which even the most democratic societies find necessary in such circumstances? This situation did not spring full-blown from the involvement in Southeast Asia. It was endemic to the cold war. At the close of World War II official press censorship was removed, but the kinds of circumstance in which any responsible government might feel that events have to be concealed from the public did not go away. The result was a contradiction impossible to resolve. The public interest was at once served and dis-served by secrecy; at once dis-served and served by openness. Whatever the case, distrust of government grew. At the outset of the U-2 affair in 1960, the United States government asserted that a weather plane on a routine mission had been shot down. The New York *Times* (May 6, 1960) reported just that. *Not* that the U.S. government *claimed* it was a weather plane, but simply that it was. Well, it wasn't. Things have not been the same since.

But there are problems between the Presidency and the press which have little to do with the cold war or with Vietnam and which—if this analysis is correct—will persist or even intensify should those conditions recede, or even dissolve, as a prime source of public concern. The problems flow from five basic circumstances which together have been working to reverse the old balance of power between the Presidency and the press. It is the thesis here that if this balance should tip too far in the direction of the press, our capacity for effective democratic government will be seriously and dangerously weakened.

I

The first of these circumstances has to do with the tradition of "muckraking"—the exposure of corruption in government or the collusion of government with private interests—which the American press has seen as a primary mission since the period of 1880–1914. It is, in Irving Kristol's words, "a journalistic phenomenon that is indigenous to democracy, with its instinctive suspicion and distrust of all authority in general, and of concentrated political and economic power especially." Few would want to be without the tradition, and it is a young journalist of poor spirit who does not set out to uncover the machinations of some malefactor of great wealth and his political collaborators. Yet there is a cost, as Roger Starr suggests in his wistful wish that Lincoln Steffens's *The Shame of the Cities* might be placed on the restricted shelves of the schools of journalism. Steffens has indeed, as Starr declares, continued "to haunt the city rooms of the country's major newspapers." The question to be asked is whether, in the aftermath of Steffens, the cities were better, or merely more ashamed of themselves. Looking back, one is impressed by the energy and capacity for governance of some of the old city machines. Whatever else, it was popular government, of and by men of the people. One wonders: did the middle- and upper-class reformers destroy the capacity of working-class urban government without replacing it with anything better so that half-a-century later each and all bewail the cities as ungovernable? One next wonders whether something not dissimilar will occur now that the focus of press attention has shifted from City Hall to the White House. (And yet a miracle of American national government is the almost complete absence of monetary corruption at all levels, and most especially at the top.)

The muckraking tradition is well established. Newer, and likely to have far more serious consequences, is the advent of what Lionel Trilling has called the "adversary culture" as a conspicuous element in journalistic practice. The appearance in large numbers of journalists shaped by the attitudes of this culture is the result of a process whereby the profession thought to improve itself by recruiting more and more persons from middle- and upper-class backgrounds and trained at the universities associated with such groups. This is a change but little noted as yet. The stereotype of American newspapers is that of publishers ranging from conservative to reactionary in their political views balanced by reporters ranging from liberal to radical in theirs. One is not certain how accurate the stereotype ever was. One's impression is that twenty years and more ago the preponderance of the "working press" (as it liked to call itself) was surprisingly close in origins and attitudes to working people generally. They were not Ivy Leaguers. They now are or soon will be. Journalism has become, if not an elite profession, a profession attractive to elites. This is noticeably so in Washington where the upper reaches of journalism constitute one of the most important and enduring *social* elites of the city, with all the accoutrements one associates with a leisured class. (The Washington press corps is not leisured at all, but the style is that of men and women who *choose* to work.)

The political consequence of the rising social status of journalism is that the press grows more and more influenced by attitudes genuinely hostile to American society and American government. This trend seems bound to continue into the future. On the record of what they have been writing while in college, the young people now leaving the Harvard *Crimson* and the Columbia *Spectator* for journalistic jobs in Washington will resort to the Steffens style at ever-escalating levels of moral implication. They bring with them the moral absolutism of George Wald's vastly popular address, "A Generation in Search of a Future," that describes the Vietnam war as "the most shameful episode in the whole of American history." Not tragic, not heartbreaking, not vastly misconceived, but *shameful.* From the shame of the cities to the shame of the nation. But nobody ever called Boss Croker any name equivalent in condemnatory weight to the epithet "war criminal."

II

An ironical accompaniment of the onset of the muckraking style directed toward the Presidency has been the rise of a notion of the near-omnipotency of the office itself. This notion Thomas E. Cronin describes as the "textbook President." Cronin persuasively argues that in the aftermath of Franklin Roosevelt a view of the Presidency, specifically incorporated in the textbooks of recent decades, was developed which presented seriously "inflated and unrealistic interpretations of Presidential competence and beneficence," and which grievously "overemphasized the policy change and policy accomplishment capabilities" of the office. Cronin cites Anthony Howard, a watchful British commentator:

> For what the nation has been beguiled into believing ever since 1960 is surely the politics of evangelism: the faith that individual men are cast to be messiahs, the conviction that Presidential incantations can be substituted for concrete programs, the belief that what matters is not so much the state of the nation as the inspiration-quotient of its people.

In his own researches among advisers of Kennedy and Johnson, Cronin finds the majority to hold "tempered assessments of Presidential determination of 'public policy.'" Indeed, only 10 per cent would describe the President as having "very great impact" over such matters.

Working in the White House is a chastening experience. But it is the experience of very few persons. Watching the White House, on the other hand, is a mass occupation, concentrated especially among the better-educated, better-off groups. For many the experience is one of infatuation followed much too promptly by disillusion. First, the honeymoon—in Cronin's terms, the "predictable ritual of euphoric inflation." But then "the Camelot of the first few hundred days of all Presidencies fades away. . . . Predictably, by the second year, reports are spread that the President has become isolated from criticism." If this is so, he has only himself to blame when things go wrong. And things do go wrong.

If the muckraking tradition implies a distrust of government, it is nonetheless curiously validated by the overly trusting tradition of the "textbook Presidency" which recurrently sets up situations in which the Presidency will be judged as having somehow broken faith. This is not just the experience of a Johnson or a Nixon. Anyone who was in the Kennedy administration in the summer and fall of 1963 would, or ought to, report a pervasive sense that our initiative had been lost, that we would have to get reelected to get going again.

Here, too, there is a curious link between the Presidency and the press. The two most important *Presidential* newspapers are the New York *Times* and the Washington *Post* (though the *Star* would be judged by many to have the best reporting). Both papers reflect a tradition of liberalism that has latterly been shaped and reinforced by the very special type of person who *buys* the paper. (It is well to keep in mind that newspapers are capitalist enterprises which survive by persuading people to buy them.) Theirs is a "disproportionately" well-educated and economically prosperous audience. The geographical areas in which the two papers circulate almost certainly have higher per-capita incomes and higher levels of education than any of comparable size in the nation or the world. More of the buyers of these two papers are likely to come from "liberal" Protestant or Jewish backgrounds than would be turned up by a random sample of the population; they comprise, in fact, what James Q. Wilson calls "the Liberal Audience." * Both the working-class Democrats and the conservative Republicans, with exceptions, obviously, have been pretty much driven from office among the constituencies where the *Times* and the *Post* flourish. It would be wrong to ascribe this to the influence of the papers. Causality almost certainly moves both ways. Max Frankel of the *Times*, who may have peers, but certainly no betters as a working journalist, argues that a newspaper is surely as much influenced by those who read it as vice versa.

The readers of the New York *Times* and the Washington *Post*, then, are a special type of citizen: not only more affluent and more liberal than the rest of the nation, but inclined also to impose heavy expectations on the Presidency, and not to be amused when those expectations fail to be met. Attached by their own internal traditions to the "textbook Presidency," papers like the *Times* and the *Post* are reinforced in this attachment by the temperamental predilections of the readership whose character they inevitably reflect. Thus they help to set a tone of pervasive dissatisfaction with the performance of the national government, whoever the Presidential incumbent may be and whatever the substance of his policies.

---

* See his article, "Crime and the Liberal Audience" in *Commentary*, January 1971.

III

A third circumstance working to upset the old balance of power between the Presidency and the press is the fact that Washington reporters depend heavily on more or less clandestine information from federal bureaucracies which are frequently, and in some cases routinely, antagnostic to Presidential interests.

There is a view of the career civil service as a more or less passive executor of policies made on high. This is quite mistaken. A very great portion of policy ideas "bubble up" from the bureaucracy, and just as importantly, a very considerable portion of the "policy decisions" that go down never come to anything, either because the bureaucrats cannot or will not follow through. (The instances of simple inability are probably much greater than those of outright hostility.) Few modern Presidents have made any impact on the federal bureaucracies save by creating new ones. The bureaucracies are unfamiliar and inaccessible. They are quasi-independent, maintaining, among other things, fairly open relationships with the Congressional committees that enact their statutes and provide their funds. They are usually willing to work with the President, but rarely to the point where their perceived interests are threatened. Typically, these are rather simple territorial interests: not to lose any jurisdiction, and if possible to gain some. But recurrently, issues of genuine political substance are also involved.

At the point where they perceive a threat to those interests, the bureaucracies just as recurrently go to the press. They know the press; the press knows them. Both stay in town as Presidential governments come and go. Both cooperate in bringing to bear the most powerful weapons the bureaucracies wield in their own defense, that of revealing Presidential plans in advance of their execution. Presidents and their plans are helpless against this technique. I have seen a senior aide to a President, sitting over an early morning cup of coffee, rise and literally punch the front page of the New York *Times*. A major initiative was being carefully mounted. Success depended, to a considerable degree, on surprise. Someone in one of the agencies whose policies were to be reversed got hold of the relevant document and passed it on to the *Times*. Now everyone would know. The mission was aborted. There was *nothing* for the Presidential government to do. No possibility of finding, much less of disciplining, the bureaucrat responsible. For a time, or rather from time to time, President Johnson tried the technique of *not* going ahead with any policy or appointment that was leaked in advance to the press. Soon, however, his aides began to suspect that this was giving the bureaucracy the most powerful weapon of all, namely the power to veto a Presidential decision by learning of it early enough and rushing to the *Times* or the *Post*.

(Or, if the issue could be described in thirty seconds, any of the major television networks.)

What we have here is disloyalty to the Presidency. Much of the time what is involved is no more than the self-regard of lower-echelon bureaucrats who are simply flattered into letting the reporter know how much *they* know, or who are just trying to look after their agency. But just as often, to repeat, serious issues of principle are involved. Senator Joseph McCarthy made contact with what he termed "the loyal American underground"—State Department officials, and other such, who reputedly passed on information to him about Communist infiltration of the nation's foreign-policy and security systems. President Johnson made it clear that he did not trust the Department of State to maintain "security" in foreign policy. Under President Nixon the phenomenon has been most evident in domestic areas as OEO warriors struggle among themselves to be the first to disclose the imminent demise of VISTA, or HEW functionaries reluctantly interpret a move to close some fever hospital built to accommodate an 18th-century seaport as the first step in a master plan to dismantle public medicine and decimate the ranks of the elderly and disadvantaged.

It is difficult to say whether the absolute level of such disloyalty to the Presidency is rising. One has the impression that it is. No one knows much about the process of "leaking" except in those instances where he himself has been involved. (*Everyone* is sooner or later involved. That should be understood.) The process has not been studied and little is known of it. But few would argue that the amount of clandestine disclosure is decreasing. Such disclosure is now part of the way we run our affairs. It means, among other things, that the press is fairly continuously involved in an activity that is something less than honorable. Repeatedly it benefits from the self-serving acts of government officials who are essentially hostile to the Presidency. This does the Presidency no good, and if an outsider may comment, it does the press no good either. Too much do they traffic in stolen goods, and they know it.

This point must be emphasized. The leaks which appear in the *Post* and the *Times*—other papers get them, but if one wants to influence decisions in Washington these are clearly thought to be the most effective channels—are ostensibly published in the interest of adding to public knowledge of what is going on. This budget is to be cut; that man is to be fired; this bill is to be proposed. However, in the nature of the transaction the press can only publish half the story—that is to say the information that the "leaker" wants to become "public knowledge." What the press *never* does is say who the leaker is and why he wants the story leaked. Yet, more often than not, this is the more important story: that is to say, what policy wins if the one being disclosed loses, what individual, what bureau, and so on.

There really are ethical questions involved here that have not been examined. There are also serious practical questions. It would be my impression that the distress occasioned by leaks has used up too much Presidential energy, at least from the time of Roosevelt. (Old-time brain-trusters would assure the Johnson staff that nothing could compare with FDR's distractions on the subject.) The primary fault lies within government itself, and one is at a loss to think of anything that might be done about it. But it is a problem for journalism as well, and an unattended one.

IV

The fourth of the five conditions making for an altered relation between the Presidency and the press is the concept of objectivity with respect to the reporting of events and especially the statements of public figures. Almost the first canon of the great newspapers, and by extension of the television news networks which by and large have taken as their standards those of the best newspapers, is that "the news" will be reported whether or not the reporter or the editor or the publisher likes the news. There is nothing finer in the American newspaper tradition. There is, however, a rub and it comes when a decision has to be made as to whether an event really is news, or simply a happening, a non-event staged for the purpose of getting into the papers or onto the screen.

The record of our best papers is not reassuring here, as a glance at the experience of the Korean and the Vietnam wars will suggest. Beginning a bit before the Korean hostilities broke out, but in the general political period we associate with that war, there was a rise of right-wing extremism, a conspiracy-oriented politics symbolized by the name of Senator Joseph McCarthy, and directed primarily at the institution of the Presidency. There was, to be sure, a populist streak to this movement: Yale and Harvard and the "striped-pants boys" in the State Department were targets too. But to the question, "Who promoted Peress?" there was only one constitutional or—for all practical purposes—political answer, namely that the President did. McCarthy went on asking such questions, or rather making such charges, and the national press, which detested and disbelieved him throughout, went on printing them. The American style of objective journalism made McCarthy. He would not, I think, have gotten anywhere in Great Britain where, because it would have been judged he was lying, the stories would simply not have been printed.

Something not dissimilar has occurred in the course of the Vietnam war, only this time the extremist, conspiracy-oriented politics of protest has been putatively left-wing. Actually both movements are utterly confusing if one depends on European analogues. McCarthy was nominally searching out Communists, but his preferred targets were Eastern patricians, while his supporters were, to an alarming degree, members of the Catholic working class. The Students for a Democratic Society, if that organization may be used as an exemplar, was (at least in its later stages) nominally revolutionist, dedicated to the overthrow of the capitalist-imperialist-fascist regime of the United States. Yet, as Seymour Martin Lipset, Nathan Glazer, and others have shown, its leadership, and perhaps also its constituency, were disproportionately made up of upper-class Jewish and Protestant youth. By report of Steven Kelman, who lived as a contemporary among them at Harvard, the SDS radicals were "undemocratic, manipulative, and self-righteous to the point of snobbery and elitism." Peter Berger, a sociologist active in the peace movement, has demonstrated quite persuasively—what others, particularly persons of European origin like himself have frequently seemed to sense—that despite the leftist ring of the slogans of SDS and kindred groups, their ethos and tactics are classically fascist: the cult of youth, the mystique of the street, the contempt for liberal democracy, and the "totalization of friend and foe [with] the concomitant dehumanization of the latter," as in the Nazi use of "*Saujuden*" ("Jewish pigs").

In any case, the accusations which have filled the American air during the period of Vietnam have been no more credible or responsible than those of McCarthy during the Korean period, and the tactics of provocation and physical intimidation have if anything been more disconcerting. Yet the national press, and especially television, have assumed a neutral posture, even at times a sympathetic one, enabling the neo-fascists of the Left to occupy center stage throughout the latter half of the 60's with consequences to American politics that have by no means yet worked themselves out. (It took Sam Brown to point out that one consequence was to make the work of the anti-war movement, of which he has been a principal leader, vastly more difficult.)

Would anyone have it otherwise? Well, yes. Irving Kristol raised this question in an article that appeared before the New Left had made its presence strongly felt on the national scene, but his views are doubtless even more emphatic by now. He wrote of the "peculiar mindlessness which pervades the practice of journalism in the United States," asserting that the ideal of objectivity too readily becomes an excuse for avoiding judgment. If McCarthy was lying, why print what he said? Or why print it on the front page? If the SDS stages a confrontation over a trumped-up issue, why oblige it by taking the whole episode at face value? Here, let it be said, the editorials of the *Times* and the *Post* have consistently served as a thoughtful corrective to the impressions inescapably conveyed by the news columns. But the blunt fact is that just as the news columns were open to astonishingly false assertions about the nature of the American national government during the McCarthy period, they have been open to equally false assertions—mirror images of McCarthyism indeed—during the period of Vietnam. And although it is impossible to prove, one gets the feeling that the slanderous irresponsibilities now being reported so dutifully are treated with far more respect than the old.

The matter of a policy of "genocide" pursued by the national government against the Black Panthers is a good example. By late 1969, preparing a preface to a second edition of *Beyond the Melting Pot,* Nathan Glazer and I could insist that the charge that twenty-eight Panthers had been murdered by the police was on the face of it simply untrue. Yet in that mindless way of which Kristol writes, the *Times* kept reprinting it. Edward Jay Epstein has brilliantly explained the matter in a recent article in the *New Yorker.* What he finds is an immense fraud. No such policy existed. There was no conspiracy between the Department of Justice, the FBI, and various local police forces to wipe out the Panthers. Yet that fraudulent charge has so profoundly affected the thinking of the academic and liberal communities that they will probably not even now be able to see the extent to which they were deceived. The hurt that has been done to blacks is probably in its way even greater. None of it could have happened without the particular mind-set of the national press.

If the press is to deserve our good opinion, it must do better in such matters. And it should keep in mind that the motivation of editors and reporters is not always simply and purely shaped by a devotion to objectivity. In the course of the McCarthy era James Reston recalled the ancient adage which translated from the Erse proposes that "If you want an audience, start a fight." This is true of anyone who would find an audience for his views, or simply for himself. It is true also of anyone who would find customers for the late city edition. T. S. Matthews, sometime editor of *Time,* retired to England to ponder the meaning of it all. In the end, all he could conclude was that the function of journalism was entertainment. If it is to be more—and that surely is what the Rosenthals and Bradlees and Grunwalds and Elliotts want—it will have to be willing on occasion to forgo the entertainment value of a fascinating but untruthful charge. It will, in short, have to help limit the rewards which attend this posture in American politics.

V

The final, and by far the most important, circumstance of American journalism relevant to this discussion is the absence of a professional tradition of self-correction. The mark of any developed profession is the practice of correcting mistakes, by whomsoever they are made. This practice is of course the great invention of Western science. Ideally, it requires an epistemology which is shared by all respected members of the profession, so that when a mistake is discovered it can be established as a mistake to the satisfaction of the entire professional community. Ideally, also, no discredit is involved: to the contrary, honest mistakes are integral to the process of advancing the field. Journalism will never attain to any such condition. Nevertheless, there is a range of subject matter about which reasonable men can and will agree, and within this range American journalism, even of the higher order, is often seriously wide of the mark. Again Irving Kristol:

> It is a staple of conversation among those who have ever been involved in a public activity that when they read the *Times* the next morning, they will discover that it has almost never got the story quite right and has only too frequently got it quite wrong.

Similar testimony has come from an editor of the New York *Times* itself. In an article published some years ago in the Sunday *Times Magazine*, A. H. Raskin had this to say:

> No week passes without someone prominent in politics, industry, labor or civic affairs complaining to me, always in virtually identical terms: "Whenever I read a story about something in which I really know what is going on, I'm astonished at how little of what is important gets into the papers—and how often even that little is wrong." The most upsetting thing about these complaints is the frequency with which they come from scientists, economists and other academicians temporarily involved in government policy but without any proprietary concern about who runs the White House or City Hall.*

This is so, and in part it is unavoidable. Too much happens too quickly: that the *Times* or the *Post* or the *Star* should appear once a day is a miracle. (Actually they appear three or four times a day in different editions.) But surely when mistakes are made they ought to be corrected. Sometimes they are, but not nearly enough. It is in this respect that Kristol is right in calling journalism "the underdeveloped profession."

Assertions that the press has a flawed sense of objectivity, or that it enjoys too cozy a relationship with the civil service, are not easily proved or disproved. But to say that mistakes are repeatedly made and not corrected is to say something which ought to be backed up with specific instances. Let me, then, offer two, taken from stories which appeared in the New York *Times* during the second half of 1970. (I was serving in the White House at the time, though I was not directly involved in any of the matters to be described.)

---

* It should not, of course, be supposed that people inside government "know" what happens. The *Rashomon* effect is universal. It is, moreover, not uncommon for men in government to be doing something quite different from what they think or intend. In such cases, the more accurate the press reporting, the more baffled or enraged the officials will be. Still, the judgment Raskin reports is near universal.

The first of my two examples is a long article which appeared in the *Times* on Sunday, November 15, 1970 under the headline, "Blacks Seek Tougher Equality Standards for Federal Hiring and Promotion." This story was not hostile to the administration; rather the contrary. It noted that the President had earlier signed an executive order requiring each department and agency to maintain an "affirmative" equal-opportunity program, and that the number of blacks in the top grades of the civil service had gone up almost by half under the "low-key approach of the Nixon Administration." The number of black lawyers in the Justice Department had declined somewhat. There were said to have been 61 (out of a total of 1,900 to 2,000) under the Democrats. This figure had dropped under the Republicans to 45, but it also appeared that the difference was to be made up by new recruits. In the meantime the Department of Transportation was promulgating new rules, the Bureau of Prisons had eliminated the written test for correction officers, and similar activity aimed at increasing the number of blacks in the higher levels of the federal government was to be encountered elsewhere. All this, however, was going on in the context of a federal employment system whose patterns of practice were lamentably at odds with its profession of being an "equal-opportunity employer," to use the federal phrase. In the words of the *Times* story:

> The most recent figures show 137,919 blacks among the 1,289,114 Government employees covered by Civil Service regulations. That is about 10.7 per cent, less than the black proportion of the population, estimated in 1970 census as 12.9 per cent.

The story went on to note that a number of black activists doubted that the federal government ever had been an equal-opportunity employer. One was particularly skeptical of executive orders: "This friendly persuasion thing has never worked in the history of our Government." Next came the question of quotas:

> Although little support for a formal quota system is evident, there is a widely held belief that Presidential statements of policy should be supplemented by more detailed instructions as to how the policies should be implemented.

There is little to take exception to in the foregoing. The official census figures for 1970 show blacks to be 12.4 per cent of the population, not 12.9 per cent, but newspapers routinely make such mistakes. It should also have been pointed out that blacks constitute only 10.9 per cent of the civilian non-institutional population of sixteen years of age or older, which is to say the population available for employment. In that sense, even accepting the figures used by the *Times*, blacks might be seen as having almost exactly "their" proportion of government employment, although an inadequate number of top positions.

The difficulty in this instance lies not with what was in the story, but what was not. What was not in the story was the fact that the category of federal worker—"General Schedule"—of which Negroes do indeed comprise 10.7 per cent is only one of three categories. In the other two categories of federal employee, the Postal Service and Wage System employees, Negroes made up 19.5 per cent and 19.7 per cent respectively. In rough terms, federal jobs are about equally divided among the three categories.* Small wonder, then, that the *Times* reported an absence of much discussion about establishing racial quotas for federal employment. Altogether, blacks have more than 15 per cent of federal jobs. If quotas were established according to the black proportion of the adult population, almost a third of black federal employees would have to be fired!

What all this comes to is that the very considerable achievement of blacks in qualifying for federal jobs and getting them far in excess of their proportion in the work force is in effect concealed and a legitimate source of black pride thereby denied. So too we are denied a legitimate sense of national progress in combating discrimination. And thus we are fed the tendentious allegations of those who wish to discredit the American "system" as inherently and irrevocably racist.

With respect to the role of the *Times* reporter, it must be said that it is simply not possible for him to have gotten the data on Classified Service employment from the Civil Service Commission releases on the subject without knowing that this is but one of three categories of employment, and that in the other categories blacks do exceptionally well. The truth would have made things look better than the reporter wished them to look. One fears it is as simple as that.

The second instance is rather more complicated. On September 14, 1970 a front-page story was published in the *Times* under the headline, "Negro College Heads Say Nixon Ignores Their Plight." The lead paragraph declared: "The presidents of nine financially troubled Negro colleges accused the Nixon Administration today of intensifying racial tensions by failing to support black education." The presidents felt that massive grants were needed and one was reported as saying that "It's five minutes before doomsday in this country." Dr. Vivian Henderson, president of Clark College in Atlanta, was reported as notably disturbed, asserting that "the Nixon Administration's utter lack of sensitivity on this

---

* These are, by the way, good jobs. In 1970, mean annual earnings of year-round full-time workers in the economy as a whole were $8,496. The average earnings of General Schedule federal employees in that year were $11,058; of Postal employees, $8,770; and of Wage System employees, $8,159. Washington, D.C. has a much higher per capita income than any state in the union for the reason that it has so many federal employees.

point, purposeful or otherwise, is feeding the flames that already roar in the hearts of many black students."

All this seemed routine enough. From the onset of mass urban rioting in the mid-1960's all manner of requests for federal funds have been backed up by not especially subtle threats of violence. Nor was it unfamiliar to learn a few weeks later that the tactic had worked. On October 2, the front page of the *Times* carried a story from the Associated Press which began: "The Nixon Administration responded to complaints that it is insensitive to Negro education by announcing today a 30 per cent increase in Federal aid for predominantly black colleges." The next paragraph explained: "The Secretary of Health, Education and Welfare, Elliot L. Richardson, said in a statement the $30 million increase was ordered by President Nixon after he heard appeals from Negro educators."

The story bumped around in the press for the next few months, culminating in a way on January 3, 1971 when another *Times* story reported that the Negro colleges were not finding it possible to draw on all of the additional $30 million. Some college presidents were reportedly angry to have learned that the law provides for a 30-per-cent matching requirement for construction aid, which made up $20 million of the additional $30 million. But the basic theme of the *Times*'s coverage of this episode remained the same. The January 3 story began: "For two years, Negro colleges called on the Nixon Administration for substantial financial help. Last September, the Administration responded, releasing $30 million for use by the schools." There are problems of detail here. The Nixon administration had not been in office for two years in September 1969; the first *Times* report of an appeal appeared (as best I can determine) that very month, and the response came a month later, in October. Be that as it may, the January 3 story declared: "Black educators have severely criticized President Nixon for allegedly ignoring the plight of their schools. The educators charged that black schools have not shared in the money and grants that go out to American educational institutions."

To repeat, a familiar theme. The way to get something out of the federal government is to blast it out. Left to itself government would never have given these financially weak institutions a break. If you want action—especially if you are black—raise hell. Right?

Wrong.

At least wrong in this instance. The true sequence of events which made up this story was turned literally upside down by the *Times*. The initiative to aid black colleges had been voluntarily taken by the administration a year before the *Times* got on to the issue. The increased support was announced months before the *Times* reported it. Far from having denounced the administration, the black college presidents had been praising it. And, for good measure, far from getting less than their share of federal aid, the black colleges had all along been getting rather more.

There are 124 "predominantly black colleges" in America, most of them small, and most in the South. They enroll somewhat more than 2 per cent of the college population, but this includes more than half of all black undergraduates.* They live with many difficulties, of which the most important—as is true of almost all colleges, large and small—is money. In 1969, they organized themselves as the National Association for Equal Opportunity in Higher Education and set out, as well they might, to get more federal funds. On October 23, 1969 a meeting on this subject was held in the Executive Office Building presided over by Robert J. Brown, a Special Assistant to the President, who as a Southern Negro was much interested in the problems of the predominantly black colleges. As a result of this meeting the Federal Interagency Committee on Education (FICE) was directed to find out what was already being done for these colleges by the considerable array of federal agencies involved in supporting education and what plans existed for the future. A preliminary report was sent to the White House in February 1970, and in June a 45-page document entitled "Federal Agencies and Black Colleges" was printed. It was a good report, full of information concerning what was being done and of recommendations for doing more. (One does not commission such reports with the expectation of being advised to do less.) In the meantime, on May 25, 1970, the President had met with a group of black college presidents, apparently the first such meeting ever to be held. In the aftermath of the Cambodian invasion Dr. James Cheek, president of Howard University, which is basically a federal institution, served temporarily in the White House as an associate of Chancellor Alexander Heard. During that time he made recommendations directly to the President on the subject of the black colleges. Much attention, then, was being given to this matter in the White House.

On July 23, 1970, a White House press conference was held by Brown and Robert Finch, formerly Secretary of HEW, now Counsellor to the President. The main purpose of the occasion was to release a statement by Heard on the completion of his advisory work on campus unrest. Obviously seeking to strike a positive note about the Heard-Cheek effort, the two White House men also brought up the subject of black colleges. The FICE report was given to the press, and Finch announced that on departing Dr. Cheek had filed a "separate document" on this "very unique" problem. He continued: "That just came in today. The President read it today. The President asked him to write such a report, and I am authorized to say, after discussing it with the President, that in HEW . . . we are going to increase [aid] . . . from $80 million to $100 million."

* In 1969 there were 171,339 students in black colleges, or 2.14 per cent of the national junior- and senior-college gross enrollment. Problems of definition complicate the statistics.

Finch's numbers were somewhat garbled. HEW aid to black colleges at the time was $96 million for the fiscal year. The additional sum now being reallocated was between $29 million and $30 million. In any event, the *Times* report of the press conference did not mention this subject.

On July 31, Dr. Herman R. Branson, president of Central State University in Wilberforce, Ohio, and the new head of the National Association for Equal Opportunity in Higher Education, wrote the President expressing appreciation for his move. On August 10 the President replied:

> The present financial plight of many of our small and the overwhelming majority of our black colleges clearly demonstrates to me that the Federal Government must strengthen its role in support of these institutions.
>
> I have committed this Administration to the vigorous support of equal educational opportunity. At the same time, we are encouraging excellence in all of our institutions of higher education.†

In a release dated August 11, 1970 the National Association for Equal Opportunity in Higher Education formally responded to the administration's move. In the accepted and understood manner of interest groups, the Association expressed gratitude for what it had got, but assured the government that it was not, of course, enough. On the other hand, it was confident that more would be forthcoming:

> We do not view this excellent first step as adequate to all our needs but rather as a model of what all agencies can do. . . . With the forthright statement of the President in his letter to Dr. Branson, we are very much encouraged and heartened about the future.

The *Times* reported nothing of this statement, as it had reported nothing of the original announcement from the White House that an extra $30 million or so was being made available to black colleges. White House announcements, Presidential letters, Washington press conferences—all were ignored. The subject was not dealt with at all until the following month when, as noted earlier, a story depicted the black college presidents as denouncing the administration's "utter lack of sensitivity" on this matter. *This* story made the front page.

The day after it appeared Dr. Vivian Henderson, of Clark College in Atlanta, to whom the remark about "utter lack of sensitivity" had been attributed, sent the following unequivocal denial to the *Times:*

† The President was referring to his message to Congress on Higher Education of March 1970, which proposed a system of student aid by which the federal government would concentrate assistance on low-income students. A proposal to establish a National Foundation for Higher Education specifically referred to the problems of black colleges.

> I am deeply disturbed by the inaccurate reporting of the conference of Presidents of Negro Colleges that appeared in the September 14 issue of the New York *Times*. The following statement is attributed to me: "Instead the Nixon Administration's utter lack of sensitivity on this point, purposeful or otherwise, is feeding the flames that already roar in the hearts of many black students." This is a gross error and misrepresentation of what actually went on at the meeting. To be sure, we were concerned with the limited response of President Nixon to our problems. The fact is, however, that President Nixon has responded. He has not been silent with regard to concerns expressed by the Presidents in the meeting with him last May. Since the meeting with Mr Nixon, about $27 million additional funds have been made available to black colleges. It would be unfair on our part not to recognize this response, limited though it is.
>
> I did not make the statement your reporter attributes to me. I do not recall such a statement being made during the course of the conference. . . .

The *Times* did not print this letter. Instead it went on to repeat the theme of the original story and gradually to establish it elsewhere as truth. In the end a small bit of history had been rewritten: even the wire services followed the *Times*'s version. *No one intended this.* That should be clear. It is simply that the journalistic system preferred a confrontation-capitulation model of events, and there was no internal corrective procedure to alert the editors to mistakes being made.

There are true social costs in all this. For one thing, a paper like the *Times* is a prime medium for internal communication within the government itself. Any Washington official following this story in the *Times* would have had to assume that the administration's attitude toward black colleges was just about opposite to what in fact it was. Such a reversal of signals can have serious consequences. Similarly there are consequences to the principals involved, in this case the college presidents who had been acting with skill and discipline and reasonable success (most notably in having gained access: within hours of the appearance of the first *Times* story a black college president was in the White House seeking reassurance that the $27.30 million had not been jeopardized) but who found themselves represented as stereotypical confrontationists. Everyone in a sense lost because the *Times* got the story wrong.

VI

In the wake of so lengthy an analysis, what is there to prescribe? Little. Indeed, to prescribe much would be to miss the intent of the analysis. I have been hoping to make two points—the first explicitly, the second largely by implication. The first is that a convergence of journalistic tradition with evolving cultural patterns has placed the national government at a kind of operating disadvantage. It is hard for government to succeed: this theme echoes from every capital of the democratic world. In the United States it is hard for government to succeed and just as hard for government to appear to have succeeded when indeed it has done so. This situation can be said to have begun in the muckraking era with respect to urban government; it is now very much the case with respect to national government, as reflected in the "national press" which primarily includes the New York *Times*, the Washington *Post*, *Time*, *Newsweek*, and a number of other journals.

There is nothing the matter with investigative reporting; there ought to be more. The press can be maddeningly complacent about real social problems for which actual counter-measures, even solutions, exist. (I spent a decade, 1955–65, trying to obtain some press coverage of the problem of motor vehicle design, utterly without avail. The press, from the most prestigious journals on down, would print nothing but the pap handed out by the automobile companies and wholly-owned subsidiaries such as the National Safety Council.) The issue is not one of serious inquiry, but of an almost feckless hostility to power.

The second point is that this may not be good for us. American government will only rarely and intermittently be run by persons drawn from the circles of those who own and edit and write for the national press; no government will ever have this circle as its political base. Hence the conditions are present for a protracted conflict in which the national government keeps losing. This might once have been a matter of little consequence or interest. It is, I believe, no longer such, for it now takes place within the context of what Nathan Glazer has so recently described in these pages * as an "assault on the reputation of America . . . which has already succeeded in reducing this country, in the eyes of many American intellectuals, to outlaw status. . . ." In other words, it is no longer a matter of this or that administration; it is becoming a matter of national morale, of a "loss of confidence and nerve," some of whose possible consequences, as Glazer indicates, are not pleasant to contemplate.

Some will argue that in the absence of a parliamentary question-time only the press can keep the Presidency honest. Here we get much talk about Presidential press conferences and such. This is a serious point, but I would argue that the analogy does not hold. Questions are put in Parliament primarily by members of an opposition party hoping to replace the one in office. Incompetent questions damage those chances; irresponsible questions damage the office. Indeed, British politicians have been known to compare the press lords to ladies of the street, seeking "power without responsibility." It would, of course, be better all around

* "The Role of the Intellectuals," February 1971.

if Congress were more alert. Thus the *Times* has reported that the GNP estimate in the 1971 Budget Message was not that of the Council of Economic Advisors, but rather a higher figure dictated by the White House for political purposes. This is a profoundly serious charge. Someone has a lot to explain. It could be the administration; it could be the *Times*. Congress should find out.

Obviously the press of a free country is never going to be and never should be celebratory. Obviously government at all levels needs and will continue to get criticism and some of it will inevitably be harsh or destructive, often enough justifiably so. Obviously we will get more bad news than good. Indeed the content of the newspapers is far and away the best quick test of the political structure of a society. Take a morning plane from Delhi to Karachi. One leaves with a sheaf of poorly-printed Indian papers filled with bad news; one arrives to find a small number of nicely-printed Pakistani papers filled with good news. One has left a democracy, and has entered a country that is something less than a democracy.

Nonetheless there remains the question of balance. Does not an imbalance arise when the press becomes a too-willing outlet for mindless paranoia of the Joseph McCarthy or New Left variety? Does it not arise when the press becomes too self-satisfied to report its own mistakes with as much enterprise as it reports the mistakes of others?

Norman E. Isaacs, a working journalist, has written thoughtfully about the possibility of establishing a "national press council." This, in effect, was proposed by Robert M. Hutchins's Commission on Freedom of the Press in 1947: "A new and independent agency to appraise and report annually upon the performance of the press." There are press councils in other democratic countries which hear complaints, hand down verdicts, and even, as in Sweden, impose symbolic fines. There is a case to be made here, but I would argue that to set up such a council in this country at this time would be just the wrong thing to do. There is a statist quality about many of the press councils abroad: often as not they appear to have been set up to ward off direct government regulation. Freedom of the press is a constitutional guarantee in the United States: how that freedom is exercised should remain a matter for the professional standards of those who exercise it. Here, however, there really is room for improvement. First in the simple matter of competence. The very responsibility of the national press in seeking to deal with complex issues produces a kind of irresponsibility. The reporters aren't up to it. They get it wrong. It would be astonishing were it otherwise.

Further, there needs to be much more awareness of the quite narrow social and intellectual perspective within which the national press so often moves. There are no absolutes here; hardly any facts. But there *is* a condition that grows more not less pronounced. The national press is hardly a "value-free" institution. It very much reflects the judgment of owners and editors and reporters as to what is good and bad about the country and what can be done to make things better. It might be hoped that such persons would give more thought to just how much elitist criticism is good for a democracy. Is this a shocking idea? I think not. I would imagine that anyone who has read Peter Gay or Walter Laqueur on the history of the Weimar Republic would agree that there are dangers to democracy in an excess of elitist attack. A variant of the Jacksonian principle of democratic government is involved here. Whether or not ordinary men are capable of carrying out any governmental task whatsoever, ordinary men are going to be given such tasks. That is what it means to be a democracy. We had best not get our expectations too far out of line with what is likely to happen, and we had best not fall into the habit of measuring all performance by the often quite special tastes, preferences, and interests of a particular intellectual and social elite. (Perhaps most importantly, we must be supersensitive to the idea that if things are not working out well it is because this particular elite is not in charge. Consider the course of events that led to the war in Indochina.)

As to the press itself, one thing seems clear. It should become much more open about acknowledging mistakes. The *Times* should have printed Dr. Henderson's letter. Doubtless the bane of any editor is the howling of politicians and other public figures claiming to have been misquoted. But often they *are* misquoted. At the very least, should not more space be allotted to rebuttals and exchanges in which the issue at hand is how the press performed?

Another possibility is for each newspaper to keep a critical eye on itself. In the article previously cited which he did for the Sunday *Times Magazine,* A. H. Raskin called for "a Department of Internal Criticism" in every paper "to put all its standards under re-examination and to serve as a public protection in its day-to-day operations." The *Times* itself has yet to establish such a department but the Washington *Post* has recently set a welcome example here by inaugurating a regular editorial-page feature by Richard Harwood entitled "The News Business." Harwood's business is to check up on what his paper runs, and he is finding a good deal to check up on. (To all editors: *Please* understand there is nothing wrong with this. It is a routine experience of even the most advanced sciences. Perhaps especially of such.) Harwood has made a useful distinction between mistakes of detail—the ordinary garbles and slips of a fast-moving enterprise—and mistakes of judgment about the nature of events:

> The mistakes that are more difficult to fix are those that arise out of our selection and definition of the news. Often we are unaware of error until much time has passed and much damage has been done.

> In retrospect, it seems obvious that the destructive phenomenon called "McCarthyism"—the search in the 1950's for witches, scapegoats, traitors—was a product of this kind of error. Joseph McCarthy, an obscure and mediocre senator from Wisconsin, was transformed into the Grand Inquisitor by publicity. And there was no way later for the newspapers of America to repair that damage, to say on the morning after: "We regret the error."

Which will turn out "in retrospect" to seem the obvious errors of the 1960's? There were many, but they are past. The question now is what might be the errors of the 1970's, and whether some can be avoided. One Richard Harwood does not a professional upheaval make, but he marks a profoundly important beginning. All major journals should have such a man in a senior post, and very likely he should have a staff of reporters to help him cover "the news business."

As for government itself, there is not much to be done, but there is something. It is perfectly clear that the press will not be intimidated. Specific efforts like President Kennedy's to get David Halberstam removed as a *Times* correspondent in Vietnam almost always fail, as they deserve to do.* Non-specific charges such as those leveled by Vice President Agnew get nowhere either. They come down to an avowal of dislike, which is returned in more than ample measure, with the added charge that in criticizing the press the government may be trying to intimidate it, which is unconstitutional.

What government can do and should do is respond in specific terms to what it believes to be misstatements or mistaken emphases; it should address these responses to specific stories in specific papers and it should expect that these will be printed (with whatever retort the journal concerned wishes to make). Misrepresentations of government performance must never be allowed to go unchallenged. The notion of a "one-day story," and the consoling idea that yesterday's papers are used to wrap fish, are pernicious and wrong. Misinformation gets into the bloodstream and has consequences. The *Times* ought by now to have had a letter from the Chairman of the Civil Service Commission pointing out the mistakes in the November 15 story on minority employment, and the even more important omissions. If the first letter was ignored, he should have sent another. Similarly the *Times* ought long since have had a letter from an HEW official exposing the errors of its coverage of federal aid to black colleges. Failing that, someone should have called in the education writers of the *Times* and asked why they let other men misreport their beat. Etc. Hamilton's formulation has not been bettered: the measure of effective government is energy in the executive.

---

* See Halberstam's account of the incident in "Getting the Story in Vietnam," *Commentary*, January 1965.

In the end, however, the issue is not one of politics but of culture. The culture of disparagement that has been so much in evidence of late, that has attained such an astonishing grip on the children of the rich and the mighty, and that has exerted an increasing influence on the tone of the national press in its dealings with the national government, is bad news for democracy. Some while ago the late Richard Hofstadter foresaw what has been happening:

> Perhaps we are really confronted with two cultures (not Snow's), whose spheres are increasingly independent and more likely to be conflicting than to be benignly convergent: a massive adversary culture on the one side, and the realm of socially responsible criticism on the other.

But given what has been happening to the press in recent years and what is likely to go on being the case if current trends should continue on their present path, where is such "socially responsible criticism" to come from? Or rather, where is it to appear in a manner that will inform and influence the course of public decision-making?

7.

THE PRESS AND THE PRESIDENT

Max Frankel

To the Editor of Commentary:

Daniel P. Moynihan was most kind and generous in his reference to me in "The Presidency & the Press" [March]. But the more I studied the article, the more troubled I became by his rather sweeping and unpleasant generalizations. And the more I studied his particular complaints against the New York *Times*, the more I found him to be confusing a most serious and difficult problem with trivial, inadequate, and basically unfair criticism. My first impulse was to ignore him—benignly.

But others found the specific charges against the *Times*'s performance to be so serious that they required either public confession or rebuttal. This led to a most wasteful examination of the more frivolous aspects of

---

Reprinted from *Commentary*, Vol. 52 (July, 1971), pp. 7–20, by permission of the author and publisher.

the indictment. If, in what follows, the more substantial parts of Mr. Moynihan's essay are not treated as fully as I would like, we at least share the blame.

First, about the two horror stories from the *Times*.

The story in November 15, 1970, about blacks seeking tougher equality standards in the Civil Service, was by no fair standard a crusade for the blacks, an attack on the Nixon administration, a campaign for racial quotas or for anything else. As Mr. Moynihan himself noted, the story was in fact friendly to the administration. It recorded the blacks' complaints about jobs and promotion to senior jobs "under either party." It said that few critics of hiring and promotion practices would have the government establish formal racial quotas and found most of them acknowledging that movement, although slow, is occurring under the present system. If that was the work of a reporter who wished to make things look worse than they are, as the article suggested, then I am naive and Mr. Moynihan is clairvoyant.

The only concrete complaint here was that our reporter did not choose to write about something she was not writing about—the Postal Service and non-Civil Service categories of federal employment. Adding those statistics, it is argued, would have shown blacks occupying a relatively larger share of all government jobs. I believe they also should have shown blacks getting a still smaller share of senior and supervisory positions. To pick that fault in one sentence of a long and commendably judicious article suggests to me that Mr. Moynihan wants not only reasonably sophisticated rendering of a situation but positive help in defeating all complaints from blacks, militant or otherwise. If we erred at all, it was in accepting the employment figures of several departments that we now have reason to believe exaggerated the status of blacks. (The further petty complaint that our reporter had the black population "estimated in the 1970 census as 12.9 per cent"—whereas Mr. Moynihan knew the "official census figures" to have shown 12.4 per cent—deserves a petty answer: both numbers are wrong, but at least our reporter properly labeled hers as an estimate. The "official" figure, when finally produced, was 11.2 per cent. In Mr. Moynihan's language, this would justify the scoffing remark that nagging academicians "routinely make such mistakes.")

In any case, I fail to understand what place this story and critique has in what attempts to be a serious and broadly philosophical discussion of journalism. It proves nothing about our business, good or bad, not even that our reporters are more vulnerable to one type of propaganda and statistical juggling than another. Ideally, of course, every such story is not a matching of claims and complaints, charges and responses, but a scientific and independent analysis of a question. It could be argued that we should never report either what critics say or what defenders retort, but only what we ourselves have established to our own satisfaction as irrefutably true, not only in fact but in spirit. We would have a very thin newspaper; perhaps none at all.

The second complaint about the *Times* is more complicated and points to some interesting sins of commission and omission both at the *Times* and in the administration. Overall, I will let others decide which are the more serious.

The criticisms, in chronological order:

1) That we did not report the "somewhat garbled" numbers Robert Finch disclosed on July 23, 1970 at the briefing on the Heard report, about some additional aid for black colleges.

2) That we did not carry the press release dated August 11, 1970, in which the National Association for Equal Opportunity in Higher Education welcomed this "excellent first step," termed it not adequate, but looked hopefully for more in the future.

3) That on September 14, 1970 we *did* carry and feature on page one a story about the presidents of nine Negro colleges charging the administration with neglect and insensitivity.

4) That we did not print a letter from one of the above presidents complaining that he had been misquoted in the "lack of sensitivity" remark, commending the President for responding with $27 million in additional funds, and describing that response as "limited."

5) That we carried another front-page story from the Associated Press on October 2, 1970, reporting that HEW Secretary Elliot Richardson disclosed a $30-million increase in aid as Nixon's response to appeals from Negro educators.

6) That we again referred to the blacks' complaints and criticism of the President in a story on January 3, 1971, reporting their inability to draw on much of the new aid because they could not meet the matching requirement.

In order:

1) Bob Semple's superb story on the Heard report did not include the sneaky and "garbled" announcement of some new aid for black colleges, even though it dealt with the report's discussion of black colleges by Alexander Heard and James Cheek. Why not? Semple does not know. He suspects that when the 40-page Heard report was dumped on reporters at 4:30 that afternoon, he felt compelled to delve into it so quickly that he either ran off to the office or sat through the briefing without really listening to the addenda.

Let us be very straight here about the order and magnitude of sins. The Heard report was not to the liking of the administration and it was shoveled out late one afternoon to complicate the life of any reporter who might wish to deal with it in a big or careful way. As Mr. Moynihan remarks, the news about some new money for black colleges was thrown in "to strike a positive note about the Heard-Cheek effort"; or, as I would have put it, thrown in to undermine even further the attention that might be given to Heard's major conclusions. It was thrown in hastily and sloppily, *not* for the purpose of informing the public in a careful way but to serve the propaganda purposes of the White House. And the figures given out were not "somewhat garbled." They were wrong.

I can regret Semple's oversight without in the slightest faulting him.

Had Mr. Moynihan chosen to list his complaints against us in a straightforward chronological order, *the entire episode,* and all the stories that troubled him would have been seen to follow from this very cheap stunt. (In truth, I did not expect, in looking into his complaints, to find such a good example of the reasons for our mistrust of government, and of the White House in particular.)

But let us also tally up our mutual sins of omission.

I can find no evidence that Ziegler, or Finch, or anyone else at that meeting set out the next morning to call our attention to the fact that we had missed what the White House regarded as an important story. Indeed, *I find no evidence that anyone apologized for issuing the wrong figures or tried to set the record straight.* (The wrong Finch figures remain wrong in the weekly compilation of Presidential documents.) What a lovely opportunity to summon the reporters and apologize for misleading them, cheering the good fortune that they had overlooked the garbled announcement, and inviting them to treat it fully and accurately on the second bounce! Should I conclude that hardly anyone gave a damn now that there was no longer any need to deflate Heard?

If the White House felt it important to get the story into print, it surely did not lack the means or know-how.

Later that year, in ignoring Heard's very explicit advice and setting out to make political capital of campus disturbances, the President and his aides showed themselves to be very skillful indeed in getting their message across. And when two stones were thrown in the direction of the President's car in Vermont—out of sight of most of the reporters in his party—Ziegler and Company showed extraordinary zeal and imagination in making certain that the news reached the nation, over and over again. My point is—and it relates to the essay's larger question about the balance of forces between press and government—that a President demonstrably has no difficulty publicizing any news or attitudes about which he feels strongly.

2) I do not know anything about the press release of August 11, 1970, except Mr. Moynihan's brief quotation from it. In a sense, I am glad we did not encounter it, for the chances are fifty-fifty that a story about the reaction of the black educators would have combined their expression

of gratitude with their complaints of inadequacy, and only deepened Mr. Moynihan's anger.

He may feel free to run down the group's motives by suggesting that their verdict of insufficiency was delivered not from the facts but from "the accepted and understood manner of interest groups." But we usually feel compelled to stop short of such a public judgment. (Should we have reported the famous Moynihan farewell address as a statement "in the manner of departing White House officials who want to retain some influence with the boss"? I thought it more than that, but others clearly did not.)

Anyhow, two days before the distribution of that press release, on August 9, 1970, the *Times* devoted one-and-a-half columns, which were featured with a picture on page one, to an interview with Robert Brown, the only black aide on the White House staff. The story, by Paul Delaney, covered Brown's review of the full range of Mr. Nixon's relations with blacks. Brown said things were getting better, both because the President had become "much more sensitive" to the problems of blacks and because he had decided to do something about it. Brown said Mr. Nixon was especially stung by some of the harshest charges of Negro leaders. (He was, as portrayed by his aide, *responding!*)

And lo, the last third of the story dwelt on the President's "immediate concern" for getting more federal money for black colleges. And at the very end of the story—appropriately for the kind of story it was, though not the kind of headline announcement the White House could have fashioned—was the news that the Department of Health, Education and Welfare had increased the allocation for black schools. The figures were there, though still not clearly enough, because it was a little hard to tell whether the administration was redirecting $120 million in *new* aid or merely redirecting some money to raise the total from $87.2 million to $120 million. But the ambiguity was in the administration's favor, and as far as I can tell we still did not receive a clarifying call from the White House.

Nor have we had any complaints about our willingness to feature Mr. Brown's representation of Presidential attitudes about blacks. His account was not "balanced" in every other paragraph with demands for courtroom evidence, nor with recollections of the Carswell episode and other relevant clues to policy. It was not a definitive study of Nixon-Negro relations. The only detours from Brown's comments, after he talked of "more and more" meetings with blacks, were to cite the case of the rebuffed black Congressmen and to record the President's two visits to black communities. All in all, a very one-sided account that neither brought nor merited any complaint.

It *might* have had a small mention, however, in Mr. Moynihan's review of our coverage last summer, though I suspect it would have virtually exploded his whole argument with us. Here we were doing for his side of the case exactly what he deplored our having done for the other side.

3) The story about the charges by nine presidents of Negro colleges, by James Wooten from Chicago, was by all accounts a fair and accurate rendering of the mood and substance of their meeting. I gather Mr. Moynihan does not dispute this. They were complaining about the federal government, about the churches, about American society, about the inadequacy of financial help, and about the inappropriateness of the help that was available. They used strong language. If they had mentioned the increased aid offered them by the administration, they would clearly have denounced it as inadequate and in no way erased the effect of the story. I do not know how much of their rhetoric came from a feeling of genuine despair and how much was meant merely to earn credentials among more militant constituents. I would guess that both motives were involved.

The fact that they chose to speak in that fashion, justifiably or not, is legitimate news. At least as legitimate as the Brown interview. News, as treated in our society, is not the same as *truth*, though it should always be *true*. The truth is cumulative and rarely discernible on any given day; it embraces motivation and consequence. Newspapers should cumulatively test the news for truth, but they cannot reasonably do so every day and with every story. We are, alas, a forum, not an almanac.

We could argue whether the Wooten story deserved to be on page one. Perhaps not, although this raises a still further question of distortions due to the *relative* value of any day's developments. These are all profound and difficult questions that our craft must face, and in some cases is facing most seriously.

But when all is said and done, we must make value judgments. Mr. Moynihan's logic propels him to the claim that a black man yelling "help" in America today should be treated journalistically as we all now wish we had treated a demagogic Senator yelling "traitor." He is saying that his every assertion should be drained of its emotional purpose and forced to meet the standards of courtroom evidence, or else be played down or even ignored.

Philosophically and politically, he is wrong. A pressure group for neglected citizens, even when it demands exaggerated attention and reparation, is not the same as an organized and officially protected goon-squad attacking individual liberties. The balance of power between the heads of black colleges and the Nixon administration is not the balance that prevailed between Joe McCarthy and his victims. (There is, alas, more similarity between the latter and what many blacks did to my friend Pat Moynihan a few years ago. He was a victim of McCarthyism. But not Nixon. I would hope that despite Mr. Moynihan's wounds he could still recognize the difference.)

It all really does come down to his enormous pity for our poor and enfeebled Presidency! How glad I am that he will now have a chance to observe it from the outside and to amend his thoughts of who is strong and who is weak in our society.

4) We did not print Vivian Henderson's letter complaining about misquotation because of our certainty that he had not been misquoted and the further judgment that he was trying to attribute error to us so as to ameliorate the morning-after consequences of his remark. (The story, in any case, and even by Henderson's testimony, would not have been altered by the omission of his remark.) He did not press us to print the letter and has told Wooten he didn't care whether we printed it or not.

Here again there lies a larger question for the press that touches on the wider meaning of the essay. We do need to provide more space where readers and persons in the news can extend, explain, and correct views and facts attributed to them in the news columns. Slowly, our profession is moving in that direction. But I fear the judgments made in this case will still have to be made in that new space. And once again we would face the question of relative power—whether the President's claim on such space, considering his opportunities to make known his views *and* propaganda, should be equal to the claims of weaker groups and citizens. I don't think so.

5) The AP story about Richardson's "disclosure" of $30-million more in aid for black colleges did, finally, get that fact out on page one. I cannot locate the material on which the story was based, but I doubt that Richardson clearly explained that the new money had actually been made available and announced *ten weeks earlier.* The administration was not responding to the Chicago complaints but it *was* responding, as the story said, to the appeals of blacks.

6) The final story, by Paul Delaney of the *Times*'s Washington bureau, reported that the new money did not, after all, do much to meet the needs of the colleges. It does not accuse anyone of perfidy or trickery. It cites a sad misunderstanding about what the new money could achieve. And it reports the black educators still dissatisfied with the amount of help they have been given.

Mr. Moynihan may have a quarrel with their view. He doesn't have much of a quarrel with that story, nor should he have.

What, then, are we really dealing with here? By his own account, a group organized (early?) in 1969 and received at the White House in October 1969, asked for urgent help. A study was commissioned and a preliminary report was delivered to the White House in February 1970. A fuller report was "printed"—though not publicized?—in June, by which time, Cambodia being Cambodia, and Kent and Jackson state being what they were, there had been another meeting between the President and black college presidents and James Cheek, working with Heard, on temporary White House assignment. And it was when *their* reports, so disappointing to the President and others, had to be published in July that there was rushed out an announcement about some more money for the black colleges, which we were late to report but which in the end, or at least so far, hasn't helped them very much. And the *Times*—no, the whole system of journalism—is roasted by Mr. Moynihan for not dealing intelligently with the issue!

Now to the central point, which I take to be Mr. Moynihan's anguish about a reversal in the "old balance of power" between President and press. He thinks the press is well on the way to upsetting that "balance" to the detriment of effective government.

I found it odd, and negligent, that he never even attempted to define either the *old* balance of power or *any* balance that he deems desirable. This makes it a rather difficult thesis to rebut, especially after he gets through conceding the President's "near limitless capacity" to make news, to dominate events of public concern, to reward friends and punish enemies (and not only in the press corps), and to carry off "formidable deceptions." He can, of course, do much more. He can exhort, rally, and inspire. He can ruin and degrade. He can breathe life into American attitudes and, often, institutions. Or he can distort and discard them. And surely at the apex of anyone's list of Presidential powers is the power to make war, nuclear war, ten-year war, undeclared war, unchecked war, unpopular war, holy war, or pointless war. (If some of our histories are correct in suggesting that the Hearst and Pulitzer press were once able to goad or frighten the country and its President into war, then it would seem that there has been, indeed, a most remarkable shift in the balance of power, though hardly in the direction Mr. Moynihan suggests.)

But if I read the story correctly, he is not even talking about the collective, though incoherent, power of the press and the television. He is talking largely about the dangerous power of the New York *Times* and the Washington *Post*. This is flattering, but hardly persuasive. The great majority of black citizens, whose thoughts he wishes to protect from their own leaders and agitators, do not read either of those newspapers. The papers that they read, across the country, would probably score quite well on his special loyalty test. As for television, I will let him decide, after some months in civilian life, whether it favors the champions of the space program or its critics, whether it is dominated by the ethics of our President or those of his critics, whether on balance it proclaims the old American and governmental virtues, or the virtues of what he calls, in Lionel Trilling's phrase, the "adversary culture."

But all right. It is the *Eastern* press that is threatening us. How?

Point one is that our muckraking tradition has fallen into the hands of a new breed of reporter of middle- and upper-class background, Ivy

League, elitist. In Washington, this group constitutes a *social* elite, "with all the accoutrements one associates with a leisured class." We are not leisured, he quickly notes, but our "style is that of men and women who *choose* to work." And the political consequence of this social status is that "the press grows more and more influenced by attitudes genuinely hostile to American society and American government." And the evidence for this is that we have been brainwashed by the "moral absolutism" of George Wald!

Others have taken this absurd standard of pedigree and tallied the preponderance of non-Ivy degrees in the upper reaches of the Washington press corps. Still others, indeed, have noted with a little more relevance that the upper reaches are, in fact, dominated by the "silent generation" that was allegedly cowed into docility in the era of Eisenhower and Joe McCarthy. As for the "charges" of social elitism and our "style of leisure"—these really would have been better expressed if he had simply repeated, "effete snobs."

But how very odd that, in a paragraph devoted to the debunking of moral absolutism—in which Mr. Moynihan complains that people call the Vietnam war shameful instead of tragic, heartbreaking, or misconceived—he would dare to characterize the attitudes of reporters in the press not as wrong, or tragic, or misconceived, but as "hostile to American society and American government." Wow! Let's make it effete and *un-American* snobs.

We are, of course, guilty of having switched, over the last generation, to a more educated corps of reporters, if only to keep up with the credentials and footwork of the holders of public office (and our new critics). The fact is that we are not nearly smart enough yet to cope with the scientific, technological, pseudo-sociological expertise that is peddled to the public by both the government and its critics. And it is a further fact, and perhaps one of the most enduring attractions of our business, that any bright lad of proletarian or other origin can rid himself of the social and hierarchical pressures of our society to participate, as a journalist, in the political process of our country.

(I found it quaint, by the way, that the witnesses summoned against our new elitists were of such clearly non-Eastern and proletarian pedigree as Roger Starr, Lionel Trilling, Thomas E. Cronin, James Q. Wilson, Seymour Martin Lipset, Nathan Glazer, Irving Kristol. Shouldn't we all start printing our colleges beside our names, to facilitate such analysis?)

It is also true, and more relevant to the essay's point, that there are among some of the newest recruits to our business young men and women who are impatient with the "objective" or, more accurately, "neutral" standards of journalism to which their elders aspired. Some of them share Mr. Moynihan's sense of that standard's inadequacy and wish to adjust it. A few of them are impatient with *any* standard that would prevent them from placing their own views before the public. It is an important subject and an interesting debate that news writers have conducted periodically over the decades. More of this in sequence.

Point two suggests that along with hostility toward the Presidency we purvey an absurdly inflated picture of the President's importance and ability to influence events, thus setting a tone of pervasive dissatisfaction with the performance of government, under any President. The *Times* and the *Post* are particularly guilty here, it is argued, because Mr. Moynihan agrees with my contention that a newspaper is as much influenced by those who read it as vice versa.

This is apples and oranges.

We Americans do have an exaggerated expectation of our Presidents and only a handful of them ever fulfill their own promise and boast, even in hindsight. Such is the power and aura of this office that a politician, no matter how poorly regarded over the years, how often suspected and vilified and run down, can assume the office and earn at once not just what you call a "honeymoon" period of grace but a new reputation for nobility and intelligence. And when he begins in lofty manner, promising to heal some of the nation's wounds and to lower his voice, he is made to feel welcome and given the chance to appear as he wishes to appear before his countrymen. The press reflects these expectations of the public and records the efforts of our Presidents and Presidential candidates to nurture them. This faith is either an element of Presidential power, to be cherished and applied with skill by those who can, or it is a terrible burden, as Mr. Moynihan would have it.

If it is a burden, then only a President who insists from the start that he does *not* know everything, cannot change too much, and will aspire only to a modest program of action can correct the nation's view. How about a President who will work for a *year* of peace at a time, instead of a *generation?* Or one who begins by saying that a new Attorney General will *not* solve much of our crime problem? Or one who tells us how many loafers there really are on welfare and how much more sophisticated he has become, once in office, about the "welfare mess"?

We do try to match promise against performance and cumulatively we manage, I think, to draw a pretty good portrait of the strengths and weaknesses of the Presidency and any particular occupant thereof. But those who find the underlying truths obscured, must begin by noting not the power for occasional deception in the White House but the *habit* of *regular* deception in our politics and administration.

By and large, it is the President and the federal government who establish the agenda of public discussion and they must choose whether their purpose shall be uplifting and educational or merely manipulative. It is the damnable tendency toward manipulation that forces us so often into the posture of apparent adversaries.

We have indeed progressively lost our naiveté about the truthfulness of Presidents and government, starting with the U-2 affair a decade ago. A. J. Liebling found the awakening after U-2 to be the "beginning of wisdom" in the country and in the press. We lost the habit of reporting as fact what was only a contention or claim of our highest officials. And there is nothing in the record of the current administration, ten years later, to break us of the new habit of treating virtually every official utterance as a carefully contrived rendering that needs to be examined for the missing word or phrase, the sly use of statistics, the slippery syntax of semantics. Planes fly to "interdict supplies" but not in support of combat infantry, until such support becomes an "ancillary" benefit and until, finally, it becomes exposed as the *real* purpose of the flights. Troops do not engage in "ground combat" as long as they hover *two feet above the ground* in helicopters. Estimates of the gross national product turn out, within weeks, to be only targets.

If this shift from simple credulity to informed skepticism is the change of balance Mr. Moynihan deplores, then I plead guilty.

He will have to take it on faith that we practice this skepticism not in the spirit of persecution or prosecution, but from a sense of wishing to serve our readers with reports of what is really going on. I will not deny that, once discovered, governmental trickery in and of itself often becomes more "newsworthy" than the report itself. But a President or government dedicated to truth-telling and eager to inform the public could very rapidly turn the wolves of the press into lambs.

My contention that readers shape a newspaper as much as it shapes them bears on this, but only indirectly.

Our skepticism *does* reflect that of our readers and it is mutually reinforcing. As George Reedy so wisely reflected in thinking back on his tours as President Johnson's press secretary, "The reality is that a President has no press problems (except for a few minor administrative technicalities), but he does have political problems, all of which are reflected in their most acute form by the press."

A few more excerpts from Reedy's *The Twilight of the Presidency:*

> There is a deep-seated human tendency to confuse unhappy news with unhappy events and to assume that if the news can be altered, so can the events.
>
> In reality, the problem of a President in dealing with the press is precisely the same as his problem in dealing with the public at large. But no President can find it within his ego to concede that he has failed in any degree with the public. It is far more satisfying to blame his failures on the press because his problems then can be attributed to a conspiracy. He can blame the "Eastern press," the "Republican press," or the "liberal press." He then does not stand indicted within his own consciousness (the most terrible court of all) as having failed.

We reflect, or refract, but we do not simply create skepticism or dissatisfaction.

But I was speaking in a still larger sense. What is it, I asked, that makes newspapers accept some value judgments and not others? Why do we write in a different spirit about one kind of crime, say simple murder, than we do about another, say civil disobedience? Why do Northern and Western newspapers write, unquestionably, from the point of view of those who regard official segregation as not only illegal but also wrong, while some Southern newspapers give the racist equal standing in the court of opinion?

This is how I came to my answer that we are mutually influenced by the attitudes and values of our communities. The newspaper that is candidly written from the viewpoint of the home folks finds nothing wrong in sports coverage that is candidly partisan for the home team. But when the teams in contention are from the same community, the coverage suddenly turns "neutral." Why? Because the community is divided. We covered World War II from the partisan viewpoint of the Allies. Not so, by and large, the war in Vietnam. We did not, on a large scale, question or ignite debate on the crossing of the 38th Parallel in Korea in 1950, but we did examine and feed controversy on the bombing across the 17th Parallel in Vietnam. Not because we alone decided that one war was more clearly just than another, or one frontier more inviolate than another, but because the communities to which we reported were divided on the issue of Vietnam in sufficient degree to alter our perspective.

If I am right, then the interconnection is quite different from the one Mr. Moynihan suggests. A President does not enhance his power to govern by converting a few reporters or selling them on his point of view. He will more likely gain the trust—if not always the active support—of the press by gaining the trust and confidence of the community.

Point three is that we are "fairly continuously" involved in the receipt of information passed to us by disloyal bureaucrats. Mr. Moynihan terms this as something "less than honorable" on our part, though he implies that receiving special information from bureaucrats who are "loyal" is okay. He says no one knows much about the process of "leaking" and that it has not been "studied."

Well, I know a great deal about it. The first thing that needs to be said is that the *deliberate* disclosure of information for the purpose of injuring the President is relatively rare. But what is rarer still is that such information finds its way into print without "the other side," whatever that may be in our judgment, being questioned about the matter and given a chance to discuss the deeper issues and even the motives of those who may have done the leaking. The great majority of deliberate "leaks" are not secret documents and papers, but guarded suggestions that a reporter look into a matter that he might otherwise neglect. More often than not, he is not even told what he will find.

And the absolute majority of unwanted "leaks" are not deliberate at all. They result from a diligent study of public papers and diligent inquiry among dozens of officials, with reporters carefully playing one set of clues against another, until they find a part of what they seek. Most of these officials make themselves available not because they wish to abet the effort but because over time they have found their accessibility to be desirable for loyal purposes. It is true that in this process, when reporters have some interesting facts, but by no means all the facts, and find themselves shut out by government, they will then publish what they know for the purpose of lighting a fire that will smoke out a good deal more. For even when a first, unwanted story is incomplete or superficial, if it touches on an important subject, it will almost always arouse the attention and curiosity of other reporters who will, together, move it much closer to the essence of the tale.

Yet even if deliberate "leaking" were as harmful as Mr. Moynihan suggests, is it his contention that the press should ignore such information and pretend it was never received? That would be an interesting discussion indeed.

Point four deals with the "rub" that he finds adhering to our concept of objectivity. It comes, he observes, "when a decision has to be made as to whether an event really is news, or simply a happening, a non-event staged for the purpose of getting into the papers or onto the screen." (I note that television has been allowed back into the defendant's box.)

It is not the experience with Joe McCarthy that should be used to instruct us on this point. We were deficient in treating him—in part because we reflected and responded to the deficiency and gullibility of our communities—but as long as men who remember that experience are alive, we will probably apply the lessons learned.

The difficulty comes in the way in which Mr. Moynihan states the problem: "*simply* a happening, a non-event staged for the purpose of getting into the papers." A quarter of a million persons marching on the White House? A series of "teach-ins"? An agitator yelling "burn"? A Vice President attacking the papers (and the screen)? Lee Harvey Oswald? The quest for recognition, to be heard, to be noticed, to be heeded—it often takes the form of a happening staged for the purpose of getting into the papers, but it is rarely "*simply*" that in either motivation or consequence.

The problem for thoughtful journalism is that we can never be sure about motivation and we certainly cannot know consequence. And in some small measure, at least, we know that we contribute to consequence. These are horrendous problems and we lose sleep over them, but they are not solved by the automatic assumption in our editorial suites of the absolute power to decide that Moynihan deserves to be heard, and another man does not. And has he thought about the agitator who *may* be encouraged in his extremism because he finds it to be "newsworthy"? What would he do to project his cause and gain attention for himself if he were shut out of the news? Burn, perhaps, instead of only shouting "burn"?

Point five raises the "absence of a professional tradition of self-correction." In one sense, of course, we correct ourselves every morning, a requirement and an opportunity that most other institutions, including the Presidency, lack.

Mr. Moynihan's evidence does not make this point very well, but there is need, in another sense, for more correction or expansion and amendment of what we report. Persons who figure in our news coverage do occasionally need more space to explain their points of view or involvement in affairs than is provided in existing columns for guest-writers and Letters to the Editor. And clearly the need is greater in some papers than others. But as I suggested earlier, such opportunity for correction is rarely denied to the White House. Men of power—or presumed power—are able to make their views known, almost by definition. It is ordinary citizens, sometimes, of late, including the editors of the Eastern press, who require an outlet.

If our Presidents are seriously concerned about "protracted conflict" with a large enough segment of our population and genuinely believe, with Mr. Moynihan, that they are steadily losing that conflict, they had better look well beyond the bearers of the bad news and certainly well beyond the morning paper. They might even look in a mirror.

MAX FRANKEL

The New York *Times*
Washington, D.C.

PART THREE

The Governmental Context

Although presidents have played a central role in national politics since the inauguration of George Washington, the development of the presidency as a major institutional force is a more recent phenomenon. The transformation of the presidential office began during the administration of Franklin D. Roosevelt and has proceeded through successive presidencies to the point where it is now appropriate—indeed, necessary—to conceive of the presidency and the bureaucracy as separate institutional components of the executive branch. The selections in Part Three examine some of the consequences of the development of the presidential institution. They focus on the internal dynamics of the presidency in the formulation and implementation of policy, the interaction of the presidency with the bureaucracy, and the relations of the presidency with Congress, the principal institution involved with the presidency in making public policy.

It has become commonplace to speak of the institutionalized presidency and of institutionalization as an ongoing process. Some observers, however, have questioned the validity and utility of institutionalization as a concept for analyzing the development of the presidential office. Still, the office is obviously much more today than the few clerks and assistants that comprised it from 1789 until early in the twentieth century. It has grown in size, structures, and functions to become a complex organization—an institution. In order to analyze the performance of the presidency in national policy making, it is important to understand the processes of its growth and change as an institution. Robert S. Gilmour takes a critical look at the concept of institutionalization, finds that much confusion has surrounded it and that it has been misapplied, but concludes that if properly defined it is a useful conceptual tool for studying the development of the presidency.

The focus of my article, which falls second in this part, is on the consequences of institutionalization for presidential leadership in policy formulation. The conclusion reached is that effective presidential performance requires highly developed staffing arrangements and advisory mechanisms, but that there is no optimal arrangement nor any guarantee that what suits one president will work equally well for another. In reading the article, it would be well to bear in mind two important developments since it was written. First, the appointment of Henry Kissinger as secretary of state in 1973. This appointment probably will reduce the role of the National Security Council staff in making foreign and military policy —at least temporarily. At the same time the assumption of the secretary's post by such a dominant personality seems likely to increase the policy-making role of the State Department, although the full measure of such changes will become clear only over time. A second development concerns the Domestic Council. Thus far it has not become a high-level policy-planning staff, but rather it has served to house political operatives who have aided in policy adoption and implementation. Its initial significance in the policy-making process stemmed from the high standing of its first director, John Erlichman, with President Nixon rather than from its subject-matter expertise. After Erlichman's departure, in April, 1973, the Council's staff shrank in size and apparent importance. Melvin Laird, its second director, served less than a year and was more involved in protecting President Nixon from Watergate fallout than with policy development. The Council's third director, Kenneth R. Cole, a White House staff member since 1969, had no independent status prior to his appointment. Its future under him and under the Ford administration is uncertain.

In a related vein, Thomas E. Cronin explores the problems of directing the federal bureaucracy from the White House. He finds conflict to be the prevailing pattern of White House-departmental relations. Some of the conflicts are unavoidable; some are even functional; and coordination and cooperation are not rare or unobtainable. The desirable state of affairs, Cronin concludes, should not be effective means of conflict resolution (which might well amount to bald coercion) but rather a "political climate in which uncomfortable questions can be asked of a President" and a more realistic set of expectations for presidential leadership.

Conflict has also characterized presidential relations with Congress. The Founding Fathers saw rivalry between the two branches as a means of avoiding tyranny, and they deliberately engineered it into the Constitution. As Madison explained in a well-known passage from *Federalist No. 51:*

> . . . the great security against a gradual concentration of the several powers in the same department, consists in giving to those who administer each department, the necessary constitutional means and personal motives to resist encroachments of the others. . . . Ambition must be made to counteract ambition. The interest of the man must be connected with the constitutional rights of the place. . . .

In addition to such constitutional checks and balances as the presidential veto and senatorial participation in the appointive process, there are institutional sources of conflict. These include their different constituencies—the president having the entire nation and members of Congress diverse portions of it; their different time perspectives—the president serving for no more than two four-year terms, while congressmen serve an indefinite number of two- or six-year terms limited only by their constituents and their health; and the different information bases of the two branches.

Since the late 1960s congressional-presidential conflict has manifested itself sharply in the controversy over executive privilege. The argument arose during President Nixon's first term in regard to the making of national security policy and continued in his second term with respect to congressional and judicial investigations of the Watergate break-in and subsequent cover-up. Ostensibly the point at issue was the adequacy of the information that President Nixon made available to Congress and to Special Prosecutor Leon Jaworski. But the more fundamental disagreement was over how much congressional involvement there should be in executive branch policy making. Congress believed that there should be closer congressional-presidential cooperation, while President Nixon used the doctrine of executive privilege as a means of excluding Congress from the inner workings of the presidency.

The statement of Senator J. William Fulbright, made in hearings before the Senate Separation of Powers Subcommittee on a 1971 bill to limit presidential use of executive privilege, reflects the congressional concern. His complaint is not so much about executive privilege as about how President Nixon organized the conduct of national security policy making to avoid congressional participation and interference. Fulbright is expressing a negative reaction to such consequences of the institutionalization of the presidency as the influential role of presidential aides and advisers. Assistant Attorney General William Rehnquist (now an associate justice of the Supreme Court) states the president's position and crystallizes the issues that Fulbright raises.

The controversy over executive privilege assumed a major role in the

Senate Watergate investigation of 1973 and in the House Judiciary Committee's inquiry into the impeachment of President Nixon and the trials of Watergate defendants in 1974. The predominant congressional position in this situation was that the president was using executive privilege as a device for shielding possible wrongdoing from legitimate legislative inquiry. The special prosecutor argued that executive privilege could not function to frustrate the operation of the judicial process in criminal proceedings. The presidential view was that executive privilege was a necessary and legitimate means of preserving the constitutional separation of powers and maintaining the president's capacity to govern.

The Supreme Court's ruling, in the landmark case of *United States* v. *Nixon,* resolved the arguments in favor of the special prosecutor and, indirectly, the congressional committees seeking information. Speaking through Chief Justice Burger, the Court (absent Justice Rehnquist, who had disqualified himself) stated that "neither the doctrine of separation of powers, nor the need for confidentiality of high-level communications, without more, can sustain an absolute, unqualified, presidential privilege of immunity from judicial process under all circumstances." The Court qualified its ruling, however, by distinguishing between a "broad undifferentiated claim of . . . confidentiality" and a "claim of need to protect military, diplomatic or sensitive national security secrets." The Court also clarified the status of the doctrine by explicitly noting that a "constitutional base" exists for a "limited executive privilege."

It is perhaps one of the paradoxes of the Constitution that the checks and balances between the branches also constitute a strong pressure for cooperation between them. The joint participation of the presidency and Congress in the legislative process makes the development of some mode of accommodation imperative if either is to accomplish many of its objectives. The success or failure of a president's legislative and budgetary proposals is dependent, to a substantial degree, on the nature of his relations with Congress. All of our recent presidents have assigned congressional liaison responsibilities to members of the White House staff, but the efficacy of those efforts has varied markedly.

Abraham Holtzman, in the closing selection, examines how President John F. Kennedy organized his staff to handle congressional liaison. The strategies, tactics, and resources that he discusses are available to all presidents (with the exception of Lawrence O'Brien, a singularly skilled political operative). Although Holtzman describes their employment in favorable terms, it should be noted that Kennedy was not overly successful in obtaining favorable congressional responses to his legislative proposals.

President Johnson began his presidency after a long period of highly successful congressional service and was quite sensitive to the needs of congressmen. Initially, he was spectacularly effective in developing presidential-congressional harmony. As the frustrations of the Vietnam war pushed domestic policy leadership aside in the allocation of his time, his difficulties with Congress mounted. Considerations of national security policy did not, Johnson apparently believed, call for the same careful consultation and nurturing of congressmen as did the passage of domestic legislation. After Johnson had announced his decision not to seek reelection, his relations with Congress, which had become quite strained and acerbic in the controversy over his war policy, improved somewhat.

President Nixon had a particularly difficult task in the area of congressional liaison because he confronted sizable Democratic majorities in both the House and Senate during his tenure in office. It is generally recognized that he paid insufficient attention to the development of congressional support, and many observers feel that his political difficulties in the Watergate affair were exacerbated by this neglect.

The presidential-congressional relationship can vary, then, with the style and character of the president, with the policy areas that are uppermost in his mind, and with the electoral situation. The importance of those relations remains constant.

8.

THE INSTITUTIONALIZED PRESIDENCY: A CONCEPTUAL CLARIFICATION

Robert S. Gilmour

"Institutionalization" of the American presidency has been acclaimed, assaulted, even debunked as a "myth" by dozens of observers and critics since World War II. Most have entered the field as reformers, urging pet solutions—usually institutional additions to the Executive Office—to "help the President" shoulder his increasing burdens. A few others have been less optimistic about institutional reform of the highest office, pointing to the enigma of organizing and staffing the presidency for effective management without at the same time constraining the President's capacity to lead. Yet none of these reformers or analysts has seriously developed a definition of "institutionalization," let alone come to grips with the problems of empirically assessing the effects of institutional growth. As a result, both the conception itself and the interpretations of its consequences have been contradictory and confused.

While sharing with other observers the hunch—and it is, empirically, little more than that—that institutional structures and institutional growth are of crucial importance, the author's purpose in this paper is to reexamine institutionalization solely as an independent variable, or potential predictor, of presidential behavior and leadership capability. The object is to construct a conception of presidential institutionalization which is at once consistent with recent strides in sociological and political development theory and which conclusively indicates the direction of institutional change. Admittedly, this skirts the more significant and difficult problem of assessing the relationship between institutionalization and other more interesting dependent variables of presidential behavior. However, careful reelaboration of this much used and confused variable seems clearly the logical first step in a project that would well exceed the scope of a journal article.

The author is also mindful of the possibility (and erstwhile reality) that a narrow focus on presidential institutionalization may elevate the concept as one of single, intrinsic importance. This is hardly the intent. Yet institutionalization is widely regarded as a powerful factor in the equation of constraints and potential for presidential leadership. Accepting this assumption for the moment, and bearing in mind contemporary plans to further institutionalize the presidential office, a more precise understanding of the phenomenon itself appears very much in order.

AN "INSTITUTIONALIZED" MUDDLE

The obvious if inauspicious point of departure in the development of a refined concept of presidential institutionalization is with the conceptual formulations of political scientists and governmental analysts. Largely, these observer-commentators have been of two types: those who would "help" the chief executive by creating new and permanent staff organizations in the Executive Office, and those who view increasing presidential institutionalization with reserve or even alarm.

Among the institutionalizers, often as not the real aim is to capture the President's attention, transfer power, or both. A recent example combining both of these objectives is the cabinet-level Domestic Council staff proposed by President Nixon's Advisory Council on Executive Organization (the Ash Council) and set in motion by Reorganization Plan No. 2 of 1970. Billed as an "institutionally-staffed group charged with advising the President on the total range of domestic policy," the Domestic Council is to be supported with a group of professionals "like the National Security Council staff," working in harmony with the President's assistants but with an "institutional identity" of its own, "established on a permanent, institutional basis . . . designed to develop and employ the 'institutional memory' so essential if continuity is to be maintained, and if experience is to play its proper role in the policy-making process." [1] One active participant in the Ash Council proceedings candidly advised the author that the Domestic Council staff was intended not only as an NSC counterpart but also as a direct competitor:

> It was the view of the Ash Council that to place the responsibility for domestic policy-making in the Office of Management and Budget [formerly the U.S. Bureau of the Budget], leaving the National Security Council outside as a separate organ, creates an imbalance for the seventies. It was our hope that with the Domestic Council the Presidents of the seventies would be more directly charged with the domestic area so that they will not be able to slough it off. The tradeoffs of domestic for foreign affairs expenditures should be made explicitly by the President. The Domestic Council would help make these choices explicit to the President.

INSTITUTIONAL CONCEPTS

In the sociological tradition, institutionalization has been defined both as a social pattern and as a developmental process. Talcott Parsons defines institutions in a somewhat static mode as "patterns of governing behavior and social relationships which have become interwoven with a system of common moral sentiments which in turn define what one has a 'right to expect' of a person in a certain position." Parsons' emphasis is placed on the expectations associated with specific roles and statuses in a social system which defines standards of legitimate performance by persons in particular positions and by others associated with them.[2] In Philip Selznick's model, "institutionalization is a *process*" in which an organization begins over time "to *infuse with value* beyond the technical requirements of the task at hand . . . largely a reflection of the unique way in which it fulfills personal or group needs. Whenever individuals become attached to an organization or a way of doing things as persons rather than as technicians, the result is a prizing of the device for its own sake." [3] Charles Loomis adds the notion that this development makes

---

[1] U.S., President, 1969– (Nixon), Message to the Congress of the United States, Washington, Office of the White House Press Secretary, March 12, 1970. (Mimeographed.)

[2] Talcott Parsons, *Essays in Sociological Theory* (rev. ed.; Glencoe, Illinois: Free Press, 1954), p. 143.

[3] Philip Selznick, *Leadership in Administration: A Sociological Interpretation* (Evanston, Illinois: Row, Peterson and Co., 1957), pp. 16–17.

"human behavior . . . more predictable and patterned. Through this process social systems are given their own distinguishing elements of structure and the processes of function." [4] The sociological conception of institutionalization thus involves both formal organizational structures and informal rules—norms and expectations—which may be used to explain human behavior in a dynamic context.

In an effort to make "institutionalization" more useful in political development and modernization studies, Samuel Huntington has refined the concept as one having four properties: adaptability, complexity, autonomy, and coherence of organization and procedures. Huntington argues that if criteria to define and measure each of these properties can be found, then "it will also be possible to measure increases and decreases in the institutionalization of particular organizations and procedures within a political system." [5] Anyone who has wrestled with such concepts as "adaptation," trying to make them operational in empirical work, will appreciate the difficulty of this particular "if." Fortunately, a few concrete indicators are provided. Organizational "complexity," for example, is understood to involve a greater number and variety of subunits, hierarchical division of labor, and diversification of function.[6] Simple counts of organizational divisions and specialized tasks would offer ready indicators of longitudinally developmental or comparative institutionalization. But in the main Huntington has employed subconstructs which are just as elusive as the larger variable he seeks to define. Even more damaging is the apparent logical inconsistency among his four conceptual ingredients. The tension between organizational complexity and coherence seems self-evident. Surely, as an institution becomes larger and more fully differentiated, these very aspects of organizational complexity will serve as impediments to the maintenance of an internally coherent structure. Similarly, the successful adaptation of an organization to its environment may, at some crucial juncture, run at cross-purposes with autonomy. Organizational complexity achieved in some rigid mold may prevent adaptation, and so on. Yet all of these variables are assumed by Huntington to be indicators of a unidimensional concept of institutionalization.[7]

A more successful effort is made by Nelson Polsby. In a three-part definition of institutionalization, devised for his study of the U.S. House of Representatives, Polsby explicitly adopts only one of the indicators of

---

[4] Charles P. Loomis, "Social Change and Social Systems," *Sociological Theory, Values, and Sociocultural Change,* ed. Edward A. Tiryakian (Glencoe, Illinois: Free Press, 1963), p. 198.

[5] Samuel P. Huntington, *Political Order in Changing Societies* (New Haven: Yale University Press, 1968), p. 12.

[6] *Ibid.,* p. 17.

[7] An additional critique of Huntington's model is offered by Mark Kesselman. See his "Overinstitutionalization and Political Constraint," *Comparative Politics,* III (October, 1970), 25.

institutionalization so far discussed, that of "complexity." This indicator is defined as an internal separation of functions so that organizational parts are not wholly interchangeable. "There is a division of labor in which roles are specified, and there are widely shared expectations about performance of roles." [8] However, the operational definition of this indicator drops the reference to roles and shared expectations, which seem out of place here anyway. Increasing complexity of the House is then shown by "the growth in autonomy and importance of committees, in the growth of specialized agencies of party leadership, and in the general increase in the provision of various emoluments and auxiliary aids to members. . . ." [9]

Two additional properties of institutionalization identified by Polsby are: (1) "boundaries," which differentiate an organization from its environment, set standards for membership, and promote the recruitment of leaders from within; and (2) "universalistic-automated decision making," as opposed to particular and discretionary means of conducting internal business. According to this second characteristic, "Precedents and rules are followed; merit systems replace favoritism and nepotism; and impersonal codes supplant personal preferences as prescriptions for behavior." [10] Like complexity, each of these components of the primary concept is operationalized by a set of quantitative indicators. Boundary definition is established by the declining percentages of first-term House members, increasing average terms of service, increasing terms of service prior to first selection as Speaker, and so forth. Changes in the system of internal decision making are measured by the rising importance of the seniority system in the selection of committee chairmen and the decline in the percentage of seats contested per Congress (that is, electoral outcomes disputed in the House and settled in camera).

While Polsby's definition of institutionalization omits a few appealing elements established by the sociological literature—the attribution of special values to the organization over time, for example—it is by all odds the strongest and best operationalized of the lot. Polsby's conception is clearly tailored for a developmental study of the House of Representatives, but his procedure is suggestive of methods that might be employed to measure institutionalization of the presidency.

---

[8] Nelson W. Polsby, "The Institutionalization of the U.S. House of Representatives," *American Political Science Review,* LXII (March, 1968), 145.

[9] *Ibid.,* p. 153.

[10] *Ibid.,* p. 145.

PRESIDENTIAL INSTITUTIONALIZATION

Relative to its political importance at all levels, the presidential institution remains comparatively understudied. Having defined the presidency in the singular, many of the most able political scientists have turned to the more obvious collectivities such as congressional committees, political parties, and courts, where data sources appear to be richer and contemporary theory more relevant. "Institutionalization" is thus an important conceptual handle if only for the reason that it focuses attention on corporate aspects of the presidency which transcend individual artistry. Presidential institutionalization is understood here as a variable that may fluctuate in either direction, taking on different values depending upon the time of measurement. These values are in turn dependent upon forces generated within the Executive Office or by the external environment of the presidency.

Drawing on the conceptual components and indicators suggested by the foregoing sociological theorists and developmental analysts, presidential institutionalization will be defined as an index of: *boundaries, organizational complexity, routinization and role development,* and *symbolic attachment.* No exhaustive attempt will be made to trace historical change in the presidency according to each of these indicators. Instead, the effort is directed toward a demonstration of their theoretic efficacy in the presidential context. Moreover, even the most cursory review of presidential development with the perspective of this composite of institutional traits shows unmistakable institutional growth.

If *boundaries* are understood as the degree of differentiation between a collectivity and its environment, there is no doubt that boundaries of the American presidency have been fundamentally altered, both as to size and permeability, during the past four decades. Indicative of this growth is the formal organization of a presidential advisory system within the Executive Office or attached to it in the form of advisory commissions and task forces.[11] In each case, presidential bureaus have replaced or at least supplemented the informal advice presidents have historically received on a regular basis from counselors outside the government. With the major exception of an elite corps of aides in the White House staff, presidential employees (clerks and professionals alike) are for the most part career civil servants, in effect, a permanent presidential secretariat. Recruitment to leadership positions, except for the most visible and sensitive posts, comes largely from within the Executive Office establishment, thus reinforcing boundary maintenance. The presidency also has

---

[11] The best single collection of materials on this subject is contained in Thomas E. Cronin and Sanford D. Greenberg, eds., *The Presidential Advisory System* (New York: Harper and Row, 1969).

its own formally designated emissaries and elaborate communications systems to superintend routine relationships with other institutions. The continued deployment of an identifiable congressional liaison team within the White House,[12] the appointment of White House-coordinated assistant secretaries for congressional liaison in the departments,[13] and the strictures of both the budgetary and legislative clearance processes placed on line agencies, all seem to be clear cases in point.[14]

While boundaries of the presidency have expanded and become more distinct, *organizational complexity* of the Executive Office has also increased, both in terms of its internal division of labor and sheer size. This second aspect of presidential institutionalization was initially a consequence of intense executive activity during the New Deal. Of course, formal creation of the Executive Office of the President which, among other things, relocated the U.S. Bureau of the Budget as a presidential agency, was not accomplished until passage of the Executive Reorganization Act of 1939. More recent developments, notably World War II, the onset of the Cold War, and rapid technological advance have continually reinforced the pressures toward increases in executive staffing and, indeed, presidential bureaucratization. Figures gathered by the President's Advisory Council on Executive Organization in early 1970 describe a presidential staff of approximately 1,640 professional and nonprofessional employees during the preceding year.[15] Staff members are largely concentrated in the White House Office (208 employees) and in two additional agencies, the Office of Management and Budget (550) and the Office of Emergency Planning (441). The important Council of Economic Advisers and Office of Science and Technology staffs are still small but growing in recent years (numbering 74 and 62, respectively, in 1969). Staff of the National Security Council totaled only 35; however, the Council itself superintends the immense security bureaucracies of the CIA and the National Security Agency.[16] In short, the presidential estab-

---

[12] See Abraham Holtzman, *Congressional Liaison* (New York: Rand McNally, 1970).

[13] Russell Pipe, "Congressional Liaison: The Executive Branch Consolidates Its Relations with Congress," *Public Administration Review*, XXVI (March, 1966), 14–24; Alfred de Grazia, "Congressional Liaison–An Inquiry Into Its Meaning for Congress" (Washington: American Enterprise Institute, 1965).

[14] Aaron Wildavsky, *The Politics of the Budgetary Process* (Boston: Little, Brown and Company, 1964); Richard E. Neustadt, "President and Legislation: The Growth of Central Clearance," *American Political Science Review*, XLVIII (September, 1954), 641–671; Robert S. Gilmour, "Central Legislative Clearance: A Revised Perspective," *Public Administration Review*, XXXI (March-April, 1971), 150–158.

[15] This total does not include the Office of Economic Opportunity, which in 1970 had 1,164 employees in its permanent Washington headquarters and 1,155 in its regional offices.

[16] Popular magazine accounts in 1971 reported that the National Security Council staff had been enlarged and reconstituted under Henry Kissinger's leadership to an overall size of more than 100.

lishment has grown very considerably since the late 1920s when Herbert Hoover had three presidential aides and the assistance of a hundred or so clerks.

The growth of the specialized presidential staff agencies and commissions created by every administration since the 1930s is itself indicative of an increasing division of labor within the Executive Office. Not surprisingly, the establishment of a well-ordered chain of command reaching down to highly specialized subdivisions and individuals in each staff bureau is the rule rather than the exception. For example, the Office of Emergency Planning (OEP) has assistant directors for telecommunications management, natural resource analysis, and emergency operations, among others. In addition, each OEP assistant director has division chiefs to supervise such areas as satellite communications, stockpile management, and disaster assistance. Accordingly, job descriptions in each of these subdivisions are further differentiated.

Even the least hierarchical and most personalized unit of presidential machinery, the White House staff, has developed reasonably well defined sets of tasks and formal designations for professional assistants. Despite Franklin Roosevelt's commitment to a staff of generalists with unfixed and ad hoc, even competitive assignments, several specific positions were created during his administration which had lasting importance—press secretary, appointments secretary, and special counsel.[17] President Truman's staff was somewhat more tightly organized than Roosevelt's, its assignments more definite.[18] But it was President Eisenhower who introduced an intra-staff hierarchy with multiple official titles —special assistants for foreign economic policy, science and technology, and security operations coordination, to name only a few—and a chief of staff to superintend communications from the staff and from line departments as well.[19] President Kennedy recoiled from this degree of formalism, scuttling Eisenhower's cabinet secretariat and subcabinet coordinating committees, but some of the Eisenhower legacy remained. In 1962, the position of special assistant for science and technology was given status under law, at Kennedy's request, as the President's science adviser and director of the new Office of Science and Technology (OST). Moreover, Kennedy was disinclined to abolish either of the Eisenhower-designated special assistantships for national security affairs or for congressional

---

[17] Richard E. Neustadt, "Approaches to Staffing the Presidency," *American Political Science Review*, LVII (December, 1963), 855–863.

[18] See especially Grant McConnell, *The Steel Seizure of 1952*, Inter-University Case Program, No. 52 (University: University of Alabama Press, 1960), pp. 22–24.

[19] Sherman Adams, *Firsthand Report* (New York: Harper and Brothers, 1961), pp. 50–58.

liaison. Actually, Kennedy strengthened both of these positions, as did his successors, Presidents Johnson and Nixon.[20]

Closely related to organizational complexity is a third, dual aspect of institutionalization, *routinization and role development.*[21] At least in part, routinization of the presidency represents a formalization of presidential actions that were once thought to be extraordinary. President Cleveland's intervention in the Pullman strike was wholly unprecedented in 1894, and Theodore Roosevelt's arrangement for arbitration of the bitter anthracite coal strike of 1902 was in the long run an even more important innovation and precedent. Arbitration became an operative principle of both the Railway Labor Act of 1926 and the National Labor Relations Act of 1935. Later, the presidency received direct powers of intervention to prevent strikes under provisions of the Taft-Hartley Act. FDR's assumption of a major presidential role in managing national economic affairs was similarly unprecedented in 1933, but the President's mandate in this realm is now set, albeit with some ambiguity, by the Employment Act of 1946. Additional legal ratifications of powers already assumed by sitting presidents in time of deep national crisis include the Atomic Energy Act of 1946, requiring presidential approval for the use of atomic weapons, and the National Security Act of 1947, which formalized defense and security coordinative structures similar to those developed during World War II and extended them into peacetime.

Only some of the formal powers and executive staff agencies were expressly desired by the presidents who received them. Transfer of the Bureau of the Budget into the newly created Executive Office under FDR and establishment of OST under Kennedy clearly were. Others were the gratuitous contributions of Congress. As Lester Seligman has pointed out, passage of the Employment Act creating the Council of Economic Advisers represents in part a congressional "desire to confine and limit . . . personal leadership." [22] Apparently, President Truman reacted to the NSC as an institution created for much the same purpose.[23] Of course, Truman's opposition to provisions of the Taft-Hartley Act is legendary.

There has been a parallel development of routines that would be extraordinarily difficult for a President to discontinue. These routines

---

[20] Stanley L. Falk argues that, far from minimizing the importance of the special assistant for national security affairs, President Kennedy added considerable strength to the position. "The National Security Council Under Truman, Eisenhower, and Kennedy," *Political Science Quarterly,* LXXIX (1964), 433.

[21] Unquestionably, the most comprehensive treatment of presidential routinization is found in Dorothy Buckton James, *The Contemporary Presidency* (New York: Pegasus, 1968), Chap. II.

[22] Lester G. Seligman, "Presidential Leadership," *Journal of Politics,* XVIII (August, 1956), 418.

[23] Falk, pp. 405–417.

largely conform to sets of expectations held for the presidency by surrounding actors of the political system—Congress, the line bureaucracy, the communications media, presidential party, and others. As a result, various roles of the presidency as initiator, crisis manager, appeals court, and supervisor of administrative detail in many contexts are rather sharply defined. And most other actors hold potential sanctions over the presidency's incumbents should they fail to perform in accord with expectations. For example, when President Eisenhower did not live up to the congressional expectation of an identifiable presidential program, intending to return that power to Congress in 1953, he was widely criticized, even by congressional members of his own party. More recently, President Johnson felt the sting of waspish reporters when he deviated from the traditional press conference styles and schedules most convenient to the communications media. In fact the historical development of a formalized ("institutionalized") presidential press conference is a story in itself.[24] Such processes as executive budgeting, legislative clearance, security briefings, and periodic Executive Office economic and cost-of-living reporting are now so well routinized that set timetables are rarely violated.

The final indicator of institutionalization, *symbolic attachment*, refers to the development of an organization's symbolic life—prestige and organizational esteem, distinctiveness, presumed traditions, and importance—to the extent that it is differentiated from, and perhaps becomes even more important than the organization's ostensible purpose. This is another way of saying what Selznick had in mind by an organization's infusion with value "beyond the technical requirements of the task at hand," or Huntington in his conception of the "triumph of the organization over its function." However, adaptable social indicators of the organizational esteem-satisfaction variety are commonly available and well tested.[25] In the case of the presidency, symbolic attachments take on especial meaning because of the fact that there are subinstitutions, that is, Executive Office agencies, living under and enhanced by the presidential umbrella.

At its worst, symbolic distinctiveness of subordinate organizations may be detrimental to a concerted performance of presidential intelligence and decision-making machinery, thus to successful leadership. John Kennedy's Bay of Pigs disaster is illustrative. The Central Intelligence Agency, as the President's foremost though certainly not his only intelligence-gathering resource, held tight reins on Cuban invasion plans to the point that secondary Cuban information and advisory sources such

---

[24] See especially Elmer E. Cornwell, Jr., *Presidential Leadership of Public Opinion* (Bloomington: Indiana University Press, 1965).

[25] John P. Robinson, Robert Athanasiou, and Kendra B. Head, *Measures of Occupational Attitudes and Occupational Characteristics* (Ann Arbor, Michigan: Survey Research Center, Institute for Social Research, 1969).

as Intelligence and Research of the State Department were purposely kept in the dark.[26] What is more, CIA officials, most notably Agency Director Allen Dulles and Deputy Director Richard M. Bissell, became "emotionally committed" to the adoption of plans that had been developed in the agency over many months time.[27] The Secretary of State and members of the Joint Chiefs of Staff meanwhile sought defensively positive positions protective of their respective agencies and deferential to the CIA for the thrust of pro-invasion argument. The outcome, as Arthur Schlesinger records it, was that "the prestige of the presidential office had been lightly regarded. . . ."[28] Schlesinger ascribes this to a failure in "primary loyalty," underscored by the fact that both Dulles and Bissell were Eisenhower appointees. Yet had Eisenhower remained in office, he would just as certainly have suffered the Cuban debacle—barring massive U. S. military intervention—as did Kennedy. The difficulty was most surely one of competing loyalties—organizational versus personal—and in this instance the organizational dynamic of subpresidential institutions was more compelling than the needs of the President himself. "Primary loyalty" was devoted to the individual agencies.

More typically, symbolic attachment takes less visible forms that are not so open to comment and criticism. The Office of Management and Budget, for example, is regarded by insiders and outsiders alike as an elite agency, the "fiscal arm of the President." Insiders busily announce that there is no room here for the "bureaucratic mentality." The implicit demand of these symbolic ascriptions is not only high level performance, but also that the Office will always be right, or at least almost always. Aaron Wildavsky aptly notes:

> Everyone knows that agencies make end-runs around the Bureau [now OMB] to gain support from Congress. If they do so too often, the Budget Bureau finds that its currency has depreciated. Hence the Bureau frequently accepts consistent Congressional action as a guide.[29]

On these grounds alone, the OMB's usefulness to the President must be said to have been altered by its own organizational sense of identity and importance.

Similarly, the Council of Economic Advisers has become a symbol of economic preeminence. In consequence, CEA staff reports often earn higher marks for sophisticated economic elegance than for helpful advice

---

[26] Roger Hilsman, *To Move a Nation* (Garden City, New York: Doubleday and Co., 1967), p. 31.

[27] *Ibid.*, pp. 30–34.

[28] Arthur Schlesinger, Jr., *A Thousand Days: John F. Kennedy in the White House* (Boston: Houghton Mifflin Co., 1965), p. 296.

[29] Aaron Wildavsky, *The Politics of the Budgetary Process*, p. 41.

to a lay economist such as the President. The symbolic life of the CEA demands a different kind of performance than it was initially designed to achieve.

INSTITUTIONAL EFFECTS

As a conceptual tool to trace the development of a political organization, "institutionalization" has been shown to have considerable utility. Even this brief synopsis of institutional characteristics of the Executive Office—defined for this purpose as boundaries, organizational complexity, routinization-role development, symbolic attachment (and consistent with the most coherent elaborations of the concept now emerging in the theoretical literature)—identifies unmistakable institutional growth. Assertions such as Henry Fairlie's that ". . . there is no evidence that any White House lore, any body of precedent or rules or conventions, is being built up, to be passed on from one Presidency to the next"[30] may be dismissed out of hand.

However well we may establish institutional growth, any assertion about appropriate levels of institutionalization of the presidency (or any other organization) will remain wholly arbitrary until firm relationships between institutional development and leadership capability, policy impact, and other dependent variables are also established. After reviewing much the same data, contemporary studies of the presidency have concluded both that the President is an institutional "captive" or "clerk" in his own house and, conversely, that this highly personalized leadership position is surrounded by "chaos" and lacks "institutional order." Such conclusions have depended entirely upon the identity and purpose of the analyst.

Beyond the difficulties of definitional precision and dispassionate observation, the larger problem is surely that of understanding the outcomes in any given political context. This is no small order for, in the first place, a solution would presume the existence of satisfactory operational definitions for such conceptions as "leadership," "policy effectiveness," and so on. Furthermore, institutionalization is only one among many possible factors which might strongly influence behavioral or structural results. It seems likely that levels of institutionalization are even more highly related to political outcomes than leadership style, rational decision making, or other highly touted predictors, but at this stage of analytic development, the nonintrinsic importance of institutionalization is a matter of conjecture. In assessing "the consequences of the House's institutionaliza-

---

[30] Henry Fairlie, "Thoughts on the Presidency," *The Public Interest*, No. 9 (Fall, 1967), p. 37.

tion," Polsby takes care to describe his conclusions as "tentative."[31] Others have not felt so inhibited when stating their speculations as fact, but they have given food for the thought that institutionalization may not be monotonically related to other variables of greater inherent interest. Statements of over- and under-institutionalization suggest that institutional development may be related to its consequences in a curvilinear fashion, its specific ideal point dependent on any number of contextual variables.

Put another way, institutionalization may have greater or lesser effect on presidential performance depending upon the circumstances of particular situations. President Kennedy's Cuban invasion experience suggests to most of us, as it apparently did to him, that he was not best served by existing institutional arrangements. His Executive Council contrivance for the Cuban missile crisis later vividly reflects this view.[32] Moreover, different presidential personalities are differentially affected by institutionalization. President Truman largely regarded institutional additions to his office (especially those proffered by Congress) with considerable reserve. FDR and Kennedy apparently viewed institutional structures with mixed feelings, accepting some and firmly rejecting others while consciously attempting to maintain an "open door" policy to communications inflow and, commonly, an ad hoc approach to arrangements even for crucial decision-making processes. President Eisenhower, on the other hand, was a consummate presidential institution builder, and Richard Nixon had similarly made his need for institutional protection perfectly clear.

It is also clear that the presidency is now heavily institutionalized in many respects and likely to become more so. Employed as a descriptive and developmental concept, "institutionalization" better enables us to discern the specific attributes and scale of this growth over time. Nonetheless, a sitting President may or may not be a "captive" of the institution. The reasons why, under what circumstances, and to what effects remain the legitimate and important objects of study.

---

31 Polsby, p. 165.

32 Richard E. Neustadt, "Politicians and Bureaucrats," *The Congress and America's Future,* ed. David B. Truman (Englewood Cliffs, N.J.: Prentice-Hall, 1965), p. 113.

9.

PRESIDENTIAL ADVICE AND INFORMATION: POLICY AND PROGRAM FORMULATION

Norman C. Thomas

The "Hickel letter" incident of May, 1970, occurring in the context of the movement of American forces into Cambodia and the campus crises that precipitated and followed the killing of four Kent State University students by National Guard troops, raised in dramatic fashion the questions that are asked about every national administration in time of trouble. "Who sees the President?" "To whom does he listen?" "Is the President isolated?" "What are his sources and means of obtaining information?" Although not nearly so widely publicized, similar and related questions concerned the members of two subcommittees of the House of Representatives as they conducted hearings in the Spring of 1970 on presidential advisory committees and on President Nixon's proposed Reorganization Plan No. 2 of 1970, to restructure significantly the Executive Office of the President. These concerns reflect the general recognition among observers of and participants in high level national politics that responsive presidential policy leadership is as dependent upon the formal and informal processes whereby the President obtains advice and information as it is upon his personal characteristics such as political style and tactics. Academicians have understood the institutional as well as the personal dimension of presidential leadership for some time, but it often tends to be overlooked by sophisticated observers and is not recognized by the public. Undoubtedly, this condition exists because of the extent to which the mass media have personalized politics and, more importantly, because personal traits and characteristics have always offered simpler and more visible explanations of presidential behavior. It is easier for the analyst to develop and for the public to understand explanations that focus on the individual who occupies the White House than it is to wrestle with the complex questions of where ideas come from and how they are translated into policies that lead to operating programs of action.

Reprinted with permission from a symposium on the institutionalized presidency appearing in *Law and Contemporary Problems*, Vol. 35, No. 3 (Summer, 1970), pp. 540–572, published by the Duke University School of Law, Durham, North Carolina. Footnotes have been abridged and renumbered for this volume.

In this paper I will examine the formal and informal advisory and informational devices that modern Presidents employ in the formulation of policies and programs. My primary concern is with information inputs to presidential decision-making processes and with the conversion of those inputs to policy choices. The questions that will guide the analysis include: (1) What are the President's major sources of information and advice? (2) What kinds of people tend to become presidential advisors? (3) What are the limitations of the various advisory mechanisms? (4) What are the advantages of the different mechanisms? (5) What kinds of relationships exist between the President and his advisory system? (6) What are the characteristics of a viable advisory system? (7) What trends and developments are emerging in the patterns of advising, informing, and assisting the President with respect to his policy-making responsibilities?

I. PRESIDENTIAL COUNSELLING: AN OVERVIEW

A. *Staffing the Presidency.* Since the late 1930's, Presidents, their principal assistants, and students of the presidency have regarded as axiomatic the presidential dependence on advice and information and the need for assistance in securing and utilizing them. The Brownlow Committee Report of 1937, the Reorganization Act of 1939 which established the Executive Office of the President, the Employment Act of 1946 which created the Council of Economic Advisers, the reports of the two Hoover Commissions in 1949 and 1955, the development of an elaborate formal staff under President Eisenhower, the use of informal and *ad hoc* study groups, task forces, and committees by Presidents Kennedy and Johnson, and, most recently, President Nixon's creation of the Domestic Council are manifestations of the continuing effort to respond to the presidential need for assistance. That effort is often referred to in governmental circles as "staffing" while academically it has been encompassed within the broader and more ambiguous term "institutionalization."

According to William D. Carey, a former Assistant Director of the Budget who spent 25 years with the Bureau of the Budget, staffing should assist the President with respect to policy analysis, communications, outreach, and command and control.[1] In the process of policy and program formulation as distinguished from implementation, policy analysis, communication, and outreach are of more direct importance than the operational problems of command and control that lie at the center of policy implementation. Staffing for policy and program formulation has varied

---

[1] Carey, "Presidential Staffing in the Sixties and Seventies," 29 *pub. Ad. Rev.* 450 (1969).

from the Roosevelt to the Nixon Administrations along a continuum of structural formality ranging from the elaborate staff arrangements favored by President Eisenhower to the free-wheeling administrative chaos that characterized the early years of the New Deal under President Roosevelt. The determination of an administration's position on that continuum is a matter of subjective judgment that rests on several factors: the President's desire to innovate; the frequency and duration of policy crises; the necessity and desire for secrecy in presidential decision-making; the President's leadership style; the President's personal relations with his immediate staff, his principal subordinates, and congressional leaders; the President's administrative orientation—his preference for systematized or random procedures, written memoranda or oral briefs, etc.; and the President's priority ranking among the great quantity of matters pressing on him for attention.

While I have not attempted to operationalize these factors so as to permit a quantitative measurement of recent presidential administrations, I will explore qualitatively their possible relationships with the degree of structural formality that might be anticipated in the presidency. It seems quite apparent that a President seeking to develop new policy departures will tend to prefer flexible staffing arrangements. This was the case with Presidents Roosevelt, Kennedy, and Johnson, all of whom were innovation-minded, but not with Eisenhower or Nixon, who both tended to favor improvement and refinement (some might say consolidation) of of existing policies and programs.[2] The President who seeks to change policies more than incrementally finds it helpful and necessary to obtain a steady flow of ideas, suggestions, and information from a wide range of sources outside as well as within the government. His emphasis is likely to be more on the scope and variety rather than the precision and detail of his policy intelligence. He is more apt to run the risk that his decisions may be based on less than a comprehensive analysis of the situation than to risk missing a promising new proposal that could lead to a breakthrough. However, the costs of the structural flexibility required by an innovative President can be substantial in terms of the lack of coordinated effort and the erosion of policy control. Activist Presidents have tolerated chaotic advisory processes and have often received sloppy if not shoddy advice. Policy crises can also affect staffing arrangements. A low incidence and short duration of crises tends to favor the growth of formalized staffing. As long as information can be obtained and processed routinely, formal arrangements can serve the President quite effectively. Crisis con-

[2] I am aware of the innovativeness of the Family Assistance Program that President Nixon proposed in 1969. The major domestic policy orientation of the Nixon Administration is not activist, however. At most it can be characterized as mildly reformist or restorative.

ditions, however, have a way of forcing the development of special temporary devices to deal with the particular situation. Information is needed quickly; there is no time for carefully prepared analyses embodied in position papers. Persons not normally in the formal policy-making structure may be needed for advice and consultation. The pace of events is so rapid that decisions must be reached without the usual process of checking and approval. These and similar considerations lead to flexible staffing arrangements. Of course, recurrent crises are now a fact of our national political life—"emergencies in policy with politics as usual," Neustadt wrote over ten years ago—and to a degree they can be handled through predetermined routines. But to the extent that each crisis presents a unique threat to the nation and to the President it will call forth a special set of arrangements to deal with it. The more crises that arise, the more the President will require flexible devices to meet them.

Staffing arrangements are also a product of presidential personality and temperament. A President who has a penchant for secrecy and surprise, like Johnson or Roosevelt, finds flexible arrangements much more suitable than formal ones. Also, some Presidents—e.g., Roosevelt and Kennedy—are more free wheeling and less bureaucratically oriented than others in their approach to administrative tasks.

Finally, to the extent that national security policy matters intrude upon domestic politics formal staffing arrangements tend to be favored over informal. The handling of national security policy lends itself more readily to systematic intelligence gathering and evaluation and to structured decision-making than do domestic affairs. The opportunity for internal maneuvering and bargaining is greatly reduced in situations affecting national security. The need for consensus behind the President's course of action is a powerful stimulus to close ranks. This facilitates formalization. In addition, the sheer volume of information that must be processed in the national security policy realm requires a considerable amount of systematization. Also, since most Presidents find they must devote the bulk of their time and attention to national security policy, and some prefer to do so anyway, there are strong pressures toward formalized staffing.

It should be apparent, however, that not all of these factors work with the same intensity, and that they may work against each other in any given presidency. For example, Kennedy's strong foreign policy orientation, a formalizing influence, was apparently overcome by the steady flow of crises and by anti-formal personal preferences and traits. Thus, it is difficult to estimate precisely the degree of structural formality in recent administrations. It is possible on the basis of scholarly studies, however, to locate them in a rough ordering that gives some idea of relative formalization.

FIGURE 1

Formalization of Staffing Arrangements in Modern Presidential Administrations

Roosevelt	*Kennedy*	*Johnson*	*Truman*	*Nixon*	*Eisenhower*
Highly Informal		Mixed			Highly Formal

The intervals between the Administrations are proximate and some may quarrel with the position of the Johnson and Truman Administrations near the middle of the scale. Yet it can be said with some confidence that the Roosevelt and Eisenhower Administrations mark the opposite extremities of the continuum, that the Kennedy and Nixon Administrations are next in the degree of staffing informality and formality respectively, and that the Johnson and Truman Administrations do fall in the midsection with the former tending toward somewhat more informality.

The consequences of the level of staffing formalization are mixed. Both highly formal and extremely informal arrangements have accompanying costs and benefits for the President who adopts them. The principal advantage claimed for formally structured policy formulation lies in the comprehensive codification of decisions which results in increased presidential control of the bureaucracy and provides a basis for common understanding of policy goals and programs. It is also argued that a formal approach results in the more systematic, careful decisional processes that are essential to the management of large bureaucracies. The primary costs of formalization are asserted to be the loss of flexibility of action, premature closure of policy options, and the ultimate triumph of technique over purpose. It should be emphasized that no President will adopt a completely formal or informal approach to staffing. There is a considerable built-in tendency to formalization in the structures and routines of the component elements of the Executive Office, e.g., the budgetary process, that cannot be abandoned for both practical and legal reasons. Likewise, there is such a continual flow of crises and new problems that no amount of systematic contingency planning or routinization can obviate the necessity for at least occasional resort to *ad hoc* policy guidance. But within fairly broad parameters a President may secure advice and information in a variety of ways. As noted above, much depends on the President's interests and style, but since it is not possible to measure let alone predict those qualities with any degree of confidence, I will focus the analysis that follows on the control of staffing for policy formulation through structural forms and institutionalized procedures.

B. Information and Advisers in the Government Context. Advising Presidents is complicated by the nature of the information process in government. That process has been characterized as "institutionalized self-deception." [3] This condition arises from two factors: the hierarchical structure of bureaucracy and the adversary nature of American politics. The men in the higher echelons require information—facts and arguments—to defend themselves against attack. Their subordinates and their staffs undertake to provide it to them. In order to serve their chiefs and to protect themselves, advisers and information sources inside the government tend to make their presentations in the most favorable light possible. The result is that "a kind of propitiatory optimism creeps into government reports" and "what is taken to be true, therefore, is what it is politically desirable to believe." It is incumbent on top officials, Frankel concludes, to recognize this flaw in governmental communications and to develop corrective instruments that will introduce a measure of skepticism to the decision-making process sufficient to insure more balanced judgments. One of the most effective and widely utilized correctives is seeking advice from outsiders, particularly from the so-called "experts." This practice also has its limitations, however.

Outside advisers, especially intellectuals and/or technical experts, encounter substantial difficulties in attempting to challenge the criteria that are the basis of existing policies. True, they bring to their task prestige, extensive information, intensive experience, and perspectives grounded more in theory and first principles than pragmatic compromises with perceived reality. But these assets are fragile and are accompanied by liabilities. Laski has warned that in the political realm, expertise runs the danger of sacrificing "the insight of common sense to the intensity of experience." [4] Since experts often lack humility and broad perspective, Laski argues that they can only make a valuable contribution to government if they can manage to relate their judgments to the values and aspirations of the public. Also, experts should take care not to oversell their advice. This is perhaps particularly applicable to social scientists whose theories and understanding of human behavior are limited—in spite of extensive information and sophisticated research. Yet, in an effort not to appear incompetent when asked for advice, they will often make recommendations that are either unrealistic or politically infeasible when the wiser course of action would be merely to suggest what common

---

[3] C. Frankel, *High On Foggy Bottom* 80 (1969). Frankel, a distinguished philosopher, served from July 1965, until December 1967, as Assistant Secretary of State for Cultural Affairs. This discussion draws upon his incisive account of his bureaucratic experience.

[4] Laski, "The Limitations of the Expert," in *The Intellectuals* 167 (G. De Huszer ed. 1960).

sense dictates. Kissinger, in a perceptive discussion,[5] asserts that the central problem that the intellectual faces when called upon for advice is that his contribution is invoked and utilized in terms of bureaucratically determined criteria. He thus finds that he may be providing information that becomes the basis for endorsing and legitimizing existing policies rather than serving as the basis for judgment regarding the efficacy of those and alternative policies. In addition, the intellectual must be careful not to formulate his contribution so abstractly as to destroy its value to the political leaders who requested it. The challenge to the intellectual whose expertise is invoked is, therefore, to reconcile "two loyalties: to the organization that employs him and to values which transcend the bureaucratic framework and provide his basic motivation." Most of all, the intellectual who serves the government must retain his independence and his disinterestedness. It is no easy task to accomplish, but the effort must be made as long as the advice of intellectuals and experts is essential to effective leadership in policy formulation.

The information process in government is also complicated in its efforts to incorporate expertise effectively by the extensive reliance placed upon committees as vehicles for coordinating advice, synthesizing information, and framing proposals. Kissinger states that reliance on committees arises from the lack of substantive competence by high-level political executives. As policy is identified with committee consensus it loses any sense of direction and becomes a matter of adjustments to the lowest common denominator. Committees, asserts Kissinger, emphasize conversation and fluency rather than reflectiveness and creativeness. They tend to suppress disagreement in the quest for consensus which most often favors the familiarity of the *status quo.* In their normal functioning, committees, whether they are composed of government officials or outside experts, are subject to substantial weaknesses. They cannot provide top leaders with the sense of purpose that will enable those officials to make effective use of the committee system. So far it has not been possible to develop a presidential advisory and information system that overcomes the limitations of governmental information processes, including the defects of committees. This analysis of presidential staffing devices will consider their potential for resolving such problems.

II. THE VARIOUS ADVISORY MECHANISMS

The President obtains advice and information from the presidency itself, the executive branch, Congress, and the public. The utilization and evaluation of this "intelligence" is accomplished through four principal mech-

[5] H. Kissinger, *The Necessity for Choice* ch. 8 (1960).

anisms: the Cabinet and its appurtenant committees, the Office of Management and Budget, the White House staff, and a variety of presidential advisory groups including task forces, councils, commissions, conferences, and committees. These advisory devices are not arrayed in a neat series of concentric institutional rings around the President. There is often overlap between the channels of the devices so that information flows from one to the other or it may be simultaneously processed by two or more of them. The utilization of specific advisory mechanisms is in part a function of their proximity to the President, but it is also determined by his relationships with individual advisers and their access to him. Although this analysis of advisory mechanisms has an institutional focus, it is undertaken with a recognition of the importance of individual interaction between the President and his advisers.

A. *The Cabinet.* The advent of a new national administration is always heralded by extensive speculation concerning the composition of the Cabinet. This speculation usually centers on leading members of the President's party, but it takes into consideration certain criteria of appointment designed to give the Cabinet a broadly representative character. For example, the Secretary of the Interior is traditionally a Westerner, Agriculture goes to a farm state figure, the Attorney General must be a lawyer, and Commerce and Treasury are usually filled by men from the business community. Not infrequently the President-elect has announced his determination to utilize the collective talents of his Cabinet, which of course will include "the best men the nation has to offer," in the conduct of his administration. The Cabinet, it is promised, will become a meaningful instrument of leadership and not a ceremonial organ with little functional value. By implication the previous administration failed to utilize the Cabinet's great potential as an advisory council for high-level policy formulation. With equally predictable frequency, the new President finds after no more than a few months in office that the Cabinet is hardly a suitable vehicle for collective decision-making. Its value, as a collectivity, is more symbolic than operational; as an institutional embodiment of the representational scope of the administration rather than an instrument of collective choice.

The problem that Presidents encounter when they attempt to utilize the Cabinet is that it is a far more suitable means of consolidating and extending political strength than of advising with respect to policy development. It is an aggregation of highest level presidential advisers, but not a viable high-level advisory group. This condition is a consequence and reflection of the "pluralistic conditions of departmental growth and of Cabinet appointment." [6] Cabinet departments developed over time to

---

[6] R. Fenno, *The President's Cabinet* 131 (1959).

perform a variety of functions in response to the felt needs of many divergent groups. This pattern of growth encouraged the departments to act more or less independently of each other. The selection of Cabinet members on the basis of geographic and clientele interests encourages in Cabinet members a particularistic loyalty to their subordinates and to their clientele groups that competes with loyalty to the President. This conflict of loyalties works against the formation of any informal sense of mutual responsibility. But without a "sense of corporate unity and common purpose," the Cabinet's potential as an advisory body cannot be realized.

The President can, and frequently does attempt to build support through individual Cabinet members and their departments. But even this use of the Cabinet is limited by the conflict of loyalties. To the extent that Presidents choose Cabinet members who will be unbending in their fealty to him, they risk weakening the supportive potential of the appointments. The departmental pressures that impinge on Cabinet members are so strong, however, that they "may make even a personal supporter act as the President's 'natural enemy' when he heads a major department." [7] The resignation of Health, Education and Welfare Secretary Robert Finch in May, 1970 provides a contemporary illustration of this old problem. A close personal friend and long-time political associate of President Nixon, Finch experienced great difficulty in reconciling his intense personal loyalty to the President with the expectations of the HEW bureaucracy and the demands of its clientele. His seventeen month tenure as Secretary was marked by his refusal to exploit his relationship with the President on behalf of his departmental constituency and that constituency's consequent disenchantment with him. When Finch left the Cabinet it was to assume a position on the White House staff as a counsellor to the President that was more compatible with their special relationship.

The Finch case raises the question of the degree to which it is possible for Cabinet members to be the President's men. While no President can tolerate a Cabinet in which all members regularly choose departmental over presidential interests. it is also true that unquestioning loyalty to the President is equally dysfunctional. What is called for is a Cabinet-presidential relationship that is "at once highly autonomous and deeply responsive."

The unsuitability of the Cabinet as an advisory mechanism does not mean, however, that the President is not dependent on his department heads for advice. But the advice and political assistance which Cabinet members can provide must come from them as individual political actors of considerable standing. As the head of a large bureaucracy with sub-

[7] D. Truman, *The Governmental Process* 406 (1951).

stantial information gathering and evaluating capabilities, with at least some independent sources of power, the Cabinet member has resources that are valuable to the President. They can be utilized in various ways. Cabinet members are usually consulted extensively regarding the development of presidential policies in their areas of activity. They participate in the development of legislative proposals for their departments and in deliberations that lead to the formulation of the President's legislative proposals. Frequently Cabinet members serve on interdepartmental committees and task forces that formulate policies and resolve differences between agencies. Also, depending on their departments, Cabinet members serve on either the National Security Council or the newly established Domestic Council.

There is, then, a substantial amount of unified presidential policy control over departments and agencies, but it is not achieved through the Cabinet. It arises through the use of other instruments and through direct relationships between the President and individual Cabinet members. In this latter regard, the Cabinet official often acts as a broker between the President and his staff and the bureaucracy and its clientele. Occasionally a Cabinet member may become a close confidant of the President on policy matters that range beyond the jurisdiction of his own department. In such instances, mutual respect and attraction permit the Cabinet member to be more than a formal adviser. The cases of Attorneys General Robert Kennedy in his brother's Administration and John Mitchell in the Nixon Administration illustrate this type of relationship. In all cases, however, a Cabinet member is only as important as the President wants him to be. The influential men in the Cabinet will shift depending on presidential preferences and values and external circumstances.

In the final analysis, it is necessary to look at devices below and beyond the Cabinet to understand fully the dynamics of presidential intelligence for policy formulation. Cabinet members are major participants in the policy-making process in their roles as heads of executive departments and by virtue of individual personal and political resources and not as members of a group of top level advisers. But the Cabinet member is more than a presidential staff resource or personal adviser. He is the principal political executive in his particular policy arena. In this capacity he often speaks for the administration. Neustadt's remarks on the role of the Secretary of State are particularly instructive regarding the situation of the Cabinet member:

> The Secretary has work of his own, resources of his own, vistas of his own. He is in business under his own name and in his name powers are exercised, decisions taken. Therefore he can press his personal authority, his own opinion, his adviser's role, wherever he sees fit across the whole contemporary reach of foreign relations . . . his status and

> the tasks of his Department give him every right to raise his voice where, when and as he chooses.

The Cabinet member draws much of his advisory strength from his departmental responsibilities; yet he cannot devote himself too extensively to running his department, else important policy choices will be made with little input from him.

The inefficacy of the Cabinet as a formal advisory mechanism and as a policy-making body does not obviate the need for collective action at some point in the process. Differences in perspective and objectives are bound to exist between agencies. Somewhere, not too far removed from the President, there must be a means of identifying alternatives, clarifying goals, and settling upon compatible courses of action. In short, policy coordination is necessary. Given the phenomena of departmentalism and of social and political pluralism, that coordination can only be secured through committees or through routinized procedures. It cannot be obtained by presidential fiat.

Cabinet-level committees for policy-making and policy coordination include those appointed to deal with a specific subject or problem, such as the Cabinet committees on economic policy and on environmental quality, and formal policy councils like the National Security Council (NSC) that are established by law or executive order and that operate with sizeable staff support. The most widely utilized means of securing coordination, however, is the interagency committee which generally operates at the sub-cabinet and agency head level.

Cabinet committees can be an effective means of handling a specific situation or policy problem. They can focus attention on it quickly and have flexibility in developing situations. But they are limited by other demands and claims made on their members. If Cabinet committees are provided with supportive staffs of significant size they quickly tend to become routinized operations and to lose the sense of urgency and the flexibility that justified their initial establishment. Cabinet committees that acquire permanent status tend to lose their high initial visibility and also their capacity to hold the attention of their members. They become one of many groups operating in the presidential arena. The committee that President Nixon established to facilitate school desegregation illustrates the problems encountered by a continuing Cabinet-level committee. The committee was chaired by the Vice President and included the Attorney General, the Secretary of HEW, and a number of subordinate officials. Because desegregation involves unsettled questions of constitutional interpretation and is a highly sensitive issue, the committee has not been able to develop a uniform national policy. Presidential statements on the subject have reflected the differing approaches of the Justice Department and HEW. Continuing controversy has forced the committee into the background.

B. The National Security Council. An important institutional participant in the presidential advisory system is the National Security Council, a body which "constitutes the most ambitious effort yet made to coordinate policy on the Cabinet level." Since its establishment the NSC has been both central and peripheral to the formulation of national security policy. A review of the uses that Presidents have made of the NSC reveals the alternative ways of allocating responsibility for policy planning and coordination in his crucial area.

President Truman saw the NSC, which was established by the National Security Act of 1947, as a necessary facility for study, analysis, and the development of policy recommendations. Truman did not, however, regard it as a policy-making body. He was concerned lest the NSC encroach on his constitutional powers and thus he did not meet with it until the Korean war began. Even with its increased activity and status after that point, the NSC was no more than a convenient staffing mechanism with a limited policy-making role.

In sharp contrast, President Eisenhower expanded the NSC into a comprehensive policy system. He regarded the council as a top level forum for vigorous discussion of carefully prepared policy papers. These NSC discussions contained statements of divergent interpretations and approaches and ultimately produced resolutions of the issues. The NSC was, in Eisenhower's view, a corporate body of advisers rather than a group of departmental and agency spokesmen. He chaired NSC meetings and led discussions of papers prepared by the Planning Board, one of the two staff arms of the Council. The other staff unit, the Operations Coordinating Board, concerned itself with problems of policy implementation. After a subject had been raised for NSC consideration by anyone from the President on down in the system, an analysis would be conducted under the direction of the Planning Board and involving the agency with the major interest in it. Eventually a policy paper would come before the Council for discussion and action. Once approved, NSC policy actions were sent to the departments and agencies for execution under the direction of the Operations Coordinating Board. The process has been described as a "policy hill" with the NSC at the summit and policies moving up the formulative side through the Planning Board and down the implementation side through the Operations Coordinating Board to the departments. The NSC also dealt with current policy matters, although smaller groups of officials usually handled important issues.

President Eisenhower's NSC staff system imposed a comprehensive framework of order on all aspects of national security affairs. Its defenders argued that it insured that the President would receive all relevant information and points of view, that it provided a reservoir of policy guidance, and that it afforded rational coordination of policy formulation and execution. Its critics charged that the system was so ponderous that it was incapable of responding effectively to emergencies or of developing new policy departures. It was asserted that the NSC system rigidified an incremental approach in a policy arena where flexibility was of great value. Furthermore, the critics claimed, the system purchased consensus at the price of ambiguity. Differences were said to be papered over with vague policy statements that had no value as guides to action.

The alleged defects of President Eisenhower's NSC system were highlighted in a senatorial inquiry conducted by Senator Henry M. Jackson (D-Wash.) during 1960 and 1961.[8] The Jackson subcommittee made a series of proposals that would have "deinstitutionalized" the system. It recommended that the Council be a smaller group, limited in membership to top officials and meeting only to advise on critical issues and problems. The support staffs would be abolished and their functions reassigned. Finally, the subcommittee suggested that the Secretary of State take the lead in formulating national security policy and that coordination of policy implementation be accomplished by an action officer or an informal interdepartmental committee.

President Kennedy, acting along the lines proposed by the Jackson committee, proceeded to dismantle most of the Eisenhower NSC system. All that remained was the statutory council consisting of the President, Vice President, the Secretaries of State and Defense, and the Director of the Office of Emergency Planning, and a small staff headed by McGeorge Bundy, the Special Assistant for National Security Affairs. The Council was but one of many ways of solving problems and President Kennedy consulted its members more often individually than collectively. The NSC staff became involved in various activities and was a major source of information for the President. It worked closely with the bureaucracy, the Bureau of the Budget, and the Office of Science and Technology. Its principal task was to identify and manage issues. When it became apparent that the State Department was unable to assume the major responsibility for initiating and coordinating national security policy, the NSC staff assumed much of that important role.

The NSC itself was primarily used to consider long term policy problems that could be dealt with through planning. The NSC staff worked more directly for the President than for the Council. It concentrated on the action oriented processes that President Kennedy's approach to foreign affairs required. The Eisenhower distinction between planning

---

[8] Subcomm. on National Policy Machinery of the Senate Comm. on Government Operations, 86th Cong., 2d Sess., *Organizing for National Security* (Comm. Print 1960).

and operations was abolished in favor of a commitment to action with policy serving as the rationale.

The abrupt transition from the Kennedy to the Johnson Administration was marked by the new President's desire to minimize the shock of the assassination. Gradually a distinctive Johnson pattern emerged. It was characterized by the President's reduced dependence on the national security staff in dealing with the bureaucracy and by increased reliance on the State Department for policy coordination. The NSC met fairly often, but rarely to consider major current issues. More important to presidential policy formulation were weekly luncheon meetings, held on Tuesdays, of the President and selected top officials. These informal gatherings served as vehicles for making key decisions, receiving advice, and establishing policy guidance. The informality of the meetings permitted an extensive interchange of viewpoints and stimulated a flow of information, but they were defective in that items often arose without advance staff work and no record of decisions was kept.

The Johnson presidency was one in which the President received a heavy flow of information through personal contacts and written memoranda. His responses, usually transmitted verbally by the Special Assistant for National Security or the NSC staff, served as guidelines for the bureaucracy. But there was no mechanism for locating issues and centralizing their management. The President disposed of most issues on the basis of memoranda processed by the Special Assistant. Decisions were made after discussions with a wide range of individuals in and outside of the government. There was, however, "no predictable pattern to such consultation. . . . At the end a decision emerged."

In order to reduce the need for the NSC staff to function as an *ad hoc* interdepartmental coordinator, President Johnson delegated to the Secretary of State, in National Security Action Memorandum 341 of March 1966, responsibility for "over-all direction, coordination, and supervision of interdepartmental activities." The vehicles for accomplishing this mission were the Senior Interdepartmental Group (SIG) headed by the Undersecretary of State and Interdepartmental Regional Groups (IRG's) headed by assistant secretaries of state. The operational consequences of this system were not as intended. Whenever the President or the NSC staff assumed control, as they did with respect to most critical issues, "the existence of the system was of little significance."

President Johnson's approach to national security policy had two distinguishing characteristics—informality and heavy reliance on the NSC staff under the direction of the Special Assistant. The NSC staff was not actively involved in policy initiation, however. What it did was act as an intermediary and brokerage agent for the President, offering advice and providing support when required. The President retained much direct power over national security matters in his own hands, leaving largely to chance and his personal resources the formulation of coherent and rationally interrelated policies.

It is somewhat premature to speak with certainty about the Nixon Administration's arrangements for managing national security policy. President Nixon appears to have concluded that a substantial National Security Council staff under the direction of his Special Assistant, Henry Kissinger, and the reestablishment of the formal NSC system are both necessary. The Kissinger staff, considerably expanded and more formalized than its predecessors, plays a major role in coordinating interdepartmental policy planning. The NSC has been reactivated as "the principal forum for presidential consideration of foreign policy issues." [9] The NSC met 37 times in 1969 and considered over 20 major problems. It operates in a manner similar to the Eisenhower NSC only without the formal staff units. Initial policy analyses are prepared by Interdepartmental Groups chaired by an assistant secretary of state. (These resemble the IRG's of the Johnson Administration.) Then an interagency review group of senior officials, which is chaired by Kissinger, examines the papers "to insure that the issues, options, and views are presented fully and fairly." Finally, the matter under consideration is presented to the President and the NSC.

Nixon's NSC system seeks to involve all relevant agencies in a process that insures that the President and the Council have all the available pertinent information. It obtains a measure of flexibility through special interagency groups, such as the Verification Panel in the area of strategic arms limitation and the Vietnam Special Studies Group. It makes provision for crisis planning and management through a special group of high officials, the Washington Special Actions Group.

The Nixon NSC system combines White House and departmentally centered control of policy formulation through use of both a sizeable NSC staff and interagency groups. It relies on systematic formal procedures but seeks to retain flexibility through special committees. Most significantly, according to the President, it is built upon a realistic appraisal of the tasks that it faces.

C. The Domestic Council. As Wildavsky has observed, there are two presidencies, one concerned with national security policy, the other with domestic affairs.[10] Substantial differences distinguish the two policy realms. In national security policy, events often move at a rapid pace with potentially grave consequences. Very little that happens can be dismissed as inconsequential and actions may be irreversible once taken.

---

[9] Report by President Nixon to the Congress, "U.S. Foreign Policy for the 1970's: A New Strategy for Peace," in 116 *Cong. Rec.* H927 (daily ed. Feb. 18, 1970).

[10] Wildavsky, "The Two Presidencies," *Trans-Action,* December, 1966, at 7. This discussion draws on Wildavsky's excellent analysis.

In domestic affairs, policy decisions are usually incremental adjustments in previous courses of action. Major policy changes occur only infrequently and then only after prolonged pressure and deliberations or in periods of crisis. Most domestic policy decisions are reversible; if they fail to meet the pragmatic test of results, something else will be tried. Another difference involves presidential control over policy. As a matter of constitutional and practical necessity Presidents have greater discretion in national security matters. There are fewer rivals for policy control and the ability of those rivals to obtain and use information is much less than in domestic affairs. The range of options and competitors is much broader in the domestic realm where interest groups and Congress possess greater capacity to bargain with the President. Wildavsky calculates that in the period 1948–64, positive congressional responses to presidential initiatives were almost twice as great in national security matters as in domestic affairs.

The differences between the two policy realms have resulted in contrasting staffing patterns. National security policy formulation has transpired with the benefit of the elaborate intelligence capabilities of the Central Intelligence Agency and the armed services and with the support of the NSC and its staff. There has been no comparable formalization of structure and process in the domestic arena. Coordination of policy formulation has been a responsibility of many agents: the Bureau of the Budget, the Council of Economic Advisers, the Office of Science and Technology, and more recently, the councils on rural and urban affairs, as well as devices such as interagency task forces, the concept of a lead agency, and reliance on individual presidential assistants. There has been an informal and often unsystematic approach to policy formulation as compared with the national security policy arena. To the extent that there has been a coordinating force, it has been provided by the budget bureau. But the Bureau was never intended to function as a top level policy council that considered proposals for action after careful staffing had been completed. Rather, it was a staff agency with about 500 career professionals that cleared legislation drafted in the bureaucracy, analyzed proposals emanating from the departments, agencies, and other sources, and prepared the budget. All this was done with a view to maintaining the integrity of the President's overall program.

The pattern of domestic policy coordination has varied between administrations. For example, President Johnson utilized a small staff headed by Joseph A. Califano, a presidential assistant. President Kennedy assigned responsibility to a group of his White House staff aides with special assignments to his brother. Under President Eisenhower, Sherman Adams, acting in the manner of a military chief of staff, personally directed the process of domestic policy coordination. President Nixon, after a year in office and on recommendation from his Advisory Council on

Executive Organization, established the Domestic Council through Reorganization Plan No. 2 of 1970. The Domestic Council is composed of the President, the Vice President, the Attorney General, the Secretaries of Agriculture, Commerce, HEW, HUD, Interior, Labor, Transportation, and Treasury, and other officials as may be deemed appropriate on an *ad hoc* basis. The Council is to have a staff of professional experts and is headed by a presidential assistant whom the President designates as its executive director.

At this writing, the Domestic Council is still establishing its procedures and recruiting its staff. The pattern of its operations is not sufficiently clear to permit a description, let alone an analysis, to be made. However, the rationale for the Council and the Administration's expectations for it were made quite explicit in the House hearings on the reorganization plan. According to Roy L. Ash, the chairman of the Advisory Council on Executive Reorganization, the major organizational premise was that presidential staff functions for policy and program formulation should be separated from those for program implementation and administration. This reaffirmation of the old politics-administration dichotomy, which academicians had thoroughly discredited by the early 1950's, rested on the belief that it was "unsound" to have the same organization perform both functions because different kinds of information, skills, and attitudes are required for each and because policy formulation requires a longer time perspective and is less subject to daily pressures than implementation is. Such a formal separation of functions characterized the NSC system under President Eisenhower, but it had not previously been employed in presidential staffing for domestic affairs. Its effectiveness remains to be demonstrated. It does recognize the increased necessity for effective program evaluation and the complexities of program implementation.

The Ash commission envisioned the Domestic Council as "a way to bring together under one roof many, but not necessarily all, of the sources for developing domestic policy." It is intended to provide a more effective means than reliance on interagency task forces and informal contact by the White House staff of bringing necessary information and opinions to the President and of resolving interagency disputes. The Domestic Council formalizes previous arrangements which, according to the Ash commission, were random and haphazard. The staff will gather information, analyze issues, and present the Council with opposing lines of reasoning. The task of the staff will be to make certain that policy alternatives have been fully presented so that the President and the Council can make informed, rational choices. It is anticipated that the President and the Council will act with a "common data base" developed by the staff. The Ash commission realized that Presidents will vary in their utilization of the Domestic Council. Its expectation was, however, that the Council will prove to be a useful managerial tool that increases the President's control over policy formulation and reduces somewhat the time required to achieve it.

The establishment of a domestic analogue to the NSC raises several questions. Although the Domestic Council staff is supposedly to refrain from reconciling any issues in its analyses, is it realistic to expect that the staff will not have a major substantive impact on policy? Such an impact can perhaps be minimized if recruitment is on professional grounds. But the pressures to insist on political criteria will be great if not overpowering. The establishment of a technical career staff comparable to that of the former Bureau of the Budget seems unlikely. One of the advantages of the Bureau was its devotion to the needs of the presidency. This was made possible, at least in part, by its separation from the political pressures of the White House. The Domestic Council—if it is to be the high-level forum for discussion, debate, and ultimate policy determination that its creators envision—will operate in closer proximity to the President. It will necessarily have a highly political staff. Can this staff provide a continuing institutional memory for domestic affairs?

A second set of questions pertain to the Domestic Council's relationships with other presidential staff units, with the bureaucracy, and with Congress. At the reorganization hearings, Representative Chet Holifield (D-Calif.) argued that the Council would become a barrier between the President and the new Office of Management and Budget (OMB). This would downgrade the OMB, Holifield reasoned, since the policy functions formerly exercised by the budget bureau would be performed by the Council staff. Furthermore, Holifield feared, that staff will be unavailable to Congress and yet be able to affect the decisions of the OMB. The question of congressional-Domestic Council staff relations remains to be determined. The role of the OMB in policy formulation does appear likely to be substantially reduced. The OMB will no longer participate in formulating legislative proposals and following them through. The useful feedback of program results and knowledge of program defects that enabled the budget bureau's program divisions to help the bureaucracy develop amendments to existing legislation and to formulate new legislative proposals will be channeled to a different policy staff. Raymond Saulnier, who served as chairman of the Council of Economic Advisers (CEA) during the Eisenhower Administration, raised objections at the hearings to the absence of the Budget Director and the Chairman of the CEA from the Council's statutory membership. He argued that this would deprive the Domestic Council of the "intimate knowledge of budget resources and demands" and the CEA's special competence in economic matters. He recommended that the CEA be assigned responsibility for staffing Domestic Council agenda items in its area. Whether the importance of the OBM, CEA, and other staff units will be lessened is an unanswered question. Their status may be jeopardized by the new arrangement, but it is too early to make such a judgment.

Finally, it is unclear how the existence of the Domestic Council will affect interagency relations and agency access to the President. The department heads will undoubtedly have access to him through the Council and also directly as in the past. But their subordinates will not have these points of contact. Agency heads and subcabinet officers will have to deal with the Council staff on matters involving policy formulation and with the OMB on matters of budget and policy implementation. To the extent that the OMB retains its former policy formulation roles, there will be duplication of effort (with the risk of considerable confusion) and the rationale for the reorganization will be defeated. There is also a question regarding access to the White House. In the Johnson and Kennedy Administrations, presidential assistants served as points of contact for agencies and interest groups and acted as brokers between the White House, the bureaucracy, Congress, and the attentive public. For example, Douglass Cater was President Johnson's liaison man for educational policy. Even after two years of the Nixon presidency, there is still (in early 1971) great uncertainty regarding the points of contact. The Domestic Council may increase rather than reduce the communication gap between the White House and the bureaucracy, especially below the Cabinet level. The Council and its staff may isolate the President rather than bring him closer to the operational problems of domestic politics as intended.

The Domestic Council is, then, a major but uncertain factor in presidential policy formulation. Ideally it will prove to be an effective staffing arrangement that permits the administration to arrive at the "best solution after weighing carefully all viable choices." On the other hand, it could become a rigidified policy control structure that impedes initiative, blocks alternatives, stifles originality, and is incapable of quick, flexible responses. The best guess is that its performance will fall between these two stools.

D. Office of Management and Budget. As every student of American government learns in the introductory course, the Bureau of the Budget (BOB) did far more than prepare the annual presidential budget. It had a major responsibility for coordinating and safeguarding the integrity of the President's overall program. It had an impact on policy formulation through the preparation of budget requests for departments and agencies, the clearance of all views expressed by federal agencies on pending legislation, review and evaluation of legislative proposals originating in the bureaucracy, and coordination of the process of developing and preparing presidential legislative proposals. In performing its duties, the budget bureau worked closely with the bureaucracy. It developed a professional expertise of its own based on substantive knowledge acquired over time and committed to serving the President. In recent years, BOB played a key role in staffing and organizing the work of presidential advisory groups. Bureau officials served on advisory committees or their staffs, the Bureau analyzed advisory committee reports and recommendations, it participated in high-level consideration of those reports, and it was the mechanism for linking committee proposals and other suggestions for policy change to the annual budgetary process.

Operating with no constituency other than the President, BOB provided objective staff assistance over time. Its biases were those of professional careerists in public service. Bureau officials developed a skeptical attitude toward other participants in the policy process—bureaucrats, congressmen and their staffs, and pressure group representatives—and they routinely challenged all suggestions and ideas in the context of their conception of the President's program goals. The Bureau did not, however, serve as a source of information. It was an institutional screen through which all kinds of information and advice was filtered and assayed in terms of its value to the President and his program.

The changes instituted under Reorganization Plan No. 2 will undoubtedly affect the central role of BOB in policy formulation. The emphasis in the new OMB is more on management than on policy development. The Domestic Council and its staff will presumably assume many of the functions formerly performed by BOB. This shift occurred in the realm of national security policy in 1947. It is too soon to determine if OMB's domestic policy role will parallel the rather limited one that it has played with respect to national security matters. Certainly the domestic policy format will be different. Decisions which Budget Bureau officials and White House staff members formerly made apart from department heads will presumably be made in a forum that includes them as principal participants. OMB will be involved but as a supportive staff whose major concern is with costs and with implementation. However well these changes work in practice, it is their clear objective to reduce the significance of the budget staff in presidential policy formulation and to utilize it more extensively as a device for coordinating and rationalizing the implementation of policy. Given the great value of BOB to Presidents since Roosevelt it is, in my judgment, questionable whether the revision of its mission and the consequent separation of policy formulation from implementation will "enable the President to have more facts and better options at his disposal when he makes his decisions." It is doubtful if structured enforcement of the politics-administration dichotomy will endure and, if it does survive, whether presidential policy leadership will be enhanced rather than weakened.

E. The Inner Circle and White House Staff Advisers. The absence of formal institutional support for the President in Congress, the fragmented parochialism of the bureaucracy, and the lack of an integrating party structure grounded in an ideology combine to make the task of leadership in policy formulation one of bargaining and manipulation. As Neustadt has so aptly stated, "presidential power is the power to persuade." In approaching the task of policy leadership, modern Presidents have depended heavily on the group of friends, counsellors, secretaries, and other aides who constitute the White House Staff and on an informal inner circle of close associates and confidants. These two sets of advisers are continuously and directly involved with him in the formulation of policy. They have some overlapping members and their composition and operational pattern varies between administrations and over time within a single presidency.

Inner circles, which have also been referred to as "kitchen cabinets," "the invisible presidency," and similar terms, tend to be comprised of a few key White House staff members, one or two Cabinet members who enjoy the special confidence of the President, and occasionally a few personal friends of the President. There is a tendency to attribute great power to these intimate presidential advisers and they no doubt have exercised considerable (but indeterminate) influence over recent Presidents. For example, John Foster Dulles and Sherman Adams apparently predominated over all other advisers to President Eisenhower for the first several years of his presidency. The intimate personal and intellectual relationship between President Kennedy and his brother Robert is well known. And President Johnson placed great reliance on two of his Cabinet members, Secretaries Rusk and McNamara. Although interaction between the President and his informal inner circle is a central feature of policy formulation, it is necessary to guard against overemphasizing this phenomenon. There exists a collective presidential decision-making process that is not so much the work of a few individuals as the organized effort of many groups including the inner circle, the White House staff, OMB, and a host of presidential advisory committees. Furthermore, national policy-making may center in the presidency, but it involves a considerable number of political elites in different policy areas. These elites, which overlap only occasionally, participate actively with the presidency in shaping national policy.

The innner circle provides the President with broad gauge advice on critical policy choices that is unrestrained by departmental, agency, or pressure group interests. It is held together by a mutual bond: the President's need for advisers who share his values and goals but who can broaden his perspective and the advisers' capacity and desire to meet that need. Membership in the inner circle is prestigious (despite Brownlow's plea for men with "a passion for anonymity") but it may be short-lived. The tasks that its members perform are demanding, and the President's needs and preferences change. According to Seligman, inner circle members function as "buffers," "catalysts," "liaison men," "fixers," "needlers," "communications experts," "policy advisers," and "sometime ideologists." Its members may be selected because of their ability to perform tasks for which the President is unsuited. In this respect, the inner circle complements the President's personality. It compensates for his limitations.

The White House staff, which usually includes some inner circle members, is larger and more formalized. The President enjoys great freedom in setting up his office and selecting his staff, but its functions are fairly well established. Its primary job is to furnish the President with sufficient information and analysis to permit him to make decisions with an awareness of the available alternatives and their probable consequences. The specific tasks of the White House staff include press relations and communications, speechwriting, congressional liaison, pressure group and general public liaison, management of the President's schedule, and policy advice and counsel.

The management of press relations and communications is crucial to building and maintaining a favorable presidential image. The persons who perform these tasks, however, seldom manage to exert influence on major decisions. Their advice relates to tactical rather than strategic matters. Speech writers are also involved in presidential communications. Their role affords them the opportunity to exert some influence on substantive policy decisions, but only to the extent that the President has confidence in the judgment of the individual speech writer. For instance, Theodore Sorensen was one of President Kennedy's principal speech writers. His style, tone, and ideas merged with those of his chief so that they were often indistinguishable. On the other hand, the identity of President Nixon's wordsmiths is virtually unknown. They remain anonymous White House artisans who mold presidential addresses to specifications determined by their superiors.

Presidential liaison with Congress and with pressure groups is a White House staff function of twofold importance. It shapes the scope and content of input from Congress and pressure groups to the policy-making process and it affects the level of support for the President's policy goals. Failure to involve congressional leaders adequately at a sufficiently early stage can spell the defeat of the President's legislative program. As a practical political matter, congressional sentiment must be assessed and congressional leaders consulted in determining the administration's policy agenda. The operating responsibilities of the congressional liaison staff include presenting the administration's position on legislation to individual congressmen, coordinating and directing the administration's legislative program on Capitol Hill, gathering information, including congressional sentiment, analyzing legislative issues, assessing the potential impact of presidential statements and actions, and performing auxiliary services for members of Congress. Under Presidents Eisenhower and

Nixon congressional liaison has been a line operation somewhat removed from direct access to the Chief Executive. Their liaison staff directors, Wilton Persons and William Timmons, did not enjoy direct access to them. The policy impact of the liaison staff under these circumstances has come from its assessments of probable congressional opinion and actions. Under Presidents Kennedy and Johnson, congressional liaison occupied a more central position in the White House staff. With Lawrence O'Brien, a skilled political tactician, directing the lobbying staff, congressional relations were significantly upgraded, although it took O'Brien and his team some time to master their work. Both Democratic Presidents worked directly with O'Brien in shaping the content of their legislative programs as well as in developing legislative strategy. While all Presidents are dependent on their liaison staffs to shepherd legislation through Congress, the role of that staff in policy-making varies substantially. All presidential lobbyists are agents, salesmen, and contact men. They can become advisers and counsellors if the President wishes.

Until the Nixon Administration, liaison with politically important interests was handled by the congressional relations staff and through the practice of assigning primary responsibility for liaison with groups in specific policy areas to presidential assistants. Access to the White House was generally channeled through these individual contact men who acted as brokers between the presidency and the pressure groups. Outside groups knew whom to see if they wished to make a presentation of their views. The assistants who acted as contacts performed these tasks in addition to their other duties. They did not formally coordinate information gathering or the rendition of advice, but were available to groups seeking access. In varying degrees and ways, they filtered the input to the President from external sources. President Nixon, in keeping with his preference for formalizing staffing arrangements, assigned responsibility for contact with organized constituencies to a separate staff. The outside liaison staff acts as a broker between pressure groups and administration policy-makers. The lodging of this responsibility in a special staff is an attempt to improve the scope and content of informational input and to more effectively convert the resources of private interests into support for the President. It has the advantage, from the presidential perspective, of systematizing what previously was a random process. Its disadvantages are not yet clear, but one possible difficulty may stem from the inability of a small liaison staff to develop sufficient familiarity with all policy sectors to be able to deal selectively and effectively with them. The liaison staff may simply become a crew of messenger-errand boys with no function other than to receive and direct communications and to perform special chores such as organizing meetings and checking out presidential appointments. An outside liaison staff with no recognized policy impact could become a liability if pressure groups perceived them as buffers between themselves and the real policy-makers. As with congressional liaison, the President must rely on the White House staff to manage relations with organized constituencies. They have great potential value to him as sources of political leverage but they can also be sources of frustration. Dealing effectively with pressure groups requires a skill and tact that gives them a sense of efficacious involvement in policy formulation. The most appropriate approach to this staff function is not yet apparent.

The management of the President's time is another vital task of the White House staff. There are two dimensions to this function: the screening, condensation, and digesting of information that reaches the President and the control of his schedule. Obviously, time is a most precious presidential resource. No President can read all the memoranda, reports, newspapers, and other printed matter that he should to be ideally well-informed. Therefore, he must attempt to minimize the costs of his ignorance. The White House staff performs this task in accordance with presidential reading habits and tastes, but regardless of its directives it necessarily exercises substantial discretion over what the President reads. There is an inescapable policy impact in this staff function that should be recognized even though it cannot be controlled.

The staff members who manage the President's schedule perform an ancient political task, that of doorkeeper. Since the beginnings of organized government those who guarded the ruler's door have exercised substantial influence and power. Henry Fairlie describes the White House as "pre-eminently a staff of competing doorkeepers," and he argues that the medieval office of chamberlain still exists. The President depends on his schedule makers to reserve his time for those persons and activities which are politically beneficial and to protect him from unnecessary wasting of time. The policy preferences of the President's doorkeepers can determine who sees him and thus, to a degree, exert an influence on his decisions. To minimize the power potential that inheres in their "chamberlains" Presidents have tended to select men whose personal loyalty is unquestioned and whose policy interests are either so limited as to pose no problem or closely identical to those of the President, such as President Nixon's assistant, H. R. Haldeman.

The members of the White House staff also provide the President with policy advice and counsel. (Those who particularly "have his ear" become, by definition, members of the inner circle.) White House staff advisers fall into two general categories. First, there are the experts and intellectuals whose skills, knowledge, and experience make them valuable as idea generators and as evaluators of policy alternatives. Their professional or academic perspectives complement the political outlook of the President. In the early years of the Nixon Administration, Henry Kissinger in national security policy, Daniel Patrick Moynihan in domestic affairs, and Arthur Burns in economic policy furnished this type of advice. The second basic category of White House advisers includes close political associates and personal friends of the President. These are truly the President's men whose main value lies in their ability to perceive an issue or situation in terms of its effect on the President and his political objectives. Their advice and counsel is political and personal. In the Nixon administration, John Erlichman, and Robert Finch, after his departure from HEW, exemplify the close political-personal adviser. Such advice is necessary and essential to a President, but hardly sufficient. It must be combined with expert and professional advice within the White House and with a wide array of external advice and information.

White House staff advisers are a mobile and transient group. Their ranks seldom hold firm as most Presidents move through several sets of advisers in the course of their administrations. In part this is due to the expendability of presidential staffers who not infrequently drop out when policies they have espoused fail or lose favor. It also stems from changing policy goals and situational factors which alter presidential staffing requirements.

F. Presidential Advisory Committees. The formulation of policy in the presidency and the executive branch also involves extensive utilization of advisory committees. A General Accounting Office survey, conducted in late 1969, revealed the existence of 1,573 boards, committees, commissions, panels, councils, conferences, task forces, and other advisory groups. The survey identified 198 "presidential committees," that were so designated when one or more of their members was appointed by the President. These presidential groups are created by statute, executive order, or less formal directive. Their manifest task is to advise and make recommendations, but they perform other functions as well. An analysis of the full range and activity of presidential advisory committees is beyond the scope of this paper. I will limit my discussion to the most salient aspects of those groups which have played a prominent role in presidential policy formulation: public commissions, White House task forces, and White House conferences, all of which operate for a limited time period, and permanent advisory bodies, such as the CEA and the President's Science Advisory Committee (PSAC), that are lodged in the Executive Office of the President.

Modern Presidents have used short-term advisory bodies for the study of specific problems or issues. The end product of these groups is usually a report and a set of recommendations for action. Public commissions are the most well-known temporary advisory committees. Presidents employ commissions for various purposes. The establishment of a commission is a safe response to a serious situation or problem. It dramatizes the President's concern and his desire to obtain expert information and advice. The unstated presumption is that presidential action will follow the report and recommendations of the commission. Although the commission may prove to be an important source of advice, its immediate function is to reassure the public, ease tensions, and alleviate pressures on the President. The Warren Commission, the Kerner Commission, and the Scranton Commission performed this function for Presidents Johnson and Nixon. Their proposals, however, did not serve as major sources of policy initiatives. Commissions have also been used to study less salient but persistent problems such as housing (the Kaiser Committee of 1967–68) and executive organization (the Ash Commission of 1969–71). These groups, although less publicized, tend to be more able to perform fact-finding and analytical activities that will generate viable policy suggestions for the President.

Most commissions, being public bodies, are necessarily broadly representative. This means that all relevant functional constituencies are included in the membership, a condition that has effects on the work of the commission. On the one hand, it may lead to a thorough airing in a highly visible forum of the central policy issues involved. On the other hand, it may result in a blurring of critical differences of opinion because of pressures to produce a consensual document. In most cases the representative character of presidential commissions contributes to their failure to serve as important sources of new ideas. (The 1970 report of the Commission on Obscenity and Pornography is a notable exception, although its proposals were publicly rejected by the President.) As one critic of the Kerner Commission observed, its purpose was "not so much to develop innovative solutions as to legitimize existing untried solutions."[11]

Sometimes a presidential commission can prove quite embarrassing to the Chief Executive. President Johnson chose largely to ignore the Kerner report's sweeping proposals for new and expanded domestic programs. They were strikingly incompatible with a tight federal budget and with the proud claims of accomplishment for the Great Society. Two years later, in 1970, President Nixon's alleged lack of leadership was a major finding of the Scranton Commission's report on campus disorders. Although Nixon's response to the report was moderate in tone, other members of his Administration rushed to attack the report and castigate its authors. The report of the commission on obscenity and pornography—a group appointed by President Johnson—received open criticism from Nixon, who used it to inject an anti-smut dimension into the 1970 congressional election campaign.

Because the use of public study commissions entails substantial costs

---

[11] G. Marx, "Report of the National Commission: The Analysis of Disorder or Disorderly Analysis?" (paper presented at the annual meeting of the American Political Science Association, Washington, D.C., 1968).

that may outweigh their potential benefits, Presidents since John F. Kennedy have also sought information through the employment of other devices such as task forces. These flexible, informal groups have been used to collate a wide range of thinking and generate new proposals in specific policy areas. Presidents Nixon and Kennedy used them as vehicles for easing the transition to their administrations. President Johnson relied upon them as primary sources of ideas for his legislative program. The Johnson task forces were more systematically operated than Kennedy's or Nixon's have been to date. In all three administrations, however, task force personnel and procedures have contrasted sharply with public commissions and with permanent advisory councils. A primary rationale for task forces is that they are not confined by the narrow institutional perspectives of the bureaucracy and Congress or by the parochial concerns of clientele groups. Rather, they permit the President to call upon people outside the government with a proper balance between imagination and practical political considerations for advice in the form of brief appraisals and tentative suggestions. Task force members tend to be university and foundation based experts who have some knowledge of and experience with the government. They are not necessarily representative of all relevant constituencies.

Task forces work with limited staff assistance. Unlike commissions, they do not produce long, documented analyses. Their reports usually are not published and they have no official status. The President may keep the task reports confidential or make all or parts of them public. The ideas contained in them can be accepted or rejected with limited risk of political embarrassment.

The limitations of task forces arise from the very informality and flexibility that constitute their greatest value to the President. They cannot carry as much weight as more formalized and publicized bodies. Their reports tend to be quite tentative and speculative and are unlikely to stand alone as the basis for new policies. They require supportive recommendations and additional studies by other groups in the bureaucracy and the Executive Office of the President. To the extent that task force reports are kept secret, as they were in the Johnson Administration, they engender resentment in the agencies, on Capitol Hill, and in clientele groups. But if the reports are made public, pressure tends to build for the President to react to the proposals regardless of how tentative they may be. Task forces also risk becoming routinized if they are used too extensively. Their success may lead to the destruction of their informal, flexible character. Task forces are a useful but limited means of obtaining the experience, information, and ideas from outside the government.

White House conferences have been held on occasion to draw attention to a specific problem by bringing together a group of distinguished citizens for a public discussion under presidential auspices. In the past decade conferences have been held on such subjects as education, civil rights, and international cooperation. The principal function of such gatherings is support-building through publicity. White House conferences have been criticized as explorations of "the lowest common denominators of their subjects." They have been lauded as manifestations of "meaningful dialogue between citizen and government official." In any case, it would seem that being organized into numerous committees and operating with temporary staff assistance, the conferences are not likely to be of great value as sources of new ideas and information. Their principal utility lies, by virtue of their nature, in the base that they potentially provide among professionals, political leaders, and relevant constituencies for presidential leadership in meeting the problems at issue. There are always risks of staging White House conferences. At least some of the notables who attend are likely to have ideas that are quite at variance with the values and goals of the President and his administration. These participants may be able to make the conference move in unintended and embarrassing directions. Another difficulty that the conferences pose is the generation of expectations that cannot be met. While a good many participants are not so naive as to regard a conference as the solution to the problem, the affected sectors of the public and even some participants tend to assume that there is a presidential commitment to action. In any case, although White House conferences can attract and build support and impart legitimacy to new policy initiatives, they have substantial limitations.

While modern Presidents have had varying success in utilizing temporary advisory groups, they have generally found two permanent advisory councils with supportive staffs, CEA and PSAC, to be of substantial value in the formulation of national economic and science policies. These two bodies are an integral part of the Executive Office of the President and thus represent the most extensive formalization of presidential advisory committees. Both possess independent staffs, but their structure and operating methods are quite dissimilar. The CEA consists of three distinguished economists who devote full time to their task and are supported by a professional staff. The CEA studies economic trends, analyzes macroeconomic policy alternatives, and examines the economic impact of substantive policy proposals in areas such as housing, welfare, and defense. It furnishes the President with sophisticated analysis that provides a rationale for presidential decisions and is a major conduit for funneling new economic ideas to the President. In the Kennedy and Johnson Administrations the CEA often competed with the Treasury and the Federal Reserve Board in shaping economic policy. Under President Johnson the Council became involved as a major participant in certain policy sectors such as housing. It moved beyond a purely advisory to a policy-making role. Presidents Eisenhower and Nixon tended to rely somewhat less on the CEA for basic policy suggestions and used it more as an analytical resource. The CEA's value to presidential staffing lies in its professional character and in the absence of any formal ties to a clientele group (other than the academically based American Economic Association).

The science advisory structure is also highly professionalized, but is somewhat more complex than the CEA operation. PSAC consists of seventeen persons, most of them distinguished academicians, and is chaired by the Special Assistant to the President for Science and Technology. The special assistant, who is the only full-time member of PSAC, also functions as director of the Office of Science and Technology (OST) and chairman of the Federal Council for Science and Technology, an interagency coordinating committee. PSAC conducts much of its business through panels consisting of one or two of its members plus additional personnel. These panels examine specific subjects and problems and file reports and recommendations. OST furnishes staff assistance to the PSAC panels, evaluates scientific research programs, and assists OMB in the development of science agency budgets. Since the establishment of OST in 1962, it along with PSAC and the special assistant have advised Presidents on such topics as the nuclear test ban treaty, the space program, domestic uses of science, and the development and support of scientific research and education. The science advisory system is geared to enable a non-scientist President to make decisions involving the support and use of science that are compatible with his political, social, and economic goals. In an increasingly complex technological environment this is an advisory mechanism of great importance. Presidents since Eisenhower have relied heavily on it to help them shape science policy.

Thus far I have not mentioned the myriad of committees and other groups that advise the President, Cabinet members, and lesser officials. These include two basic types, interagency committees and public advisory committees. The interagency committee is primarily a coordinating device and is used mainly to monitor policy and program implementation. Occasionally in the Kennedy and Johnson Administrations, interagency task forces were assigned responsibility to develop presidential legislative proposals. Interagency groups are apparently necessary to overcome the structural dispersion of the federal bureaucracy. They have had varying degrees of success depending, at least in part, on the rank and prestige of the chairman. In testimony before the Monagahan subcommittee, William Carey, a long-time budget bureau official, cited the Federal Interagency Council on Education (FICE) as an example of an ineffectual group. FICE, which an Assistant Secretary of HEW chaired, "never did get around to giving advice to the President." On the other hand, Carey observed that the Federal Council on Marine Resources and Engineering Development, which the Vice President chaired, was highly successful.

Public advisory committees are a pervasive phenomenon in national politics. They can provide a steady flow of new ideas to the President and members of the administration and in so doing improve the quality and widen the range of policy options that are open. They can also serve to broaden the participation of individuals and groups in the processes of policy formulation, thus improving communication between the government and the public and increasing popular support for various programs. But advisory committees are subject to limitations if not abuse. Agencies tend to use them as crutches or shields. Advisory committee members may be coopted to support narrow bureaucratic rather than broader presidential and public values. It is also possible that committees may attempt to exercise control over the agencies. To the extent that they succeed democratic responsibility to the public is blunted.

The most troublesome problem that advisory committees present the President is not the lack of information and advice, nor the absence of effective means to obtain it. Rather, it is the difficulty of organizing and using the advisory system effectively. What the President does not and cannot know is immeasurable. Most of the proposals, recommendations, and reports of the numerous committees that are advisory to him never reach the President. As William Carey told the congressional subcommittee investigating the matter:

> . . . Government is getting a great deal of advice, and some information, from the legions of advisory bodies which it creates. I am much less clear on what happens to the advice, or who is listening. I do know that very little of the advice emanating from most advisory bodies ever seeps through to the President himself. Most of it is lost through evaporation, some of it leaks out on staff advisers to the President, and no one can say with certainty how much of it feeds into policy decisions. There is no catch basin to filter and synthesize committee advice and recycle it through the executive branch system.

The need for evaluation and analysis of information on a systematic basis has been long recognized and is at the heart of the rationale for Reorganization Plan No. 2 of 1970. There have been some successful ventures in this direction, such as the CEA and the science advisory system, but they were not comprehensive. The policy analysis performed by the former Bureau of the Budget, as important and vital to presidential leadership and planning as it was, did not provide the integrative and synthesizing functions at a level of analysis that would solve the problems Carey describes. Perhaps the new Domestic Council will do so.

Advisory committees of all types are indispensable instruments of presidential policy leadership. However, they have been used indiscriminately in recent years with the result that their credibility has been damaged and their potential value reduced. Furthermore, their findings and recommendations have not always been systematically analyzed or regularly used as the basis for further policy development. No doubt Presidents will continue to employ them, but a more realistic appraisal of their capabilities is in order.

III. THE ADVISORY FUNCTION: A SUMMARY

It has been asserted on more than one occasion, both by former participants in the work of the presidency and by students of it, that much of what happens escapes the attention of the President. This is not at all surprising given the complexity of governmental operations, yet there remains the need for effective presidential leadership in the making of basic policy decisions. That leadership is heavily dependent on the advice and information that the President receives. To a considerable extent the President's office and powers are defined in the Constitution and by statute, he must function as head of one of three equal branches of government, Congress and established customs have imposed numerous duties upon him, and as the nation's major political leader he is expected to respond to the demands of partisans and established constituencies. In meeting the many expectations that surround their various roles, modern Presidents have found it convenient and necessary to utilize some basic sources of advice and information that inhere in the institution and the situation in which they must operate.

In this paper I have examined some of the principal advisory mechanisms that Presidents have employed in the process of policy formulation. The Cabinet and its committees, the top echelon councils for national security and domestic policy, the Office of Management and Budget, the White House staff and its inner circle, and the permanent and temporary presidential advisory committees all carry accompanying benefits and costs. For example, the Cabinet as the symbolic embodiment of the representative character of the administration appears ideal for building support and developing consensus when used as a policy-making body. But it is so severely hampered by the fragmentation inherent in the pluralistic basis of departmentalization that frustration often results when Presidents try to use it. Or, when various types of advisory committees are employed to tap vitally needed external sources of information, they may prove unmanageable or even embarrassing to the President. Or, devices designed to provide systematic identification, analysis, and management of issues and problems, such as the NSC system, may be instituted at the expense of policy rigidity that limits the capacity for flexible response in emergencies.

The use of many advisory mechanisms—the White House staff and its inner circle, the OMB, and some type of NSC system—is inescapable and each President must adapt them to his personal administrative and leadership styles and to his policy objectives. The use of other mechanisms—the Cabinet and its committees and presidential advisory committees—is much more discretionary. How Presidents employ them is likely to vary between administrations according to a rough cost-benefit calculus that also incorporates elements of style and political goals.

Generally, it appears that Democratic Presidents have tended to prefer a less formalized, more open advisory system characterized by relatively easy access of individuals and groups to the President, a heavy flow to the President of reports, memoranda, and other written material that has only been partially refined or screened, an absence of strict functional specialization within the system, and a pragmatic flexibility that is adaptable to emergencies but poorly suited to any kind of long-range planning. Conversely, Republican Presidents have tended to organize their advisory systems more formally and elaborately. Their arrangements have featured greater reliance on the Cabinet as an advisory and decisional body, more finely prescribed procedures and routines for obtaining and processing information, more careful management of the President's time through controlled access to him and highly selective filtration of the flow of paper, an insistence on functional separation of intelligence tasks, and strong emphasis on long-range planning seemingly at the expense of adaptability to emergency situations. The greater propensity of most Democratic Presidents to innovate in domestic policy also appears to be associated with their preference for more open staffing arrangements. The Republican Presidents' preference for structural formalism and prescribed routines is, however, at its strongest in the realm of national security policy where there is much less partisan difference of opinion over policy alternatives. This suggests that the partisan factor is an independent determinant of staffing arrangements for presidential policy formulation.

Regardless of party affiliation, the inclination to develop new policies, and personal operating style, the President needs substantial assistance in obtaining and utilizing advice and information. Successful presidential policy leadership requires that the President's goals be sufficiently well defined that governmental performance can be directed and measured according to the standards that the goals provide. The refinement of presidential policy preferences is not an easy task, for the presidency is the strategic focal point of pressures and demands that emanate from independently powerful elites that function in the numerous policy areas. The President acts as a broker and mediator between these competing and usually non-overlapping elites. He can provide leadership and direction in those policy areas that he regards as important, but only if he has secured the needed intelligence.

Unfortunately, there is no specific formula for an effective advisory and information system. As President Nixon has so appropriately observed:

> There is no textbook prescription for organizing the machinery of policy making, and no procedural formula for making wise decisions. The policies of this Administration will be judged on their results, not on how methodically they were made.[12]

Perhaps the most that can be stipulated is that presidential advice and information should be as wide ranging as possible and that it should encompass diverse social, economic, and political perspectives. The advisory system should be structured so that the President is not isolated, yet he must be protected from fatuous incursions on his time and energy. At key points close to the President there should be situated two sets of advisers, one with unquestioning personal loyalty to him and the other with broader professional and political loyalties. Within these limits, the President may use whatever combination of advisers and advisory mechanisms he wishes. The system that he develops will always be characterized by nagging uncertainties as well as promising potential. Consequently there needs to be continuous analysis and evaluation of the presidency and its intelligence system. Yet the basic pattern is set and, even with structural shifts such as Reorganization Plan No. 2, is likely to undergo only marginal adjustments. Ultimately it may well be that muddling through is the most that we can hope for. If so, the challenge that remains is still demanding: to manage the muddling so as to produce satisfactory, if not optimal presidential policy leadership.

---

[12] Report by President Nixon, *supra* note 9, at H929.

10.

"EVERYBODY BELIEVES IN DEMOCRACY UNTIL HE GETS TO THE WHITE HOUSE . . .": AN EXAMINATION OF WHITE HOUSE-DEPARTMENTAL RELATIONS

Thomas E. Cronin

I. ON DIRECTING THE FEDERAL ESTABLISHMENT FROM THE WHITE HOUSE

A President is expected to perform three overriding functions: to recast the nation's policy agenda in line with contemporary needs, to provide symbolic affirmation of the nation's basic values, and to galvanize the vast machinery of government to carry out his programs and those he has inherited. The slippage and gap between the first and third functions is the primary concern of this discussion. The annual unveiling of a President's legislative program now has much in common with Madison Avenue's broadsides advertising each year's "spectacular new line" of Detroit-made combustion engine automobiles: the perceptive citizenry is increasingly sensitive to performance standards of both.

And so it is that the recently arrived President, aspiring to "unite the nation" and "get the country moving again," expecting that he and his lieutenants will succeed where previous administrations faltered, customarily feels he must order first his own executive branch "household." Recent Presidents often have gone out of their way to solicit the loyalty and support of senior civil servants. President Nixon, for example, immediately after his inauguration, personally traveled to each executive department and met with and addressed thousands of these senior officials. Presidents and their inner circle of aides continuously strive to secure greater internal managerial control over the executive departments. They even learn (after awhile) that one way to do this is to forge a

Reprinted with permission from a symposium on the institutionalized presidency appearing in *Law and Contemporary Problems,* Vol. 35, No. 3 (Summer, 1970), pp. 573–625, published by the Duke University School of Law, Durham, North Carolina. Abridged; footnotes renumbered for this volume.

unity on policy priorities among the general American public *outside* of the executive branch.

But, as Bailey has pointed out, the executive branch of the federal government is a many-splintered thing. The President is soon acquainted with the considerable difficulty of promoting unity in the face of the basic pluralism of the American political system. Presidents Kennedy, Johnson, and Nixon have each complained bitterly about the recalcitrance of the federal bureaucracy, and seemingly turned more and more to their personal White House staffs for help in gaining control of their own executive establishment. And the collective record of Kennedy, Johnson, and Nixon as chief executive, especially with respect to the achievement of their domestic policy goals, has raised considerable questioning and criticism. As Rexford Tugwell concluded:

> The truth is that Kennedy did not function as an executive. He had only the most meager contacts with the secretaries of the domestic departments, largely because he had no interest in their operations. This inability of a president—who must be political leader and chief legislator and who is sole custodian of the national security—to direct the domestic establishment has become almost total.[1]

Kennedy, after being in office two years, publicly complained that the nation's problems "are more difficult than I had imagined" and "there are greater limitations upon our ability to bring about a favorable result than I had imagined."

One Kennedy White House aide put the frustration more bluntly: "Everybody believes in democracy until he gets to the White House and then you begin to believe in dictatorship, because it's so hard to get things done. Everytime you turn around, people just resist you, and even resist their own job." Again, the same John Kennedy who in many ways inspired the country, was moved to quip about a relatively low priority project, the architectural remodeling of Lafayette Square across from the White House, "let's stay with it. Hell, this may be the only thing I'll ever really get done." President Johnson also expressed disappointment over seemingly slow and uncooperative departmental responses. He attempted to "ride herd" on a multitude of programs by insisting on getting up-to-date figures on varied federal and international grant programs and routinely required departmental written reports. But he eventually resorted to vesting more and more authority for departmental coordination in the White House domestic policy aides and his Budget Bureau director. It was a no doubt disillusioned President Johnson, tired with continually battling the bureaucracy, who solemnly warned the incoming Nixon Ad-

---

[1] Tugwell, "The President and His Helpers: A Review Article," 82 *Pol. Sci. Q.* 253, 262, 265 (1967).

ministration that they should spare no effort in selecting thoroughly loyal people to man key departmental positions. It is as though Johnson believed that a significant portion of the Great Society programs, for which he had fought so hard, had been sabotaged by indifferent federal officials. And, in the wake of the Great Society legislative victories, both Presidents Johnson and Nixon held that the scaffolding of the federal government and the federal system needed extensive revamping, if not major surgery. Said Nixon: ". . . I have concluded that a sweeping reorganization of the Executive Branch is needed if the government is to keep up with the times and with the needs of the people."[2]

The thesis running implicitly if not explicitly through this paper is that White House staffs and executive department officials, upon whom contemporary Presidents are exceptionally dependent, are more specialized, professionalized, and differentiated than has been generally acknowledged. Presidents find themselves continuously surrounded—some would say afflicted—by problems of complexity, diversity, and a seemingly endless series of jurisdictional and territorial disputes. Presidential staffs, cabinet members, and advisors are invariably associated with, if not captured by, professionally, politically, or personally skewed sets of policy preferences. No cabinet officer or White House advisor consistently and singularly acts for "Everyman" or "the public interest." Priority setting, budget cutting, and preferred procedural strategies necessarily promote selective interests at the expense of others. Hence, Presidents are constantly, and rightfully, faced with conflicting claims; calibration and management of conflict is the core of presidential leadership. Those who would somehow reorganize the federal government so as to remove or elevate the American presidency away from bureaucratic or societal conflicts should be fully aware that they may at the same time be stripping the presidency of the strategic occasions for exercising essential leadership skills.

To the extent that White House staff and senior department officials maintain close communications and negotiations—or exchanges—we can speak of the existence of an executive branch exchange system. Both sides are needed to perform the functions of the executive branch; each wants certain types of help from the other, and each seeks to avoid overt antagonism toward the other. White House staff members can be viewed as performing important linkage roles in this exchange system, connecting a President with a vast network of administrative officials. Presidents and most of their staff grow well aware that cooperation from the permanent federal departments is earned rather than taken for granted. Loyalty and support as well as crucially needed expertise are eagerly sought, for a

---

[2] Nixon, State of the Union address, Jan. 22, 1971, in 117 *Cong. Rec.* H92, H94 (daily ed. Jan. 22, 1971).

basic premise in the exchange system is that departmental officials, especially civil servants, play, or can play, a strategic role in administering federal government activities.

Some of the relationships within this exchange system can be briefly suggested here. Richard Neustadt has commented:

> Agencies need decisions, delegations, and support, along with bargaining arenas and a court of last resort, so organized as to assure that their advice is always heard and often taken. A President needs timely information, early warning, close surveillance, organized to yield him the controlling judgment, with his options open, his intent enforced. In practice these two sets of needs have proved quite incompatible; presidential organizations rarely serve one well without disservice to the other.[3]

And Bill Moyers adds:

> The job of the White House assistant is to help the President impress his priorities on the Administration. This may throw him into a sharp adversary role between two Cabinet members who are also competing with the President for their views of what the priorities should be. . . . Their [White House assistants] job is to make sure that decisions get implemented; it is not to manage the implementations. The follow-through aspect of it is very, very important. In recent years, the White House staff may have tended to become far too much of a managerial operation and less an overseer.[4]

The general White House view reflects a concern for teamwork, cohesiveness, interdepartmental coordination, follow-through on the President's program, and protection of the President's reputation. White House aides generally spend a sizable portion of their time engaged in intra-executive branch alliance building. How best to communicate what the President wants done? How to give the departmental leaders a sense of involvement in presidential decisions? How politely but firmly to tell "them" of the President's dissatisfaction with department performance? How to motivate them to give added energy to get "our" programs moving? Should we promote an inside man into that new vacancy or bring in someone from the outside? How can we extricate this program operation from that nearly impossible group of people over there? A standard joke during the 1960's had White House staff members trying to figure out how to contract out to private enterprise or foundations the work

---

[3] Neustadt, "Politicians and Bureaucrats," in *The Congress and America's Future* 102, 113 (D. Truman ed. 1965).

[4] Quoted in an interview by Sidey, "The White House Staff vs. the Cabinet," *The Washington Monthly*, Feb. 1969, at 4.

that the State Department was assigned to perform. A standard exercise during the late 1960's, especially within the Nixon Administration, was the design of programs that might shortcircuit the federal bureaucracy with the hope of getting federal monies and programs more swiftly into the hands of state and local officials. In short, the problem becomes how to employ the resources and sanctions of the presidency to make the machinery of government act in accord with the administration's overriding goals?

Senior departmental officials are no less involved in exchanges with the presidential staff. Some of them are temporary political appointees, most are career civil servants with a long legacy of dealing with the presidency, especially with the budget officials attached to the Executive Office of the President. Their concern is often a blend of wishing to satisfy and cooperate with the objectives of the current presidential team, but at the same time attending to departmental priorities and the always present need for maintaining departmental integrity. White House requests for the most part are honored; pressure and arrogant communications are resented. But the day-to-day concerns are reflected in the following types of questions: How can we get White House endorsement and increased budget approvals for this new department initiative? How can we get the White House to side with us in this jurisdictional matter? How can we make an end run around that unsympathetic and amateur White House aide and make sure the President hears about this new idea? When should we supply a potentially great news announcement to the White House and risk not being able to use it here to gain publicity for "our" cabinet officer and departmental programs? In short, how do we deal with the White House when necessary, or when it can help us, but otherwise preserve our autonomy?

Simple but previously neglected questions such as the following need to be asked: How much tension and strain exist between White House staff and departmental executives? Why do some White House staffers see considerable conflict whereas others view departmental relations as essentially harmonious? What variance exists over time or among the departments? What are the major sources of perceived conflicts? To what extent should and can conflict be resolved?

II. WHITE HOUSE-DEPARTMENTAL CONFLICT: PRESIDENTIAL AND DEPARTMENTAL PERSPECTIVES

The focus on conflict here deserves a note of explanation. In the strictest sense, conflict occurs when different people "seek to possess the same object, occupy the same space or the same exclusive position, play incompatible roles, maintain incompatible goals, or undertake mutually incompatible means for achieving their purposes." [5] Conflict, as well as its closely interrelated opposite, integration or harmony, is always more or less present in any large organization, and indeed in all human relations. If one looks for it, one will surely find it. One of the ironies of our government is that, although it exists to resolve conflict, *i.e.*, to pull together diverse class, regional and ethnic interests and accentuate the common goals of prosperity, liberty, etc., it strives at the same time to make this nation safe for and supportive of certain types of conflict, *e.g.*, business competition in the marketplace, diversity in religion, and the clash of contending ideas and values. Within the federal executive branch there is more contention about the priorities and tempo of federal activity than there is about the basic ends or legitimacy of the government. In this sense, the executive branch exchange system operates much like a trading arena in which different participants hope that their preferences might prevail.

Conflict is not always an indicator of weakness or ill health of an organization. Critical adversary relationships may provide a much needed jolt toward system adaptation and renewal, and hence be a notable asset. Coser's suggestions are relevant:

> Conflict prevents the ossification of social systems by exerting pressures for innovation and creativity; it prevents habitual accommodations from freezing into rigid molds and hence progressively impovershing the ability to react creatively to novel circumstances.[6]

Several former members of the executive branch have made a case that certain federal policies and practices have suffered not from too much conflict, but from too little. But assessing the utility or disutility of conflict requires an extremely sensitive appraisal of a large number of variables. The analysis here is limited to an exploration of participant perspectives on the existence and presumed sources of conflict in the White House-departmental exchange system.

It is hoped that studying the existence and nature of conflicts in the executive branch exchange system may add to our understanding about what makes the presidency work—or not work. Though contemporary Presidents have been able to provide some semblance of integrating unity via their legislative messages and budgetary controls, Presidents seem otherwise increasingly buried beneath their own institutional machinery. Conservatives and liberals alike join in faulting the executive branch as a bulwark against change, and as largely unresponsive to contemporary needs. The phenomenal growth and differentiation of the executive es-

---

[5] North, "Conflict—Political Aspects," in 3 *International Encyclopedia of the Social Sciences* 226 (D. Sills ed. 1968).

[6] Coser, "Conflict—Social Aspects," in 3 *International Encyclopedia of the Social Sciences, supra* note 13, at 232, 235.

tablishment and the attributed independence of the permanent government (civil servants, foreign service and military officials, and so forth) from the presidential government (the President, his inner circle of White House counselors, and those politically appointed cabinet officials who can be thoroughly relied upon) make assessing the strength of the presidency quite complicated.

Let us examine the major competing schools of thought about functions and responsibilities belonging at the White House and those belonging within the departments. Just as there are those who want to strengthen Congress in all executive-legislative relations and thereby make Congress the "first branch of government," so also there are heated arguments about whether the cabinet and the departments need to be strengthened vis-à-vis the White House staff and the Executive Office of the President. While not doing justice to the richness of varied arguments, it is helpful to sum up the contending polar perspectives characterizing much of recent practice and prescription: the presidential perspective and the departmental. These are presented here as ideal type constructs and as such are not necessarily held by any one person or group. It is likely that admixtures of these perspectives will be found in instances of conflict and in proposals for reducing conflict.

A. *The Presidential Perspective.* This perspective, popular among most presidential advisors, university liberals (at least during the 1950's and 1960's), and probably a majority of the Washington press corps, holds that the presidency should be a strong and visible force in making sure that presidential policy objectives get effectively translated into desired policy performance. "This is the great office, the only truly national office in the whole system." The basic premise corresponds with Alexander Hamilton's point of view—that the requisite unity and drive for our political system would only come from a strong executive. Only the presidency should retain discretion over budget choices and over the way federal policies are administered. And only the presidency can provide the needed direction and orchestration of complex, functionally interdependent federal programs. Presidents and their staffs, if properly organized, can assure that the laws of the land not only will be administered faithfully, but also imaginatively. There is an explicit assumption that a strong presidency can make a major difference in the way government works and that this difference will be in the direction of a more constructive (desirable) set of policy outcomes.

Presidentialists invariably also argue that the presidency is not properly organized, staffed, or funded. The presidency needs not just "more help" but a major infusion of skills, talent, tools, and loyalty if it is to gain control over the permanent federal departments. Implicitly, if not explicitly, "More Power To The White House" is the slogan. Partly because so many previous Presidents have bypassed existing departments and set up their own new independent agencies, and partly because of the sheer size and diversity of the executive establishment, the White House too often serves at the pleasure of the bureaucracy, rather than vice versa. McGeorge Bundy speaks for many believers of the presidential persuasion when he observes that the executive branch in many areas "more nearly resembles a collection of badly separated principalities than a single instrument of executive action." [7]

The presidential camp never completely trusts civil servants, and frequently mistrusts political appointees as well. Whatever of importance needs doing either ought to be done directly from the White House, or should be done with the expectation that the departmental people will temper or undermine the desired policy intentions. The goal of the presidentialists in its crudest form is "to presidentialize" the executive branch. Toward that end there are catalogues of reform proposals, a few of which can be mentioned as examples:

> The strong Presidency will depend upon the Chief Executive's capacity to control and direct the vast bureaucracy of national administration. Ideally, the President should possess administrative powers comparable to those of business executives. . . . What the President needs most can be simply formulated: a power over personnel policy, planning, accounting, and the administration of the executive branch that approaches his power over the executive budget.[8]

Other variations on this theme call for better policy evaluation and program management staffs within the Executive Office. Presidentialists with narrow policy interests are always asking that the formulation and administration of their particular policy concerns be brought closer within the presidential orbit "much along the lines of the Council of Economic Advisers." Another suggestion would give the presidency some field agents or "expediters" (federal domestic program "czars") located in federal regional offices or large metropolitan areas to insure that presidential priorities are being properly effected at the grass roots level.

B. Departmental Perspective. This perspective holds that the success or failure of the federal government's efforts to manage federal programs rests almost entirely on the quality and competence of the executive departments. An assumption here is that all programs at the federal level possess considerable discretionary aspects. Those holding a departmental perspective say that for programs to be effectively administered, discretion and authority must (at least to a large extent) be vested in depart-

---

[7] M. Bundy, *The Strength of Government* 37 (1968). *See also id.* ch. 2.
[8] L. Koenig, *The Chief Executive* 417 (rev. ed. 1968).

mental and bureau leaders. The sentiment here is that the role of the White House, particularly in regard to the administration of domestic programs, should be a highly selective one, and one that is tremendously and rightfully dependent on career civil servants and professional departmental expertise. Certain department officials, for example, deplored the amount of White House involvement in AID grant clearances, HUD model city selections, and HEW desegregation proceedings. To be sure, even the most extreme departmentalist would agree that crisis situations and various types of national security matters necessarily should be subject to substantial presidential discretion.

The departmentalist view has varying support among professional civil servants, among some former cabinet officers, and even among some former White House staff assistants. Moreover, there are increasing numbers of skeptics who are persuaded that a larger and more "resourceful" presidency (or more "institutionalization" of the presidency) is not a realistic answer to the problem of managing a responsive federal government. There are even those who argue that it probably does not make much difference which of the various presidential candidates gets elected. "You can elect your favorite presidential hopeful at the next election but the basic problems of government non-responsiveness will still be with us!"

Some advocates of the departmental perspective come to their position because of a recognition that the political facts of life just do not permit intensive or extensive presidential involvement in most matters of federal policy administration. The limits of the presidency are cited, such as in David Truman's appropriate cautions:

> [the president] cannot take a position on every major controversy over administrative policy, not merely because his time and energies are limited, but equally because of the positive requirements of his position. He cannot take sides in any dispute without giving offense in some quarters. He may intervene where the unity of his supporters will be threatened by inaction; he may even, by full use of the resources of his office, so dramatize his action as to augment the influence he commands. But he cannot "go to the country" too often, lest the tactic become familiar and his public jaded. Rather than force an administrative issue, he may choose to have his resources for a legislative effort . . . [For effectiveness he] must preserve some of the detachment of a constitutional monarch.[9]

And while the President remains detached or "above" the day-to-day operations of the federal government, cabinet members and their staffs want both a relative independence and a vote of confidence with which to carry on their work. As one prerequisite, they insist that White House

---

[9] D. Truman, *The Governmental Process* 407–08 (1951).

staff members should not have authority independent from the President to issue directives to cabinet and agency leaders. And when they need it cabinet members and agency heads should have the right to direct access to the President. It follows too that Presidents should get involved only in broad policy questions, not in the nuts and bolts concerns of program execution and application. White House people are viewed as "amateurs and terribly ill-informed nuisances" who are seen as "breathing down our necks."

The more the White House usurps functional responsibilities from their "proper" home in the departments, the more the White House may undermine the goal of competent departmental management of presidentially sponsored programs. A cabinet member who is made to look weak within his department will be treated with less respect by subordinates as well as by relevant congressional and client support groups. Department officials who must fight strenuously to maintain access and rapport with the White House have correspondingly less energy left over for their internal department management concerns. When the White House staff or other presidential advisors step in and temporarily take over certain departmental functions, the action may further diminish the capacity of the department to streamline or revitalize its capability for managing these functions in the future. Too frequent intervention from the White House creates morale problems within the departments. Resentment and hostility are likely to impede subsequent cooperation. Imaginative professional people will not long remain in their departmental posts if they are frequently underused or misused.

Departmentalists, charging that White House aides get rewarded for "meddling" in department affairs, note that on closer inspection it is frequently a disadvantageous strategy for everyone involved, excepting perhaps the White House aide who has to look "busy."

III

A. Amount of Conflict Perceived by White House Staffers. Conflicts in the executive branch system are widely acknowledged by most recent White House staff members. The forty-three aides interviewed for this study were asked whether they experienced major difficulties in working with the federal executive departments: "can you give your view of this; is this really a problem?" As shown in Table 1, approximately two-thirds answered that there were extensive and considerable troubles in dealing with the departments. Some talked of this as the single greatest problem in contemporary government. One man who had worked for both Presidents Kennedy and Johnson said that "it was an absolutely terrible problem. . . . There are major problems with cabinet members and civil servants alike. Even the great cabinet members like McNamara and Freeman were terrible in evading their share of many of our efforts." A senior Johnson Administration counselor observed that the "separation of governments is not so great between Congress and the president as between a president and those people like sub-cabinet and bureau officials, who become locked into their own special subsystems of self-interested policy concerns." Others talked about the increasing defiance of department people toward the White House:

> It's a terrible problem and it's getting worse, particularly with the State Department. The major problem is the lack of any identification [on their part] with the president's program priorities. At State they try to humor the president but hope he will not interfere in their complex matters and responsibilities. It is equally a problem with civil servants and cabinet types. It is amazing how soon the cabinet people get captured by the permanent staffs. Secretary [David] Kennedy [of Treasury] under Nixon, for example, was captured within days . . . and Nixon's staff didn't even try to improve things. They just assumed there was a great problem. Personally, I think you can't expect too much from the bureaucracy. It is too much to expect that they will see things the president's way.

TABLE 1

White House Staff Perception of Conflict with Departments

Problem of tensions and conflict in these exchanges was:	*Percentages N = 43*
Considerable	65%
Moderate	25
Insignificant	10
Total	100

Source: Personal interviews with forty-three White House staff members serving between 1961 and 1970.

Some aides were more inclined to note that conflicts varied with different departments and with different cabinet members. For example: "yes there are certainly many problems, but it differs from area to area and from president to president. I think the amount of friction is related to the role of the White House staff and what they undertake and what presidents let them do." Another example of a more tempered assessment of the existence of conflict comes from a Congressional relations aide to the Kennedy-Johnson White House:

> Oh, yes–there are problems to an extent. There is deep suspicion around the whole government toward the new president when he comes into power. . . . But the fights you get in are different all around town. . . . We had some excellent men around town, and some bombs. The important thing for a president to do is to get good men and then

> decentralize the responsibility. Let the department people do their job and don't let your [White House] staff interfere too much. . . .

Some White House staff who had less involvement with departments were the most likely to acknowledge little if any serious conflict.

On balance, a substantial majority of recent presidential staffers complain of considerable difficulty and conflict in their work with the federal executive departments.

B. What White House Staffers See as Sources of Conflict. Conflicts in the executive branch exchange system can be attributed to both subjective and objective factors. The difference in allegiance to the presidential or departmental perspectives illustrates a major subjective factor. Some other subjective factors include differing definitions of priorities and roles, personality clashes, and personal ambitions. Objective factors would include such things as sheer size of the federal effort (and the time and communications restrictions that stem from that size), restrictive budget limitations (Presidents and cabinet heads find they have little control over ninety per cent or more of "their" budgets), centrifugal pulls inherent in federalism and in the functionally independent departments, and various knowledge gaps (for example, "we don't have all the answers!"). Presidential staff members seem to be well aware of most of these sources, but seem to stress the subjective differences and the ill effects of the divorce between presidential and departmental perspectives.

Extended interviews with White House staff yield the persuasive impression that no one set of difficulties lies at the root of executive branch conflict. Their discussions often moved back and forth from noting causes to complaining about symptoms. But their multiple citations here (see Table 2) are instructive both for their diversity and for unexpectedly candid criticism of the way the White House itself contributed to these difficulties.[10]

1. *On White House "Sources" of Conflict.* White House staffers suggest that their own definition of their roles, and the pressures they had to work under frequently exacerbate relations with cabinet and department officials. Presidents and their staffs arrive at the White House charged up to get things done, to produce results, to make good on the pledges of their campaign. The frenzy and simplification of problems and issues generated in the campaign, coupled with the post election victory euphoria result in strategies of over-extension and insensitivity:

---

[10] The staff perceptions of the sources of conflict shown in Table 2 do not adequately reflect the intensity of the respondents' views. Although they blamed White House staff operations approximately as often as they faulted the departments, the author feels their criticisms of department officials and civil servants were more intense than their criticisms of their White House colleagues.

> Well, a Kennedy staff hallmark was to seize power from around town. In retrospect I think they often were insensitive to the channels of the existing government. They came in after the campaign with a pretentious "know it all" attitude and they hurt their case by this stance. For example, I think the White House staffers often called people low in the departments and deliberately undercut cabinet people too much in the early years. . . . In retrospect I don't think you can coordinate much from the White House. You just don't have the people and the numbers . . . [and] you can't evaluate all that much [not to mention managing it]. . . .

Staff insensitivity to cabinet and department executives occurs for a variety of reasons. Presidents often want to "put the heat on" some cabinet member or bureau chief, but prefer not to take the blame for being tough. Presidents understandably eschew the "bad guy" role, hence the bearing of unpleasant news befalls various staff assistants.

Discussions about the problem of staff insensitivity were often ambiguous. On the one hand, aides somewhat contemptuously talked of the need for more "care and feeding" of cabinet members (as though some of the cabinet were kept symbols for window dressing alone). But they would also insist that one just has to be aggressive and "hard-nosed" in order to get anything accomplished.

TABLE 2

Presidency Staff Perspectives on the Sources of Conflict and Strain in White House-Executive Department Relationships

Types and Sources of Conflict	*Percentages N = 41*
White House "Sources":	
WH staff insensitivity toward department officials	51%
WH staff and President communications failures	44
WH staff usurpation of department roles and/or excessive interference in department affairs	37
WH "tried to do too much too quickly"	29
Departmental "Sources":	
Civil servant and bureaucratic parochialism	49
Cabinet "leadership" too weak or unimaginative	46
Departmental leaders captured by narrow special interests	46
Red tape, and inept staff work	37
Departments unable to work together	24
Complexity/Diversity Factors:	
Sheer size and complexity of federal efforts	37
Lack of time for the needed follow-through/coordination/implementation	27
Substantive and ideological differences about policy choices within the federal system	27

Source: Personal interviews conducted by the author with forty-one presidential staff members who served at the White House during 1961–70. Respondents could give more than one reply.

Some aides stressed that the always delicate distinction between *staff* or advisory roles at the White House, and operational administrative *line* responsibilities in the cabinet departments became overly blurred during the Kennedy and Johnson years. Too many of the staff tried to do more than they were supposed to be doing and gradually came "to give orders" rather than transmit requests. But as mentioned earlier, Presidents frequently encouraged this development and some cabinet members respect decisive and competent White House aides, brusque though they may be. Impatient or disillusioned with some of their cabinet, Kennedy, Johnson and Nixon turned more and more to their White House staff for advice, coordination, and particularly for help in resolving jurisdictional disputes between executive agencies. One result, in the words of one top Johnson aide, was that "after awhile he [Johnson] never even bothered to sit down with most of the cabinet members (domestic cabinet) even to discuss their major problems and program possibilities." Partly because of the war, and partly because he had grown used to leaning on his own staff so heavily, "Johnson became lazy and wound up using some of the staff as both line managers as well as staff and, I think in retrospect, *it frequently* didn't work out!"

Some of the most instructive commentary was devoted to the problem of intra-executive branch communications. Numerous aides mentioned that a "basic reason for conflict is the lack of communications." Fault in this regard is generally placed upon White House staff and sometimes on the President. Often it is not that cabinet and departmental officials fail to respond to White House policy directives, but rather that those directives are too hazy or inadequately communicated. Sometimes it is because Presidents and their aides just have not made up their minds. Occasionally, different White House aides send out contradictory messages to the departments. For example, the domestic program and legislative development staff might be pressing a department or new program ideas while the budget director and his staff are warning department officials of the need to reduce their activities, especially their more costly programs. Often the President has not made his view known forcefully enough to overcome uncertainty and confusion. Presidents are handicapped in this sense because they often have multiple audiences in mind when preparing their remarks. The capacity of the departments to understand what the President means and to believe that he really means it should never be taken for granted.

One other problem discussed by close to a third of the White House aides (again, see Table 2) was that their Administration tried to do too much too fast. Even President Johnson was quoted to this effect in the last days of his presidential term. It was not that Great Society programs were ill-intentioned or mis-placed, but rather that not enough planning had preceded implementation. One veteran budget counselor to Presidents explained his view of the conflict this way:

> Too much was attempted under LBJ. We didn't ask ourselves enough questions about whether we could do these things. Expectations outran the capability to work things out. There were too many other demands or problems in the mid and late 60's. Vietnam, inadequately trained manpower at all levels of government, and the structure of intergovernmental relations was inadequate. The space and missile programs had the backing of the people, but public support was terribly splintered over the War on Poverty, etc. . . . It was like a Tower of Babel with no one interested in the other people's programs.

If the departments are, in fact, occasionally "parochial" in their behavior, Presidents and presidential staff can often be overly "political" in their behavior. For example, Nixon's vetoes of various health and education bills—for balancing his political budget—incurred the hostility of several HEW officials. Likewise President Kennedy's highly political decision to support federal subsidies for the construction of the Cross-Florida Barge Canal angered many budget and conservation counselors within his own administration. Likewise the typical Executive office attitude toward the Agricultural Department—"keep prices down and the farmers off our back!"—annoyed many department officials who held expansionary hopes for turning their department into a rural development and a major conservation agency. The point to be appreciated in several of these illustrations is that the political perspectives and substantive preferences of Presidents and their staffs produce their share of executive branch conflicts.

2. *On Departmental "Sources" of Conflict.* There is an increasingly popular view that much of the conflict in the federal executive branch can be explained by the fact that the departments are "specialized, parochial, self-interested," while the President and his advisors have "a government-wide point of view." The extent to which this is the overriding explanation is easily overestimated. White House staff members (whom we would expect to be prime enthusiasts for this interpretation) fault the White House and its operations about as often as they fault the cabinet and the departments.

Approximately half of the White House aides mentioned a seeming inability of many government workers to adopt "the presidential perspective." This latter commodity, always ill-defined, seems capaciously to include "the public interest," responsiveness to the electorate, maturity of judgment, virtue, and wisdom. Whatever all this is, quite a number of the White House policy staff assistants are convinced that department people either do not understand it or just stubbornly resist it. "Mostly the bureaucrats are unresponsive, they view themselves as the professionals and see your [White House] impact as purely political. They don't fight you openly, but they don't cooperate if they can help it!"

Another way for White House aides to explain departmental sources of conflict is to question the competence or loyalty of the cabinet member. Cabinet members get faulted for being "too much of an individualist," "too aloof," "too stubborn" and sometimes for not being "a take charge type." In any event, the traditional complaint that cabinet members get captured by narrow special interests was a frequent response.

One of the most significant factors promoting conflict between the departments and the White House staffs is their different time perspectives. This same variable is also at play in White House-congressional relations. A president and his staff think in terms of two and four year time frames—at the most. They strive to fulfill campaign pledges, convention platforms, and earlier announced priorities as soon as possible, seeking always to build a respectable record for forthcoming election campaigns. The haste with which the White House rushed the announcements of the Model Cities and the Teacher Corps programs may well have damaged the chances for effective design and launching of these programs. Career civil servants, on the other hand, will be around after the elections regardless of outcomes, and more importantly, they are held accountable to the General Accounting Office, the Office of Management and Budget, or to congressional investigation committees for the way federal programs are administered (and for any mistakes that might be made). The work incentives for most careerists are stacked in the direction of doing a thorough, consistent, and even cautious job, rather than any hurried dancing to the current tunes of the White House staff.

C. Conflict as a Result of Complexity. Nearly all of the White House aide commentary on executive branch conflict can be traced back to problems of government size and problem complexity. White House aides become arrogant and insensitive because they are often asked to do too much in too short a time. White House aides "breathe down the necks" of cabinet and department leaders because Presidents become impatient and restless for results. Departments appear inert or unresponsive because they are having difficulty in pulling together diverse specialists to work on complex questions. Cabinet members give the impression of being "weak" (and sometimes are) because they must preside over huge holding companies of diverse, functionally specialized enterprises. White House aides are continuously disillusioned and disappointed by the lack of coordination both within and among departments; but the White House vision of coordination unrealistically presupposes that department people share an understanding of complex problems, and a sophisticated appreciation of the relatedness of one problem to another, of one agency to another. Communications problems exist because large numbers of people are involved in administering programs all over the country and are confronted by constantly changing and shifting circumstances. Legislative or executive intent, or the GAO and Civil Service Commission "rulebooks and regulations," even if they could be memorized, do not have all the answers for all seasons. Uncertainties, changing environment, and shifting priorities all make policy implementation harder (and pleasing the White House near impossible). One White House counselor to President Eisenhower summed up what he refers to as the pervasive fact of political life that continually affected the Eisenhower Administration:

> The sheer size and intricacy of government conspire to taunt and to thwart all brisk pretensions to set sensationally new directions. The vast machinery of national leadership—the tens of thousands of levers and switches and gears—simply do not respond to the impatient jab of a finger or the angry pounding of a fist.[11]

There is, finally, the constantly faced dilemma of choosing between competing values. Ideological preferences enter here. That not many White House aides mention ideological factors as a source of conflict may imply that a relatively common political culture unites executive department officialdom with recent members of the presidential government. But there are differences of view, sometimes reflecting political party points of view, but more often reflecting differences about the role of the federal government in solving local or international problems. There is always the problem of making the critical distinction between what the federal government can do and what it cannot do. The occasional quest to push the governmental system to great levels of commitment and compassion gets generated in presidential elections and later by major presidential policy addresses (*e.g.*, the quest *to end* poverty, *to achieve* equality of opportunity, *to renew* our cities, *to help develop* Latin America, *to return power* to the people, and so forth). However, even the "best laid plans" of Presidents or Congress often get rescinded because of the "bottlenecks" of problem complexity and jurisdictional interdependency. As White House aides well know, however, "you have to start somewhere"—despite manifest opposition and complexity.

Listening to White House aides' views of these conflicts heightens one's appreciation for the responsibilities of the chief executive. The President has to act, even in the face of uncertainties, complexity, and opposition; eventually the consequences of inaction may outweigh the results of an ill-fated action. The President can ask the right questions, can act as educator, can preside over appropriate compromises, and can do much

---

[11] E. Hughes, *The Ordeal of Power* 59 (1963).

to shape and sharpen new policy directions, but the constraints on directing an effective application of those policies to problems are enormous. As the general public expects more and more of the presidency, and as its responsibilities for performance become greater and greater, the President is often thrust in the middle of a disillusioning squeeze play.

IV. A DIFFERENTIATED WHITE HOUSE STAFF

Much has been written about the continuous growth and increasing importance of the White House staff. The popular verdict is that the White House staff is the "center of the action" within the executive branch, and that it, more than any other body of counselors, is now the prime mechanism for helping Presidents shape and execute decisions. We are told that recent White House staffs have included favored assistants who have overshadowed the cabinet executives and challenged the importance of the "Distinguished Outsiders" to whom previous Presidents may have turned. Senior presidential assistants often deny any superordinate status over the cabinet and claim they are there merely to help the President communicate with the departments.

To be sure, White House staff have been quite strategically important in policy formulation stages of federal policy. But their apparent "effectiveness" in this one sphere too often obscures an unimpressive record in policy direction or "follow-through." While White House staff may contribute to the distillation of a vast amount of incubating legislative proposals, congressional subcommittees along with departmental officials are often able to go about the work of steering and administering federal domestic programs with seeming immunity from White House influence.

Presidents, of course, use their staff differently from term to term, and from one season to the next. But several generalizations about the White House staff in the 1960's can be suggested. It is my estimate that the patterns of continuity and similarity of the way recent Presidents (1960–1971) have organized and used their White House staffs far outweighed the differences. First, while the role of the White House staff has grown generally, its greatest increase in responsibility has been in information gathering and "policy distillation" activities: the culling of new ideas from task force and advisory group reports, the drafting of legislative messages, and the subsequent design of legislative strategies. As mentioned above, the execution or direction of far-flung federal enterprises have been less easily assumed by the White House (although there have been attempts). Second, the increased importance of the White House staff in policy making comes not so much at the expense of cabinet and departmental influence, as in proportion to the measurably expanding commitments of the federal government. Furthermore, just as current White House staff are significantly more important as a collectivity than most previous presidential staff, contemporary department leaders (excepting perhaps one or two) have vastly increased mandates, more administrative responsibilities, and larger staffs of their own, than did their predecessors of some twenty or forty years ago. Finally, relatively few White House aides enjoy anything near the prominence of the more important members of the cabinet. Under recent Presidents, only a small number of White House aides (ranging from six to a dozen) have had close and frequent access to the President. In practice, the large majority of White House aides deal much more frequently with sub-cabinet and cabinet secretariat staffs than directly with cabinet members. And White House aides have their largest influence on matters of small importance or in matters with which the President is indifferent.

The day of the "general purpose aide" with an entirely undefined portfolio seems a thing of the past for White House staff. To be sure, many of the White House jurisdictions are not rigidly prescribed, but those claiming to be generalists thrive not "at large," but in particular functional or substantive assignment areas, within, for example, public relations, foreign policy, or domestic program areas. It is easier than one might suspect to divide recent White House staff into five relatively distinct functional operations. (More could be defined, but a typology of five is sufficient for our purposes.) Overlapping assignments do exist and not a few White House aides claim they serve (or served) as bridges between factions within the staff. But with rare exceptions, presidential aides can be identified as members of one of the following staff units: (1) domestic policy and legislative program, (2) budget and economic policy, (3) national security and foreign policy, (4) congressional relations, and (5) administrative and public relations.[12]

As seen in Table 3, perceptions of executive branch conflict vary quite measurably with the type of White House task assignment. The White House aides with more programmatic or policy oriented responsibilities are far more likely to observe "considerable conflict" with the departments than are the more political or public relations staff assistants to Presidents. Is this just because they have more contact with the departments? Or is the nature of the work assignment responsible? Or is the type of man who is likely to be cast in one job at the White House basically different from the type of man he must deal with in the depart-

[12] One of the more distinguishing characteristics of the expanding Nixon White House has been its newly-created Office of Communications for the Executive Branch —a public relations and image-making functional group that will no doubt continue to exist in the same or somewhat similar format under future Presidents. *See* Bonafede, "Men Behind Nixon—Herbert G. Klein: Spokesman for the Administration," *Nat'l J.* 258–62 (Dec. 6, 1969).

ments? A closer examination of this differentiated White House staff (at least as it existed from 1961–1970) may suggest some of the features about White House work and staff "operational codes" which both make life difficult within the White House and shape varying performances.

TABLE 3

Varying Staff Perceptions of Conflict in Presidency—Executive Department Relations, with Staff Functions Held Constant

	Presidency Staff Functional Groupings				
Levels Of Conflict	*Domestic Policy & Legis. Prog. N = (12)*	*Budget/ Economic (6)*	*National Security/ Foreign (8)*	*Congress Relations (5) (Total N = 43)*	*Administrative Public Relations Staffs (12)*
Considerable	100%	83%	75%	20%	25%
Moderate	0	17	12.5	80	50
Insignificant	0	0	12.5	0	25
	100%	100%	100%	100%	100%

Source: Personal Interviews of White House Staff Members serving between 1961 and 1970.

A. *Domestic Policy and Legislative Program Staff.* Recent developments have had the effect of enhancing the need for a larger and more professional domestic policy and legislative program staff: the sheer growth of federal domestic programs, the fact that the initiative for setting the budget and formulating legislation has swung over to the President, and the vast increase in jurisdictional questions which are raised by multi-departmental programs such as Model Cities, mass transit, manpower training, early childhood education, and environmental protection. Another new dimension of White House staff domestic policy work has been the increased use and major reliance on presidential advisory networks outside of existing channels (*i.e.,* besides those within or connected with the executive departments).

Most of the Kennedy and Johnson domestic policy staff members were trained as lawyers (see Table 4). Most also had previous and sometimes extensive Washington experience; the Kennedy aides came directly from the campaign and from Capitol Hill staff positions, the Johnson aides mainly came from within the executive departments. Many had both legislative and executive branch work experience. Presidents Kennedy and Johnson used their domestic policy staff to summarize and analyze departmental proposals, refine conflicting views (insofar as possible), and generally define issues or proposals that deserved presidential attention. The domestic policy staff have been particularly sensitive to the fact that they should help the President "make his decisions [based] on the full range of *his* considerations and constituencies, which no Cab-

TABLE 4

Background Characteristics of Various White House Staff Groupings During the 1960's

Background Factors	*STAFF GROUPINGS* Domestic Policy & Legis. Prog. N = (12)	Budget/ Economic (6)	Nat. Security, For. Affairs (8)	Congress Relations (5)	Administrative Personal Staff (12) (Total N = 43)
Lawyer	75%*	0%	0%	40%	17%
Economist	0	50	50	0	0
University Professor	8	50	38	0	0
Public Relations Journalist	0	0	0	0	58
Former Congressional Staffer	42	0	12	20	33
Former Executive Branch Employment	75	100	75	40	17
Political Activist	50	0	25	100	67

Source: Personal interviews. * Percentages to be read down the column.

inet member shared." These staff usually see their works in terms of "getting things started," "getting bills to Capitol Hill," and later, once programs start getting enacted, "making things work."

The domestic aides, more frequently than any other group within the White House, usually fashion a distinctively adversary relationship with their counterparts in the domestic executive departments. Patrick Anderson captures some of the disquietude toward Johnson aide, Califano:

> Serving as the chief expediter for an impatient and demanding President, Califano has made many enemies. Cabinet members seeking to carry an issue to the President are often told to "talk to Joe" and this breeds resentment. Part of Califano's job is to knock heads together, and this wins him no friends among those whose heads are knocked. Some Cabinet members call him "Little Joe" behind his back, and they say it without smiling. Others who have crossed his path have called him a "hatchet man," and worse.[13]

These White House staff tend to be younger than the cabinet and senior civil servants with whom they conduct most of their business. In-

[13] P. Anderson, *The President's Men* 367 (1968).

variably, the White House lawyers explicitly view themselves as counsels to the President (who, of course, is "their" client). Often these lawyers interrogate or prod "their" departmental adversaries much in the spirit of the prosecuting attorney, and with the same tutored and dispassionate disregard for niceties, they soon earn the disapprobation of many of a departmental official. Priding themselves on possessing a superior capacity to think analytically, and the insight and foresight of that mysterious element called the "presidential perspective," White House domestic policy lawyers often view themselves as the necessary and indispensable catalysts who must stimulate and prod the departments into compliance with presidential intentions. Insensitive and arrogant as this appears, these aides are encouraged in this behavior by their perceptions of the constant need for speed, and by an often disillusioned and disbelieving President hardened by his inability to bend departmental bureaucracies in the direction of his policy priorities.

B. Budget and Economic Counselors. During the 1960's several members of the Council of Economic Advisers and of the Budget Bureau directorate functioned as full-fledged members of the White House staff. The previous distinctions between "Executive Office of the President" and "White House staff" became increasingly blurred as the White House domestic policy lawyers needed more sophisticated counsel on unemployment, tax policy, inflation control and numerous related questions involved in "managing" the national economy. Concomitantly, budget directors and economists—assigned to the Executive Office—assumed a presidential perspective largely indistinguishable from that of senior White House policy aides.

Budget Bureau leadership in the past decade was recruited from among the economics profession or from respected "old hands" who successfully worked themselves up the career ladder within the Bureau. In theory at least, the President's domestic aides and political counselors serve the short term, immediate policy interests of *a President,* whereas the Budget Bureau serves the longer term perspective of *the presidency,* with particular responsibilities for program evaluation and budgeting analysis. By the mid-1960's both the Bureau of the Budget and the Council of Economic Advisers were involved in White House program formulation tasks as well as in quasi-operational activities such as inflation control or anti-poverty program activities. As these so-called Executive Office "staff" became increasingly involved in White House and cabinet-level operations, the distinctions between White House and "Executive Office of the President" *and* the distinctions between presidential *staff* and executive branch *management* became at best hazy, and often confusing.

The Bureau of the Budget—now the Office of Management and Budget—has long played a central role (although with differing success) as an intermediary between White House and the departments. The Bureau has been expected to raise tough questions about program promise and performance: "What will this program really do?"; "Why has this program taken so long to get off the ground?"; "Why does this cost so much?"; "Why haven't you been in closer collaboration with other departments on this part of that program?"; and so forth. Not surprisingly, and in no small part intentionally, these investigative questions and the budgetary examination processes themselves beget a more or less adversary relationship with the departments. Moreover, Presidents and their senior White House staff assistants expect their budget and economic advisors to identify and bring to their attention department inconsistencies and specific program activities that run counter to the President's intentions.

Budget officials, even more than White House staff domestic policy aides, are now well accustomed to their often unfashionable role as the "abominable no-men" of the executive branch. Presidents frequently transmit some of their most unpleasant decisions for cabinet leaders *via* Budget Bureau leadership. One former director points out that conflict between the departments and the Budget Bureau is not only inevitable but, on balance, healthy. How else can you ferret out all the problems and possibilities? Said another Budget Bureau leader: "there is actually an inverse relationship between a cabinet member's effectiveness for the administration and his popularity with the Budget Bureau." That is to say, malleable and agreeable department people probably lack the capability for inventing and incubating needed new policy proposals and/or managerial strategies.

C. National Security and Foreign Policy Staff. It might seem that the President's national security staff would enjoy more harmonious relationships with "their" executive departments than is the case between the domestic policy staff and the domestic departments. Presumably the national security staff deals primarily with only two departments, State and Defense, in contrast to domestic policy aides who must deal with about ten departments plus numerous independent agencies. Moreover, it is generally held that the President is granted much greater leeway in determination of foreign policy than is the case in the various domestic policy spheres. But such a view is somewhat deceptive, for the Defense Department alone is really several departments rolled into one huge umbrella, employing at least three times as many *civilians* (not to mention military personnel) as the entire list of domestic departments (with the Post Office now excluded). In practice, the White House national security staff has responsibilities for at least seven or eight major departments and agencies, including Defense, State, Central Intelligence Agency, The Military (Joint Chiefs of Staff), the United States Information Agency,

Agency for International Development, and frequently, when appropriate, for Treasury, Agriculture, and Commerce as well.

The hope that a strong Secretary of State and a well organized State Department could act as the central coordinator for United States foreign policy has grown increasingly unrealistic. Contemporary Presidents have generally held that United States national security policy is and must be presidential policy, and concomitantly, there has been a major shift in policy formulation and direction to the White House and away from the various departments.

All recent Presidents have relied heavily on their national security staffs for keeping in close communication with the executive agencies making up the national security establishment.

D. White House Congressional Relations Staff. White House congressional relations aides differ from their fellow staff having substantive policy responsibilities in several ways. Their concern is less with policy formulation than it is with policy promotion. While the program and policy staff are busy trying to win support and cooperation for White House policy interests within the departments, congressional relations aides spend their time seeking political support from within congressional committees and among diverse factions on Capitol Hill. Not surprisingly, program and congressional liaison aides sometimes differ over the relative merits and feasibility of newly suggested program ideas. And at least under the recent Democratic administrations, the congressional relations aides have frequently mirrored the more conservative views of congressional chairmen in internal White House staff deliberations. Congressional relations aides only infrequently pay attention to policy implementation activities and on those occasions, more often than not, they argue the case as viewed on Capitol Hill to their White House colleagues.

Several factors help explain the congressional relations staff's more moderate estimates of contention between White House and departments. First, the White House congressional relations staff by vocation are far more geared to political accommodation and compromise than others on the White House staff. Consensus-building rather than policy incubation and program generation is their life style and preoccupation. They define their task as helping the President get his program passed by Congress. They consciously work for the reelections of the President (or his party) and the President's supporters within the Congress. To these ends they necessarily seek to minimize conflict and maximize cohesion. A reasonably unified executive branch is an added advantage for successful enactment of major legislation. Division and dissension within or among these departments will usually hurt a bill's chances for passage. Because they, more than any other staff at the White House, are conscious of the ingredients (*i.e.*, new proposals) that go into the making of the box scores of wins and losses that (albeit simplistically) characterize presidential-congressional relations, the legislative liaison aides favor "practical" proposals. While domestic and budget White House staff often remain disappointed by the dearth of new ideas or the hesitancy of the President to back a controversial proposal, the congressional relations officers are more easily satisfied by modest accomplishments and are also less inclined to encourage new or complicated legislative initiatives that might be difficult to pass—"we obviously don't want to be put in the position of having to sell programs that don't have a reasonable chance of passing."

Second, at least during the 1960's, the congressional relations officials had explicitly designated lieutenants in all major departments. For the most part these department officers were loyal partisans who owe allegiance almost equally to their cabinet members *and* to the White House congressional relations office, for the White House legislative liaison team had authority to remove or fire departmental legislative relations aides. These department contacts frequently had "graduated" to their posts from campaign or Capitol Hill staff work. In general, the White House staff enjoyed cordial and close (often with weekly meetings) relations with these "compatible" counterparts in the departments. In marked contrast with the White House domestic and budget aides it was quite rare for the White House congressional relations aides to have much if any contact with non-partisan civil servants or "bureaucrats." To some extent, their departmental lieutenants took the brunt of and absorbed department conflicts, thereby leaving the White House congressional relations aides relatively free to deal with senior congressional officials and preside over White House-congressional relations strategies.

Finally, the primary preoccupation of White House congressional relations aides is dealing with the leadership and committee chairmen in Congress. Since congressional aides are employed first and foremost to help forge viable coalitions of congressional support from bill to bill and from one legislative season to the next, their chief opposition consists of dissident members of their own party or influential opponents on the other side of the congressional aisle. Departmental concerns, especially departmental debates about alternative programs, are less appreciated and probably less well understood by congressional relations White House aides; these latter concerns necessarily take a back seat to their principal attention which is devoted to congressional and partisan strategy and tactics. In sum, then, both the fact that congressional relations aides have less actual contact with cabinet members and civil servants and the fact that they have distinctively different functional responsibilities account for less perceived conflict with departments.

E. Administrative and Public Relations Staff. As can be seen in Table 3, the non-policy administrative and personal staff assistants to the President were the least disposed to see serious conflict between the White House and the departments. Strictly speaking, no one on the White House staff is far removed from policy matters, but in a relative sense, there is measurable variation in staff involvement in detailed substantive policy deliberations. We now have White House organizations with large staffs of communication specialists, campaign counselors, ceremony coordinators, and dozens of others who handle speechwriting, mail, T.V. and radio arrangements, travel arrangements, and so forth. One reason for their "happier" evaluation of departmental relations is that they are measurably less involved with the vast executive establishment. Their contact with the departments is either with the usually responsive Office of the Secretary or with their own carefully planted network of political aides.

It is not so much that many of these aides do not have some problems in their relations with department officials, as it is that they have grown accustomed to accentuating the positive. That is, they are hired to secure maximum press and TV coverage for presidential accomplishments and, not surprisingly, to insure that the appealing rather than the appalling stories, the harmonious rather than the contentious character of a presidential administration are communicated to the American general public. Just as congressional relations aides experienced their conflicts more with certain members of Congress rather than departmental officials, so also many, if not most, of the administrative and public relations aides to Presidents have their occupational difficulties with columnists, editors, and TV commentators outside the government rather than with department officials inside the government.

V. A DIFFERENTIATED CABINET

In the previous section it is suggested that the differentiated White House staff organization may be one of the contributing factors to the variance in staff perceptions of conflict with the departments. So also it is likely that diversity and dissimilarity of the executive departments may also contribute to a variance in White House staff perceptions of conflict. An essential premise here is that an understanding of White House-departmental relations must take into account the differences in the way cabinet and department roles are viewed from the White House.

Though the cabinet is not mentioned in the United States Constitution, Presidents have appointed and consulted with their department heads ever since George Washington began the practice. President Washington actively solicited advice and counsel from his three department heads—State, Treasury, and War. In time he called these three together with his part-time Attorney General (who continued a private practice on the side). Subsequently, cabinet meetings became tradition and almost all Presidents used their cabinets as a political sounding board and as a convenient communications network. Over time, the cabinet changed greatly, especially affected by its growth from three to a dozen departmental members by 1967. While the notion of a cohesive presidential cabinet of collegial and interchangeable advisors persists with remarkable staying power, the cabinet as a collectivity has rarely been a policy making or program coordinating body. Indeed, the cabinet as a meaningful "collectivity" appears to be passing into oblivion (though not out of existence). And as Rossiter predicted more than twenty years ago, in its place there has grown up "a congeries of functional cabinets with reduced and appropriate membership." [14] The following discussion sketches several variables that undoubtedly affected White House assessments of and working relations with the cabinet departments under recent presidential administrations.

Any discussion of the cabinet, of course, should note that personality and individual levels of competence often affect the degree to which cordiality exists between White House and departments. Each cabinet usually has one or two cabinet members who excel in one way or another and become the dominant personalities in their cabinet.

Occasionally, too, there are times when the politics of the period and the functions of a department thrust particular cabinet members into prominence, and simultaneously, into close collaborative relations with the White House. Dean Acheson's unusually close and cordial ties with the Truman White House and Lyndon Johnson's highly respectful appreciation of Dean Rusk illustrate the cases of internationally tense periods in which diplomatic political strategy looms large. Secretary John Gardner (HEW 1965–68) enjoyed great prominence and relatively good relations with the Johnson White House during the middle 1960's around the time in which major educational and health legislation were being ratified and placed into operation. Soon thereafter, however, when the Vietnam war began overshadowing all else and consuming more and more of the President's time and potential budget increases, White House communications with HEW's Gardner began to resemble those of most other domestic cabinet members—less frequent and less supportive.

The rise in prominence or fashion of an issue relevant to a department's activities can occasionally also work to the detriment of White House-department relations. The "law and order" issue in the late 1960's occasioned cutting partisan attacks to be mounted against President Johnson's Attorney General. Ramsey Clark resisted most temptations to act in any retaliatory or repressive manner. But, evidently, Clark's response was viewed as overly dispassionate and tolerant by his President.

---

[14] Rossiter, "The Constitutional Significance of the Executive Office of the President," 43 *Am. Pol. Sci. Rev.* 1206, 1216 (1949).

And the more recent case of former Secretary Walter Hickel and his varied efforts apparently illustrates the case of a cabinet member who decides to champion popular issues (environmental protection and youth) measurably further than the Administration of which he is a part.

There are, of course, numerous other reasons why Presidents and their staff may deliberately choose to have "cool" relations with a cabinet member. Sometimes this may be due to presidential lack of interest in a department's domain. Sometimes there is ill will existing between a strong President and a strong and quite stubborn cabinet member. Part of the problem undoubtedly arises because Presidents just don't have time to spend with cabinet officers, not to mention the leaders of independent agencies and major bureau chiefs. The blunt fact of the contemporary period is that approximately two-thirds of presidential time has been spent on national security and foreign policy considerations.

An apparent pattern characterizes White House-cabinet relations over time. Just as there is a distinctive presidential "honeymoon" with the press and with partisan critics, so also White House-department ties usually are the closest and most cooperative during the first year of an administration. The first six months of the relationship is usually cordial, "healthy," and often bordering on the euphoric. The election victory is still being celebrated. A new team of "leaders" has arrived in Washington. New faces provide for extensive news copy. A new federal policy agenda is being recast. The newly staffed executive branch gives everyone an impression of bubbling over with new ideas, new possibilities, and imminent break-throughs. In contrast to the much publicized arrival of the cabinet members, White House staff receive less publicity at this time.

But as policy formulation is accentuated in the early years of a presidential term, program management and implementation receive increasing attention in the later period (especially if a President has been successful in passing a fair amount of new legislation by then). Critical domestic developments and international crises begin to monopolize the presidential schedule. Presidents gradually find that they have much less time for personally dealing with cabinet members as they had in the administration's early months. Cabinet members become less inclined to refer "too much" to the President, knowing full well that they may prematurely exhaust their personal political credit with him. Additionally, the President's program becomes somewhat fixed; priorities get set and budget ceilings produce some new rules of the game. Ambitious, expansionist cabinet officers become painfully familiar with various Executive Office staff refrains, usually to the effect that "there just isn't any more money available for programs of that magnitude," "budget projections for the next two or three years just can't absorb that type of increment," and perhaps harshest of all—"yes, I agree that this is an excellent proposal, but excellent though it may be, it will just have to wait until the next term."

When, in the course of an administration, cabinet members grow bitter about the way they are treated and increasingly left out of White House affairs, they seldom make their opinions public. There are, of course, some exceptions and privately a good number of cabinet officers will talk about the problem. The case of Interior Secretary Walter Hickel is perhaps an extreme case; the fact that he had only two or three private meetings with his President during a two year period seems an unusually restrictive arrangement. Most recent cabinet officers have had more frequent relations with their White House superiors, but few of the domestic cabinet members have been wholly pleased by the quantity or quality of these meetings.

Conventional rankings of the departments are based on their longevity, annual expenditure outlays, or their personnel totals. Rankings according to these indicators can be seen in the first three columns of Table 5. A preliminary appreciation of department diversity can be gained by even a casual comparison of these columns. For example, while the State Department is more than 175 years older than some of the newest departments, its expenditures rank as the lowest of any department. On the other hand, the Department of Health, Education and Welfare although formally less than twenty years old ranks second only to Defense in having more personnel and higher annual expenditures.

Some other ways of classifying the departments deserve note. One is suggested by Stewart Alsop's journalistic appraisal of real political "power and impact." [15] Alsop's 1967 ranking takes into account not only the conventional data mentioned above, but also the Washington, D.C., status considerations toward contemporary cabinet members and departmental activities. Upon closer inspection the Alsop listing varies only slightly from longevity or seniority rankings with minor adjustments added to acknowledge the higher budget allocations of Defense and HEW as well as the personal Washington "celebrity" status of Robert S. McNamara and John W. Gardner (HEW).

The contemporary cabinet can also be differentiated into "inner" and "outer" departmental clusterings as illustrated in the fifth column of Table 5. The inner cabinet, at least throughout the 1960's, was generally recognized as the primary presidential counseling as well as strategic information gathering departments. (A cabinet counselor is a source of information and advice, someone to whom a President can turn for appraisals and consultation on highly sensitive or critical problems.) The outer cabinet are the explicitly domestic policy departments (Justice excepted). By custom, if not by designation these cabinet officers assume a relatively

---

[15] *See* Alsop, *The Center* (1968), ch. 9.

TABLE 5

Various Ways of Viewing the Executive Departments

SENIORITY	*EXPENDITURES*[a]	*PERSONNEL*[b]	*A JOURNALIST'S ASSESSMENT OF "REAL POLITICAL POWER & IMPACT"*[c]
1 State	1 Defense	1 Defense	1 Defense
2 Treasury	2 HEW	2 HEW	2 State
3 War/Defense	3 Treasury	3 Agriculture	3 Treasury
4 Justice	4 Agriculture	4 Treasury	4 Justice
5 Interior	5 Labor	5 Interior	5 Interior
6 Agriculture	6 Transportation	6 Transportation	6 HEW
7 Commerce	7 HUD	7 State	7 Labor
8 Labor	8 Commerce	8 Justice	8 Agriculture
9 HEW	9 Justice	9 Commerce	9 Commerce
10 HUD	10 Interior	10 HUD	10 HUD
11 Transportation	11 State	11 Labor	11 Transportation

INNER & OUTER CLUSTERINGS[d]	*SUPER-CABINET PLAN A*[e]	*SUPER-CABINET PLAN B*[f]	*PRESIDENT NIXON'S 1971 PROPOSAL*[g]
State Defense Treasury Justice	National Security Economic Stability and Growth Domestic Policy	Foreign Affairs Economic Affairs Natural Resources Science and Technology Social Services and Justice	State Defense Treasury Justice
Agriculture Interior Transportation HEW HUD Labor Commerce			Human Resources Natural Resources Economic Development Community Development

[a] Estimated budget outlays of the executive departments in 1971.
[b] *Statistical Abstract*, data for 1970.
[c] *See* S. Alsop, *The Center* 254 (1968).
[d] Generic clustering according to counseling/advocacy dimensions—see text discussion.
[e] The way some White House aides view aggregate departmental concerns, and the apparent priority of these concerns as viewed by recent Presidents.
[f] An example of cabinet consolidation that is one of many plausible but politically unlikely reforms.
[g] Richard M. Nixon, State of the Union message to Congress, January 22, 1971.

straight-forward advocate orientation that overshadows their counseling role. (An advocate is someone who argues for a cause, who supports, defends and on occasion pleads in behalf of some special concern.)

State, Defense, Treasury, and Justice, each for different reasons (discussed below), are the cabinet posts most consistently considered as part of the inner cabinet. The pattern in the past few presidential administrations suggests somewhat strongly that these counseling cabinet positions are vested with high priority responsibilities that almost naturally bring Presidents and their top staff into close and continually collaborative relations with the occupants of these inner cabinet leadership posts. Sorensen wrote that it was the "nature of their responsibilities and the competence with which they did their jobs" that brought certain department executives particularly close to President Kennedy in this counseling manner. Speaking of the Eisenhower period, Emmet J. Hughes sees a convergence of raw strength of personality and leadership with the Defense, Treasury, and State cabinet posts. Sorensen cites six cabinet members as enjoying particularly close ties to John Kennedy, and one gathers that the general order of their importance and closeness to Kennedy amounted to this: Defense Secretary Robert McNamara, Attorney General Robert Kennedy, Secretary of State Dean Rusk, Treasury Secretary Douglas Dillon, and in varying ways Labor Secretary Arthur Goldberg and Vice President Lyndon Johnson. And it is abundantly clear that Rusk and McNamara continued to hold superordinate status in the Lyndon Johnson cabinet vis-à-vis their cabinet colleagues. On balance, the period between 1961 and 1971 can be characterized by having had an "inner cabinet" group made up of the Defense, State, and Treasury secretaries along with the Attorney General. Then, too, as will be discussed a little later, certain White House staff counselors were also included in an inner circle if not in the inner cabinet.

The inner cabinet grouping of this inner/outer breakdown suggested here corresponds identically to George Washington's original foursome, to Stewart Alsop's journalistic appraisal, and also to Sorensen's account of the Kennedy Administration. Moreover, the inner cabinet departments were the only ones immune to President Nixon's proposed overhaul of the executive branch; all others were nominated for abolition. My own classification of inner/outer derives from the examination of how White House aides viewed the departments. The status accorded these cabinet roles is, of course, subject to ebb and flow, for the status is rooted in performance and the fashions of the day as well as reputation. But, in general, White House staff during the 1960's acted far more deferentially toward these inner cabinet positions and the men who occupied them than toward outer cabinet officials.

With the exception of the State *Department*, as distinguished from the *Office of the Secretary* of State, the inner cabinet and the inner cabinet departments were almost always viewed as executive branch allies of the White House staff. An implicit operational code to this effect seemingly guided the manner in which most White House staff aides participated in executive branch activities during the 1960's. For this reason, these ties deserve further attention.

The State and Defense Departments have long been considered counseling and inner-cabinet departments. And the special closeness of Secretaries Rusk and McNamara with both Kennedy and Johnson is illustrative. One Johnson aide said it was his belief that President Johnson personally trusted only two of his cabinet—Rusk and McNamara (though it appears that the trust relationship between Johnson and McNamara diminished somewhat in 1967). Contemporary Presidents view national security and foreign policy matters as life and death considerations; President Kennedy, for example, noted that while mistakes in domestic policy "can only defeat us [at the next election, mistakes in] foreign policy can kill us." The seemingly endless series of crises (Berlin, Cuba, Congo, Dominican Republic, Vietnam, and the Middle East to name just a few) during the 1960's make it mandatory for recent Presidents to maintain close relations with these two national security cabinet heads. Just as George Washington had met almost every day with his four "cabinet" members during the national security concern over the French crisis of 1793, so also John Kennedy and Lyndon Johnson were likely to meet at least weekly and be in daily telephone communication with their inner cabinet of national security advisors.

It needs to be added, however, that throughout the past decade there has been more than a little White House discontent with the operational lethargy of the State Department. We see here an anomaly in which the Secretary of State clearly was regarded as a member of the President's inner cabinet, but the Department of State was regarded as one of the most deficient and inadequate cabinet departments. More than twenty-five per cent of the White House staff interviewed for this study cited the State Department as an excellent illustration of the problem of White House-department conflicts. White House staff scorned the narrowness and timidity of the encrusted and elitist foreign service officers and complained also of the custodial conservatism reflected in State Department working papers. Part of this problem may stem from the threats and philosophy of the Joseph McCarthy era which intimidated State Department careerists into holding only the puristic interpretations of the accepted policies of the day, thereby inhibiting their imaginative and inventive policy faculties. No doubt though, part of the problem stems from the way recent Secretaries, especially Secretary Rusk, defined their job. The demands on the Secretary were such that the State Department and its management were not Rusk's personal top priority. John Leacacos has surmised that the priorities appeared to have been:

> . . . first, the President and his immediate desires; second, the top operations of the current crisis; third, public opinion as reflected in the press, radio and TV and in the vast inflow of letters from the public; fourth, Congressional opinion; fifth, Rusk's need to be aware, at least, of every thing that was going on in the world; and only sixth and last, the routine of the State Department itself.[16]

The fact that the Secretary of State so frequently serves as the President's representative abroad or his number one witness on foreign policy

---

[16] Leacacos, *Fires in the In-Basket* 110 (1968).

matters before the Congress undoubtedly is another reason so few Secretaries of State have had the time or energy available for managing the State Department's widely scattered staff. It needs to be added that more than sixty federal departments, agencies, and committees are involved some way in the administration of our foreign policy. Recent Presidents increasingly have vested authority in their own White House-based NSC staff partly to compensate for State's uneven performance as a coordination arm for foreign policy matters and partly because Presidents need instant analysis during international crisis periods. In this regard, McGeorge Bundy's White House national security staff was dubbed by the press as "Bundy's little State Department." In another step to centralize and coordinate basic foreign policy activities, Richard Nixon has instituted a White House-level Council of International Economic Policy with broad authorities. Nonetheless, the Secretary of State still enjoys a relative closeness to the incumbent President and even with the rise in importance of White House national security counselors the Secretary of State is likely to continue as a full-fledged member of future presidential inner cabinets.

The Justice Department, also a counseling department, is frequently identified with the "inner circle" of cabinet agencies and its chieftains usually associated with the inner cabinet. That both Kennedy and Nixon appointed their most trusted campaign managers to the Attorney Generalship is an indicator of the importance of this position as a presidential counseling location. The Justice Department traditionally serves as the President's attorney and lawyer. This special obligation results in continually close professional relations between White House domestic policy lawyers and Justice Department lawyers. Few people realize that the White House is constantly dependent on Justice Department lawyers for counsel on civil rights developments, presidential veto procedures, tax prosecutions, anti-trust controveries, presidential pardons recommendations, regulatory agency oversight, and a continual overview of the congressional judiciary committees. That this particular exchange sees lawyer working with lawyer may well account for some of the generally higher levels of satisfaction characterizing White House-Justice Department transactions.

The Treasury Department continues to play an all important role as an interpreter of the nation's leading financial interests and as key presidential advisor on both domestic and international fiscal and monetary policy considerations. At one time, of course, the Bureau of the Budget existed within Treasury. Now the budget staff and numerous economists, particularly within the Council of Economic Advisers, are attached to the White House itself, thereby somewhat diminishing the monopoly of economic counsel once available only from the Treasury. But, Treasury is a department with major institutional authority, having considerable responsibility for income and corporate tax administration, currency control, public borrowing and counseling the President with respect to questions of balance of gold, the federal debt and international trade, development, and monetary matters. By custom, if not by law, the Secretary of the Treasury sits in on deliberations of important national security controversies. Indeed, Treasury Secretary Douglas Dillon played a significant role in Kennedy's Cuban Missile Crisis policy determinations. There is here, as in the case of the Justice Department lawyers, a common professional linkage among economists and financial specialists at Treasury and their professional counterparts on the White House staff.

The inner circle of cabinet members are noticeably more interchangeable than the outer circle cabinet. Henry Stimson, for example, alternated from Taft's Secretary of War, to Hoover's Secretary of State, and then back once more as FDR's Secretary of the War Department. Dean Acheson was an FDR Under Secretary of the Treasury but later a Truman Secretary of State. C. Douglas Dillon reversed this pattern by being an Eisenhower Under Secretary of State and later a Kennedy Secretary of the Treasury. When Kennedy was trying to lure Robert McNamara to his new cabinet he offered McNamara his choice between Defense and Treasury. More recently, former Attorney General Nicholas Katzenbach went from Justice to an Under Secretaryship of State, and former Attorney General William Rogers is now the thirteenth Justice Department head to have served in another inner cabinet position. John Connally, once a Secretary of the Navy, became a Nixon Secretary of the Treasury. There have been occasional shifts between inner and outer cabinet (*e.g.*, Harriman–Commerce to State, and Richardson–State to HEW), but such examples are an exception to the general pattern. What this interchangeability means is hard to discern, but it suggests perhaps that Presidents find it easier as well as more necessary to work with inner cabinet members and that inner cabinet members find it easier for their part to adopt a counseling style that allows them to identify more closely with the presidential "perspective" than is the case for outer cabinet members.

Quite related to the interchangeability of inner cabinet roles is the little-appreciated fact that, at least in recent years, White House staff aides recruited from within the executive branch have come mainly from among the inner-cabinet departments, often directly from service as assistants to cabinet members. And many of the recent White House staff who did not come from the executive branch had served (at one time or another) as departmental consultants to inner cabinet officials.

In recent years several members of the White House staff have performed cabinet-level counselor roles. Eisenhower, for example, explicitly designated Sherman Adams as a protocol member of his cabinet. Kennedy clearly looked upon Theodore Sorensen, McGeorge Bundy, and some of his economic advisors as co-equals if not more vital to his work than most of his cabinet members. Johnson and Nixon have likewise assigned many of their "staff" men to cabinet-type counseling responsibilities. Indeed, President Nixon, quite reasonably, has appropriated this term—cabinet counselor—for several of his personal staff, including Messrs. Burns, Moynihan, Harlow, and Finch. These counselors, whether in department posts or on the White House staff, are expected to rise above the narrowing frame of reference of the conventional advocate and, in Moynihan's view "It is not enough [that they] know one subject, one department. The President's men must know them all, must understand how one thing relates to another, must find in the words the spirit that animates them. . . ." The people to whom Presidents turn for White House overview presentations to congressmen and cabinet gatherings provide another indicator of inner "cabinet" status. When Kennedy wanted to have his cabinet briefed on his major priorities, he would typically ask Secretary of State Dean Rusk to review foreign affairs considerations, Chairman of the Council of Economic Advisers Walter Heller would review major questions about the economy, and Ted Sorensen might sum up and give a status report on the domestic legislative program. In like manner, when Lyndon Johnson would hold special "seminars" for large gatherings of congressmen and their staffs, he would invariably call upon the Secretaries of State and Defense to explain national security matters, and then ask his Budget Director and his Chairman of The Council of Economic Advisers to comment upon economic, budgetary, and domestic program considerations. More recently, President Nixon would typically call upon his Secretary of State, his director of the Office of Management and Budget, and one of his chief White House domestic policy counselors to inform and instruct members of his assembled cabinet and sub-cabinet. These illustrations indicate that recent Presidents often believe that members of their own Executive Office are better equipped to talk about and counsel "significant others" regarding the "President's" program rather than let most cabinet members attempt to do the same. Kallenbach's reasoning in this regard seems appropriate:

> [A]s the departments have grown and supervision of their operations has become more burdensome, the heads have less opportunity to concern themselves with questions of general policy outside their own spheres of interest. Another factor is the steady enlargement of the Cabinet group itself. . . . This creates a condition which tends to induce the President to rely more heavily upon one or more individuals in the group for general advice, rather than upon all equally.[17]

What has generally happened in recent years is that the Secretaries of State and Defense still remain as prominent national security advisors

[17] J. Kallenbach, *The American Chief Executive* 439–40 (1966).

though the National Security Assistant to the President has joined them as an inner-circle counselor. In domestic and economic matters Treasury Secretaries and most Attorney Generals still play a major role in rendering advice and broad-ranging policy counsel, but they have been joined in the inner "cabinet" by the Budget Director, and variously prominent White House and staff economists and domestic policy coordinators. President Nixon's 1971 cabinet reform proposal is an apparent recognition of the problem of the outer cabinet's "distance" from the presidency. His proposals would abolish some of the outer cabinet departments and attempt to bring four newly packaged or consolidated "outer" departments into closer proximity if not full-fledged status with his inner cabinet. It is impossible to tell whether his recommendations will make any significant difference in this regard, although his motives for proposing this change are no doubt related to the seemingly estranged relationships between the outer departments and the White House.

The outer cabinet is the collection of cabinet posts and departments most often nominated as candidates for reform or abolition. These are the cabinet posts that experience the great cross pressures from clientele groups and congressional interests that often run counter to presidential interests or priorities. It is the outer cabinet departments that have the most intensive and competitive exchange with White House and Budget Bureau staff, and many an outer cabinet member has complained bitterly about the political pressures on and unmanageability of their departments.

Most of the White House domestic and budget policy aides interviewed for this study cited five departments as the ones with which they had the most difficult or truculent working relations—HEW, HUD, Labor, Commerce, and Interior. Invariably, the White House staff suspects that outer cabinet departmental executives often accentuate the concerns of their department and their department's more obvious clientele over the concerns that might be broadly ascribed to the President or the President's party.

Most of the reform proposals espoused by White House aides (two of which are noted as columns 6 and 7 in Table 5), would reduce the number of cabinet posts in the hope of strengthening the President's ties with the outer cabinet and increasing the stature of the outer cabinet vis-à-vis the inner cabinet. The implicit (but by no means clear) assumption behind most of these reforms is that the fundamental conflict in the executive branch is not between the President and various cabinet members, but it is rather between special and general (or presidential) interests. Some of the outer cabinet departments could and perhaps will eventually be collapsed into a few broader purpose departments. Alternatives depicted in Table 5 indicate that department reduction could conceivably be pushed to five or even three basic core departments (even more "revolutionary" than the Nixon proposals). As is usually the case, talk about the need to reform and the move in this direction (however gradual) has been preceded by an implicit or unconscious set of practices that have already recognized a distinctively differentiated cabinet. The way White House aides define their work and how Presidents allocate their time and energy indicate that there currently exist three specialized "cabinet" concentrations—national security, aggregate economics, and domestic policy affairs. And at least during the 1960's it happened that these three areas were attended to in approximately this same order of importance or deference.

In the future it is likely that regardless of how organization charts are drawn, presidential use of the cabinet and White House staff will take into greater consideration the realities of the differentiated roles and activities of the federal departments. It is likely, too, that Presidents will move in the direction of utilizing specialized "cabinets" for concentrated purposes of the federal government. This is to say, the generalized cabinet will more or less pass into oblivion as a national security "cabinet," an economics directorate and a domestic policy "cabinet" continue to emerge, each of which will be presided over by some combination of presidential counselors, some based in redesigned executive departments and others located on the President's personal staff. Cabinet advocates will surely still exist, but it may be possible to have them operate from posts within rather than on top of the executive departments. (It may well turn out, of course, that these concentrated and realigned cabinets will find that their internal rivalries become so intense and so often tumultous that new reform movements will then champion the goal of breaking up the super cabinet framework.) On balance, the White House staff for the forseeable future is not likely to become much smaller or see its importance measurably diminished by these reorganizational developments, but a redesigned and consolidated outer cabinet might enable White House staff to abstain more often from the temptation of pulling administrative responsibilities into itself than has been the case in the last ten years.

VI. STRENGTHENING WHITE HOUSE-DEPARTMENT RELATIONS?

There is little difficulty in establishing the existence of considerable White House frustration with department "unresponsiveness" or parochialism and the existence of cabinet and department distress at the sometimes unnecessary political and abrasive behavior of the White House staff. But it is much less easy to evaluate the varied prescriptions that are put forth as a means toward improving White House-department relations.

We have seen in preceding sections that there is no one single cause of White House-department conflicts; moreover there is no one simple solution. Indeed, it would seem reasonable that the appropriate reforms will vary not only with the type of problem but also according to staff functions at the White House and the differentiated departments involved. Most of the White House aides at least implicitly acknowledge that numerous remedial or regenerating efforts are needed within the White House as well as between the White House and departments.

Many former presidential aides began their discussion of reforms by pointing out the obvious: no two Presidents are exactly alike; styles differ as well as policy preferences. Hence, "each president should organize his office more or less as he sees fit."

As seen in Table 6, rather than uniformly calling for the presidential or "more power to the White House" perspective, these aides support what might be called an integration model just as much, and many of them support a department/cabinet approach as well. Almost eighty per cent of the domestic and budget policy aides offered suggestions that would strengthen White House policy planning and management capabilities. Even those who complained about White House staff arrogance often concluded that Presidents must have tough and aggressive staff help.

TABLE 6
Presidency Staff Perspectives on the Question of Improving Cooperation and Reducing Conflict Between White House and the Executive Departments

Strategy Perspectives[b]	*Percentages*[a] *N = 43*
I. *Presidential Perspective:*	
—Stronger WH Management-Monitoring System	45%
—More Aggressive WH Sanctions and Controls over Executive Departments	41
—Stronger WH Policy Determinating Capability	33
II. *Integrative Perspective:*	
—Make It More of a "Two-Way Street"	45
—More Collaboration and Departmental Involvement in Policy Setting	40
—More WH Staff Sensitivity and Homework Re: Intra-Departmental Concern	36
III.. *Departmental—Cabinet Perspective:*	
—Strengthen Cabinet Secretaries and Cabinet-President Linkage	26
—Delegate More to Departments—Less WH Interference and Primacy; More Trust and Better Communications	24

Source: Personal Interviews of White House Staff Members Who Served During 1961–1970 period.

[a] Percentages here reflect multiple responses.

[b] Aggregate responses to the three perspectives were as follows: 69% of the respondents recommended the presidential perspective, 69% recommended the integrative perspective, and 40% recommended the departmental/cabinet perspective.

Although there is a good deal of overlap between those supporting the presidential and integrative perspectives, the integration approach was relatively more supported among the administrative and public relations assistants and among the national security policy aides than among the domestic and budget policy advisers. Integrative recommendations are seemingly based on the assumption that the White House is not likely to have much of an effect on federal program implementation unless it can win supportive cooperation from among the middle and higher echelons of the executive branch departments.

Some forty per cent of the former White House staff aides noted that a strong presidency could only succeed in an executive branch which also was characterized by the existence of strong cabinet and departmental leadership. Many of these aides felt that Kennedy, and Johnson, and their senior staff had neglected the cabinet members and underestimated their importance in making the government work. One aide insisted that it was a major mistake to let the domestic cabinet departments become so divorced from the White House:

> One way to improve things is to have the president and the cabinet members, particularly in domestic areas, meet at least six or seven times a year and talk in great detail, and in highly substantive terms, about the major priorities of the administration. You have to have better communication. Basically you have to make the cabinet less insecure.

Other aides criticized certain of their colleagues for having taken over operational responsibilities of the regular agencies, adding that too often these aides neither expedited program implementation nor accomplished anything else except possibly enlarging their own importance. Those aides who held sub-cabinet positions in one of the departments or agencies (either before or immediately after they worked on the White House staff) were significantly more sympathetic to the departmental/cabinet perspective than most of their White House colleagues who had not served "in the other fellow's shoes."

VII. CONCLUSION

A democracy must serve as a forum or arena for the practical and just mediation of conflicts. If our elected chief executive and his lieutenants were not constantly surrounded, or "afflicted," by a wide diversity of conflicts, they would probably be avoiding their legitimate public responsibilities. The conflicts discussed in this paper are those that exist within the executive branch, but it seems fair to assume that executive branch conflicts in large part mirror the existing and potential conflicts of society at large and as such they deserve far more detailed scrutiny. In general, however, we can conclude with Lewis Coser that such conflicts as exist are multilateral rather than unilateral, multidimensional rather than unidimensional, and occasioned by mixed rather than single motives. This paper suggests, if anything, that the conflicts which abound in the executive branch admit no single source, nor are they generated by any one set of political actors or agents. Size, complexity, specialization, and differing policy preferences are but a few of the factors contributing to that richness of contention that often exists within the American executive establishment.

The intent of this paper has been to answer only the most simple and elementary of questions pertaining to conflict and cooperation within the executive branch. It is tempting to pontificate about "solutions" and "remedies" that might ameliorate these conflicts and "strengthen" White House-department relations. But such an exercise would be premature and diversionary from the much needed analysis that must precede sophisticated political engineering. For example, we know little about the impact of conflict on the way public policies are selected and applied, or the conditions under which conflict in the executive branch is useful or necessary or valuable rather than a liability. It might be feasible to devise some indicators or scales on which to measure the amount and intensity of conflict, and the degree to which it helps or hinders certain sets of actors or certain sets of preferences within given decisional arenas. The very definition of conflict deserves more attention: how to distinguish between *routine* and *critical* conflicts; is there a point at which creative or constructive conflict becomes debilitating to the institutions within which they have been fostered? What are the effects of varied types of conflicts on system stability, system renewal, and system innovation?

But having duly displayed the appropriately detached professional caution, let me at least stick a toe into the water, and indulge just a little in a few suggestions that emerge from this analysis. Some readers may find these suggestions to be mere common sense or unnecessarily overbearing. And to some extent so they are. I would only add that these suggestions are offered in the spirit of experimentation and tentativeness and urge that these too be tested.

Ted Sorensen has written that President John Kennedy was always more interested in policy than in the administration of policies. We can extend that observation to President Johnson and the White House staffs of both Presidents as well. The way in which our elections and campaign systems are run makes it easy to accentuate discussions about policy issues rather than policy strategies, and this emphasis seemed overextended during the 1960's. At the beginning of a presidential term White House staffs are initially comprised of policy-generating and policy-distillating activists who attempt to make good on the sweeping proposals that were vaguely articulated in previous campaigns. The emphasis is on policy change and the development of brand new sets of policies rather than the adaptation or improvement of existing policy. It may well be that the initial investment in a staff gathered for the purpose of developing and selling new policies skews the White House counseling resources in such a way that the White House is less effective in managerial and implementation aspects of policy leadership. Since it appears that White House work emphases are somewhat subject to cycles of accentuated policy formulation or accentuated policy implementation, it may be that staffing patterns should similarly be subject to shifting composition. During the Kennedy-Johnson presidencies, however, the internal composition of the staff did not noticeably change. The domestic policy staff, for example, continued to be comprised of youthful Washington lawyers who were geared to putting together new programs for the next State of the Union. But during periods when program implementation and interdepartmental jurisdictional disputes become the overriding concerns of a presidential administration it may not be enough to rely solely upon this type of staff. And to overcome some of the operational deficiencies of major new programs such as those making up the core of the War on Poverty, Alliance for Progress, and Great Society it may not be enough to have White House lawyers and economists occasionally seek the advice of management consultants or appoint managerial project directors to secondary departmental posts.

Even if Presidents reshuffle their executive branch departments, even if Presidents could redesign the congressional committee structure to their own preference and banish lobbyists from the metropolitan Washington community—conflicts would still exist and flourish within the executive establishment. Therefore, no matter what other reforms are attempted, Presidents and their senior-most advisors ought to give far more consideration to the need for skilled management mediators, who will not be afraid occasionally to widen the scope of conflict, who can selectively step in and divide up controversial pieces of the action. By custom if not by preparation, White House aides have increasingly been forced to serve as arbitrators among competing agencies, competing policies, and competing priorities. Indeed, the increasing prominence and importance of domestic, budget, and national security policy aides at the White House derive from their sitting as judges on the high court of executive branch jurisdictional claims. But ironically many of these people were recruited to the White House not because of their special talents in this area, but because of their help on the campaign trail or as an academic advisor to a presidential candidate or a President-elect in search of a legislative program. It is an understatement to suggest that the White House is in great need of decisive executive branch mediators who can, with the full confidence of the President, preside over the thorniest of complicated claims and counter-claims by competing cabinet members and know when worthy and important elements of a debate are being seriously neglected or misrepresented within these cabinet level negotiations. In the recent past Presidents have used people who were already "on-board" to perform tasks for which they were ill-suited or unprepared.

Presidents and their White House staff should never assume that departmental executives will intuitively divine presidential intentions. White House staff themselves have sometimes not clearly understood their own and their own President's policy positions and often do not adequately communicate their policy positions when they do know their position. While it is true that department officials sometimes do not want to hear or understand what the White House is saying, just as often White House aides have misunderstood the degree to which their job is that of a communications agent. Ironically, those White House staffs who have had most experience in the field of communications are those assigned to deal with external groups and publics, such as the Congress, the press, and the general public, rather than the various components of the executive branch itself.

We have suggested in this paper the distinction between an inner and outer clustering of the cabinet. Inner cabinet members seem to enjoy closer and more collaborative ties with the White House; outer departments are more characterized by centrifugal pulls that dissipate close counseling relationships with the White House. But there are some implications of this dichotomy which are not entirely clear at first glance; the problem for the White House may not be to try to make the outer cabinet precisely like the inner cabinet, but to consider whether the inner cabinet might not benefit from some aspects of the way in which the White House relates to the outer cabinet. That is, the cordial and frequent contact between White House and Defense, Justice, Treasury, and the Secretary of State may actually camouflage substantive problems that should be contended, and issues that should be subject to the clashing of adversary viewpoints. United States policy in Vietnam, the Bay of Pigs episode, inadequate tax reform, and too casual a concern for civil liberties are general illustrations that come most readily to mind as by-products of the inner cabinet in the 1960's. It may be that because White House relationships with the counseling departments seem so close, comfortable, and professional in comparison with White House relationships with the overt advocate departments, that the White House too readily accepts the judgments of these departments, overlooks potentially divisive issues, and neglects the creation of an effective system of multiple and critical advocacy for the substantive and operational aspects of these departments. Too often in the 1960's the debates and adversary proceedings came too late or were procedurally foreclosed with reference to inner cabinet policy choices. If this be so, then many of the more conventional structural reforms (including some of those which President Nixon proposed in his 1971 State of the Union address) misunderstand an important aspect of White House-department relationships. Efforts must be made to increase certain types of conflicts and advocacy proceedings to ferret out differences of views, to generate alternative policy choices (and their rationale), and to estimate the likely consequences of diverse policies.

Many of the White House staff with executive branch experience previously served within inner cabinet departments, and this may explain both their greater difficulties with the outer cabinet and their preference for reforms which would place presidential counselors, as opposed to advocates, in charge of realigned and consolidated outer cabinet departments. But an assumption by which these aides are guided is that the policies or products of the inner cabinet have somehow been more acceptable or wise than those of the outer departments. There may be a tendency here, mistakenly to interpret closeness and loyalty to the presidency as equivalents of intelligent policy and competent administrative performance. In any event, Presidents should be wary of receiving their counsel exclusively from inner cabinet and staff who maintain only a presidential perspective. I am among those who feel that people who protest that a President is drastically isolated are, more often than not, merely signifying that a President has rejected or ignored their pet preferences, but there is nonetheless often a tendency for Presidents to indulge in only those views and opinions that sound like music to the ear, a situation that can of course lead to a state of alarming deficiency.

No one should dispute that our modern presidency is charged with enormous new obligations to act as an overseer of executive branch *responsiveness* and *integrity*. Who else can recruit talented department leadership? Who else can better motivate, educate, and inspire federal officials to higher levels of public commitment? And who else can both authoritatively mediate interdepartmental squabbles and wage vigilant pressure campaigns against those within the federal government who see themselves as the chief constituency of their own federal departments? All this and more is expected of the modern presidency and the expanded super staffs at the White House. But notions of government integrity and responsiveness are always slippery and should necessarily be subject to continuous definitional disputes. Responsiveness to whom? Is the presidentialists' perspective really free of special interests, or does this depend almost entirely on whether one happens to like the sitting President?

We come back, invariably, to a realization that Presidents are limited in the degree to which they can eliminate executive branch conflicts, and alternatively try to strengthen White House-department ties. Presidents have been and will continue to be frustrated by the sluggishness of the federal executive branch's response to new priorities. And increasingly,

Presidents are disillusioned by the seeming incapacity to inspire and recharge the batteries of the sprawling federal government. But there are occasions, I think, when Presidents and their staff are justifiably thwarted from any easy resolution of substantive and procedural conflicts. We must be careful to maintain a political climate in which uncomfortable questions can be asked of a President from within—or without—the White House. Sometimes an issue is of sufficient divisiveness that it is not then amenable to any majoritarian point of view, and displacement or avoidance of conflict may be the best approach. Moreover, certain types of conflict-resolution or coordination are essentially forms of coercion that might threaten the rightfully independent bases of influence and opposing viewpoints in Congress or society.

We might measurably contribute to the health of our presidency by examining and ultimately appreciating those conflicts that are avoidable or unavoidable, appropriate or inappropriate, and by trying to understand how these conflicts can limit as well as strengthen the presidency. Properly conceived and carried through, such analyses will undoubtedly help to limit and refine our expectations and assessments of democratic presidential leadership.

11.

THE CONTROVERSY OVER EXECUTIVE PRIVILEGE

Statement Before the Senate Subcommittee on Separation of Powers, July 27, 1971

Senator J. William Fulbright

The term "credibility gap" which we have heard so frequently in recent years, is a tame euphemism for a deep malady of our society. The malady is a loss of faith on the part of the American people in the truthfulness and integrity of their own Government. A recent Harris poll indicated

Abridged from U.S. Congress, Senate, Subcommittee on Separation of Powers, *Hearing on Executive Privilege: The Withholding of Information by the Executive,* July 27, 28, and 30; and August 4 and 5, 1971 (Washington: U.S. Government Printing Office, 1971), pp. 18–31.

that 71 percent of the American people believed that the "real story" from Washington seldom reaches the people. Another survey shows that 64 percent of our people believe the country is "off on the wrong track," and still another indicates that 47 percent of the American people are pessimistic about the Nation's future and believe there could be a "real breakdown in this country."

I would just interject, Mr. Chairman, to say that your own statement and that of Senator Mathias and the activities of this committee, I think, more than anything else I can think of, might restore some faith in the Government.

The controversy generated by the Pentagon papers is only the latest manifestation of the dissembling and subterfuge which have undermined popular confidence in our leaders and—far worse—in our institutions. Again and again, from the time of the U–2 incident in 1960 to the Bay of Pigs, the Dominican intervention, and all of the well-known misrepresentations concerning the war in Vietnam, our Government has been exposed in falsifications of its own practices and policies. Inevitably, this has taken a heavy toll on public confidence in our Government.

Sophisticated students of international affairs may scoff, pointing out that all governments engage in subterfuge in their foreign policies; it is, so they tell us, in the "nature" of politics, especially power politics. Perhaps it is, but until recently we Americans had supposed that we were guided by a higher, democratic standard. It comes, therefore, as something of a shock to have it suggested—in the understated words of The Guardian of London—that "The McNamara papers show that superpowers make decisions much the same way the world over—with scant concern for the opinions or the feelings of those they represent." [1]

When a government refuses to put its trust in the people, the people in turn will withdraw their trust from that government, and that I fear, is exactly what has been happening in America in recent years. You, yourself, Mr. Chairman, have been in the forefront of the effort to resist and reverse this trend. Along with other Senators and citizens, I have followed with admiration your effort to curb the surveillance of civilians by the military, and I concur in your suggestion—as reported in a recent press article—that the Pentagon has conveyed "the appearance, if not the reality, of a contempt for the right of Congress and the American people to full information about the operations of their Government." [2]

Secrecy and subterfuge are themselves more dangerous to democracy than the practices they conceal. Totalitarian devices such as military surveillance of civilians cannot long survive in the full light of publicity.

---

[1] Quoted in Washington Post, June 17, 1971, p. A12.

[2] Quoted in "Congress, Executive Continue Conflict over Withdrawal Data," Baltimore Sun, July 4, 1971, p. 7F.

An ill-conceived war, once recognized as such by the people and their representatives, must eventually be brought to an end. But without publicity and debate there is no redress. Secrecy not only perpetuates mistaken policies; it is the indispensable condition for their perpetuation. Twenty-three years ago in a different context, Congressman Richard Nixon of California endorsed that production:

> The point has been made that the President of the United States has issued an order that none of this information can be released and that, therefore, the Congress has no right to question the judgment of the President. I say that that proposition cannot stand, from a constitutional standpoint, or on the basis of the merits. . . .[3]

In the words of the great early American legislator Edward Livingston of New York:

> No nation ever yet found any inconvenience from too close an inspection into the conduct of its officers, but many have been brought to ruin, and reduced to slavery, by suffering gradual impositions and abuses, which were imperceptible, only because the means of publicity had not been secured.[4]

Contrary to the intent of Congress, the spirit of the Constitution and democratic principle, there has grown up within our government a whole new bureau or department, vested with the most crucial decisionmaking power on matters of war and peace but responsible to neither the Congress nor the people. The new bureau is more than the National Security Council, although that is its heart and core. Functionally it consists of the entire organization which has grown up around the President, nominally in the capacity of personal advisers and assistants but actually, because of their number and organization, constituting a new superbureau, separate from and superior to the regular Cabinet departments and shielded from Congress and the people behind a barricade of executive privilege.

No one questions the propriety or desirability of allowing the President to have confidential, personal advisers. President Wilson relied heavily on the advice and friendship of Colonel House, and President Roosevelt relied similarly on Harry Hopkins. President Nixon is certainly entitled to the private and personal counsel of Mr. Kissinger, but Mr. Kissinger in fact is a great deal more than a personal adviser to the President. Unlike Colonel House and Harry Hopkins, who had no staffs

---

[3] Congressional Record, April 22, 1948, p. 4782.

[4] Quoted in Raoul Berger, "Executive Privilege v. Congressional Inquiry," UCLA Law Review, May 1965, p. 1332.

of their own, and even unlike Mr. Rostow, who at the end of 1968 had a substantive staff of no more than 12 persons, Mr. Kissinger presides over a staff of 54 "substantive officers" and a total staff of 140 employees.

In addition, Mr. Kissinger serves as chairman of six interagency committees dealing with the entire range of foreign policy and national security issues and is also in charge of "Working groups" which prepare the staff studies on which high level policy discussions are based. The National Security Council staff budget, which includes funds for outside consultants, stood at $2.2 million in fiscal year 1971, which is more than triple Mr. Rostow's budget in 1968. Mr. Kissinger's role is comparable to that of Colonel House in about the same way that a moon rocket is comparable to the Wright brothers' airplane; both could fly but there all meaningful comparison comes to an end.

Mr. Kissinger's principal function—so we are told—is to define "options" for the President. On its face this might be taken for a disinterested, more or less clerical activity. But as people with experience in government know very well, the power to "define" options is the power to choose some and eliminate others, and that is a significant power indeed.

One official has been quoted as saying that it gives Mr. Kissinger a "hammerlock" on foreign policy. Or, in the words of one reporter who has made a study of the Nixon administration's foreign policy methods, "Mr. Kissinger has become the instrument by which President Nixon has centralized the management of foreign policy in the White House as never before. . . ." [5]

I do not consider Mr. Kissinger's influence, or that of his new foreign policy bureau, as being in any way sinister, illegitimate, or even inappropriate—except in one respect: their immunity from accountability to Congress and the country behind a barricade of executive privilege. The President is entitled, within the limits of the law, to organize his advisers and delegate authority among them as he sees fit. He is not, however, at liberty to create—nor is Congress at liberty to accept—a policymaking system which undercuts congressional oversight and the advisory role of the Senate in the making of foreign policy.

Were the President disposed to dismantle the elaborate National Security Council staff and retain the services of Mr. Kissinger as a personal adviser, I would see no reason to challenge the invocation of executive privilege on Mr. Kissinger's behalf. That, however, is not the case, nor does such an arrangement seem likely to commend itself to the present administration.

As matters stand, Mr. Kissinger appears on television shows, provides "background" briefings for invited members of the press—who are per-

[5] Hedrick Smith, "Foreign Policy: Kissinger at Hub," New York Times, January 19, 1971, p. 1.

mitted to ask questions—and on few occasions has asked the leadership to provide special facilities so that he can provide briefings to selected Senators under his own rules. At the same time Mr. Kissinger and members of this staff have steadfastly refused to appear before any congressional committee, either in public or executive session.

As one reporter has sardonically commented:

"Presidential aides are talking nonstop to just about every group except official committees of Congress." [6]

The result is that the people's representatives in Congress are denied direct access not only to the President himself but to the individual who is the President's chief foreign policy adviser, the principal architect of his war policy in Indochina, and the emissary for his forthcoming trip to China.

The China visit provides a striking example of the way in which the new foreign policy apparatus in the White House circumvents the Congress. Although not technically essential, it would have been useful and appropriate for the President, through his National Security Adviser, to have consulted with the Foreign Relations Committee in executive session prior to Mr. Kissinger's secret visit to Peking, all the more since the committee has recently held a series of highly illuminating hearings on China policy. It would now be useful and appropriate for Mr. Kissinger to report to the Foreign Relations Committee on his trip to Peking and to consult on substantive matters, the recognition of China or the status of Taiwan, as these pertain to the President's forthcoming "journey for peace."

The elaborate new foreign policy apparatus in the White House is not an oddity or innovation of the present administration but rather the consummation of a long-term trend toward the centralization of foreign policy powers in a small elite of experts and intellectuals surrounding the President. One of the most striking revelations to emerge from the Pentagon papers was the extraordinary secrecy with which the inner circle of the Johnson administration made their fateful decisions of 1964 and 1965. Mr. George Reedy, who is scheduled to testify before this subcommittee, is well qualified to tell how far this concealment was carried.

For my own part, reading the excerpts from the Pentagon papers published in the press, I was struck by the almost total exclusion of Congress from the policymaking process. Insofar as Congress is mentioned at all in the Pentagon papers as published in the press—and that is not often—it is referred to as an appropriate object of manipulation, or as a troublesome nuisance to be disposed of.

---

[6] Alan L. Otten, "Too Much Privilege?" Wall Street Journal, March 18, 1971, p. 18.

The issue is not one of the character or honesty of the foreign policy experts surrounding the President but of their lack of accountability—and the resulting lack of Presidential accountability. Congressmen and Senators usually do not possess specialized or expert knowledge, but they do have that single indispensable attribute which the experts do not have: accountability. Like the businessman who has to meet a "payroll," the Congressman or Senator has to respond to the wishes and whims, the prejudices and preferences, of his electorate. This anchor in reality is the elected Representative's one indispensable credential for participation in the policymaking process.

The barrier to participate is secrecy. It is in order to breach that barrier that I commend to the subcommittee this legislation relating to executive privilege, both as it relates to the withholding of information and as it has been extended to shield individual officials from the give and take of face-to-face discussion. As matters now stand, and until a legislative remedy is adopted, Congress has neither the information it required in order to discharge its constitutional responsibilities nor the opportunity to question and consult with the ranking figures in the new superbureau of foreign affairs.

In his memorandum to agency heads of March 24, 1969, outlining a procedure for compliance—or noncompliance—with Congressional requests for information, President Nixon refers in passing—as if it were axiomatic—to the executive branch's "responsibility of withholding certain information the disclosure of which would be incompatible with the public interest." Until and unless legislation is adopted by Congress to restrict executive privilege both as it applies to information and as it has been extended to shield individuals in high policy positions, the executive will continue to be the sole judge of that amorphous category called the public interest and of what is compatible or incompatible with it. It will still retain the power to decide for itself whether and to what extent it will be investigated. It will still be the judge and jury in cases of its own malfeasance and failures of judgment, of which there have been a great many in recent years.

For over a century executives upon occasion have refused information to Congress, and Congress, for the most part, has acquiesced. No doubt, as in the case of Presidential use of the war power, these unwarranted denials of information will be cited as precedents conferring legitimacy on the claim to a right of unrestricted and unreviewable executive privilege. My own view—which I believe to be an accepted principle of jurisprudence—is that usurpation is not legitimized simply by repetition, nor is a valid power nullified by failure to exercise it. The valid power involved is that of legislative oversight, which cannot survive in the face of an absolute and unrestricted executive privilege.

No one questions the propriety of executive privilege under certain circumstances; what is and must be contested is the contention that the President alone may determine the range of its application and, in so doing, also determine the range of the Congress' power to investigate. As Senator George Norris once said:

> Whenever you take away from the legislative body of any country in the world the power of investigation, the power to look into the executive department and every other department of the government, you have taken a full step that will eventually lead into absolute monarchy and destroy any government such as ours.

Statement Before the Senate Subcommittee on Separation of Powers, August 4, 1971

Assistant Attorney General William H. Rehnquist

The doctrine of executive privilege, as I understand it, defines the constitutional authority of the President to withhold documents or information in his possession or in the possession of the executive branch from compulsory process of the legislative or judicial branch of the government. The Constitution does not expressly confer upon the executive any such privilege, any more than it expressly confers upon Congress the right to use compulsory process in the aid of its legislative function. Both the executive authority and the congressional authority are implicit, rather than expressed, in the basic charter. Thus, the Constitution nowhere sets out in so many words either the power of Congress to obtain information in order to aid it in the process of legislating, nor to the power of the executive to withhold information in his possession the disclosure of which he feels would impair the proper exercise of his constitutional obligations. Yet, both of these rights are firmly rooted in history and precedent.

It is well established that the power to legislate implies the power to obtain information necessary for Congress to inform itself about the subject to be legislated, in order that the legislative function may be exercised effectively and intelligently. *McGrain* v. *Daugherty*, 273 U.S. 135, 175 (1927) upheld this authority against a private citizen who was the brother of a former Attorney General of the United States.

Abridged from U.S. Congress, Senate, Subcommittee on Separation of Powers, *Hearing on Executive Privilege: The Withholding of Information by the Executive*, July 27, 28, and 30; and August 4 and 5, 1971 (Washington: U.S. Government Printing Office, 1971), pp. 428–438.

Conversely, the authority of the executive branch to withhold information from compulsory process under the doctrine of executive privilege has been sustained by the courts in the case of *United States* v. *Reynolds*, 345 U.S. 1, 8 (1953). That case involved a claim of executive privilege against compulsory process of the judicial branch, rather than the legislative branch, but it is significant that the Supreme Court there recognized the existence of such a privilege. The Court did not accord the executive *carte blanche* in asserting the claim of privilege, but the Court's description of the extent of judicial review of the propriety of the claim indicates that such a review would be a narrow one. The Court specifically provided that such judicial determination would have to be achieved "without forcing a disclosure of the very thing the privilege is designed to protect," 345 U.S. at p. 8, and went on to say that where the government makes a prima facie showing that the evidence involved military matters which should not be divulged in the interest of national security, "the Court should not jeopardize the security which the privilege is meant to protect by insisting upon an examination of the evidence, even by the judge alone in chambers." 345 U.S. at p. 10.

While the Supreme Court has recognized the authority of Congress to use compulsory process in aid of a legislative investigation, and has likewise recognized the authority of the executive branch to assert a claim of privilege against compulsory process where the public interest would be harmed by disclosure, there is no authoritative decision settling the extent to which Congress may compel the production of documents or testimony on the part of members of the executive branch. One of the reasons for this lack of precedent may be that the relationship between the two branches during most of our country's existence has been not that of conflict, but of cooperation, albeit a cooperation which was on occasion an uneasy one. The vast majority of requests by congressional committees for testimony from the executive branch are freely complied with, and every year hundreds of executive branch witnesses appear and testify before committees of the Congress. It is only in the rare case—indeed, the very rare case—the case in which a committee of Congress after mature consideration feels that information in the possession of the executive branch is essential to the discharge of the legislative function, and where the executive feels that the constitutional principle of separation of powers would be infringed by its furnishing of such information —that the question of executive privilege arises.

The problem of executive privilege arises primarily in those areas in which congressional demands for information clash with the President's responsibility to keep the same information secret. Senator Fulbright suggested in his introductory statement that Congress cannot be expected "to abdicate to 'executive caprice' in determining whether or not the Congress will be permitted to know what it needs to know in order to discharge its constitutional responsibiliies." But can the executive conversely be required to abdicate to "congressional caprice" and release to Congress information which in the view of the President should not be made public? This conflict becomes all the more serious because some members of Congress claim the right to determine not only what information should be made available to Congress, but also whether that information once made available to it should be released to the public.

The President's authority to withhold information is not an unbridled one, but it necessarily requires the exercise of his judgment as to whether or not the disclosure of particular matters sought would be harmful to the national interest. As is the case with virtually any other authority—including the authority of Congress to compel testimony—it has potential for abuse.

Executive privilege does not authorize the withholding of information from Congress where disclosure may prove merely embarrassing to some part of the executive branch. The privilege is limited to those situations in which there is a demonstrable justification that executive withholding will further the public interest. Frequently the objection of the executive is not to the furnishing of information to members of Congress, but to the attendant complete release of the information to all interested parties throughout the world which necessarily accompanies disclosure at a public hearing. The executive branch has on more than one occasion made available to Congress in executive session this sort of information.

The doctrine of executive privilege has historically been pretty well confined to the areas of foreign relations, military affairs, pending investigations, and intragovernmental discussions.

The need for secrecy in the first two categories, foreign relations and military affairs, has been well recognized by the Judicial Branch. Most recently in the *New York Times* v. *United States,* decided on June 30, 1971, Mr. Justice Stewart stated in his concurring opinion:

"Yet it is elementary that the successful conduct of international diplomacy and the maintenance of an effective national defense require both confidentiality and secrecy. Other nations can hardly deal with this Nation in an atmosphere of mutual trust unless they can be assured that their confidences will be kept. And within our own executive departments, the development of considered and intelligent international policies would be impossible if those charged with their formulation could not communicate with each other freely, frankly, and in confidence. In the area of basic national defense the frequent need for absolute secrecy is, of course, self-evident."

Congress has recognized the need for Presidential discretion in the disclosure of information in the field of foreign relations.

The reasoning behind the claim of executive privilege in these four classical categories seems to me to be as thoroughly defensible in principle as it is well established by precedent. In the field of foreign relations, the President is, as the Supreme Court said in the *Curtiss-Wright* case, the "sole organ of the nation" in conducting negotiations with foreign governments. He does not have the final authority to commit the United States to a treaty, since such authority requires the advice and consent of the United States Senate; but the frequently delicate negotiations which are necessary to reach a mutually beneficial agreement which may be embodied in the form of a treaty often do not admit of being carried on in public. Frequently the problem of overly broad public dissemination of such negotiations can be solved by testimony in executive session, which informs the members of the committee of Congress without making the same information prematurely available throughout the world. The end is not secrecy as to the end product—the treaty—which of course should be exposed to the fullest public scrutiny, but only the confidentiality as to the negotiations which lead up to the treaty.

The need for extraordinary secrecy in the field of weapons systems and tactical military plans for the conducting of hostilities would appear to be self-evident. At least those of my generation and older are familiar with the extraordinary precautions taken against revelation of either the date or place of landing on the Normandy beaches during the Second World War in 1944. The executive branch is charged with the responsibility for such decisions, and has quite wisely insisted that where lives of American soldiers or the security of the nation is at stake, the very minimum dissemination of future plans is absolutely essential. Such secrecy with respect to highly sensitive decisions of this sort exclude not merely Congress, but all but an infinitesimal number of the employees and officials of the executive branch as well.

Finally, in the area of executive decision-making, it has been generally recognized that the President must be free to receive from his advisers absolutely impartial and disinterested advice, and that those advisers may well tend to hedge or blur the substance of their opinions if they feel that they will shortly be second-guessed either by Congress, by the press, or by the public at large, or that the President may be embarrassed if he would have to explain why he did not follow their recommendations. Again, the aim is not for secrecy of the end product—the ultimate Presidential decision is and ought to be a subject of the fullest discussion and debate, for which the President must assume undivided responsibility. But few would doubt that the Presidential decision will be a sounder one if the President is able to call upon his advisers for completely candid and frequently conflicting advice with respect to a given question.

The recent episode of the publication of the so-called "Pentagon Papers" by the press has focused public attention on the executive decision-making process. It has been urged in some quarters that the spotlight of publicity be focused, not upon the responsible head of the executive branch who must bear the ultimate responsibility for the decision, but upon his subordinate advisers, in order that they may be subjected to the various cross-currents of public opinion in formulating their recommendations to the President. Any decision to move in this direction would represent a sharp departure from the distribution of powers contemplated by the Constitution. The executive branch of the federal government has one head, and that is the President of the United States. It is he, and he alone, who must face the electorate at the end of his four-year term in order to justify his stewardship of the nation's highest office. The notion that the advisers whom he has chosen should bear some sort of a hybrid responsibility to opinion makers outside of the government, which notion in practice would inevitably have the effect of diluting their responsibility to him, is entirely inconsistent with our tripartite system of government. The President is entitled to undivided and faithful advice from his subordinates, just as Senators and Representatives are entitled to the same sort of advice from their legislative and administrative assistants, and judges to the same sort of advice from their law clerks. The notion that those engaged in directly advising members of any of the three branches of the government should have their work filtered through a process of analysis and criticism by columnists, newspaper reporters, or selected members of the public before that advice reaches their constitutional superior is entirely at odds with any system of responsible popular government.

I would add, finally, that the integrity of the decision making process which is protected by executive privilege in the executive branch is apparently of equal importance to the legislative and judicial branches of the government. Committees of Congress meet in closed session to "mark up" bills, and judges of appellate courts meet in closed conference to deliberate on the result to be reached in a particular case. In each of these instances, experience seems to teach that a sounder end result—which will be the fullest object of public scrutiny—will be reached if the process of reaching it is not conducted in a goldfish bowl.

While reasonable men may dispute the propriety of particular invocations of executive privilege by the various Presidents during the nation's history, I think most would agree that the doctrine itself is an absolutely essential condition for the faithful discharge by the executive of his constitutional duties. It is, therefore, as surely implied in the Constitution as is the power of Congress to investigate and to compel testimony.

United States v. *Nixon* *Opinion of the U.S. Supreme Court*

Mr. Chief Justice Burger delivered the opinion of the Court.

These cases present for review the denial of a motion, filed on behalf of the President of the United States, in the case of *United States* v. *Mitchell et al.* to quash a third-party subpoena *duces tecum* issued by the United States District Court for the District of Columbia, pursuant to Fed. Rule Crim. Proc. 17(c). The subpoena directed the President to produce certain tape recordings and documents relating to his conversations with aides and advisers. The court rejected the President's claims of absolute executive privilege, of lack of jurisdiction, and of failure to satisfy the requirements of Rule 17(c). The President appealed to the Court of Appeals. We granted the United States' petition for certiorari before judgment, and also the President's responsive cross-petition for certiorari before judgment, because of the public importance of the issues presented and the need for their prompt resolution.

On March 1, 1974, a grand jury of the United States District Court for the District of Columbia returned an indictment charging seven named individuals with various offenses, including conspiracy to defraud the United States and to obstruct justice. Although he was not designated as such in the indictment, the grand jury named the President, among others, as an unindicted coconspirator. On April 18, 1974, upon motion of the Special Prosecutor, a subpoena *duces tecum* was issued pursuant to Rule 17(c) to the President by the United States District Court and make returnable on May 2, 1974. This subpoena required the production, in advance of the September 9 trial date, of certain tapes, memoranda, papers, transcripts or other writings relating to certain precisely identified meetings between the President and others. The Special Prosecutor was able to fix the time, place and persons present at these discussions because the White House daily logs and appointment records had been delivered to him. On April 30, the President publicly released edited transcripts of 43 conversations; portions of 20 conversations subject to subpoena in the present case were included. On May 1, 1974, the President's counsel, filed a "special appearance" and a motion to quash the subpoena, under Rule 17(c). This motion was accompanied by a formal claim of privilege. At a subsequent hearing, further motions to expunge the grand jury's action naming the President as an unindicted cocon-

Reprinted and abridged from the *Congressional Record*, daily edition, July 25, 1974, pp. H7199–H7204.

spirator and for protective orders against the disclosure of that information were filed or raised orally by counsel for the President.

On May 20, 1974, the District Court denied the motion to quash and the motions to expunge and for protective orders. It further ordered "the President or any subordinate officer, official or employee with custody or control of the documents or objects subpoenaed," to deliver to the District Court, on or before May 31, 1974, the originals of all subpoenaed items, as well as an index and analysis of those items, together with tape copies of those portions of the subpoenaed recordings for which transcripts had been released to the public by the President on April 30. The District Court rejected jurisdictional challenges based on a contention that the dispute was nonjusticiable because it was between the Special Prosecutor and the Chief Executive and hence "intra-executive" in character; it also rejected the contention that the judiciary was without authority to review an assertion of executive privilege by the President. The court's rejection of the first challenge was based on the authority and powers vested in the Special Prosecutor by the regulation promulgated by the Attorney General; the court concluded that a justiciable controversy was presented. The second challenge was held to be foreclosed by the decision in *Nixon* v. *Sirica,* – U.S. App. D.C. –, 487 F. 2d 700 (1973).

The District Court held that the judiciary, not the President, was the final arbiter of a claim of executive privilege. The court concluded that, under the circumstances of this case, the presumptive privilege was overcome by the Special Prosecutor's prima facie "demonstration of need sufficiently compelling to warrant judicial examination in chambers. . . ." The court held, finally, that the Special Prosecutor had satisfied the requirements of Rule 17(c).

On May 24, 1974, the President filed a timely notice of appeal from the District Court order, and the certified record from the District Court was docketed in the United States Court of Appeals for the District of Columbia Circuit. On the same day, the President also filed a petition for writ of mandamus in the Court of Appeals seeking review of the District Court order.

Later on May 24, the Special Prosecutor also filed, in this Court, a petition for a writ of certiorari before judgment. On May 31, the petition was granted with an expedited briefing schedule. On June 6, the President filed, under seal, a cross-petition for writ of certiorari before judgment. This cross-petition was granted June 15, 1974, and the case was set for argument on July 8, 1974.

I. JURISDICTION

The threshold question presented is whether the May 20, 1974, order of the District Court was an appealable order and whether this case was properly "in," the United States Court of Appeals when the petition for certiorari was filed in this Court. Court of Appeals jurisdiction under 28 U.S.C. § 1291 encompasses only "final decisions of the district courts."

The finality requirement of 28 U.S.C. § 1291 embodies a strong congressional policy against piecemeal reviews, and against obstructing or impeding an ongoing judicial proceeding by interlocutory appeals. See *e.g., Cobbledick* v. *United States,* 309 U.S. 323, 324–326 (1940). This requirement ordinarily promotes judicial efficiency and hastens the ultimate termination of litigation. This Court has "consistently held that the necessity for expedition in the administration of the criminal law justifies putting one who seeks to resist the production of desired information to a choice between compliance with a trial court's order to produce prior to any review of that order, and resistance to that order with the concomitant possibility of an adjudication of contempt if his claims are rejected on appeal." *United States* v. *Ryan,* 402 U.S. 530, 533 (1971).

The requirement of submitting to contempt, however, is not without exception and in some instances the purposes underlying the finality rule require a different result. Here too the traditional contempt avenue to immediate appeal is peculiarly inappropriate due to the unique setting in which the question arises. To require a President of the United States to place himself in the posture of disobeying an order of a court merely to trigger the procedural mechanism for review of the ruling would be unseemly, and present an unnecessary occasion for constitutional confrontation between two branches of the Government. Similarly, a federal judge should not be placed in the posture of issuing a citation to a President simply in order to invoke review. The issue whether a President can be cited for contempt could itself engender protracted litigation, and would further delay both review on the merits of his claim of privilege and the ultimate termination of the underlying criminal action for which his evidence is sought. These considerations lead us to conclude that the order of the District Court was an appealable order. The appeal from that order was therefore properly "in" the Court of Appeals, and the case is now properly before this Court on the writ of certiorari before judgment.

II. JUSTICIABILITY

In the District Court, the President's counsel argued that the court lacked jurisdiction to issue the subpoena because the matter was an intra-branch dispute between a subordinate and superior officer of the Executive Branch and hence not subject to judicial resolution. That argument has been renewed in this Court with emphasis on the contention that the dispute does not present a "case" or "controversy" which can be adjudicated in the federal courts. The President's counsel argues that the federal courts should not intrude into areas committed to the other branches of Government. He views the present dispute as essentially a "jurisdictional" dispute within the Executive Branch which he analogizes to a dispute between two congressional committees. Since the Executive Branch has exclusive authority and absolute discretion to decide whether to prosecute a case, *Confiscation Cases,* 7 Wall. 454 (1869), *United States* v. *Cox,* 342 F. 2d 167, 171 (CA5), cert. denied, 381 U.S. 935 (1965), it is contended that a President's decision is final in determining what evidence is to be used in a given criminal case. Although his counsel concedes the President has delegated certain specific powers to the Special Prosecutor, he has not "waived nor delegated to the Special Prosecutor the President's duty to claim privilege as to all materials . . . which fall within the President's inherent authority to refuse to disclose to any executive officer." The Special Prosecutor's demand for the items therefore presents, in the view of the President's counsel, a political question under *Baker* v. *Carr,* 369 U.S. 186 (1962), since it involves a "textually demonstrable" grant of power under Art. II. The mere assertion of a claim of an "intrabranch dispute," without more, has never operated to defeat federal jurisdiction; justiciability does not depend on such a surface inquiry.

Our starting point is the nature of the proceeding for which the evidence is sought—here a pending criminal prosecution. It is a judicial proceeding in a federal court alleging violation of federal laws and is brought in the name of the United States as sovereign. Under the authority of Art. II, § 2, Congress has vested in the Attorney General the power to conduct the criminal litigation to the United States Government. 28 U.S.C. § 516. It has also vested in him the power to appoint subordinate officers to assist him in the discharge of his duties. 28 U.S.C. §§ 509, 510, 515, 533. Acting pursuant to those statutes, the Attorney General has delegated the authority to represent the United States in these particular matters to a Special Prosecutor with unique authority and tenure. The regulation gives the Special Prosecutor explicit power to contest the invocation of executive privilege in the process of seeking evidence deemed relevant to the performance of these specially delegated duties.

So long as this regulation remains in force the Executive Branch is bound by it, and indeed the United States as the sovereign composed of the three branches is bound to respect and to enforce it. Moreover, the delegation of authority to the Special Prosecutor in this case is not an ordinary delegation by the Attorney General to a subordinate officer: with the authorization of the President, the Acting Attorney General provided in the regulation that the Special Prosecutor was not to be removed without the "consensus" of eight designated leaders of Congress.

The demands of and the resistance to the subpoena present an obvious controversy in the ordinary sense, but that alone is not sufficient to meet constitutional standards. In the constitutional sense, controversy means more than disagreement and conflict; rather it means the kind of controversy courts traditionally resolve. Here at issue is the production or nonproduction of specified evidence deemed by the Special Prosecutor to be relevant and admissible in a pending criminal case. It is sought by one official of the Government within the scope of his express authority; it is resisted by the Chief Executive on the ground of his duty to preserve the confidentiality of the communications of the President. Whatever the correct answer on the merits, these issues are "of a type which are traditionally justiciable." *United States* v. *ICC*, 337 U.S., at 430. The independent Special Prosecutor with his asserted need for the subpoenaed material in the underlying criminal prosecution is opposed by the President with his steadfast assertion of privilege against disclosure of the material. This setting assures there is "that concrete adverseness which sharpens the presentation of issues upon which the court so largely depends or illumination of difficult constitutional questions." *Baker* v. *Carr*, 369 U.S., at 204.

In light of the uniqueness of the setting in which the conflict arises, the fact that both parties are officers of the Executive Branch cannot be viewed as a barrier to justiciability. It would be inconsistent with the applicable law and regulation, and the unique facts of this case to conclude other than that the Special Prosecutor has standing to bring this action and that a justiciable controversy is presented for decision.

III. RULE 17(C)

The subpoena *duces tecum* is challenged on the ground that the Special Prosecutor failed to satisfy the requirements of Fed. Rule Crim. Proc. 17(c), which governs the issuance of subpoenas *duces tecum* in federal criminal proceedings. If we sustained this challenge, there would be no occasion to reach the claim of privilege asserted with respect to the subpoenaed material. Thus we turn to the question whether the requirements of Rule 17(c) have been satisfied.

Rule 17(c) provides:

"A subpoena may also command the person to whom it is directed to produce the books, papers, documents or other objects designated therein. The court on motion made promptly may quash or modify the subpoena if complicance would be unreasonable or oppressive. The court may direct that books, papers, documents or objects designated in the subpoena be produced before the court at a time prior to the trial or prior to the time when they are to be offered in evidence and may upon their production permit the books, papers, documents or objects or portions thereof to be inspected by the parties and their attorneys." A subpoena for documents may be quashed if their production would be "unreasonable or oppressive," but not otherwise.

Against this background, the Special Prosecutor, in order to carry his burden, must clear three hurdles: (1) relevancy; (2) admissibility; (3) specificity. The most cogent objection to the admissibility of the taped conversations here at issue is that they are a collection of out-of-court statements by declarants who will not be subject to cross-examination and that the statements are therefore inadmissible hearsay. Here, however, most of the tapes apparently contain conversations to which one or more of the defendants named in the indictment were party. Recorded conversations may also be admissible for the limited purpose of impeaching the credibility of any defendant who testifies or any other coconspirator who testifies. Generally, the need for evidence to impeach witnesses is insufficient to require its production in advance of trial. Here, however, there are other valid potential evidentiary uses for the same material and the analysis and possible transcription of the tapes may take a significant period of time. Accordingly, we cannot say that the District Court erred in authorizing the issuance of the subpoena *duces tecum.*

Enforcement of a pretrial subpoena *duces tecum* must necessarily be committed to the sound discretion of the trial court since necessity for the subpoena most often turns upon a determination of factual issues. Without a determination of arbitrariness or that the trial court finding was without record support, an appellate court will not ordinarily disturb a finding that the applicant for a subpoena complied with Rule 17(c).

In a case such as this, however, where a subpoena is directed to a President of the United States, appellate review, in deference to a coordinate branch of government, should be particularly meticulous to ensure that the standards of Rule 17(c) have been correctly applied. From our examination of the materials submitted by the Special Prosecutor to the District Court in support of his motion for the subpoena, we are persuaded that the District Court's denial of the President's motion to quash the subpoena was consistent with Rule 17(c). We also conclude that the Special Prosecutor has made a sufficient showing to justify a subpoena for production *before* trial. The subpoenaed materials are not available from any other source, and their examination and processing should not await trial in the circumstances shown.

IV. THE CLAIM OF PRIVILEGE

A

Having determined that the requirements of Rule 17(c) were satisfied, we turn to the claim that the subpoena should be quashed because it demands "confidential conversations between a President and his close advisors that it would be inconsistent with the public interest to produce." The first contention is a broad claim that the separation of powers doctrine precludes judicial review of a President's claim of privilege. The second contention is that if he does not prevail on the claim of absolute privilege, the court should hold as a matter of constitutional law that the privilege prevails over the subpoena *duces tecum.*

In the performance of assigned constitutional duties each branch of the Government must initially interpret the Constitution, and the interpretation of its powers by any branch is due great respect from the others. The President's counsel, as we have noted, reads the Constitution as providing an absolute privilege of confidentiality for all presidential communications. Many decisions of this Court, however, have unequivocally reaffirmed the holding of *Marbury* v. *Madison,* 1 Cranch 137 (1803), that "it is emphatically the province and duty of the judicial department to say what the law is." *Id.*, at 177.

No holding of the Court has defined the scope of judicial power specifically relating to the enforcement of a subpoena for confidential presidential communications for use in a criminal prosecution, but other exercises of powers by the Executive Branch and the Legislative Branch have been found invalid as in conflict with the Constitution. Since this Court has consistently exercised the power to construe and delineate claims arising under express powers, it must follow that the Court has authority to interpret claims with respect to powers alleged to derive from enumerated powers.

Notwithstanding the deference each branch must accord the others, the "judicial power of the United States" vested in the federal courts by Art. III § 1 of the Constitution can no more be shared with the Executive Branch than the Chief Executive, for example, can share with the Judiciary the veto power, or the Congress share with the Judiciary the power to override a presidential veto. Any other conclusion would be contrary to the basic concept of separation of powers and the checks and balances that flow from the scheme of a tripartite government. The Federalist, No. 47, p. 313 (C. F. Mittel ed. 1938). We therefore reaffirm that it is "emphatically the province and the duty" of this Court "to say what the law is" with respect to the claim of privilege presented in this case. *Marbury* v. *Madison, supra,* at 177.

B

In support of his claim of absolute privilege, the President's counsel urges two grounds one of which is common to all governments and one of which is peculiar to our system of separation of powers. The first ground is the valid need for protection of communications between high government officials and those who advise and assist them in the performance of their manifold duties; the importance of this confidentiality is too plain to require further discussion. Human experience teaches that those who expect public dissemination of their remarks may well temper candor with a concern for appearances and for their own interests to the detriment of the decisionmaking process. Whatever the nature of the privilege of confidentiality of presidential communications in the exercise of Art. II powers the privilege can be said to derive from the supremacy of each branch within its own assigned area of constitutional duties. Certain powers and privileges flow from the nature of enumerated powers; the protection of the confidentiality of presidential communications has similar constitutional underpinnings.

The second ground asserted by the President's counsel in support of the claim of absolute privilege rests on the doctrine of separation of powers. Here it is argued that the independence of the Executive Branch within its own sphere, insulates a president from a judicial subpoena in an ongoing criminal prosecution, and thereby protects confidential presidential communications.

However, neither the doctrine of separation of powers, nor the need for confidentiality of high level communications, without more, can sustain an absolute, unqualified presidential privilege of immunity from judicial process under all circumstances. The President's need for complete candor and objectivity from advisers calls for great deference from the courts. However, when the privilege depends solely on the broad, undifferentiated claim of public interest in the confidentiality of such conversations, a confrontation with other values arises. Absent a claim of need to protect military, diplomatic or sensitive national security secrets, we find it difficult to accept the argument that even the very important interest in confidentiality of presidential communications is significantly diminished by production of such material for *in camera* inspection with all the protection that a district court will be obliged to provide.

The impediment that an absolute, unqualified privilege would place in the way of the primary constitutional duty of the Judicial Branch to do justice in criminal prosecutions would plainly conflict with the function of the courts under Art. III. In designing the structure of our Government and dividing and allocating the sovereign power among three coequal branches, the Framers of the Constitution sought to provide a comprehensive system, but the separate powers were not intended to operate with absolute independence. To read the Art. II powers of the President as providing an absolute privilege as against a subpoena essential to enforcement of criminal statutes on no more than a generalized claim of the public interest in confidentiality of nonmilitary and nondiplomatic discussions would upset the constitutional balance of "a workable government" and gravely impair the role of the courts under Art. III.

C

Since we conclude that the legitimate needs of the judicial process may outweigh presidential privilege, it is necessary to resolve those competing interests in a manner that preserves the essential functions of each branch.

The expectation of a President to the confidentiality of his conversations and correspondence, like the claim of confidentiality of judicial deliberations, for example, has all the values to which we accord deference for the privacy of all citizens and added to those values the necessity for protection of the public interest in candid, objective, and even blunt or harsh opinions in presidential decisionmaking. A President and those who assist him must be free to explore alternatives in the process of shaping policies and making decisions and to do so in a way many would be unwilling to express except privately. These are the considerations justifying a presumptive privilege for presidential communications. The privilege is fundamental to the operation of government and inextricably rooted in the separation of powers under the Constitution. In *Nixon* v. *Sirica*, – U.S. App. D. C. –, 487 F. 2d 700 (1973), the Court of Appeals held that such presidential communications are "presumptively privileged," and this position is accepted by both parties in the present litigation. We agree with Mr. Chief Justice Marshall's observation, therefore, that "in no case of this kind would a court be required to proceed against the President as against an ordinary individual." *United States* v. *Burr*, 25 Fed. Cas. 187, 191 (No. 14,694) (CCD Va. 1807).

But this presumptive privilege must be considered in light of our historic commitment to the rule of law. This is nowhere more profoundly manifest than in our view that "the twofold aim [of criminal justice] is that guilt shall not escape or innocence suffer." *Berger* v. *United States*, 295 U. S. 78, 88 (1935). We have elected to employ an adversary system of criminal justice in which the parties contest all issues before a court of law. The need to develop all relevant facts in the adversary system is both fundamental and comprehensive. The ends of criminal justice would be defeated if judgments were to be founded on a partial or speculative presentation of the facts. The very integrity of the judicial system and public confidence in the system depend on full disclosure of all the facts, within the framework of the rules of evidence. To ensure that justice is done, it is imperative to the function of courts that compulsory process be available for the production of evidence needed either by the prosecution or by the defense.

In this case the President challenges a subpoena served on him as a third party requiring the production of materials for use in a criminal prosecution on the claim that he has a privilege against disclosure of confidential communications. He does not place his claim of privilege on the ground they are military or diplomatic secrets. As to these areas of Art. II duties the courts have traditionally shown the utmost deference to presidential responsibilities. In *C. & S. Air Lines* v. *Waterman Steamship Corp.*, 333 U.S. 103, 111 (1948), dealing with presidential authority involving foreign policy considerations, the Court said:

"The President, both as Commander-in-Chief and as the Nation's organ for foreign affairs, has available intelligence services whose reports are not and ought not to be published to the world. It would be intolerable that courts, without the relevant information, should review and perhaps nullify actions of the Executive taken on information properly held secret." *Id.*, at 111.

In *United States* v. *Reynolds*, 345 U.S. 1 (1952), dealing with a claimant's demand for evidence in a damage case against the Government the Court said:

"It may be possible to satisfy the court, from all the circumstances of the case, that there is a reasonable danger that compulsion of the evidence will expose military matters which, in the interest of national security, should not be divulged. When this is the case, the occasion for the privilege is appropriate, and the court should not jeopardize the security which the privilege is meant to protect by insisting upon an examination of the evidence, even by the judge alone, in chambers."

No case of the Court, however, has extended this high degree of deference to a President's generalized interest in confidentiality. Nowhere in the Constitution, as we have noted earlier, is there any explicit reference to a privilege of confidentiality, yet to the extent this interest relates to the effective discharge of a President's powers, it is constitutionally based.

The right to the production of all evidence at a criminal trial similarly has constitutional dimensions. The Sixth Amendment explicitly confers upon every defendant in a criminal trial the right "to be confronted with the witnesses against him" and "to have compulsory process for obtaining witnesses in his favor." Moreover, the Fifth Amendment also guarantees that no person shall be deprived of liberty without due process of law. It is the manifest duty of the courts to vindicate those guarantees and to accomplish that it is essential that all relevant and admissible evidence be produced.

In this case we must weigh the importance of the general privilege of confidentiality of presidential communications in performance of his responsibilities against the inroads of such a privilege on the fair administration of criminal justice. The interest in preserving confidentiality is weighty indeed and entitled to great respect. However we cannot conclude that advisers will be moved to temper the candor of their remarks by the infrequent occasions of disclosure because of the possibility that such conversations will be called for in the context of a criminal prosecution.

On the other hand, the allowance of the privilege to withhold evidence that is demonstrably relevant in a criminal trial would cut deeply into the guarantee of due process of law and gravely impair the basic function of the courts. A President's acknowledged need for confidentiality in the communications of his office is general in nature, whereas the constitutional need for production of relevant evidence in a criminal proceeding is specific and central to the fair adjudication of a particular criminal case in the administration of justice. Without access to specific facts a criminal prosecution may be totally frustrated. The President's broad interest in confidentiality of communications will not be vitiated by disclosure of a limited number of conversations preliminarily shown to have some bearing on the pending criminal cases.

We conclude that when the ground for asserting privilege as to subpoenaed materials sought for use in a criminal trial is based only on the generalized interest in confidentiality, it cannot prevail over the fundamental demands of due process of law in the fair administration of criminal justice. The generalized assertion of privilege must yield to the demonstrated, specific need for evidence in a pending criminal trial.

D

We have earlier determined that the District court did not err in authorizing the issuance of the subpoena. If a president concludes that compliance with a subpoena would be injurious to the public interest he may properly, as was done here, invoke a claim of privilege on the return of the subpoena. Upon receiving a claim of privilege from the Chief Executive, it became the further duty of the District Court to treat the subpoenaed material as presumptively privileged and to require the Special Prosecutor to demonstrate that the presidential material was "essential to the justice of the [pending criminal] case." *United States* v. *Burr, supra,* at 192. Here the District Court treated the material as presumptively privileged, proceeded to find that the Special Prosecutor had made a sufficient showing to rebut the presumption and ordered an *in camera* examination of the subpoenaed material. On the basis of our examination of the record we were unable to conclude that the District Court erred in ordering the inspection. Accordingly we affirm the order of the District Court that subpoenaed materials be transmitted to that court.

Affirmed.

Mr. Justice Rehnquist took no part in the consideration or decision of these cases.

12.

WHITE HOUSE LEGISLATIVE LIAISON

Abraham Holtzman

The President and White House Lobbyists: A Hypothesis. A White House liaison unit has been institutionalized now under five Presidents. Lyndon B. Johnson employed a liaison unit throughout his administration and Richard M. Nixon has appointed Eisenhower's former chief liaison officer, Bryce N. Harlow, to serve him in that capacity. Although the pattern in which subsequent Presidents will organize their personal staffs remains to be seen, a hypothesis may be advanced that future chief executives, regardless of their particular styles, will continue to depend upon a special staff of White House officers for liaison with the Congress. The role of chief legislator imposes tremendous demands upon Presidents. At the same time an effective instrument for helping the President carry out this role has already been institutionalized under Republican as well as Democratic administrations. The personality and style of a President undoubtedly shape his own relations with the Congress and with his immediate assistants, but it is questionable whether future chief executives can forgo relying upon a special staff for congressional relations or fail to appoint such actors to a major rank in the White House.

This study did not cover the administration of President Johnson. By continuing to utilize his liaison agents as important actors in dealing with the Congress, even after he had been elected on his own program and record in 1964, Johnson demonstrated that the needs of the President for such instruments to carry out his leadership in the Congress remain significant despite the style and personality of the incumbent.

President Truman was a congressional type who enjoyed the battles of politics and involved himself actively in his legislative campaigns. His special liaison staff, though, was ineffective and insignificant compared with those of his successors. It has been suggested that President Eisenhower was less interested in domestic politics than in national security problems and foreign policy, and that he did not relish the bargaining of

---

Reprinted from the book *Legislative Liaison: Executive Leadership in Congress* by Abraham Holtzman, pp. 244–258. © 1970 by Rand McNally and Co. Published by Rand McNally and reprinted with permission of the publisher. Abridged; footnotes renumbered.

presidential-congressional relations. Hence his congressional liaison unit became very important in the White House. Arthur M. Schlesinger, Jr., an intimate associate of President Kennedy in the White House and a historian of the Kennedy Administration, observes that working with the Congress did not afford Kennedy the "greatest pleasure or satisfaction. This made his congressional liaison staff all the more important. . . ."[1] It is unwarranted, however, to conclude from these three cases that a White House liaison unit will be utilized in an important manner only if a President is less concerned with domestic legislation or is by temperament detached from congressional politics.

Lyndon B. Johnson did enjoy congressional politics. He was an expert in the area of congressional relations and legislative maneuvering. His personality disposed him to personal, direct involvement in the Congress on a massive scale to ensure the adoption of his program. Clearly Johnson was a different type than his predecessor, and his arrangements with his staff reflected his unique style and personality. He retained O'Brien as chief liaison officer even after elevating him to be Postmaster General, and he built Vice President Hubert H. Humphrey into the President's liaison team in a manner unique in American politics. Yet he continued to employ the principal members in the Kennedy liaison unit as an essential set of staff officers up to 1967, when he eventually replaced them with others. The importance of a liaison unit in the White House was fully recognized by a President who pursued a personal, aggressive role in offering leadership to the Congress.

WHITE HOUSE LOBBYISTS: STRATEGIES, TACTICS, AND RESOURCES

Strategy and tactics are closely associated with the resources of actors. The White House controls a greater amount and a wider range of potent resources than any of the departments. And the White House has the priority in strategy and tactics as well as the broad responsibility for the program of the administration which cuts across the departments.

The President: The Most Important Resource. The awesome office of the presidency endows its occupant with prestige and power that no comparable individual in the national government or the country possesses. He is party leader, chief executive, chief legislator, and chief of state, all in one. Decisions made at his level are final for most of the executive system and extend deeply into national-state-city relations.

---

[1] Arthur M. Schlesinger, Jr., *A Thousand Days: John F. Kennedy in the White House* (Boston: Houghton Mifflin, 1965), p. 711.

From the point of view of the legislators, the interest groups, his Cabinet, and his lobbyists, the President is therefore the most significant executive actor in congressional relations. The President can be used to influence the Congress indirectly via his press conferences or through more immediate appeals to the general public. The messages that accompany his bills are carefully designed to affect both congressional response and public opinion.

President Kennedy and his chief lobbyists believed, however, in the personal approach as the most effective one for establishing good relations with the Congress. Direct contact between the Chief Executive and the legislators was pursued in a variety of ways. Congressmen in groups of fifteen or so were invited to the White House to socialize with the President, and at such occasions each legislator was afforded an opportunity for an informal chat with him.[2] Appointments with the President were arranged for individual legislators, and the President's liaison staff brought congressmen into the White House for off-the-record sessions. Committee chairmen were accorded much more deferential treatment, each being invited for a personal conference with the President. And the Democratic party leaders in the Congress met regularly with the President. Congressmen were invited among others to the social evenings in the White House. When the President wished to offer a grand gesture to someone of consequence in the Congress, he went personally to that legislator. Such occasions were rare, but one example was President Kennedy's unexpected trip by helicopter to a gathering in Virginia honoring the chairman of the Senate Finance Committee. While the Kennedy White House probably systematized these contacts with the Congress more than had the preceding administration, one of Eisenhower's chief lobbyists, Bryce N. Harlow, contended that Eisenhower had similarly been involved in congressional action.

> He was a heavy participant in it, infinitely more than he has been publicly given credit for. A lot of it was off the record. He phoned, had meetings with congressmen at breakfast and dinner and in private sessions in the evenings. A great part of this the press was unaware of.

President John F. Kennedy recognized fully the importance of cultivating the Congress, and he was willing to assume this responsibility. Nevertheless, O'Brien expressed the theory that the President should be protected from being involved too much. "I'm cautious about overextending him." As chief assistant to the President for congressional relations, he felt responsible for making as many decisions as possible by himself.

---

[2] "Twice this week," noted O'Brien in an interview with the author in 1963, "we've invited congressmen to the Executive Mansion, in the President's living quarters. It's called coffee hours but it's really cocktails, and they let their hair down."

"I try to avoid using him with congressmen; there are too many demands already on his time." The two conferred frequently over strategy, O'Brien having easy access at all times to his political superior and the President calling him in for discussions three or more times a day. Only if a problem were totally out of control did the liaison officer turn to the President for his personal intervention. "I say: 'Here is the situation. I've tried and failed. Either we have to try something else or you have to get involved.'" On priority legislation, O'Brien did not hesitate to employ the President to shore up the administration's position with a committee chairman. "If I get nervous regarding Wilbur Mills and the timetable on the tax bill, I can reach a point where I want Mills to restate to the President what his position is. He is put on record with the President and this relieves me."

The White House staff reported that it avoided using the President to call congressmen for their votes. President Kennedy did call frequently during the crucial Rules Committee fight of 1961, but on the whole the White House resisted employing this tactic. "We discovered that we have to keep him off the phone when things get tough," explained Wilson. There were actually very few such phone calls by the President because his staff concluded that if he started using the phone for votes, all the members would expect to be asked by the President personally. His staff and the whips would then begin to accumulate a tremendous number of "uncertains" in replies from congressmen who wished to exploit the situation. Consequently it was rare that the President called to round up votes. More often, he would call after a victory to congratulate a legislator, or to seek someone's advice.

The President was also the source of O'Brien's mandate. The liaison officer required from the President a type of intervention that legitimized his own authority to act decisively within the Congress and the executive system. When O'Brien took over White House-congressional liaison, Harlow warned him that the President himself would pose a major problem for him, one that would have to be solved. Inevitably, the President would become personally engaged in relations with congressmen on his own initiative or in response to direct calls from them. The danger lay in the President's becoming so busy that he overlooked the necessity of "filling you in on what he's done. You have to plead with your President never to call over your head without telling you and always to keep you informed of what he has done." It was a problem that departmental lobbyists also faced with their superiors. Secondly, Harlow advised O'Brien that as chief lobbyist he would have to make certain that Cabinet members as well as congressmen knew that he spoke for the President, that their relations were very close. Unless he was established as the President's man in the eyes of legislative and executive leaders, they would bypass him, downgrade his opinions and decisions, and doubt his capacity to commit the President. "You have to establish yourself. Make certain that you ask the President to address questions to you in their presence so that they see he relies upon you."

According to O'Brien, he encountered no trouble in either respect. "There is very little slip-up between the President and me," he reported. While occasionally the President would talk on the phone with someone on the spur of the moment, the President's secretary always forwarded to O'Brien memos of the President's calls. But it was rare that the President and he had not coordinated their approaches to the Congress well in advance. As for representing the President in the eyes of executive leaders and legislators, O'Brien was satisfied that no problem existed. "The key to my spot is that I do speak authoritatively for the President, and the others know it." He participated in Cabinet meetings as the President's liaison officer and also in the President's Tuesday breakfasts with the Democratic leaders of the Congress, where strategy and tactics were discussed. O'Brien reported that he and his staff were also involved in policy-making in the White House. "We have a voice in the preparation of legislation and the President's messages. Not a veto, but a strong voice regarding the political and legislative possibilities." In the fall of each year, when the substantive assistants to the President were preparing the legislative program for the next session of Congress, a member of the liaison staff represented the chief lobbyist in their discussions. O'Brien himself spent a week at the Palm Beach White House while the State of the Union and other major messages were being hammered out.

The Personal Approach of the Liaison Staff. The chief lobbyist for President Kennedy emphasized the value of a personal approach to Congress, and he patterned the entire approach of his office upon that premise. This meant that the White House liaison staff had to know the Democratic congressmen as individuals and to be prepared to deal directly with them. The President had made mention of the fact that when he was a congressman, no one from the White House staff had ever contacted him. "I recall my fourteen years on the Hill, and I cannot recall during that . . . period having any direct or meaningful contact with a member of the White House staff."

On both an informed and a formal basis, Kennedy's chief liaison officer attempted to establish personal links between himself, his staff, and the Congress. On assuming his post, he had sought to become personally acquainted with as many congressmen as possible. He met separately with the liberals in the House who composed the Democratic Study Group. And throughout each congressional session, the O'Briens entertained important members of the Congress at their home for Sunday brunch.

In the formal day-to-day work with the Congress, each liaison officer was responsible for a specific group, thereby reinforcing the personal relations he had established with the legislators. In general, O'Brien as chief lobbyist worked primarily with Democratic party leaders, with committee chairmen, and with Republican leaders. Congressional Democratic leaders met with and called the President directly, but in the main it was the President's principal liaison officer to whom they addressed themselves and who sought them out. As has been pointed out, O'Brien participated with them in the leadership meetings at the White House. In the Congress he collaborated with them on strategy, nose counting, and the persuasion of legislators. His staff was instructed to deal with the rest of the Congress, although he was available to resolve difficult problems.

His two principal assistants, titled administrative assistants to the President, also worked with committee chairmen and the Democratic leadership. One, Mike N. Manatos, was assigned solely to the Senate, although O'Brien continued to consider the Senate his special responsibility in view of the status of the senators and their insistence in many cases upon dealing personally with the most responsible executive leaders. His lieutenant for the House of Representatives, Henry Hall Wilson, was assisted by other liaison agents since the House was considered too large to be assigned to any one liaison officer, and it posed the greatest challenge to the Kennedy program.

The White House recognized, moreover, that the Democratic membership in the House was divided into discernible segments, each of which required special attention. The most important of these groups was the southern contingent. Defection among these congressmen—unless contained within manageable limits—threatened every major Kennedy proposal. The careful cultivation of southern Democrats to retain them as administration supporters was a basic component of White House strategy. Hence the principal assistant for the White House was a southerner. As past state president of the Young Democratic Clubs of North Carolina and as a former state legislator, Wilson was a southern type in all but ideological orientation; he had long been associated with the liberal wing of his state party. As the chief liaison officer for the House, he worked with the Speaker, majority leader, and whip, and with the committee chairmen, but the southern and border congressmen were his special assignment.

The nonsouthern Democrats in the House were assigned to two subordinate legislative liaison officers. Initially, Richard K. Donahue, the senior of the two, had not been engaged in direct contact with congressmen; he had represented O'Brien in the development of substantive policy at the White House and he had concentrated upon patronage problems. With Wilson devoting himself to southern and border congressmen as well as to the leadership and committee chairmen, complaints had arisen from other Democrats who wanted personal attention from the White House. As a result Donahue was assigned the big-city delegations from the northeast and midwest. Subsequently an additional liaison agent was appointed to collaborate with Democrats from the West and the few noncity party members from the northeast and midwest. The responsibility of these two liaison officers was defined as affording "those who will automatically vote for us a direct link with the White House. They touch base with them, hold their hands, and in general worry with them." The two were responsible as well for making certain that these congressmen appeared for important votes, knew the White House position on legislation and amendments, and voted the correct way. "O'Brien and I have no time for the saved," explained Wilson. "Most of our work is in lining up the critical votes. Donahue and Daly are employed to cover the liberal Democrats who complain that 'we're taken for granted.'"

Patronage and Special Favors. Just as departmental liaison agents capitalized upon the needs and desires of legislators for special favors affecting their constituents, so did the White House liaison staff devote itself assiduously to this task. During his three years in the White House, reported O'Brien in 1963, he and his staff had developed a tremendous service operation. "We could never have survived unless we had had and had used patronage. We get the vote, but not just by an appeal on the basis of merit or substantive discussion with members." He and his staff were not moral crusaders, he pointed out; their job was to get the legislation through.

O'Brien had been responsible for patronage on the Democratic National Committee between the November 1960 election and the inauguration of the President. His title in the White House had originally called for him to be concerned also with personnel, a recognition that patronage and legislation were linked together. Although he was officially divested of his personnel assignment, he continued to serve as a patronage boss in the White House. The departments were alerted to keep the White House informed of important patronage opportunities and to furnish data on major contracts, projects, and services. Similarly, the White House demanded that departments give preferential treatment to Democrats so that they could capitalize upon projects directly affecting their constituencies. "It is not in the best interest of legislative harmony," counseled the White House, "to have Republican Senators announce projects directly affecting Districts with sitting Democratic Congressmen. . . . An orderly, considered treatment of the Congress will result in an expedited Administration Program." [3]

It was O'Brien's contention that by integrating and exploiting the

---

[3] See "Memorandum to All Cabinet Officials and Agency Heads," April 21, 1961, from Lawrence F. O'Brien, Special Assistant to the President, reprinted in Republican National Committee, *Battle Line*, no. 28 (May 7, 1961).

resources of the departments, the White House could provide much more extensive service than had the comparable unit in the Eisenhower Administration. The President's more ambitious program of legislation could therefore be more effectively advanced. Such services were considered to contribute to a favorable climate in which White House lobbyists and legislators could interact. The White House could also more readily affect votes, both indirectly and directly. One of O'Brien's assistants disclosed that the White House sought to "jockey into a position where they [those Democrats who did not usually support the administration] call us" in order to create a sense of obligation on their part. When such congressmen sought special favors from the departments, the latter were alerted to cue in the White House so that its officers could suggest to a member that "he can't get it unless he goes along with us." Donahue, who worked with the big-city delegations, maintained that patronage for their party organization was often much more important to these legislators than the substance of bills. At times, he told a *Congressional Quarterly* reporter, "our hearing is better than at other times," and it was more sensitive during legislative showdowns, when "we expect their hearing to be more sensitive at the other end of the line, too." [4]

On the whole, the Kennedy liaison unit did not employ constituent-oriented resources to deny legislators their requests or to deprive them of what they had. Rather the principal approach was positive—finding ways to provide grants, expedite contracts, and fill positions. Nevertheless, the White House could turn a deaf ear to requests or refuse to expedite matters in which congressmen were interested. According to the liaison officers, the knowledge that the White House controlled such resources in itself constituted an inducement to legislators to be cooperative.

"Muscle." Merit, compromise, and political rationalization were major tools employed by the White House liaison officers, as they were for their departmental counterparts. However, by the time the White House unit entered into most legislative battles, positions had tended to become hardened on substance and along party lines. Consequently White House lobbyists had to fall back upon a tougher approach to congressmen.

Both congressmen and departmental liaison officers agreed that "muscle" resided in the White House. It was this group of political actors who got tough when it was necessary. That the Kennedy White House got tough at times was not denied by anyone, although recourse to such tactics occurred only when the administration felt that there was a great deal at stake on a vote and that the results were uncertain. Under such circumstances the White House employed both direct and indirect pressure. Of course the very uncertainty associated with the disposition of

---

[4] *Congressional Quarterly Note to Editors,* pp. 2–3.

favors and services constituted a type of pressure. Hence the resources themselves added to the muscle available to the White House lobbyists. But when the liaison officers referred to muscle or pressure, they often emphasized other means for influencing legislators.

One direct type of pressure applied by the White House was insistence that it needed the member's vote and that he had to comply. "When we're down to a handful of votes, we call members and say 'We need your vote to make it.' They say, 'We're staked out already,' or 'Our constituents oppose it.' You draw it cold for them: 'This is it. You've got to take the heat.' "

The liaison officers acknowledged that they were applying pressure simply by calling to assert a White House interest in an item or to ascertain how the congressman stood on the issue. Wilson explained:

> When I call a member of a committee it's because he's on the line or undecided. The fact that I call him on a committee matter is more than just a substantive argument pro or con; it's the White House calling. They go on the defensive and we proceed from there. They know we wouldn't call unless we know they're reluctant to vote or attend.

O'Brien suggested that by invoking the name of the President in a direct appeal ("The President wants you and this is the key to his program") he made it difficult for a congressman to beg off. Common party ties helped, he contended, since in most cases Democratic congressmen started with a basic loyalty to their party and to the President as party leader. Unless special problems arose for them in their districts, appeals in the name of party loyalty and to support their party's leader tended to evoke cooperative responses from such congressmen.

The White House used other congressmen, especially legislative party leaders, to obtain or reverse votes. So, too, did it collaborate with the Washington lobbyists from allied interest groups. It reached into the state and local parties as well as to other influential groups and individuals in the legislators' constituencies. In the case of big-city congressmen, the White House was not averse to asking their local party leaders to swing them into line. The press publicized one such incident: A Roman Catholic congressman threatened to offer a parochial school amendment to a public school measure, thereby endangering the bill's chances. In response from an appeal by O'Brien, the legislator's district party leader telephoned him to ask, "Who sent you there, me or the Bishop? And who's going to keep you there, me or the Bishop?"[5] Nevertheless, when

---

[5] *Time Magazine,* September 1, 1961, p. 14. See also Richard F. Fenno, Jr., "The House of Representatives and Federal Aid to Education," in *New Perspectives on the House of Representatives,* ed. Robert L. Peabody and Nelson W. Polsby (Chicago: Rand McNally, 1963), p. 241, n. 10.

a city congressman was himself a local leader, such as James J. Delaney of New York, "there is no way we can keep him in line if he goes off; he's as independent as hell in his district."

The liaison staff also appealed to state party leaders to marshal support within their delegations for the administration. During the House Rules Committee fights of 1961 and 1963, when the White House and the House Democratic leadership strove to ensure that they could control the decisions of that committee, calls were placed to party leaders in southern states. The 1961 contest occurred too early in the year for the new administration to generate maximum pressure from state party leaders. But for the 1963 fight the White House started working on sympathetic party leaders early in November 1962. By the time Congress convened in 1963, asserted a senior White House liaison officer with reference to one state, "There was an incredible amount of pressure from the state, generated by the state party." One Washington observer reported that, in seeking to defeat an amendment to a bill expanding unemployment compensation, O'Brien had telephoned governors whose states stood to benefit from the bill, urging them to contact their senators for their votes.[6]

As a last resort the White House would in desperation reach into the constituency of Republican congressmen as well. In the 1963 fight on the Rules Committee, the White House reported that it "got to some Republicans" by contacting their sources of contributions in their districts. "We tried to find where these lines were and we made them responsive to us on this vote." It was a tortuous path, tracing the relations between the Republicans and their financial supporters and then persuading the latter to pressure their congressmen to support the Democratic position. Knowing that the businessmen were vitally concerned with the impending tax bill, which was the top-priority White House bill for 1963, the White House lobbyists and their associates employed the following logic: "We know the Congress. If you don't let us decide strategy and handle this fight, we can lose it. If we lose on the Rules fight, we'll lose labor support for the tax cut, and thus lose the tax cut itself."

Another resource that the White House mobilized was support from business executives whose companies held contracts with the national government. On the extremely tight fight in 1962 to extend the debt limit, an important bill in itself but linked closely to the politics of the Trade Expansion Act of 1962, calls were placed by certain political officials outside the White House to defense contractors. It was indicated to them that, should the debt limit not be raised, defense contracts faced a cutback. The businessmen called their congressmen, Republican and

---

[6] Helen Fuller, *Year of Trial: Kennedy's Crucial Decisions* (New York: Harcourt, Brace & World, 1962), p. 162.

Democratic, to express their concern. "We wanted it and needed it," stated a senior White House liaison officer. "I don't consider this undue pressure. Anyway, our position was that we had never heard of it. X [an actor placed in Defense by the White House] took the rap." Criticism for such action came entirely from the opposition party.

With one group of Democratic congressmen, the White House liaison officers conceded that their muscle had not provided much leverage: the southerners, particularly in the House of Representatives, who were the Democrats most likely to defect. The Kennedy White House liaison unit recognized that there was little that could be done to force the southerners into line. Other tactics were more effective, although on the whole most southern congressmen remained impervious to the strategies and tactics of the White House.

Southern Democrats were not comparable to northern city congressmen, Wilson contended. City bosses—the kind found in Chicago, Philadelphia, and New York—simply did not exist in the South. In most southern constituencies, organized labor possessed no influence; if anything, its support was often a liability. Southern Democrats looked for financial assistance neither to labor unions nor to the national party, but to local businessmen whose national interest groups opposed the administration's program. Moreover, many southern congressmen were much more concerned with winning the nomination in their primary elections than they were with the November elections. The President could offer little or no help in the first and, as head of the ticket, he wasn't a great asset in the final election either; in contrast, his name at the head of the ticket could mean votes for many northern Democrats. There was little, therefore, that southern Democrats could gain from the administration except a smile and a pat on the head.

It was clear, however, that more than a smile and a pat were available for dealing with southerners. They too could be approached through their concern with winning government contracts for their new industries and securing nationally supported projects and laboratories for their districts. Another tactic of the White House liaison staff was to reduce the political liability at home for those asked to support administration measures. "They do not want to get stuck out in left field in their states as Kennedy men." One tactic was to persuade more senior members of southern delegations to identify with an administration measure, thereby making it easier for the others to do so. "They can then feel that they can afford to vote with us." In many cases, Wilson asserted, southern Democrats wanted to be friendly. It was a matter of discovering how they could be permitted to take advantage of their common party identification and other links with the administration without hurting themselves in their districts. Often this was merely a question of helping them conclude that a supporting vote was politically feasible. Of course, southern Democrats could be prevailed upon to cooperate more easily on voice votes, standing or teller votes, or by providing bodies for a quorum—this participation was not publicly recorded. But even on roll-call votes, where they were committed on the record, some of them responded to "A vote this one time and we'll let you off the hook on the next one."

Additional Aspects of White House-Legislative Liaison. White House lobbyists, like their counterparts in the departments, engaged in the role of intelligence agent. The White House lobbyists covered a broader area of congressional relations and served as a center for integrating the entire executive system. Although they too tended to concentrate upon authorization legislation, they were much more actively involved in appropriation politics than were departmental liaison officers. And of course they also worked very closely with lobbyists from the interest groups that supported administration legislation. However, only the senior White House lobbyists reported that they sometimes tried to nullify the efforts of groups that opposed them by frightening off their lobbyists.

On the whole, the President's chief lobbyist was aware of the danger of excessive executive intervention in the Congress. The White House, he maintained, did not usually become involved in determining the membership of committees. It did pass on suggestions to the party leaders and the Democrats on the Ways and Means Committee (who served as their party's "committee on committees" in the House), "but we do *not* try to run it from here." The White House had to beware of charges that executive leaders interfered unduly in the Congress: "That can weaken us terrifically." When he first undertook to lobby for the President, he had moved somewhat cautiously; he had been uncertain whether he and his staff would be accepted and whether they would have the freedom to maneuver with the Democratic leadership and the members. "I think I was always filled with a certain degree of concern, trepidation, if you will. . . . At the outset I don't know how the Speaker felt about us, but I do know that we were very, very careful not to cross that barrier that we felt existed Constitutionally." He claimed that the White House had never crossed it, but they had discovered "you can talk across it."

The legislative liaison agents had only minimal contact with the Bureau of the Budget, a major staff unit to the President. The Bureau was engaged in its own relations with the Congress; it was not closely tied on a day-to-day basis with the liaison unit. According to one senior officer in the Bureau as well as the liaison agents, the latter did check with the Bureau occasionally to ascertain whether some transaction in which they were involved with legislators coincided with the program of the President. More often the senior members of the liaison unit went with their problems directly to their substantive counterparts—Theodore C. Sorensen, Meyer Feldman, Lee C. White—in the White House office. The liaison officers said that they respected the Bureau of the Budget as another source of political intelligence and as "very responsive and savvy." "We try to use them without totally using them." One criticism of the Bureau was its tendency to say that Congressman X or Y "won't give. We find that we need to knock their heads a couple of times and we're in business."

In the Kennedy Administration the Vice President apparently did not participate in the politics of advancing the administration's program in the Senate. None of the liaison officers reported that they had dealt with him or that he was a resource—as far as important executive leaders were concerned—whom they involved in the Congress. Rowland Evans and Robert Novak contend that President Kennedy had decided to use Vice President Lyndon B. Johnson on the Hill, but that the Vice President did little to help the administration's program and seldom offered a suggestion at the weekly leadership meetings.

Although this study did not extend into the administration of President Johnson, it should be noted that his vice president, Hubert H. Humphrey, was perfectly willing to lobby the Congress. An interview in 1965 with one of his assistants revealed that the President assigned to Vice President Humphrey the movement of legislation as his major task. At this time O'Brien was still a full-time lobbyist in the White House.

The assistant to the Vice President was responsible for helping his superior advance the President's program. "I pick up and pass on information; am in constant contact with all the committee staffs; help with the nose counts." He also carried on some discussions with senators, although this was primarily Vice President Humphrey's assignment, to which he devoted three to four hours a day. The Vice President and his assistant supplemented the White House liaison unit and coordinated very closely with it, the assistant representing the Vice President at the general meetings of legislative liaison agents convened by O'Brien at the White House. It was the assistant's contention that for the departmental liaison officers the Vice President represented a much higher level of political strength than before: "They can go so far, then they have to go one level up in the Senate to the Vice President."

Vice President Humphrey continued to serve as a special liaison actor with the Congress. It was reported by the press during 1965–67 that the administration owed certain gains in the House and the Senate to the lobbying efforts of the Vice President. In April 1967 the President designated Vice President Humphrey as his chief troubleshooter on Capitol Hill. No official announcement was made, but the press stated that the Vice President's role was spelled out by the President at a Cabinet meeting, Humphrey was to help map legislative strategy, persuade dissident southerners to vote for the administration, and "restore enthusiasm to discouraged Democratic liberals." Among the factors allegedly responsible for the Vice President's being handed this assignment were the difficulties O'Brien faced in continuing as the chief legislative liaison officer while serving as Postmaster General and the impending departure of Henry Hall Wilson.

PART FOUR

The Policy Context

THE SELECTIONS in Part Four continue the themes examined in Part Three, but with a focus on presidential policy-making activity. In performing his major task of governing the nation the president must provide leadership in the formulation, adoption, and implementation of public policy. The three selections that follow examine presidential leadership behavior in the crucial area of national security policy and in a major domestic policy area, education. They also analyze the impact of the organizational setting on presidential policy making. It is appropriate to consider the policy context of the presidency at this point, for public policy is the end toward which the president's other political activities and the organization of the presidential office are ultimately directed.

The president's dependence on the military in making national security policy is the concern of Morton H. Halperin. Halperin, a senior fellow at the Brookings Institution, examines the difficulties the president encounters in his efforts to obtain "good military advice," and he explores alternative procedures for doing so. Halperin concludes that in the final analysis much depends on the judgment of the president and on his capacity to resist strong pressures from the military. Although the military unquestionably plays a major role in developing and implementing national security policy, and the president is heavily dependent on military expertise for advice and information with respect to certain key subjects, the military is not the only source of information and advice, nor is it a monolithic force. Internal divisions exist between the three armed services and within individual services, and nonmilitary factors also come into play. The president has a greater task in making national security policy than merely dealing with the Pentagon.

One alternative method of obtaining diversity of information and advice and at the same time of rationalizing the policy-making process is the "multiple advocacy" model proposed by Alexander L. George. In presenting the case for multiple advocacy, George analyzes the limitations of the policy process and considers various means of improving it. He warns that multiple advocacy is complex and not easily achieved, but he believes that it offers great potential for improving the effectiveness of the process. In the Nixon administration, however, multiple advocacy was not implemented. Rather, the president and Henry Kissinger, first in his capacity as national security assistant and then as secretary of state, dominated the policy-making process with considerable apparent success in terms of results. George's prescriptions remain to be tested.

The president's ability to make policy by command and his leverage in bargaining with other participants are much reduced in domestic policy areas. Here presidential and executive branch control over information and expertise is not nearly so monopolistic; organized nongovernmental interests are much more active and influential; and the stakes are quite different (not as high for the nation as a whole, but greater in an economic sense for certain individuals and groups). The decisions are also not as likely to be irreversible as in the national security realm. Consequently, presidential policy preferences are less likely to prevail in unadulterated form. They must instead usually be modified through negotiation and bargaining to reflect the views of bureaucratic, congressional, and private sector participants in the policy-making process. The president's role is still central and his proposals form the basis for action, but the limitations on his capacity to determine the result are much greater.

These and other characteristics of domestic policy making are the focus of my analysis of educational policy formulation during the Johnson administration. Although this closing selection in Part Four is a case study of a single policy area during a particular period in time, it reveals the nature of the problems the president faces in developing legislative proposals. All presidents must organize the presidency for domestic policy formulation, if for no other reason than that the other participants in the policy-making process expect them to take the lead in developing the agenda for action. While President Johnson enjoyed great success in pushing new legislation through Congress during his first two years in office, too much significance should not be attached to the procedures he created for formulating policy. It should be remembered that he came to the presidency as a master legislative strategist, that he knew the key leaders of Congress intimately, and that he skillfully exploited the political situation he inherited when he assumed office.

In the last decade, as the nation has grappled with chronic inflation, the president's role in the formulation of macro-economic policy has assumed increasing importance. Political scientist Thomas E. Cronin believes that presidents now devote more attention to economic policy than to all other aspects of domestic policy. Until now, however, this area has been examined more from the perspectives of economics and substantive policy than from those of presidential politics and policy processes. Much of the extant literature dealing with presidential involvement in macro-economic policy making dates from the period ending in 1965 with the triumph of the Keynesian economic policies advocated by the academicians who served on the Council of Economic Advisers under Presidents Kennedy and Johnson. The few studies of the subject since the onset of the current inflationary era in 1966 primarily have been journalistic accounts of suggested solutions to specific problems and of personal characteristics and activities of particular economic policy makers, rather than careful analyses of the macro-economic policy process.

Consequently, I have chosen not to include a selection on this topic. A few comments on recent economic policy formulation are in order, however. The condition of the nation's economy has been a statutory responsibility of the president since passage of the Full Employment Act of 1946. The progressive severity of inflation since 1970, which forced President Nixon to devote increasing attention to economic policy, brought this responsibility back into focus. Upon taking office, President Ford identified inflation as the nation's primary problem and promised to treat it accordingly.

In spite of sharp differences among economists over how best to combat inflation without incurring unacceptably high levels of unemployment, there has been relatively little disagreement among top presidential advisers on economic policy. They have agreed with the conservative prescription of tight limits on the money supply exerted by the Federal Reserve, restraints on the growth of the federal budget, and reliance on the operation of the free market. Their position contrasts with the liberal one calling for less reliance on monetary policy, increased spending on federal domestic programs balanced by reduced defense expenditures, and selective use of governmental economic restraints ranging from private persuasion and public "jawboning" to direct wage and price controls. This viewpoint has had substantial support in Congress and among Democrats generally.

The primary conflicts in the economic policy-making process during the Nixon and Ford administrations have involved struggles for access to the president and for the premier position of influence among his principal economic advisers. The officials that have figured most prominently in these struggles have been the secretary of the treasury, the chairman of the Federal Reserve Board, and the director of the Office of Management and Budget. Cabinet members in other domestic policy areas, the chairman of the Council of Economic Advisers, and officials serving in presidential staff capacities or as heads of less prominent agencies have been more peripherally involved.

It is possible to offer a few tentative generalizations concerning the macro-economic policy-making process in the 1970s. First, no fixed pattern of presidential involvement has been established, as the president's role has varied substantially depending on political and economic conditions and on the personal characteristics of the economic policy makers. This situation contrasts sharply with the established patterns that mark presidential participation in making national security policy, shaping domestic policies, developing legislation, and preparing budgets.

Secondly, the major economic advisers to the president tend to share his ideological preferences, but they compete vigorously with each other for his favor. Success in this competition appears to be based on three factors: compatible personal relations with the president, a solid organizational base of operations, and bureaucratic political skills.

Finally, there is no assurance that such a process is capable of producing viable economic policies. Indeed, the results, as measured by the deteriorating condition of the economy in the 1970s, suggest that the process may be somewhat dysfunctional for effective presidential discharge of the statutory responsibility for the health of the economy. It must be acknowledged, also, that there is no assurance that the policies advocated by liberal economists will work any more effectively. Nor, for that matter, is there any substantive body of economic theory upon which the president can rely with confidence.

Clearly, macro-economic policy and the processes by which it is made constitute an area of major national importance. The inflation of the 1970s demonstrates that the presence of a formal Council of Economic Advisers and the requirements of the Full Employment Act of 1946 are not sufficient guarantors of prosperity. Congress and the president thus have the opportunity to develop and establish a more specific economic policy-making role for the president. While this alone will not cure the nation's economic ills, it should at least lead to the more rapid development and implementation of policies that lead in that direction. Political scientists and other students of the presidency and the policy process can make an important contribution to this effort. But first they must expand their knowledge base, to a level comparable to that which exists in the national security and domestic policy areas, through further research and study.

13.
THE PRESIDENT AND THE MILITARY
Morton H. Halperin

All Presidents are dependent on the permanent bureaucracies of government inherited from their predecessors. A President must have the information and analysis of options which the bureaucracies provide in order to anticipate problems and make educated choices. He must, in most cases, also have the coöperation of the bureaucracies to turn his decisions into governmental action. A bureaucracy can effectively defuse a presidential decision by refusing to support it with influential members of Congress or to implement it faithfully.

The President's dependence on the bureaucracy and his limited freedom to manœuvre are acute in all areas. The military, however, poses a unique set of problems for him. These arise in part from the limitations upon the President when he is seeking military advice. When the National Security Council or other presidential sessions are convened to discuss high-level foreign and national security matters, the President has a great deal of influence on the selection of all those who will attend, except the Chairman of the Joint Chiefs of Staff, who must be chosen from a small group of senior career military officers. Compare also the President's ability to appoint noncareer people to subcabinet and ambassadorial posts with the limitations on his range of selection for appointments to senior military positions or overseas military commands.

One dilemma for the President is finding alternative sources of military advice. The military, for example, has a virtual monopoly on providing information to the President about the readiness and capabilities of U.S. or even allied forces. Other groups and individuals can provide advice on many "military" questions, but their access to information is limited. The President may call for judgments from his Secretary of Defense, but the Secretary's analysis must rely on the basic factual material and field evaluations provided by the military.

Judgments about the likely effectiveness of American combat operations are also the exclusive province of the military. In assessing the

---

potential effects of a diplomatic move, the President can turn not only to career Foreign Service Officers, but also to businessmen, academics and intelligence specialists in other agencies. On the other hand, if he wishes to know how many American divisions would be necessary to defend Laos against a Chinese attack, the legitimacy of advice from groups other than the military is distinctly reduced. The military's influence on the information and evaluation of options which reach the President is further enhanced by the important role it plays in the preparation of national intelligence estimates.

Yet another source of leverage for the military is the prestige and influence that military leaders have enjoyed, at least in the past, with leading figures in Congress. Until quite recently, this influence limited presidential effectiveness with Congress and the general public. Even now, military influence continues to be strong with the leaders of the Armed Services Committees and appropriations subcommittees. Legislation clearly gives the military the right to inform congressional committees directly of their differences with adminstration policy, when asked. Senior military officers frequently exercise that right. In addition, military views on matters of major concern to the services often become known to the press. Thus, Presidents have shied away from decisions that they believed the military would take to the Congress and the public, and have frequently felt obliged to negotiate with the military.

For example, both Presidents Truman and Eisenhower carried on extensive negotiations with the military to secure its support for defense reorganization programs which appeared to have little chance of getting through Congress without military acquiescence. Later Presidents have shied away from defense reorganizations requiring congressional approval, at least in part because of the difficulty of gaining military concurrence, or congressional action without the concurrence. The backing of the military has also been vital to Presidents in other important programs. Truman, for example, relied heavily on the military to endorse his Korean War policies, especially in his disagreement with General Douglas MacArthur over limiting the war. MacArthur, who then commanded the U.N. forces in Korea, wanted to expand the war to China and to use nuclear weapons. The Joint Chiefs were not in favor of the expansion and Omar Bradley, Chairman of the Joint Chiefs and a much decorated World War II hero, strengthened Truman's position enormously when he stated publicly that MacArthur's proposal would lead to "the wrong war, in the wrong place, at the wrong time."

The political influence of the military has been substantially reduced in the last few years. The fact that the Joint Chiefs favor a particular proposal is no longer a guarantee of congressional support and may in some cases be counterproductive. For example, the Joint Chiefs were not asked by the Nixon administration to play a major role in defending the

Safeguard ABM. Nevertheless, the fact that the Joint Chiefs still wield influence with certain members of Congress and some parts of the public may inhibit the President, particularly if he fears a right-wing attack or needs a two-thirds vote to get a treaty through the Senate.

The implementation of presidential decisions by the military works both for and against the Chief Executive. The military tradition of discipline, efficiency and a clearly delineated chain of command increases the probability that precise orders will be observed and carried out with dispatch. However, the fact that the military implements decisions according to standard procedures may cause presidential orders to be misconstrued through oversimplification. The Joint Chiefs will defer to the field commander and not monitor his compliance carefully. Moreover, Presidents find it difficult to develop alternate means to secure implementation of decisions in the domain of the military. For example, the President may use special envoys in place of career Foreign Service Officers to carry out delicate negotiations while he can hardly send a retired businessman to land American forces in Lebanon or to command a nuclear missile-carrying submarine.

Presidents also have great difficulty convincing the military to create new capabilities, which they may need in the future but which might tend to alter the traditional role of a particular branch. The services emphasize the forces which conform to their notion of the essence of their role and resist capabilities which involve interservice coöperation (*e.g.* airlift), noncombat roles (*e.g.* advisers), and élite forces (*e.g.* Green Berets). At least until recently, they have also resisted the maintenance of combat-ready nonnuclear forces.

II

This is not to suggest that the President's problems with the military are greater than, for example, those with the Department of Agriculture or other agencies with strong links to domestic constituencies and congressional committees. Nor is it to suggest that the information and advice given the President by the military has over the years been less valuable than the advice of others. The point is rather that within the foreign policy field the greatest limitations on the President's freedom of action tend to come from the military. None of our Presidents has been content with his relations with the military.

In fact, Presidents have used a number of devices to overcome limitations on their power, to get the information and advice they want and to find support for implementing their decisions. Presidential strategies have varied, depending on the type of issue and depending on whether they were seeking: (1) information or options, (2) political support or (3) faithful implementation.

Their techniques include the following:

(1) *Reorganizations.* The Nixon National Security Council system and the appointment of the President's Blue Ribbon Panel on Defense Reorganization (Fitzhugh Panel) suggest a return to the emphasis on reorganization which tended to dominate thinking in the early postwar period and, indeed, through 1960. Reorganization efforts within the Pentagon have aimed at securing coördinated military advice, rather than separate advice from each service. Presidents have, in general, pressed the Joint Chiefs to transcend service biases and to come up with agreed positions based on a unified perspective. Eisenhower was particularly adverse to JCS splits. But the success of these efforts has been relatively limited. Most observers conclude that JCS papers still tend to reflect particular service views, either by way of deference or compromise, rather than the unified military judgment of a "true" Joint Staff. Secretaries of Defense have not looked upon the Joint Staff as part of their own staff.

The reorganization of the National Security Council system beginning in 1969 appears to have been designed to bring to bear a variety of different views on military problems. The evaluation of alternate military forces is centered in the Council's Verification Panel. This group first considered the Strategic Arms Limitation Talks (SALT) and then the prospects and problems of mutual force reductions in Europe, thereby going beyond traditional military and intelligence channels. The Defense Program Review Committee was designed to apply expertise to a review of budget decisions from the Budget Bureau and the President's economic advisers, as well as the State Department and the Arms Control and Disarmament Agency. The NSC system itself was designed to take into account the views of the State Department and other government agencies about military commitments, bases, overseas departments and military assistance. At the same time, these efforts assured the military of orderly consideration of its views, reflecting the judgment that the military is more willing to participate faithfully in the implementation of a decision where it has been overruled if it feels that military views have been fully taken into account.

(2) *Military adviser in the White House.* President Franklin Roosevelt relied heavily on Admiral William Leahy as the Chief of Staff to the Commander in Chief. Truman for a brief period continued to use Leahy and then, on a part-time basis, relied on General Eisenhower for advice on budget issues, while Eisenhower was President of Columbia University. Truman later turned to the Chairman of the Joint Chiefs.

Eisenhower, his own military adviser in the White House, had only a junior military officer in the person of Colonel Andrew Goodpaster who functioned in effect as a staff secretary, collecting and summarizing for the President intelligence materials from the State Department and the CIA, as well as the military.

Kennedy, after the Bay of Pigs operation, brought General Maxwell Taylor into the White House as the military representative of the President, and Taylor advised the President on a broad range of issues involving all aspects of national security policy. When Taylor moved over to become Chairman of the Joint Chiefs, a JCS liaison office was created in the White House, working primarily with the President's Assistant for National Security Affairs.

President Johnson relied primarily on other mechanisms but did use General Taylor as a White House consultant after his return from Vietnam. Taylor functioned in relation to the Vietnam issue, providing an alternate source of advice and information to the President on options open to him in Vietnam operations and negotiations.

President Nixon recalled General Goodpaster briefly during the transition period and the very early days of his administration, but since then has not had a senior military adviser in the White House. Henry Kissinger's deputy is an army major-general. He ensures, along with the JCS liaison office, that Kissinger and the President are aware of JCS concerns, but he does not serve as an alternate source of military advice.

(3) *A civilian adviser in the White House.* There has been a growing trend in the postwar period toward presidential reliance on White House staff assistance in both domestic and national security policy. In the National Security field, civilian assistance has been used not only as a source of additional information, advice and options, but also as an aid to the President in seeing that his decisions are carried through.

Truman tended to rely on his cabinet officers and the uniformed military, but there were episodic interventions by civilians in the White House. Under Truman, Clark Clifford became heavily involved in the negotiations leading to the Defense Unification Act and the National Security Council system. Later he contributed to the creation of the Atomic Energy Commission and the continued control of atomic weapons by the Commission. Averell Harriman, who became Truman's national security adviser just before the Korean War, functioned briefly during the early stages of the war as a spokesman for the President's position; his tasks included a visit to General MacArthur to explain the President's policies to him and seek his compliance.

Eisenhower had no single national security adviser in the White House. His Assistants for National Security Council Affairs were involved only in the very limited number of issues that were handled in the rather stylized machinery of the National Security Council system as then constituted. Eisenhower brought in several advisers for specific issues, including Nelson Rockefeller, but these advisers tended to interact and overlap with Secretary of State Dulles rather than with the Department of Defense. They were responsible for some new initiatives, such as Eisenhower's "open skies" proposal in 1954, but the instances are few.

The regularization and institutionalization of a civilian adviser in the White House on national security matters came with President Kennedy's appointment of McGeorge Bundy. Bundy, following the Bay of Pigs fiasco, moved to increase the independence of the White House in securing information by arranging to get a good deal of the raw material directly from the field, including State, Defense and CIA cable traffic. Bundy also assumed primary responsibility for briefing the President. Despite the expanded role which involved them in many foreign policy matters with military implications, neither Bundy nor Walt Rostow, Johnson's adviser for national security affairs, were heavily engaged in Defense budget matters. Under President Nixon, Henry Kissinger has been as active in Defense Department matters as he is in those for which the State Department has primary responsibility. Nixon appears to rely upon Kissinger as an alternative source of information and options on the broad range of military and national security matters, and as a channel for various kinds of military advice.

(4) *Reliance on the Secretary of Defense.* Truman and Eisenhower tended to rely on their Secretaries of Defense primarily to secure the implementation of their decisions, particularly Defense budget decisions. They expected the Secretaries to bear the weight of military objections to ceilings on defense spending and to force the services to develop forces within those ceilings. Even in this role the Defense Secretaries were of limited value to the President since they tended to become spokesmen for the military desire for increased spending.

The appointment of Robert S. McNamara brought to fruition a trend which had been developing gradually and had accelerated during the brief tenure of Secretary Thomas Gates. This called for the Secretary of Defense to become in effect the principal military adviser to the President, superseding the Joint Chiefs. Over time Kennedy and Johnson, at least until the Vietnam war accelerated in late 1965, tended to look to the Secretary of Defense for advice on commitments, bases, overseas deployments and military aid, as well as budget decisions. The Secretary's job included absorbing the advice tendered by the military and combining that in his recommendations to the President. Both Kennedy and Johnson did, of course, continue to meet with the Chairman of the Joint Chiefs in formal sessions of the National Security Council and in other meetings, but by and large they received military judgments and advice through the filter of the Secretary of Defense. As the Vietnam war heated up, JCS Chairman General Earle Wheeler was included in Johnson's regular Tuesday lunches and began to act as an independent vehicle for reporting JCS views to the President, at least on the range of issues discussed at those meetings. Defense Secretary Laird has continued the tradition of taking positions on substantive issues of military policy and operations, as well as defense budget issues, although the President seems to regard him simply as a second source of advice on military questions. The Secretary and the Joint Chiefs have a co-equal role in the National Security Council and in all of its subordinate institutions.

(5) *Reliance on the Secretary of State.* No President has given the Secretary of State a dominant role in decisions regarding combat operations or the defense budget. Truman did call on General Marshall—when he was Secretary of State—for support in keeping the Defense budget down, and Nixon has brought the Secretary's staff into the Defense budget process through the Defense Program Review Committee. However, on issues concerning commitments, bases, overseas deployments and military aid, Truman tended to rely largely on Acheson's judgment, and Eisenhower depended to a large extent on Dulles. Secretary Rusk played a major role in these issues along with Secretary McNamara.

(6) *Reliance on scientists.* Although scientists have occasionally been used to evaluate combat operations, by and large their role has been limited to issues reflected in the Defense budget. Eisenhower depended, particularly in the later years of his administration, on the chief scientist in the Pentagon (the Director of Defense Research and Engineering) and on his science advisers. Kennedy also looked to his science adviser, Jerome Weisner, for alternate advice on the Defense budget, as well as on arms-control matters, particularly relating to the nuclear testing issue. The role of the science advisers seems to have declined precipitously under Johnson and Nixon, with their energies going largely to non-Defense matters.

(7) *Reliance on the Bureau of the Budget.* The role of the Budget Bureau (now Office of Management and Budget) in Defense decisions has been very limited. Truman and Eisenhower relied upon the Budget Director to help set a ceiling on Defense spending, but the Bureau did not get involved in deciding how that money would be spent. Under Eisenhower, Kennedy and Johnson it became a matter of tradition that the Budget Director would have to appeal Secretarial decisions on the Defense budget to the President, the reverse of the situation in all other departments. Press reports suggested that initially Nixon had reversed this process, but he now appears to have returned to this traditional pattern. The Budget Director sits on the Defense Program Review Committee, but the extent of Budget Bureau influence is difficult to determine.

(8) *Ad hoc techniques.* Presidents have used a number of ad hoc or special techniques to secure information and options on military questions. One technique frequently used during the Truman and Eisenhower

periods was the President-appointed commission. Nixon's Fitzhugh Panel may mark a return to the use of this technique, although it has thus far been limited to organizational rather than substantive questions.

Occasionally, Presidents have sent special representatives into the field to investigate military questions. Kennedy, for example, sent an old friend and military officer to the camp preparing the Cuban guerrillas for the Bay of Pigs operations, and Richard Nixon sent British guerrilla war expert Brigadier General Thompson to Vietnam for an independent assessment.

Now and then a President has been fortunate enough to have the concurrence of the military on a particular policy, without having to bargain. That the Joint Chiefs of Staff opposed expansion of the Korean War and felt that General MacArthur had indeed been insubordinate was of critical importance to Truman in securing public acceptance of this policy. However, in most cases, the President has been forced to bargain for the public support of the Joint Chiefs. Truman had to accept the case for German rearmament in order to gain JCS approval to send American forces to Europe. Kennedy and his Secretary of Defense engaged in long hours of bargaining with the Joint Chiefs before they were able to devise an acceptable safeguard program of standby preparations for nuclear testing that made it possible for the Joint Chiefs to give their reluctant support to the Nuclear Test Ban Treaty. Johnson felt obliged to have the Joint Chiefs of Staff on board before he would order the cessation of the bombing of North Vietnam in 1968.

In some cases, the President has sought to use the prestige and power of his office to accomplish his objectives in the face of military opposition. This tactic has a better chance of success when the decisions involve only executive department action; when the Chiefs are split; and particularly when the decisions do not require the use of armed forces in combat operations. But it can be done in other cases. For example, on the matter of civilian control of atomic weapons and the creation of a civilian-dominated Atomic Energy Commission, Truman appealed to the public and Congress over the objections of the military, and was able to win. Eisenhower in the same way (although less successfully) enlisted the support of the American business community in his effort to reorganize the Defense Department against the judgment of the military.

Presidents have had the greatest success in bypassing the military on Defense budget limitations, because military demands are essentially open-ended and always have to be overruled. However, the appeal to fiscal conservatism and alternative demands for resources have also tended to check defense expenditures.

III

Techniques used to improve the information and options reaching the President can also be applied to the implementation of decisions. For example, civilian advisers in the White House have been used to monitor compliance with presidential decisions, and other Presidents have tended to rely on the Secretary of Defense to see that their decisions were carried out.

In addition, Presidents have sometimes resorted to selecting military officers who they felt shared their views and therefore would act to implement them properly. The most dramatic case came in 1953 when Eisenhower replaced all of the Joint Chiefs of Staff and appointed Admiral Radford, a known supporter of his policy of massive nuclear retaliation, as the Chairman of the Joint Chiefs and chose service chiefs who by and large were prepared to comply. After the Cuban missile crisis, Admiral George Anderson, who had not coöperated fully with the President, was not reappointed to the post of Chief of Naval Operations. However, there are severe limits to the value of such actions: General Ridgway and later General Taylor, the Army Chiefs of Staff appointed by Eisenhower, resisted the reduction in the size of the Army and the Administration's reliance on massive nuclear retaliation. When their views were ignored they resigned and protested publicly. In response to Admiral Anderson's reassignment as Ambassador to Portugal, Congress legislated statutory terms for the members of the Joint Chiefs.

Another technique that has been used to increase compliance with presidential decisions is the creation of new organizations which reflect new desires. The most successful such effort was to create within the Navy a Special Projects Office to monitor the Polaris program and to alter promotion procedures so that command of a Polaris submarine would permit promotion to senior grades. The least successful effort was Kennedy's attempt in the early 1960s to give the military a greater flexibility in dealing with counterinsurgency operations by creating the Green Berets.

IV

The decline of the prestige of the military over the past several years has given President Nixon and his successors greater freedom to determine how advice from the military reaches them, and to accept or reject that advice. The experience of the postwar period suggests two basic changes which the President could institute now that would increase his leverage vis-à-vis the military—one involving the channel by which he receives advice from senior military officers and the other concerning the role of civilian advisers.

The experience of the last 25 years suggests that the effort to reorganize the Pentagon and then to demand "unified" military advice from the Joint Chiefs of Staff has been a failure. As noted above, most observers who have had the opportunity to view the product of the Joint Chiefs would argue that unified JCS papers reflect either a compromise among the services, a form of logrolling in which the proposals of all services are endorsed, or deference to the service or field commander most concerned. As long as the function of the Joint Staff is to come up with a paper that will be endorsed by all of the Chiefs, there does not appear to be any way to alter the situation fundamentally, although some progress has been made in the last several years in increasing the flexibility and independence of the Joint Staff.

More radical changes must be effected if the President is to get good military advice. The key to improving the situation is to separate the Chairman of the Joint Chiefs of Staff and the Joint Staff from the Service Chiefs. The President and the Secretary of Defense would in this case solicit the separate views of each of the Service Chiefs and of the Chairman of the Joint Chiefs, and where appropriate, the views of the relevant unified and specified commanders (*e.g.* commanders in Europe and Asia and the head of the Strategic Air Command). These latter views might be channeled to the Secretary through the Chairman of the Joint Chiefs. The Chairman would, in turn, be the officer in the line of command through the President and the Secretary of Defense to the commanders (bypassing the Service Chiefs) for carrying out operations in the field.

The basic rationale behind this change in procedure is that the Service Chiefs and the unified and specified commands constitute the highest level at which reliable (first-hand) information and advice are available. The Joint Staff, when it needs information, must solicit either the service staffs in Washington or the field commanders. In fact, JCS information and advice presented to the President and the Secretary usually come from the services and the subordinate service commands in the field. For example, most of the positions taken by the Joint Chiefs of Staff on questions relating to Vietnam simply involved a JCS endorsement of the recommendations of General Westmoreland or General Abrams, the army commanders in Vietnam, and Admiral Sharp, Commander in Chief of the Pacific, who had particular responsibility for the bombing operations.

On questions of requirements for overseas bases, to take another example, the Joint Chiefs in most cases simply endorse the position of the Service which utilizes the base. On budget issues, the Chiefs tend to endorse all of the programs desired by each of the services. When forced to choose on an issue of policy the Chiefs compromise among the different

Service positions rather than attempting to develop a position based on a unified military point of view.

Under the proposed change of procedure the President and the Secretary of Defense would be made aware of differing positions which might otherwise be compromised. In addition this would leave the Chairman of the Joint Chiefs and the Joint Staff free from the job of developing a compromise position and therefore able to present the Secretary of Defense with a military judgment separate from the interests of the Services. If this process is to succeed the President and the Secretary will have to choose a Chairman of the Joint Chiefs with whom they can work. Then, if the system is developed properly, the Chairman and the Joint Staff would come to be seen as part of the Office of the Secretary of Defense, providing him and the President with military advice which could be weighed against the advice of the operators—the Service Chiefs and the unified and specified commanders. The influence of the Chairman would come from his record of persuasiveness with the President and the Secretary of Defense. They will take his judgments seriously if his choice is shown to be based on a broader range of considerations than the advice of the Service Chiefs.

Such a procedure would increase the probability that imaginative and innovative proposals would reach the President. It would also make it more likely that the President would become aware of the wide diversity of military opinions on a question and not act on an erroneous assumption that there was a unified view.

One of the few instances on record in which the President did seek separate opinions from the several Chiefs came in 1961 when President Kennedy was contemplating an invasion of Laos. Partly because of the Bay of Pigs episode in which the doubts of individual Chiefs about the military feasibility of the landing in Cuba never reached him, Kennedy asked each Chief separately for his views in writing and then met with them as a group. He discovered by this process that each one had a slightly different position on what should be done, what troops should be committed, and what the likely outcome of American intervention would be. Receiving this conflicting advice, it was harder for Kennedy to make a decision to intervene but it also meant that he did not make a decision under a mistaken impression that there was a unified military view either for or against the intervention.

The proposed procedure would also increase presidential flexibility in accepting or rejecting military advice because he would no longer be confronted with a unanimous but misleading statement of JCS views. He would be able to choose among service and command viewpoints rather than having to develop a new position which in essence overrules all of the military, in as much as JCS opinions now represent all the services.

In order to increase the President's freedom to choose and the likelihood that he will get faithful implementation and political support for his actions, a procedure should be developed which provides for military access to the President on issues of importance to the military. Access should be provided not only for the Chairman of the Joint Chiefs, but also for the Service Chiefs and the unified commanders most concerned. When he finds it necessary to overrule the military, the President should justify his decision on broad political grounds; he should be seen doing so personally; and he should do so in writing with a clear memorandum stating his position. All of these acts would increase military willingness to go along with presidential decisions and to implement them faithfully.

The military takes seriously the President's role as Commander in Chief and also recognizes that he has broader responsibility concerned with both domestic and international political situations. They are much more amenable to being overruled on these grounds than to being told that their military judgment is questioned. (For this reason the military resented McNamara's reliance on civilians, particularly in the Office of Systems Analysis, for judgments on what they took to be purely military questions, *i.e.* statements of military requirements.) They also implement decisions faithfully when assured that their position has been heard by the President and it has not been lost in the filter of Secretary of Defense memoranda.

Securing separate advice from the Service Chiefs and other military commanders will require that the President, or at least his White House staff, spend more time digesting the separate positions. However, this seems a price worth paying to increase the flow of new ideas or doubts about proposed courses of action to the White House.

Military compliance with presidential decisions would also be enhanced by avoiding the practice of using the military to seek public support for presidential decisions. The value of such action has become considerably reduced in recent years, and such use of the military tends to legitimize and increase the importance of their opposition when they choose to oppose policy.

V

Implicit in the new procedures as suggested is a reduced role for the Secretary of Defense from that which he assumed in the 1960s. His scope would also be affected by another proposed change—that decision-making on matters concerning Defense budgets and the use of military force be moved outside of the Pentagon and into a broader arena involving officials from the White House and other agencies.

The Nixon administration has moved rather significantly, at least in form and to some extent in substance, to change the locus of decisions. The creation of the Washington Special Action Group (WSAG) brings into existence for the first time a forum in which detailed contingency planning for the actual use of military force is carried out beyond the Pentagon. WSAG is chaired by the President's Assistant for National Security and includes senior State Department and CIA officials as well as civilian and military representatives of the Pentagon. It provides a forum where the military, diplomatic and intelligence evaluations of likely use of American military forces can be brought together in a systematic way, something which was not done in the past. This institution needs to be strengthened, probably with the addition of some White House staff assigned specifically to this task.

A second institution of significance is the Defense Program Review Committee (DPRC), which is also chaired by the President's Assistant for National Security and includes representatives not only from State but also from the Arms Control and Disarmament Agency, the Council of Economic Advisers and the Office of Management and Budget. The implications of this institution are enormous. If it is functioning effectively, decisions not only on the total size of the Defense budget but also on the major Defense programs will be made outside the Pentagon in an interagency forum where White House influence is dominant. The President would be receiving advice on Defense budget issues from several different perspectives. While the institution has been created, it does not appear yet to have either the staff or the necessary top level direction to get into a wide range of Defense issues.

For this purpose and also to make WSAG more effective, the President's Assistant for National Security probably needs a Senior Deputy who would take some of the responsibility for White House direction for budget and combat decisions, and who would be explicitly charged with bringing to bear the broader concerns of the President.

The procedures suggested here in no sense imply a downgrading of military advice. Instead they are designed to assure that the President receives the full range of the existing military opinions rather than what filters through a JCS compromise procedure or a Secretary of Defense responsible for presenting military views to the President. They also aim to give the President critical commentary on military proposals from civilian officials with a different and somewhat broader range of responsibilities. In the end, good decisions will depend on the wisdom and judgment of the President. What he decides, however, is greatly influenced by the information presented to him, as well as by his sense of freedom to choose regardless of strong military and other bureaucratic pressures.

14.
THE CASE FOR MULTIPLE ADVOCACY IN MAKING FOREIGN POLICY *

Alexander L. George

This paper discusses prescriptive theories of policy making in complex organizations with particular reference to foreign policy making in the Executive Branch. Instead of utilizing centralized management practices to discourage or neutralize internal disagreements over policy, an executive can use a multiple advocacy model to harness diversity of views and interests in the interest of rational policy making. Diversity is also given scope in "bureaucratic politics" and "partisan mutual adjustment," but in contrast to these unregulated pluralistic systems, multiple advocacy requires management to create the basis for structured, balanced debate among policy advocates drawn from different parts of the organization (or, as necessary, from outside the organization). Multiple advocacy, therefore, is a "mixed system" that combines elements of a centralized management model with certain features of pluralistic and participatory systems.

The functional equivalent of a rational model can be provided within an organization also by means other than multiple advocacy. One such organizational device, that of "adversary proceedings," is often recommended as a means for obtaining a final critical examination of a preferred policy option before it is recommended to or adopted by the top decision maker. The concept of "adversary proceedings," borrowed from the judicial system, is not a well-defined or standardized method for organizational decision making. Generally, however, it includes few advo-

* So many persons have commented on earlier drafts of this paper that it is difficult to list all of them in acknowledging my debt and appreciation. I want to thank the panel chairman, Paul Hammond, and Allen Schick and William Harris for their helpful discussion of an earlier version of this paper that was given at the annual meetings of the American Political Science Association in Chicago, September 1971. I would like to express appreciation also to the Committee on International Studies, Stanford University, for its support of my research.

Reprinted by permission of the author and publisher from the *American Political Science Review,* Vol. 66 (September, 1972), pp. 751–785. Abridged. Some footnotes omitted.

cates, and covers fewer options than would a system of multiple advocacy.

Another organizational device for obtaining a rational consideration of alternatives is the "devil's advocate." Strictly speaking, the devil's advocate performs a role; it is understood that he will argue on behalf of an unpopular option which should be considered but which no one else will speak up for, and which the devil's advocate himself does not really favor. A strong case can be made in principle for utilization of a devil's advocate, but one cannot be sanguine about its efficacy in foreign policy making on the basis of recent experience.

Still another, and far more comprehensive, organizational approach for achieving the functional equivalent of the ideal rational model can be seen in President Nixon's version of the National Security Council. Unlike a multiple advocacy system, which defines the role of the chief executive as a "magistrate" who listens in a structured setting to different, well-prepared advocates making the best case for alternative options, the present NSC relies upon staff work to distill, analyze, and present options to the President for his choice. Thus, the President is defined as a unitary rational decision maker who is shielded from too much direct exposure to undigested, "raw" disagreements over policy within the executive branch.

Both the Nixon NSC concept and multiple advocacy attempt to cope with those stubborn dynamics of organizational behavior and bureaucratic politics that undermine or destroy efforts to achieve the functional equivalent of rationality in making foreign policy decisions; but they do so in different ways. Each model has somewhat special requirements and conditions for reasonably effective performance. Before contrasting these two approaches in further detail, one should note that the burden of evaluating prescriptive policy-making models is a heavy one. Only very limited empirical evidence exists for either model. The task of comparative evaluation is complicated in any case by several factors: The reality of a policy-making system is always more opaque and inconsistent than the theoretical model which rationalizes it. Moreover, while it is useful at this stage in theory development to sharpen the differences between alternative prescriptive models, certain features of the multiple advocacy system to be discussed in this paper do appear in some form and under certain circumstances in the present NSC system; and still other prescriptions for managing foreign policy making, to be discussed later under "preventive interventions," could be incorporated into the Nixon-Kissinger model without robbing it of its distinctive features.

It is important, finally, to recognize that neither multiple advocacy nor any other management model can be expected to cope reliably with many constraints on the quality and effectiveness of foreign policy. In focusing in this paper on the way in which the policy-making system is organized and operated—i.e., the process variables—we do not ignore or underestimate the simultaneous importance of many other decision-making variables: ideology, cognitive beliefs about opponents and about the nature of the international system, operational codes, public opinion, substantive knowledge and skill (relevant, for example, to negotiation, deterrence, coercive diplomacy, crisis management, conciliation, alliance-maintenance, etc.). Because many other variables of this kind also influence the quality of decision making, even a good policy-making process—i.e., one that provides the functional equivalent of a rational model of decision making—cannot guarantee that highly adaptive decisions will be made in every case. Rather, it is a matter of probabilities, and particular attention should be given to the ability of a policy-making system to do well when dealing with critical rather than routine decisions.

One set of critical decisions in foreign policy concerns decisions involving commitment, intervention and escalation—the class of foreign policy decisions singled out for analysis in this paper. Ideological premises and cognitive beliefs about the opponent and about the nature of the international system held by policy makers are likely to play a particularly important role in determining such decisions. Indeed such values and beliefs may "dominate" on occasion whatever independent contribution even a well-designed and well-managed policy-making system can make to the quality of decisional outputs.

It is not easy to deal with these essentially normative problems in focusing on different ways of organizing the process variables of policy making, although we shall attempt to do so to some limited extent when we review historical cases in U.S. foreign policy. For the moment it may be appropriate simply to remind ourselves that these other variables also affect foreign policy decisions made via highly centralized policy-making systems such as the present NSC. To the extent that there is significant *disagreement* among policy makers on matters of foreign policy ideology and related cognitive beliefs, one can argue that a more openly competitive system such as multiple advocacy is more likely to secure a critical examination and weighing of them, outside of as well as inside the executive branch, than a highly centralized policy-making system. But we confess that there is little empirical evidence to clarify, let alone settle this question. Indeed, the performance of policy-making systems has hardly been studied from this broader standpoint. Rather, the framework usually employed regards values and beliefs of this kind as decisional premises that bound the more narrow search for "efficient" means.

THE NATIONAL SECURITY COUNCIL: SOME QUESTIONS

We shall forego a detailed description of President Nixon's reorganization of the National Security Council in 1969.[6] It will suffice for our purposes to articulate some of the underlying premises of the current NSC model and to raise some questions of theoretical and practical interest. It should be emphasized at the outset, however, that the administration does not always make foreign policy decisions in a manner consistent with its own NSC model. Any president and any administration is likely to resort to a number of different ways of making major foreign policy decisions. Even multiple advocacy can be noted from time to time in the present administration's way of making certain foreign policy decisions.[7] And, as a sympathetic observer recently noted, "The NSC system today is not the tidy blueprint of January, 1969. The older it has gotten, the more informal and overlapping its procedures have become." [8]

One of the major objectives of Nixon's reorganization of the NSC was to curb, if not altogether eliminate, the play of "bureaucratic politics" in the making of foreign policy within the executive branch. By instituting centralized control and direction of the search for and evaluation of options at the NSC level, Nixon has greatly enhanced presidential control over foreign policy decision making and weakened the ability of officials in departments and agencies to exercise independent judgment and influence over decisions. President Nixon and his Special Assistant for National Security Affairs, Henry Kissinger, have tried to impose the model

---

[6] For detailed description of President Nixon's reorganization of the NSC see, for example, Vincent Davis, "American Military Policy: Decision-making in the Executive Branch," *Naval War College Review* (May 1970), pp. 4–23; Robert H. Johnson, "The National Security Council: The Relevance of Its Past To Its Future," *Orbis*, 13 (Fall, 1969), 709–735; E. A. Kolodziej, "The National Security Council: Innovations and Implications," *Public Administration Review*, 29 (Nov.-Dec. 1969), 573–585; Frederick C. Thayer, "Presidential Policy Processes and 'New Administration': A Search for Revised Paradigms," *Public Administration Review*, 31 (September/October 1971) 552–561; and particularly Irving M. Destler, *Presidents, Bureaucrats and Foreign Policy* (Princeton, N.J.: Princeton University Press, 1972).

For accounts of the historical evolution of the NSC see, for example, Keith C. Clark and Lawrence J. Legere, eds., *The President and the Management of National Security* (N.Y.: Praeger, 1969); Paul Y. Hammond, *Organizing for Defense* (Princeton: Princeton University Press, 1961); Senator Henry M. Jackson, ed., "Jackson Subcommittee Papers on Policy-Making at the Presidential Level," *The National Security Council* (N.Y.: Praeger, 1965); Stanley Falk, "National Security Council under Truman, Eisenhower, and Kennedy," *Political Science Quarterly*, 79 (Sept., 1964), 403–434.

[7] As, for example, in the policy planning for the SALT talks. See Samuel C. Orr, "Defense Report/National Security Council Network Gives White House Tight Rein over SALT Strategy," *National Journal*, 3 (April 24, 1971), 877–886; and John P. Leacocos, "Kissinger's Apparat," *Foreign Policy*, No. 5 (Winter 1971–72), p. 19.

[8] Leacocos, p. 5.

of unitary, rational policy maker on the more loosely structured pluralistic systems of previous administrations.

It must be recognized that the present NSC system has indeed reduced some of the dysfunctional consequences associated with the freer play of "bureaucratic politics" in more loosely coordinated policy-making systems of earlier periods. As in other types of complex organizations, subunits of the executive branch tend to engage in "quasi resolution of conflict" and to avoid uncertainty in relations with each other by means of "negotiating the internal environment" within the organization.[9] Left to their own devices, those subunits which share responsibility for a particular policy area often adapt by restricting competition with each other. As a result, policy issues may not rise to the presidential level, or when they do, they often take the form of concealed compromises that reflect the special interest of actors at lower levels of the hierarchical system.

Another dysfunctional aspect of relatively decentralized "bargaining" systems of policy making stems from the tendency of an individual subunit to restrict its contribution to the organizationwide search for and evaluation of options in order to enhance its ability to influence top-level organizational choice. Thus, a subunit (for example, the State Department or the Joint Chiefs of Staff) might attempt to provide the chief executive with only one preferred option, which reflects its own internal bargaining politics and obscures or conceals information and analysis that support other options.

These and other dysfunctional aspects of "bureaucratic politics" were well known to President Nixon when he took office; his desire to avoid them influenced the redesign of the NSC. As he put it in his "U.S. Foreign Policy for the 1970's":

> The new NSC system is designed to make certain that clear policy choices reach the top, so that various positions can be fully debated in the meeting of the Council. Differences of view are identified and defended, rather than muted or buried. I refuse to be confronted with a bureaucratic consensus that leaves me no options but acceptance or rejection, and that gives me no way of knowing what alternatives exist.[11]

---

[9] Richard M. Cyert and James G. March, *Behavioral Theory of the Firm* (Englewood Cliffs, N.J.: Prentice-Hall, 1963), pp. 116–120. As Robert Axelrod (*Conflict of Interest* [Chicago: Markham, 1970, p. 123]) points out, Cyert's and March's observation regarding internal bargaining and other adaptive devices on the part of the subunits of an organization "leaves open the question of how the upper levels of the organization supervise the sub-units. . . ." This is not surprising, however, since the Cyert-March theory is not a prescriptive management theory.

[11] Richard Nixon, *U.S. Foreign Policy for the 1970's: A New Strategy for Peace,* A report to the Congress, February 18, 1970 (Washington, D.C.), p. 22. Henry Kissinger had earlier noted and deplored the play of bureaucratic politics in policy making in "Domestic Structure and Foreign Policy," *DAEDALUS*, 95 (Spring, 1966), 503–529.

Indeed, under Kissinger, presidential-level involvement in, and efforts to control foreign policy formation and implementation have substantially increased. The staff of the NSC, augmented in numbers and functions, has reached deeper into the departments and bureaus in order to identify and gain control over a wider range of issues at earlier stages. What is more, strengthening a trend begun in the Kennedy administration, the Special Assistant for National Security Affairs has emerged as a semi-autonomous actor in the policy system. Kissinger now plays an active, central role in influencing and shaping the process of policy analysis throughout the executive branch in order to formulate well-developed options for the President's consideration. The enhanced role of the Special Assistant incorporates important features of the management model developed earlier by Secretary of Defense McNamara in the sphere of defense planning. Thus, reminiscent of McNamara is Kissinger's practice of frequently initiating policy studies from the presidential level (the well-known National Security Study Memoranda, or NSSM), as a means of enabling the NSC staff to force issues that would otherwise be buried or neglected by the agencies up for ultimate presidential action.

If we grant that the present system curbs some dysfunctional features of "bureaucratic politics," we are still left with the question of the cost and limitations of so centralized a system. To be sure, interested personnel in the departments, agencies, and subunits are by no means excluded from participating in the present policy-making process. In fact, in some respects, via their membership in the various NSC-centered committees, many departmental personnel are involved more systematically and more closely at least in preparatory stages of policy making than was the case under previous administrations. At the same time, however, the roles of leading departmental officials have been subtly redefined and delimited; indeed, cabinet officials and other senior officials *have been seriously weakened in their roles as policy advocates and advisers.* While this may not have been intended by Nixon and Kissinger, it is nonetheless a consequence of the way in which they have restructured the system. In the course of developing and evaluating policy options, the intricate machinery of the NSC coopts foreign policy specialists and analytical resources in the departments. As a result, when department heads and senior officials finally do have an opportunity at top-level NSC meetings with the President to express their views on alternative options, as indeed the present system permits and encourages, they may not be in a position to offer well-considered *departmental* points of view backed by solid independent analysis.[15] In this weakening of independent analytically-ori-

---

[15] This is implied in several accounts of the Cambodian decision. See Hedrick Smith, "Cambodian Decision: Why President Acted," *N.Y. Times,* June 30, 1970; David Maxey, "How Nixon decided to Invade Cambodia," *Look,* August 11, 1970.

ented staffs at department levels, even senior departmental officials are placed at a disadvantage in performing as advisers to the President in the final stages of decision making. The question arises, therefore, whether the present system suffers from overcentralization and overbureaucratization of the preparatory "search" and "evaluation" phases of policy analysis.

It should be noted also that the present system attempts the questionable procedure of separating the "search" and "evaluation" phases of policy making as much as possible from the final process of "choice." While providing orderly procedures for widespread participation of foreign policy specialists in the departments and agencies in the "search" and "evaluation" phases, the present NSC system restricts the *process* of "choice," and not merely the final decision, essentially to the President. Those few advisers who participate in the final discussions before he makes his choice of policy all largely depend on the same body of distilled analysis of options that has emerged from the centralized, "advocate-free" search and evaluation process. The question can be posed whether the executive would be in a position to make better decisions if *multiple centers of analysis* and *stronger staffs* were available to senior departmental officials who serve as advisers to the President in the final stages of foreign policy decisions.

A number of other questions can be raised about the present NSC system. While it is nicely suited to Nixon's preference for solo decisions made in private, such as a system tends to exaggerate the all-too-familiar risk that arises whenever a president improvises at the last minute an option somewhat different from the carefully evaluated ones presented to him. As is well known, the utility of a complex option often suffers from last minute alterations of some of its components. Unless the President's improvised choice is resubmitted for careful evaluation, the value of the NSC's meticulous preparation of options can be easily defeated. This danger is enhanced in crises when time pressures for decision are urgent.

More generally, when decisions must be arrived at quickly the NSC's orderly but somewhat laborious collection and evaluation of "pure," advocate-free options from subpresidential levels in the government may break down or work ineffectively. Evidently for this reason the "Washington Special Actions Group" (WSAG), chaired by Kissinger, was established within the structure of NSC committees to deal with crises. Relatively little information is available on WSAG's performance, the unauthorized disclosures to columnist Jack Anderson of its handling of the Indian-Pakistan conflict in late 1971 being an important exception. Kissinger himself has conceded that while the NSC system "works rather well" on the whole, it does "better in noncrisis situations than in crises." [19] It would seem particularly important for crisis management, therefore, to back-stop the NSC apparatus with a system of multiple advocacy in which representatives of departments and agencies can draw upon competent analytical staffs of their own.

A highly centralized policy-making system such as the present NSC system can easily overburden the top-level decision maker. It may be necessary, as has often been said, to centralize first before effective decentralization is possible. With the passage of time, however, signs have multiplied that the present NSC suffers from dangerous overload precisely because of its inability to build "centers of strength responsive to the President in other parts of the foreign affairs government." [20]

The NSC system gives the President and his Special Assistant, Henry Kissinger, opportunities to use their control over the NSC committees to shape final policy choices, if they wish to, during the course of the centrally directed and coordinated policy analysis. One observer concludes a balanced appraisal of the workings of the NSC system with the observation that, "The kinds of analyses that are done, the way the choices are presented to the President and the NSC, and the shape of the resulting policies inevitably reflect the biases of the President and his leading officials, such as Kissinger." [21] Another observer, in an otherwise sympathetic evaluation of the NSC, asks whether the often repeated phrases such as "keeping the options open" do not have "more a liturgical than intellectual significance"; he also notes that some critics complain that the NSC-initiated studies impose busywork on the departments while the Special Assistant and his staff focus on the essential issues.[22]

More so than in any previous administration the Special Assistant for National Security Affairs is now increasingly one of the President's leading foreign policy advisers if not the most important one. Thus the basis has been created for a serious role conflict that can interfere with the performance of his other task as "custodian-manager" of the process of policy formulation.

It should be noted, finally, that by placing the President at the helm

---

[19] Quoted by Milton Viorst, "William Rogers Thinks Like Richard Nixon," *New York Times*, Magazine, February 27, 1972. On the NSC's Washington Special Actions Group, see also Leacocos, "Kissinger's Apparat," pp. 7–8.

[20] Destler believes the failure to do so is one of the major deficiencies of the Nixon Administration's organization of foreign policy making. The creation of the Planning and Coordination Staff in the State Department in 1969 has evidently not been as successful in this respect as had been hoped. In mid-1971 a new system of evaluating country programs (Policy Analysis Resource Allocation) was installed within State having as its goal to give State more weight in the implementation of foreign policy (Leacocos, "Kissinger's Apparat," p. 10).

[21] Orr, "Defense Reports," p. 881.

[22] Leacocos, p. 23.

of a more tightly controlled, depoliticized system of policy making within the executive branch, the present NSC system has also strengthened his position in the foreign policy arena vis-à-vis Congress. For by weakening the struggle over foreign policy within the executive branch, the new NSC system also limits the opportunities "outside" actors (Congress) have had to influence the making of policy by participating informally in the play of "bureaucratic politics" among the various actors in the executive branch.

While many questions can be raised about the performance of the present NSC system and the prescriptive model of rational organizational decision making that guides it, it is by no means easy to formulate an overall appraisal. In any case it is unlikely that a future president will decide whether to continue with this type of NSC system exclusively on the basis of available evaluations of its performance under the present administration. Rather, the variable that will probably dominate in shaping the NSC in a new administration, as a long-time staff member and student of the NSC reminds us, will be "the President's style of decision-making."[23] Variation in the personal styles of past presidents helps account for the zigzags in degree of institutionalization and reliance upon NSC procedures. These personal preferences are themselves likely to lead to reorganization of the NSC in the future, even apart from the deeply ingrained American faith in the virtues of organizational tinkering.

Assuming a disposition to return to a somewhat more loosely coordinated, pluralistic system of internal policy making at some point in the future, we must ask whether appropriate design models and management theories exist for that purpose. I have not been able to find any reasonably detailed ones in the literature on organization theory. It is well to make clear that we are talking about *prescriptive* theories that indicate how policy-making processes in complex organizations can be designed and managed to realize the presumed benefits of internal diversity and competition. Most theories of organizational behavior are of an explanatory-predictive type and do not provide much by way of guidelines or rigorous support for prescription. Conversely, normative theories of organizational decision making lack a firm empirical base.

CONVERTING "BUREAUCRATIC POLITICS" INTO EFFECTIVE MULTIPLE ADVOCACY

We have already noted some of the dynamics of organizational behavior and bureaucratic politics that undermine efforts to achieve rational con-

---

[23] Robert H. Johnson, "National Security Council," p. 720.

sideration of policy and decision making. As a result of these barriers, many executives and scholars take a dim view of bureaucratic politics; they deplore the fact that important policy decisions are influenced by negotiation and bargaining within the policy-making circle rather than being settled through more detached intellectual analysis. Other students of government, including the present writer, see possible merit in competitive policy making. They believe that conflict is normal, perhaps inevitable, and potentially healthy; for them, internal disagreement about policy within the organization is not necessarily an abnormal strain that must be abolished in the interest of rational decision making. Rather, conflict may help produce better policy *if* it can be managed and resolved properly.

Indeed, it is generally agreed that social conflict can promote adaptation. Social theorists of conflict have not extended their analysis of this phenomenon to decision-making systems, but laboratory studies of decision-making groups provide some evidence that conflict within the group may have a constructive effect on its problem-solving activity and on the quality of its choices. Perhaps the most interesting of these laboratory studies for our purposes is that by Joseph L. Bower, which is distinguished by the fact that it employs a multiactivity model of decision-making functions—the distinction between "search," "analysis," and "choice"—that has been the focus of some of the most useful contemporary theories of organizational behavior. This distinction has already been employed in this paper to identify some of the essential features of the Nixon NSC concept and to differentiate it from the multiple advocacy model.

Multiple advocacy [is a theory that] attempts to indicate how the policy-making system might be structured and managed so that internal disagreements might contribute to improving the quality of search and evaluation activities associated with choice of policy.

It should be made clear that as conceived here, multiple advocacy would be an integral part of a *mixed system* in which centralized coordination and executive initiative would be required. Multiple advocacy is *not* a plea for dispersing power more widely to subunits and actors within the bureaucratic politics model.

To reintroduce the prescriptive approach into the study of bureaucratic politics, in which Richard Neustadt pioneered with *Presidential Power*, we must return to leads provided by earlier scholars that have not been pursued more systematically in the past ten years. Curiously, the foremost advocate of the bargaining model of policy making, Charles Lindblom, while recognizing that it can and does perform badly on occasion, has displayed little interest in articulating the conditions necessary for its effective performance. Critics of the extreme bargaining model have been more helpful in this respect, but they have been content to argue the case for centralized management tools and stop well short of developing a theory for a sounder bargaining model.

What, then, are the conditions and requirements for converting bureaucratic politics into effective multiple advocacy? In 1959 Roger Hilsman suggested some of the "conditions" under which the bureaucratic politics process might be rather efficient in identifying and assessing major policy alternatives in the realm of foreign policy. "The chances should be good," he suggested, "that the resulting policy will be a wise one. . . . If the subject under debate is one on which the different groups of advocates are knowledgeable, if the participants are well informed, and if the top levels of government participate fully in the process or are sensitive to the verdict. . . ." [32] Hilsman's observation was offered parenthetically and linked casually with a few illustrative cases. I will attempt a fuller statement:

Since conflict over policy and advocacy are inevitable within a complex organization, one solution lies in ensuring that there will be multiple advocates within the policy-making system who, among themselves, will cover a range of interesting policy options on any given issue. Further, if a system of multiple advocacy is to function effectively, each participant must have minimal resources needed for advocacy, and certain rules of the game may be necessary to ensure proper give-and-take. A system of multiple advocacy works best and is likely to produce better decisions when three conditions are satisfied:

(1) No major maldistribution among the various actors of the following resources:

- (a) Power, weight, influence.
- (b) Competence relevant to the policy issues.
- (c) Information relevant to the policy problem.
- (d) Analytical resources.
- (e) Bargaining and persuasion skills.

(2) Presidential-level participation in organizational policy making in order to monitor and regulate the workings of multiple advocacy.

(3) Time for adequate debate and give-and-take.

To state the requirements for effective multiple advocacy is to realize at once how difficult it is to satisfy them. It is clear, as the first of these

---

[32] To these three conditions Hilsman appended an additional proviso: "that the circumstances make no demand for speed," and he suggested the usefulness of distinguishing among "crisis policy," "program policy," and "anticipatory policy." Roger Hilsman, "The Foreign Policy Consensus: An Interim Research Report." *Journal of Conflict Resolution,* 3 (December, 1959), 361–382. Hilsman's more recent views on improving the policy-making machinery (in *To Move a Nation,* esp. pp. 564–576, and *The Politics of Policy Making in Defense and Foreign Affairs* [N.Y.: Harper & Row, 1971], Ch. 10) restate and elaborate the ideas he presented in 1959.

three conditions reminds us, that *the mere existence within the policy-making system of actors holding different points of view will not guarantee adequate multisided examination of a policy issue.* Competence, information, and analytical resources bearing on the policy issue in question may be unequally distributed among these advocates. As a result, one policy option may be argued much more persuasively than another. And there is no assurance, of course, that the policy option which is *objectively* the best will be presented persuasively, for this requires that its advocate possess adequate competence, information, and analytical resources. Deprived of a persuasive presentation, that policy option may lose out to an inferior one that happens to have more effective sponsorship.

A further complication is that policy issues are often not decided solely on the basis of the intellectual merits of the competing positions put forward. Rather, the bargaining aspects of policy making may play a considerable role in shaping and determining the final decision. Hence the distribution among the actors of the other two resources listed in our theory—power (weight and influence) and bargaining skills—may be critical in shifting the decision toward one or another of the options. Thus, an option put forward by an advocate with superior competence, adequate information, and good analytical resources will not necessarily prevail over options advanced by an advocate who is less resourceful in these respects but operates with superior power and bargaining skills.

Maldistribution of resources among the various actors can take many forms. Our purpose here is not to develop predictive theories about what combinations of these five resources are most likely to enable a player or a coalition to prevail in the clash over choice of policy. Rather, we wish to help develop a theory for converting bureaucratic politics among multiple actors into a more effective and reliable system of multiple advocacy. Useful for such a theory is the working assumption that *all five resources* will be needed to some degree *by each actor or by each coalition* to perform effectively as an advocate in a system of multiple advocates.

It should be clear that the theory of multiple advocacy poses some rather sharply defined requirements for managing the policy-making system. We shall give considerable attention in the remainder of this paper to presidential-level involvement in the policy-making system—the second requirement of our theory. At this point it suffices to note three general tasks that the chief executive and his staff will have to perform to ensure that reasonably adequate forms of multiple advocacy can be created out of the vagaries of the working of bureaucratic politics. First, the chief executive may have to take steps if not to equalize resources among the advocates, then to avoid gross disparities in them. Second, the chief executive must be alert to the danger that a sufficient range of policy alternatives may not be encompassed by the advocates available for participating in the resolution of a particular policy issue; in that event, he may bring in outsiders or members of his own staff to serve as advocates for different interests or policy options. Third, he may have to develop certain rules of the game to maintain fair competition and to avoid "restraint of trade" among the advocates.

MULTIPLE ADVOCACY AND "PARTISAN MUTUAL ADJUSTMENT"

The model of competitive *but balanced* policy making I have outlined is more aptly designated as "multiple advocacy" than as "bargaining" or "partisan mutual adjustment." It is important to note that multiple advocacy is not a pure or "free market" bargaining game. Rather, it is a "mixed system" which requires centralized management to maintain and make use of internal competitive processes. Effective multiple advocacy does not just happen. It requires management to structure and interrelate several different roles within the policy-making system. Not all actors are cast in the role of "advocate." Two other distinct roles are also required on the part of top-level management: the role of *custodian* of the policy-making process and that of *magistrate* who presides at the apex.

Before proceeding, it will be useful to note that multiple advocacy differs from Charles Lindblom's concept of "partisan mutual adjustment" in several important respects.[38] Lindblom means his propositions about "partisan mutual adjustment" to apply to the workings of the political system as a whole. He does not focus his analysis, as we do here, on decision making within the executive branch. Moreover, while multiple advocacy is a model of discussion and negotiation, "partisan mutual adjustment" is a more comprehensive model of interaction of many kinds, of which discussion with negotiation is only one.[39]

---

[38] Lindblom's earlier views on the advantages of the bargaining model appear in his "Bargaining: The Hidden Hand in Government," The RAND Corporation, RM-1436-RC (22 February, 1955). A substantial broadening and fuller exposition of the bargaining model, which Lindblom renamed "partisan mutual adjustment," appears in *The Intelligence of Democracy: Decision-Making Through Mutual Adjustment* (N.Y.: Free Press, 1965). Interesting refinements and additions appear in his most recent statement, *The Policy-Making Process* (Englewood Cliffs, N.J.: Prentice-Hall, 1968).

[39] This point was made by Charles Lindblom in a personal communication (October 12, 1971); he adds that "in some forms of partisan mutual adjustment, to be specific, the mutual adjustment is achieved by mutually adaptive moves of distant parties who do not in any way communicate with each other and indeed may not even know each other or be able to identify each other." In any form of mutual adjustment, "the adjustments are made serially by persons or parties that react to preceding moves of other parties and are in turn reacted to by successive moves of further parties—all in circumstances in which no person or party sees the earlier

A comparison between "partisan mutual adjustment" and multiple advocacy, therefore, will be inappropriate and misleading unless these differences in scope and focus are kept in mind. Nonetheless, we may note a tendency in the discussion of "partisan mutual adjustment" and in Lindblom's earlier essay on "Bargaining: The Hidden Hand in Government," which was more directly concerned with the executive branch, to assume that various factors will operate naturally to induce effective coordination in the absence of centralized control or intervention. The logic of "partisan mutual adjustment" implies not merely automaticity and inevitability of coordination; it also suggests that the policy choice that emerges will be about as good as can be obtained, given the complexity of the issues and the variety of interests activated by them.

In contrast, the multiple advocacy model makes explicit the assumption that effective competition is usually necessary if the processes of bureaucratic politics within a complex organization are to produce the functional equivalent of a rational consideration of, and choice among, policy alternatives. We noted earlier several dysfunctional aspects of bureaucratic politics ("quasi-resolution of conflict" and "negotiating the internal environment") which are, in fact, examples of imperfect competition in pluralistic systems. We also noted that the Nixon administration has resorted to a centrally directed, depoliticized system of policy making in order, among other reasons, to avoid dysfunctional consequences of this kind. The alternative examined here, multiple advocacy, does not ignore the dysfunctional workings of bureaucratic politics. It attempts to deal with them, however, by utilizing the resources and involvement of the top-level executive and his staff in a different fashion than does the presently constituted NSC system.

In contrast to "partisan mutual adjustment," therefore, multiple advocacy is a *management-oriented* theory. It warns that the presumably beneficial effect of internal competition and conflict on organizational policies does not obtain if the competitors are unevenly matched, or if they divide up the market, engage in unfair competition, squeeze out or buy off weaker competitors, etc. Accordingly, multiple advocacy assigns to top-level authority in the organization the task of maintaining and supervising the competitive nature of policy making within the organization. This task belongs to the *custodian* role, which we have already mentioned and to which I shall give considerable attention in the remainder of this paper. The custodian's role can be introduced and maintained only by the chief executive. (It should be noted that the highly centralized policy-making model of the Nixon Administration also requires a custo-

---

moves of the other parties as anything but part of the environment to which he is reacting and in which it may not be at all conspicuous." Types of partisan mutual adjustment and the position of negotiation therein are indicated in Lindblom's *Intelligence of Democracy*, pp. 33–4.

dian; some of his tasks are similar to those of the custodian in a multiple advocacy system.) In a multiple advocacy system the chief executive must define his own role as that of a *magistrate* who evaluates, judges, and chooses among the various policy options articulated by advocates. The central importance of the magistrate role should not be overlooked or taken for granted. It is only because a magistrate presides at the apex of the policy-making system that multiple advocacy can be maintained and regulated. The introduction of the magistrate role into the system means that advocates are no longer competing against each other (as would be the case in a decentralized bargaining system such as "partisan mutual adjustment"); rather, the advocates are competing for the magistrate's attention. The custodian can influence such competition even if the resources of the advocates are unbalanced; in fact, it is particularly necessary for him to do so when there is a marked disparity in bargaining advantages among advocates.

As this implies, in his role as magistrate, the chief executive does not simply decide in favor of the strongest coalition of advocates. Rather, his central position and ultimate responsibility give him the obligation to evaluate the relative merits of competing positions and the power to decide against the majority. In order to discharge this responsibility, the chief executive will continue to require a strong analytically-oriented staff such as that of the NSC.

It is important to recognize that the responsibilities of the chief executive for policy making are not necessarily confined to the role of magistrate, which *he* exercises, and the role of custodian, which he would be wise to delegate to a senior assistant. In addition, from time to time the chief executive will find it desirable to initiate policy advocacy from the presidential level, particularly when departmental officials do not become advocates for policy options that deserve serious consideration, either because they do not attach high enough priority to such options or perceive departmental disadvantages in them. In such instances, the chief executive may play the advocate's role himself or encourage policy advisers on his staff to exercise the prerogatives of advocates. In the latter event, I shall argue, the chief executive should *not* ask the person whom he has charged with the custodian's role to act also as adviser-advocate.

As the preceding discussion implies, the chief executive's personal orientation to manifestations of "politics" and conflict is likely to be particularly important in determining the ways in which he will attempt to cope with bureaucratic politics and the extent to which it can be converted into an effective system of multiple advocacy.

Before proceeding we must take note of another factor that affects the ability of the chief executive to play the roles we have assigned to him in our theory of multiple advocacy. In the American system of government, as Richard Neustadt pointed out so incisively in his *Presidential*

Power (1960), the President must be an ever-wary, active and skillful participant in the arena of bureaucratic politics if he is to protect his own interests. Neustadt defined these interests largely in terms of the President's *personal power position.* As Neustadt emphasized, presidential power is not an ample and stable commodity which the incumbent receives upon entering office and which is available to him ever thereafter to be used when needed. Rather, presidential power is a highly unstable variable whose magnitude can vary greatly depending upon the incumbent's resourcefulness as a political entrepreneur and his skillfulness at the game of bureaucratic politics.

We may note that Neustadt did not attempt to develop a broader theory for strengthening multiple advocacy. He confined himself, rather, to various kinds of advice on how the president might maintain his personal power position and utilize it effectively.[43] In fact, it must be noted that Neustadt focused his advice to presidents somewhat too narrowly on the problem of protecting their personal power positions. He did not address the broader question of what the President can do to ensure that better public policy decisions will emerge from the inevitable play of bureaucratic politics. There is indeed an underlying assumption in parts of Neustadt's book—which in fact may be the major theoretical proposition he wishes to advance—that if the President succeeds in protecting his personal power stakes in controversial policy matters, he will thereby also ensure better policy decisions for the country at large. This is sometimes true, but the exceptions can be extremely important. A chief executive may resist initial indications that a change of policy is needed because he feels, and is advised, that to do so will damage his prestige and reputation. But by protecting his personal power stakes too assiduously the President may become gradually locked into a disastrous policy. I shall return later to the possibilities for genuine role conflict between the executive's interest in protecting his personal power stakes in a policy issue and his broader responsibility for involving himself in the policy-forming process in order to secure better advice and better decisions.

[43] The advice Neustadt's book offers a president by no means exhausts the possibilities available to him. In a cogent explication and critical appreciation of *Presidential Power,* Peter Sperlich argues that Neustadt overstates the President's need to rely exclusively on bargaining and persuasion to influence others and notes that the chief executive has other sources of authority and influence, such as organizational ideology and norms, at his disposal for this purpose. Sperlich also calls attention to the danger of "overload and breakdown" if a president attempts to follow Neustadt's advice too literally. (Sperlich, "Bargaining and Overload: An Essay on *Presidential Power,*" in *The Presidency,* ed. Aaron Wildavsky, [Boston: Little, Brown & Co., 1969], pp. 168–192.) On the chief executive's ability to use symbolic manipulation, not merely commands, to influence subordinates and other actors in the political system, see also Murray Edelman, *The Symbolic Uses of Politics* (Urbana: University of Illinois Press, 1964).

"MALFUNCTIONS" OF THE POLICY-MAKING PROCESS AND THE NEED FOR PREVENTIVE INTERVENTIONS

Despite numerous efforts in the past to restructure the machinery and procedures of foreign policy making, it is probably not unfair to say that improvements in policy performance have been marginal and uneven. While structural reorganization can aid in the quest for effective decision making, there appears to be no single structural formula by means of which the chief executive and his staff can convert the functional expertise and diversity of viewpoints of the many offices concerned with international affairs into consistently effective policies and decisions. This sober observation coincides with the evaluation of a broader range of experience in many different kinds of organizations. The optimistic view that principles of modern organization and administration, and indeed bureaucracy itself, provided a vehicle for achieving greater rationality in the conduct of social and governmental affairs has long since faded. As one specialist on organization, Warren Bennis, has put it: "the pyramidal, centralized, functionally specialized, impersonal mechanism known as bureaucracy—was out of joint with contemporary realities." Continuing, Bennis predicts that "adaptive, problem-solving temporary systems of diverse specialists, linked together by coordinating executives in an organic flux—this is the organizational form that will gradually replace bureaucracy." [51] While the outlines of this vision remain dim, it is clear that theorists of administration and organization are breaking new ground once again and that a period of exploration lies ahead. The theory of effective multiple advocacy and the related model of collegial (as against bureaucratic) decision making just described are very much in accord with novel road maps that organizational theorists are beginning to chart.

In arguing for a new, more flexible form of organization, Bennis recognizes the paradox that even highly flexible systems need to be managed in appropriate ways. "A question left unanswered," he notes, "has to do with leadership. How would these new organizations be managed?" [52] We face a similar problem here, one whose difficulty must be

---

[51] Warren G. Bennis, "Post-Bureaucratic Leadership," *Transaction* (July-August 1969), pp. 44–61. See also W. G. Bennis and Philip E. Slater, *The Temporary Society* (N.Y.: Harper & Row, 1968); and Alvin Toffler, *Future Shock* (N.Y.: Random House, 1970), Ch. 7, "Organizations: The Coming Adhocracy."

Charles Perrow's concept of "multiple leadership" is similar in some ways to the notion of policy making via multiple advocacy (Perrow, "The Analysis of Goals in Complex Organizations," *American Sociological Review*, 26 [December, 1961], 854–866).

[52] Bennis, "Post-Bureaucratic Leadership," p. 45. Bennis recognizes that one task will be the control of conflict within such organizational forms. It will be necessary, he believes, to develop ways of developing "group synergy" and "collaborative cultures." The new concept of leadership required will include (what we also stress

acknowledged. . . . Experience indicates that any system for policy making, however well designed, is subject to periodic failures and gross malfunctions. As Harold Wilensky has emphasized, all large-scale organizations have structural characteristics of hierarchy, specialization, and centralization that encourage chronic pathologies of information and advice.[53] As a result, organizational theorists have increasingly emphasized that the design of machinery and operating procedures for policy making must take into account the types of human failures, individual and group dynamics, organizational pathologies and malfunctions that can occur.

A sophisticated approach for designing a better policy-making system, therefore, will not be content with restructuring the organization and rewriting its standard operating procedures; it will also include mechanisms for timely identification and correction of possible malfunctions. Provision must be made for monitoring the day-to-day workings of the policy system, and strategies for "preventive intervention" must be available within the policy-making system. Clearly the chief executive has unique opportunities as well as responsibilities in this respect. "Preventive intervention" is not a novel concept. In trying to adapt and incorporate it into foreign policy making, one should draw upon experience gained in other policy arenas. Stimulating analogies are also available in biological and cybernetic models of "self-organizing systems." In John von Neumann's phrase, self-organizing systems "contain the necessary arrangements to diagnose errors as they occur, to readjust the organism so as to minimize the effects of errors, and finally to correct or block permanently the faulty component." Such systems are "able to operate even when malfunctions set in . . . while their subsequent tendency is to remove them." [55]

The strategy I have chosen for developing this kind of pragmatic

---

here) "practical theories of intervening and guiding these systems, theories that encompass methods for seeding, nurturing, and integrating individuals and groups" (p. 51).

[53] Harold Wilensky, *Organizational Intelligence* (N.Y.: Basic Books, 1967). For a more general discussion of six types of "failures or pathologies" to which every political decision system is prone, see Karl W. Deutsch, *The Nerves of Government* (N.Y.: Free Press, 1963), Ch. 13, "The Self-Closure of Political Systems." Breakdowns in presidential advisory systems are discussed and illustrated by Neustadt, *Presidential Power,* and by Aaron Wildavsky, *Dixon-Yates: A Study in Power Politics,* (New Haven: Yale University Press, 1962).

[55] John von Neumann, "The General and Logical Theory of Automata," in *The World of Mathematics,* ed. James R. Newman (N.Y.: Simon and Schuster, 1956). Vol. IV, 2085–2086. (Quoted by Martin Landau, in "Redundancy, Rationality, and the Problem of Duplication and Overlap," *Public Administration Review,* 29 [July-August, 1969], 346–358.) Stimulated by mathematical demonstrations that redundancy can help create a system that is more reliable than any of its parts, Landau argues that duplication and overlap in administrative agencies are not necessarily signs of waste and inefficiency, though he admits the task remains to distinguish between inefficient redundancies and those that are constructive and reinforcing.

management theory consists of diagnosing past policy making within the government with the object of inductively codifying the lessons of experience. This approach is favored over one that would rely on more abstract preconceptions or theoretical models about how complex organizations can be made to engage in more "rational" decision making. Such an inductive approach, it should be noted, gives our prescriptive model a strong empirical base. (At the same time, however, formal models of rational decision making can have heuristic value for diagnosing past performance and for setting general goals to be furthered by preventive interventions.)

MALFUNCTIONS OF THE POLICY-MAKING SYSTEM: A TYPOLOGY

Nine possible malfunctions of the policy-making process have been identified. These malfunctions can occur whether the policy-making system is modeled on one prescriptive theory or another, or even when it lacks any well-defined modus operandi. "Preventive interventions" by the custodian-manager of the policy-making system, therefore, are required to deal with emerging malfunctions of this kind in a system such as the present Nixon-Kissinger National Security Council as well as in a system of multiple advocacy. The nine malfunctions thus far identified are listed separately, although they may be interrelated in a particular historical case such as the Bay of Pigs.

1. *When the President and his advisers agree too readily on the nature of the problem facing them and on a response to it.*
2. *When advisers and advocates take different positions and debate them before the President but their disagreements do not cover the full range of relevant hypotheses and alternative options.*
3. *When there is no advocate for an unpopular policy option.*
4. *When advisers to the President thrash out their own disagreements over policy without the President's knowledge and confront him with a unanimous recommendation.*
5. *When advisers agree privately among themselves that the President should face up to a difficult decision, but no one is willing to alert him to the need for doing so.*
6. *When the President, faced with an important problem to decide, is dependent upon a single channel of information.*
7. *When the key assumptions and premises of a plan have been evaluated only by the advocates of that option.*
8. *When the President asks advisers for their opinions on a preferred course of action but does not request a qualified group to ex-*

amine more carefully the negative judgment offered by one or more advisers.

9. *When the President is impressed by the consensus among his advisers on behalf of a particular policy but fails to ascertain how firm the consensus is, how it was achieved, and whether it is justified.**

IMPLICATIONS FOR STRENGTHENING THE POLICY-MAKING SYSTEM

Awareness of these possible malfunctions should enable the custodian of the policy-making process to identify their emergence in a timely fashion. The kinds of intervention strategies needed to correct or compensate for any emergent malfunction are mostly self-evident and have been suggested in the preceding review of historical cases. It seems highly appropriate that responsibility for discharging this critical task at the highest level of policy-making in the executive branch should be assigned to the Office of the Special Assistant for National Security Affairs. (Staff assistants to senior officials in departments can be assigned a similar task as custodians of the process of policy formation in their own agencies.)

The Special Assistant will be able to perform the critical tasks associated with the custodian's role *only if he scrupulously refrains from becoming an advocate himself.* Both the advocate's role and the custodian's role are necessary, but effective operation of the policy-making system requires that these two roles be kept separate. To combine them in the person of one official will create the basis for a severe role conflict. When important policy issues are being decided it would be extraordinary if an individual who is actively involved himself as an advocate of a particular option could also discharge the critical tasks of custodian of the process, for to do so might well hamper his efficacy as an advocate. To say that the role conflict might be avoided if the custodian confined himself to being a *policy adviser* without engaging in advocacy is to ignore the ease with which a policy adviser is drawn into advocacy, as well as the danger of covert advocacy disguised as disinterested advice.

The role of custodian is critical for effective operation of the policy system. Performance of the role can only be eroded and eventually robbed of its integrity if its incumbent is encouraged by the chief executive to become a policy adviser, or otherwise succumbs to the temptation of becoming an advocate. In arguing that the chief executive should clearly define the role of custodian to exclude advocacy I do not

* Editor's note: Case history materials illustrating each of the nine malfunctions have been deleted. See pp. 769–781 of the original article. N.C.T.

ignore the President's equally important need for foreign policy advisers and even advocates on his personal staff. I am simply urging that the roles be kept separate and not be assigned to one person. Other persons with special competence on foreign policy matters can be appointed by the chief executive as his advisers on substantive issues, leaving the Special Assistant to focus exclusively on the procedural aspects of policy making.

It should be noted that both Truman and Eisenhower attempted to prevent leading staff personnel of the National Security Council from acting as policy advocates or advisers. (At the same time, both presidents appointed a number of other persons as personal advisers on foreign policy but, significantly, did not give them any responsibility for managing the NSC policy-making system.) Under Truman, the NSC staff was headed by an Executive Secretary whose duties were carefully circumscribed. When Eisenhower created the Office of the Special Assistant for National Security Affairs, he excluded from its duties the role of policy adviser. Robert Cutler, the first incumbent of the Office of Special Assistant, reports that his role was defined by Eisenhower as that of a nonadvocate and a nonfreewheeler. Only rarely, Cutler has written, did he undertake to suggest an independent position of his own inside or outside the NSC. Such forays "would sometimes bring down on my head an adverse storm." Interestingly, however, he adds: "But if debate was intensified on a germane issue, it was worth a knock on the head." [92]

Under Kennedy, however, a basic duality emerged in the role of Special Assistant for National Security Affairs. In the looser organization of the NSC that Kennedy introduced, the Special Assistant emerged as an ad hoc policy adviser to the President; he was no longer restricted to being the neutral manager of well defined NSC procedures. While we do not yet have a careful, informed analysis of McGeorge Bundy's effort and those of his successors (Walt Rostow and Henry Kissinger) to combine the task of custodian of the process with that of adviser, there are indications that these two roles cannot easily be combined in one position.[93]

---

[92] Robert Cutler, *No Time for Rest* (Boston: Little, Brown & Co., 1966), pp. 315–316. A useful, up-to-date review of the development of the NSC and the variations in its importance, organization and performance is provided in Clark and Legere, *President and Management of National Security* (see especially Chapter 4 by Richard M. Moose and Chapter 10 by John Ponturo). Useful materials are also contained in Patrick Anderson, *The Presidents' Men;* Robert H. Johnson, "The National Security Council: The Relevance of its Past to its Future," *Orbis,* 13 (Fall, 1969), 709–735; Paul Y. Hammond, *Organizing for Defense;* Senator Henry M. Jackson, ed., *The National Security Council* (N.Y.: Praeger, 1965).

[93] Patrick Anderson emphasizes the basic duality that affected Bundy's performance as Special Assistant. He suggests that Bundy was aware of the latent role-conflicts in the position and tried to give priority to his task of keeping the President's choices open. (*The Presidents' Men,* p. 270). Material on Bundy's alleged tendency

The same kind of role conflict is likely to emerge if the Special Assistant acts as a *spokesman* on behalf of existing policy. Whether he speaks openly to explain and support decisions taken by the administration or does so in an ostensibly off-the-record manner, this additional task may constrain his performance as neutral custodian of the process. Note that the definition of Robert Cutler's role in this respect restricted him to the classical anonymity expected of a presidential assistant. He was not to issue public statements, nor provide the press with rationales for policy decisions, nor even to discuss or write about how the NSC was organized and operated except as specifically authorized by the President.[94]

In the past decade there has been a gradual and cumulative change also in the way in which the "spokesman" component of the role has been defined. Beginning with McGeorge Bundy in 1961, the man serving as Special Assistant has increasingly acted as a major, though not the sole, spokesman for the President's foreign policy decisions. The explanation for this development is not difficult to grasp. The men selected for the job, beginning with Kennedy's choice of McGeorge Bundy, have been specialists on national security affairs to a degree that their predecessors under Eisenhower and Truman clearly were not.[95] It is understandable that such an official, so close to the President's thinking and so well informed about the basis and rationale of foreign policy decisions, should be considered an ideal choice to serve as an important communication link and public relations channel to the more alert and informed elements of the public. Performing the additional task of spokesman-apologist for foreign policy need not seriously weaken the Special Assistant's ability to organize the process of policy making and to keep options open. But policy making also includes the sensitive task of reviewing and reconsidering existing policies, and it is in this respect particularly that participation in the public explanation and justification of current policies may inhibit the Special Assistant's performance of his

to shift from arbiter to advocate on a number of occasions is reported in the highly critical appraisal offered by David Halberstam ("The Very Expensive Education of McGeorge Bundy," pp. 23, 29, 34–35.) Irving Destler's *Presidents, Bureaucrats, and Foreign Policy* helps clarify to some extent the role interpretations and performance of Bundy and his successors. David K. Hall is undertaking a comprehensive study of the development and performance of role tasks associated with the Executive Secretary and the Special Assistant within the NSC system as part of his PhD. dissertation in the Political Science Department, Stanford University.

94 Robert Cutler, pp. 315–316.

95 A former long-term member of the NSC staff notes that the individuals Eisenhower selected to be his Special Assistant for National Security Affairs "were not, with the single exception of his last appointee, Gordon Gray, experts in foreign affairs or defense policy. They were the President's agents in operating the NSC system, but they were not, by and large, independent sources of power and advice" (Robert H. Johnson, "National Security Council," p. 716).

major responsibility for helping to keep options open and to create new ones.

Another duality and potential role conflict can be identified between the custodian task and what may be called the "watch dog" task. The custodian's job is to protect the chief executive's broad responsibility for the quality of the policy-forming process. The "watch dog" task is concerned, more narrowly, with protecting the President's personal power stakes in the sense discussed earlier. "Custodian" and "watch dog" tasks cannot be comfortably combined in one role. The attempt to do so may lead, as some critics have charged, to an erosion of the Special Assistant's performance of his responsibility for maintaining the quality of the policy-making process. When he attempts to perform both functions, the Special Assistant risks losing the capacity for serving as the "honest broker" of ideas and analyses. To serve as guardian of the President's personal power stakes in a controversial policy matter can easily lead the Special Assistant to become a gate-closer; instead of helping to keep the President's options open, he helps the President to keep them closed. This is the criticism leveled at Walt Rostow's performance in the role.[96] The question has also been raised whether serving as personal adviser to the President has required Kissinger to subordinate his institutional role as kingpin of the NSC system.[97]

Finally, at risk of hopelessly complicating the problem, we must recognize still another role conflict that may affect adversely the Special Assistant's ability to discharge the custodian's task. If, as has been the case in the past, the Special Assistant is also expected to monitor and ensure the *implementation* of policy decisions once they are taken, can he preserve intact his other role as the neutral, nonadvocate custodian of the process of policy making (which of course includes policy evaluation and review)? As Thomas E. Cronin points out, White House aides who might be able to fashion a fairly objective role in the process of policy formation often become advocates and unrelenting lieutenants for fixed views in the implementation stage.[98] The importance of implemen-

---

[96] See, for example, Townsend Hoopes, *Limits of Intervention*, pp. 59–61, 116, 123.

[97] Destler, *Presidents, Bureaucrats, and Foreign Policy*, Ch. 5.

[98] Personal communication (1971). Cronin considers this and related problems in his recent study of White House "staffers" and their relations with department officials. "'Everybody Believes in Democracy Until He Gets to the White House . . .': An Examination of White House-Department Relations," *Law and Contemporary Problems*, 35 (Summer, 1970), 573–625 (published July 1971 at the School of Law, Duke University). [See selection No. 10 in this volume. ed.]

I am very much in agreement, as this paper indicates, with the suggestion made earlier by Cronin that political scientists should give more attention to examining the roles and perspectives of members of the presidential advisory system. (T. E. Cronin, "Political Science and Executive Advisory Systems," in T. E. Cronin and S. D. Greenberg, eds., *The Presidential Advisory System* [N.Y.: Harper & Row, 1969], pp. 321–335.)

tation notwithstanding, I would assume that the Special Assistant's personal involvement in it is likely to create serious constraints on his ability to perform as custodian of the policy-making process insofar as concerns reevaluation of that policy. The question is posed, therefore, whether the two tasks of custodian and implementer, both of which the executive requires, need to be combined in the same person and whether they can be kept sufficiently separate to avoid a dysfunctional role conflict.

I have argued that the Special Assistant, or someone like him elsewhere in the advisory system, should be the custodian of the process, and that this critical task should *not* be combined with becoming (1) a policy adviser-advocate; (2) a public spokesman on behalf of existing policy; (3) a watchdog of the President's personal power stakes in policy issues; or (4) an implementer of policy decisions already taken.

These four additional tasks, I feel, cannot be effectively combined with that of custodian. The attempt to do so will undermine the integrity with which an incumbent can perform the task central to the custodian's role, which is to find ways of maintaining and improving the workings of the policy-making system. This the custodian attempts to do on behalf of the executive by balancing actor resources when necessary, by strengthening weaker advocates, or compensating for their weakness, by bringing in new advisers to argue for unpopular options, by setting up new channels of information so that the President and other policy makers are not dependent on a single channel of information, by arranging for independent evaluation of decisional premises and options that are not receiving objective, competent evaluation within the system, by monitoring the policy-making process for possibly dangerous malfunctions and instituting appropriate corrective action.

This "job description" is, indeed, a composite of some of the most useful tasks performed *on occasion* by incumbents of the office. But these critical tasks have by no means been consistently undertaken, as we have seen, on all the occasions on which there was a need for them. It is suggested, therefore, that the best performances of the job in the past now be codified and institutionalized into the Special Assistant's role.

The availability of this kind of pragmatic theory should help to institutionalize and regularize self-correcting mechanisms within the policy-making system. As a result, the kind of timely intervention McGeorge Bundy made in the MLF * case to prevent a "breakdown" in the advisory system will, it is hoped, become the rule rather than the exception. As we have seen, what this Special Assistant for National Security Affairs did so well for Johnson in this case, no one did for Truman in Novem-

* In 1964 President Johnson's national security advisers proposed the establishment of a multi-lateral force for NATO. Bundy's intervention led the president to challenge his advisers and, ultimately, to reject the proposal. N.C.T.

ber, 1950, when the President should have been alerted to his advisers' agreement that something should be done about the maldeployment of MacArthur's forces despite their reluctance to raise the question. Perhaps one of Truman's assistants would have done so had essential features of the multiple advocacy model been institutionalized in the norms of the system at that time.

Similarly some of the inconsistencies noted in McGeorge Bundy's performance might have been reduced had he incorporated into his role a better understanding of the critical tasks required to "manage" the policy-making process more effectively. His insight and ingenuity in safeguarding the President's options, demonstrated so well in the MLF case, were conspicuously absent in other cases, in part because the role itself was not clearly and consistently defined at that time and because Kennedy did not develop a well-defined policy-making system to which he was willing to adhere consistently himself.

Kissinger's definition of the role suffers from even greater role conflict and overload. As was noted earlier, his functioning as policy adviser and alter ego to the President has become even more prominent with the passage of time. As he has become increasingly drawn into the vortex of presidential decision making, with its special requirements for secrecy and personal loyalty, his ability to serve as custodian-manager of the NSC-centered process has been hampered. The dilemma is acute, and as the job of Special Assistant is now defined, it will not be easy to relieve it.

CONCLUSION: SOME CAVEATS ABOUT MULTIPLE ADVOCACY

The case for multiple advocacy has been presented in undiluted form. It remains to acknowledge that, as with all other prescriptive theories, this one too has practical limits and costs attached to it.

Multiple advocacy is not offered as a panacea nor as a blueprint that covers all aspects of policymaking. We have noted that ideological values and various cognitive beliefs of policy makers (what we have called "decisional premises") may sometimes be so firmly and uniformly held as to severely constrain the choice of policy. In these circumstances the way in which policy-making procedures are organized and managed may make little difference so far as the substance and quality of the decision is concerned. Often, however, there are competing values and a variety of decisional premises within the decision-making group which, moreover, are not firmly held; in these circumstances, the workings of the policy-making process may indeed exercise a critical influence on the evaluation and choice of policy.

It would be naive, then, to argue that multiple advocacy (or indeed any other policy making model) can guarantee "good" decisions in every instance. Rather, the case for it must rest on the more modest expectation that even an imperfect system of multiple advocacy will help prevent some very bad decisions. This is not to say that malfunctions of the policy-making system of the kind we have identified always result in major policy errors. But they can.

In stating the case for multiple advocacy, I do not mean to imply that it can or should be rigidly applied in any and all circumstances. I have recognized and emphasized that presidential-level policy initiatives are needed from time to time; they are part of the "balancing" that is required to achieve a more rational consideration of policy. With the accumulation of further experience and research on these matters, perhaps we can gain a better understanding of the scope of this and other prescriptive theories. We need to develop a variety of prescriptive theories and to understand more clearly the uses and limitations of each. As such theories become better understood one may hope that a versatile president will choose among them to fit the changing demands of different situations.

I have tried to convey that an effective system of multiple advocacy is not easily achieved in practice. It is not easy to recruit able persons for all the senior positions in the policy-making system and to provide them with all the resources and staffs they need to become effective advocates—competent, analytically able, skillful in bargaining and persuasion. And, in any case, having the resources for advocacy does not ensure that the actors will actually engage in advocacy of all the options that need to be considered. They may avoid advocating some of these options because they run counter to the bureaucratic interests of their departments and agencies. They may eschew raising other options even if they believe in them for fear of ending up on the "losing side" too often, thereby losing "influence" or tarnishing their "reputations," or expending limited bargaining resources in fruitless or costly endeavors. The perception that problems of this kind were imbedded in the workings of "bureaucratic politics" no doubt contributed to the belief of those who designed the present NSC that a strong centralized policy-making system was desirable.

Quite obviously the structure and management of the policy system would have to be designed to give participants a stake in insuring multiple advocacy. Some things can be done to reduce to more tolerable proportions the tendencies noted. These would include selective recruitment, socialization of incumbents into their roles, management of rewards and punishments, selective employment of multiple advocacy for problems in which these inhibitions are less salient. One of the important tasks and responsibilities of a top-level executive (and surrogates charged with managing the policy-making system) is to define the norms and culture of participants in the system to make them consistent with the requirements of the policy-making model he wishes to employ. There is more latitude in this respect than might be imagined; witness the widely different norms and role definitions Kennedy introduced into his policy-making group in the Bay of Pigs and in the Cuban missile crisis.

While the requirements for effective multiple advocacy are not easily achieved, knowledge of the theory is itself useful. It can sensitize the chief executive and his staff to defects in the way important decisions are being made. In any case, multiple advocacy does not have to work perfectly in order to be valuable. To be sure, it is difficult to specify a *critical threshold* that defines operationally when multiple advocacy is likely to work well enough to make a difference. Such a demand on the theory seems legitimate enough at first glance, but I cannot accept it as an essential requirement for practical purposes. Because the kinds of decisions we are concerned with are subject to complex multiple causation, the notion of a fixed "critical threshold" for the performance of the policy-making process, equally applicable to all cases, is misleading. Rather, the degree of multiple advocacy that is "critical" and may suffice to obtain a more effective decision will depend upon the configuration of the other causal variables, which changes from case to case. In some cases even a modest amount of multiple advocacy may suffice; in other cases even a textbook replica of multiple advocacy at its best will not overcome the thrust of other variables (e.g., ideology, operational code beliefs, limitations of knowledge and information, personality idiosyncrasies, etc.) that favor a less effective decision.

As the foregoing implies, I agree with the observation of some critics that multiple advocacy would tend to be a "fragile, unstable" system. But this would be a more damaging limitation if a certain level of proficiency in multiple advocacy had to be achieved in every case (the "critical threshold" problem). Multiple advocacy strives to provide the functional equivalent of rationality in the policy-making process of a complex organization; something less than that may still be better than the alternative. In judging multiple advocacy one must compare it with some alternative system, not with an ideal standard. No policy-making system looks very good when compared with the ideal.

The chief executive's attitude toward multiple advocacy is, of course, critical. This model of organizational policy making is likely to suit the style and temperament of some presidents more than others. Apart from this, how shall we deal with the observation that multiple advocacy would be bad advice and unwelcome to a president who knew what he wanted to do and who regards his chief problem as that of imposing his decision on subordinates and getting them to implement it? Certainly there will be many occasions on which a president must impose his policy on other actors within the executive branch. The problem of evaluating alternative policy-making models, however, cannot be tied to the assumption that the President's *initial* policy preference is always the most effective and desirable option. It may indeed be "unwelcome" but not therefore "bad" advice to a president who "knows what he wants to do" to expect of him that he subject his preferred option to serious scrutiny and debate. One can hope that a president will see that it is to his advantage to avoid reaching premature closure in his own mind about the best option until the processes of multiple advocacy have had an adequate opportunity to illuminate the issue. Certainly the final choice of policy has to remain the President's. Most everyone agrees that he should have real alternatives from which to choose. But it is not only other actors in the policy-making system who, when bureaucratic politics works badly, can narrow and delimit the President's choice; the President himself can deprive himself of genuine alternatives and a reasoned choice.

The argument may be granted, but the dilemmas of presidential decision making are such that a remedy for one problem may create or exacerbate still another problem. Thus, to submit to multiple advocacy may entail costs that a president would rather avoid incurring. The time required for effective advocacy and for give-and-take among the advocates may on occasion impose undue delays on decision making at the executive level. In a full-blown system of multiple advocacy, competition and conflict may occasionally get out of hand, strain cohesion, impose heavy human costs, create political difficulties for the chief executive in his relations with Congress and the public. Cast in the role of advocates, officials may be quicker to go outside the executive branch in search of allies in policy disputes. The chief executive may feel the weakening of his control over final decisions outweighs the benefits he gets from multiple advocacy.

There is no denying that multiple advocacy entails costs which may be onerous and difficult to live with from time to time. On the other hand, other systems of policy making also entail costs and risks, though different and perhaps less conspicuous. The *absence* of effective multiple advocacy, as we have seen on a number of historic occasions, can also have very serious costs in terms of the maladaptive policies it generates. It is hoped that this formulation of the theory together with the historical documentation of its importance provided here will at least call attention to some of the fundamental problems, lacunae, and defects in other policy-making systems, and, in addition, stimulate efforts to meet the challenge of making multiple advocacy work.

15.

POLICY FORMULATION FOR EDUCATION: THE JOHNSON ADMINISTRATION

Norman C. Thomas

This paper views the formulation of national education policy from a systems perspective. A policy system is a process whereby inputs, i.e., demands and support, from organized interests, concerned individuals, and the mass public are converted into policy outputs and ultimately fed back in the form of new inputs. The conversion process, the making of national policy, is the basic activity of the policy system.

The educational policy system considered here, included individuals located in the United States Office of Education (USOE), the Department of Health, Education and Welfare (HEW), the Executive Office of the President, the legislative and appropriations subcommittees in both houses of Congress having jurisdiction over USOE programs, education interest groups, other lobby groups with an interest in education, and persons in the education profession or the general public with access to the official policy-makers. I identified the members of the policy system through a procedure that used position, reputation and activity as criteria (Gergen, 1968). Initially, I compiled a list of potential members including all persons holding formal positions of authority, persons having a reputation among informed observers and other potential members as influential participants in the policy process, and individuals who appeared as contributors of inputs to the policy system through such vehicles as testifying before congressional committees or service on presidential task forces and other major advisory bodies. The list contained 175 persons.

The next step involved interviews with 24 individuals possessing substantial knowledge of USOE and its programs including USOE, HEW, and Bureau of the Budget officials, congressional staff members, prom-

---

Reprinted from *Educational Researcher,* Vol. 2 (May, 1973), pp. 4–8, 17–18. Reprinted by permission of the publisher.

This article is a revision of a paper delivered at the annual meeting of the American Educational Research Association, New Orleans, February 28, 1973. I wish to thank Thomas E. Cronin and Samuel Halperin for helpful suggestions in revising the paper for publication. The University of Michigan and the Relm Foundation provided financial support during the period when the data were gathered.

inent educators, lobbyists, and journalists. I asked them to examine the list and indicate those whom they regarded as most important with respect to policy formulation, adoption, and implementation. Their responses, along with information obtained from a more general background investigation, provided the basis for narrowing the list to 77 influentials. The determination of the influentials was, necessarily, a subjective judgment although the ratings of the 24 "knowledgeables" was a major factor in making it. I am confident that the panel is a fairly accurate representation of the national policy-making elite for education as it existed in 1967–68.

At the final stage of data gathering, I interviewed 71 members of the educational policy system. The interview instrument employed primarily open-ended questions regarding the respondents' participation in and perceptions of the policy-making process. Thus, the data are mostly non-quantitative and the analysis is conducted in qualitative terms. The principal foci of the inquiry are the origination of ideas and their movement onto the agenda for action.

POLICY CONCEPTION

The question of where ideas come from is almost impossible to answer with precision. Attempts to trace the exact origin of significant new policy proposals may be fruitless, but it does seem that Yarmolinsky's (1966) suggestion of a "theory of simultaneous and seemingly spontaneous invention" applies to education. For instance, seven people including Abraham Ribicoff, Wilbur Cohen, Francis Keppel, Senator Wayne Morse, his aide Charles Lee, Representative John Dent, and Representative Roman Pucinski are credited with or claimed credit for tying aid to elementary and secondary education to the war on poverty in a manner that facilitated circumvention of the church-state issue. A major source of new ideas in education is naturally, the academic community. Academia was the origin of such suggestions as the Educational Opportunity Bank, the voucher system and open schools. Proposals for institutional grants in higher education originated with several unknown university and college presidents and were advanced by most national associations in higher education.

There was no shortage of ideas in the education policy system during the Johnson Administration. A major problem confronting the policymakers, however, was that of discriminating between feasible proposals and suggestions which, regardless of their merit, had little or no chance of adoption. As knowledgeable and expert as they were, the policy system participants still required some means of analyzing a vast amount of information and synthesizing it into an ordered agenda for action. In education, as in other national policy systems, the presidency performed this function through the preparation of the President's legislative program and the budget. These documents, i.e., presidential messages and the annual budget, and specific authorization and appropriation bills, served as the basis of congressional action. They establish a set of definite, but not inflexible, boundaries within which most serious policy deliberation occurs.

The policy formulation stage is crucial for it is where major innovations are spawned and matured. In all but the most exceptional circumstances, new policy departures and significant changes in existing policy must survive the process of agenda setting in order to receive consideration in Congress. This does not mean that modest, incremental changes are not possible without formal incorporation in the presidential policy agenda. They occur routinely through legislative and bureaucratic initiative. Nor does it deny the probability that presidentially supported proposals may be defeated or substantially modified by subsequent action elsewhere in the policy system. But it is manifest that unless and until major policy innovations, e.g., education vouchers, federally funded open schools, institutional grants to colleges and universities, unrestricted block grants to the states, full expense loans to college students with long term repayment, and similar proposals are accorded a high presidential priority, the chances of their adoption and implementation are very small.

In establishing priorities, or in setting his policy agenda, the President necessarily employs the resources of his staff, the Bureau of the Budget, and other units of the Executive Office. In this respect, it is more accurate to speak of policy formulation by the presidency, with the President as the principal individual participant in that institution. The general pattern of presidential policy formulation was developed under Presidents Roosevelt and Truman and had become a systematic routine by the early years of the Eisenhower Administration (Neustadt, 1954 & 1955).

The legislative program emerged from proposals prepared by departments and agencies who based them on administrative experience and suggestions and ideas from their clientele groups. The presidency was dependent on the bureaucracy for information, ideas, and new policy proposals. While the bureaucracy had vast information resources and no end of proposals, its perspective was limited and it tended over time to offer suggestions that were remedial and incremental rather than innovative and imaginative. The limits of bureaucratic initiative are almost an article of faith in the presidency. White House staff members and Budget Bureau officials during the Johnson Administration were particularly skeptical of the capacity of HEW and USOE to be effective agents of change in American education. A high ranking Bureau of the Budget official, Philip S. Hughes, summed up this presidential staff perspective:

> . . . The routine way to develop a legislative program has been to ask the departments to generate proposals. Each agency sends its ideas through channels, which means that the ideas are limited by the imagination of the old-line agencies. They tend to be repetitive—the same proposals year after year. When the ideas of the different agencies reach the departmental level, all kinds of objections are raised, especially objections that new notions may somehow infringe on the rights of some other agency in the department. By the time a legislative proposal from a department reaches the President, it's a pretty well-compromised product (Leuchtenberg, 1966).

TASK FORCES

The last three Presidents have sought to overcome some of the liabilities of their dependence on the bureaucracy in program development through the use of task forces of experts, knowledgeable laymen, and public officials. President Kennedy commissioned 29 and President Nixon 18 task forces to report on a wide range of policy problems prior to their inaugurations. The reports of these preinauguration task forces provided a reservoir of proposals which policy-makers used during the ensuing presidential administrations. Neither President continued to use task forces systematically, although each appointed similar groups on an ad hoc basis to deal with a variety of domestic and foreign policy problems.

Shortly after taking office, President Johnson appointed a series of task forces to study specific policy areas (Thomas & Wolman, 1969). Acting at the suggestion of advisers who were familiar with the Kennedy task forces, President Johnson sought to obtain ideas and suggestions from outside the Federal government which would serve as the basis of a legislative program that was distinctively his own. The 1964 experience with task force operations was deemed so successful that it was refined and expanded in the following years. Under the direction of Special Assistant Joseph A. Califano, the White House staff assumed the primary role in setting the framework for legislative and administrative policy-making. President Johnson brought the function of policy planning more effectively under his control through the integration of the task force operation with legislative submissions and budget review and the creation of a small policy staff under one of his key assistants (Cronin, 1968). The impact of the departments and agencies in the development of the presidential legislative program was considerable, but it tended to come more through the participation of their policy-level personnel in White House meetings where task force reports were evaluated. Commissioner Harold Howe II acknowledged that during the Johnson Administration "much policy development in education has moved from here (USOE) to the White House." Similarly, a career official in the Bureau of the Budget observed that "at the stage of developing the presidential legislative program, the task force reports play a more significant role than any documents or proposals emanating from the agencies."

The agencies proposed a substantial amount of technical legislation which corrected defects and filled gaps in existing statutes but the most important substantive contributions came from elsewhere. "The task forces presented us with meaty propositions to which we could react," recalled a former Budget Bureau official, "not the nuts and bolts stuff which we usually got from the agencies." Although the agencies made major contributions to public policy by refining and making workable the general ideas of the task forces in the course of drafting bills and implementing programs, their participation in the formulative stages was somewhat reduced during the Johnson Administration.

CHARACTERISTICS AND FUNCTIONS

Task forces were of two basic types, those composed of members drawn from people outside or from inside the government. Outside task forces were primarily employed to secure new ideas for the development of policy. Initially, in 1964, President Johnson used them as ad hoc devices to produce proposals which almost immediately were incorporated in his legislative program. By 1966, task forces were a normal aspect of presidetial operations and they were also used to take a long-range view of major problem areas.

As compared to outside task forces, inside interagency task forces functioned more to coordinate agency approaches, to obtain some measure of interagency agreement in areas of dispute, and to review, in broad terms, the recommendations of outside task forces. While interagency groups may have generated some new proposals, their major purpose was to provide the President with a coordinated overview of functional problems that cut across departmental and agency lines and to suggest alternative solutions. An important aspect of this coordinating function of the inside task forces was to conduct a "detailed pricing out of all proposals."

Once the task forces had written their reports, they submitted them to the President and deposited them with the Bureau of the Budget. Then the Bureau, HEW and USOE forwarded their comments directly to the White House.

Following the initial evaluation, the White House staff took the lead in winnowing down task force proposals. If it appeared that an outside task force report would be followed by an interagency task force, that decision was made by presidential assistant Califano, the budget director, the chairman of the Council of Economic Advisers, and the appropriate departmental and agency officials. Otherwise, in a series of White House meetings, the department and agency officials and their top assistants, representatives of the Bureau of the Budget's Human Resources Division, representatives of the Council of Economic Advisers, and members of Califano's staff examined the reports. After considerable discussion and bargaining, they developed a proposed legislative program which was presented to the President for final decision.

A total of 12 major task forces concerned with education operated during the Johnson Administration. The reports of these task forces were made public in January, 1972. The Gardner Task Force of 1964 was responsible for Title III and contributed to Title IV of ESEA. The International Education Task Force developed the proposal for the International Education Act, which Congress passed in 1966 but refused to fund. The Ink Task Force developed the plan for the 1965 reorganization of USOE. The Interagency Task Forces of 1966 and 1967 proposed amendments to existing legislation which were embodied in presidential messages in the following years and some of them were eventually adopted. The recommendations of the Early Childhood Development Task Force of 1966–67 were the basis for the "Follow Through" program and Parent and Child Centers in the Johnson Administration and for the establishment, during the Nixon Administration, of HEW's Office of Child Development. The 1967 Interagency Task Force on Child Development was involved in implementing the outside group's report and in reviewing all HEW programs for children. The Friday Task Force of 1967 contributed several recommendations that appeared in President Johnson's 1968 education message. The four remaining Task Forces produced substantial reports which are full of recommendations that comprised a lengthy agenda for future action.

Although I have not had the opportunity to examine the task force reports and consequently have not traced the fate of the myriad of recommendations and proposals they generated, it is apparent that the earlier task forces of 1964 and 1965 had greater impact on legislation. As the task forces proliferated and the scope of their inquiry broadened, their uniqueness declined and their proposals became increasingly commonplace. In the last two years of the Johnson Administration, interagency task forces were centrally involved in policy formulation and played a more important role than outside groups.

Membership on the task forces was neither carefully balanced nor broadly representative. Because the composition of the task forces was kept secret, the Administration could avoid striving for balanced representation in favor of imaginativeness. To the extent, however, that quickly saleable proposals were desired, task force membership tended to be more representative.

Usually the President and his top policy advisers selected the members of outside task forces. The criteria for selection tended to vary with the mission of the task force. Many respondents emphasized the importance of independence of viewpoint; however, it was acknowledged that persons holding radical views were unlikely to be included. A conscious effort was made to avoid formal representation of established clientele groups such as the NEA and the ACE which customarily worked closely with the HEW and USOE in developing policy. As USOE's role in policy initiation began to decline as a consequence of the task force operation, the access of the lobby groups to policy makers who set the agenda for action also began to fall.

The task forces do not appear to have used formal votes to reach decisions. The usual mode of decision was bargaining until a consensus developed. When members raised strong objections, efforts were made to satisfy them. Although the task forces were not broadly representative, their members apparently did represent institutional and professional interests to a considerable degree during deliberations.

The secrecy of the task forces was one of their most important operational characteristics. In the eyes of President Johnson and his staff, secrecy was crucial for it enabled them to ignore proposals that were politically infeasible. Recommendations could be adopted or rejected without having to expend political resources defending the choices made. The range of options was not only maximized, it was kept open longer and at very little cost. Secrecy also prevented opposition to task force proposals from developing until a much later stage in the policy process.

There seems almost unanimous agreement among persons familiar with the task forces that competent staffing was essential to the success of their operations. Most education task forces were staffed with Bureau of the Budget personnel. They tended to prod the task forces to be venturesome. Their activities included preparing or assigning the conduct of background studies, acquiring data, drafting reports, and providing liaison with the White House.

HEW and USOE played a peripheral role in the operation of the outside task forces. Since the manifest intent in using outside task forces was to bypass the bureaucracy, departmental and agency officials tended to distrust task forces and minimize their significance. As Samuel Halperin, Deputy Assistant Secretary of HEW for Legislation remarked, "The reports are kept so secret that they don't really pollinate anything." In interagency task forces, however, HEW and USOE dominated the proceedings. For example, Commissioner Howe was the key figure in the work of the 1967 inside task force in education. That group developed the Administration's 1968 legislative program on the basis of recommendations of the Friday Task Force and agency submissions.

The evaluation of the reports of outside task forces was a somewhat unstructured process. After being sent to the President and deposited with the Budget Bureau's Office of Legislative Reference, the reports went to the Bureau's examining divisions, other units in the presidency, and USOE for comment. The role of the agency was minor, however, compared with that of the Bureau of the Budget and the White House staff. Significantly, the same personnel from the Bureau and the White House who served on task force staff and sat with them as liaison men were usually involved in evaluating the reports.

The dual role of the Bureau and the White House staff meant that the reports had an Executive Office bias. One HEW official charged that "there is an incestuous relationship between the task forces on the one hand and the Budget Bureau and the White House on the other." The Bureau was aware of its dual role and the problems inherent in it. According to the staff director for Gardner and Friday Task Forces, "I leaned over backward to be fair, but I did feel like I was meeting myself coming back." Or, as William Carey, the assistant director in charge of the Human Resources Division, observed, "We are involved at the Bureau with task forces as participants and as critics." Not surprisingly the Bureau's dual role was perplexing and frustrating to those outside the presidency who were affected by its actions.

IMPACT

The flexibility and adaptability of the task forces had begun to decline as their operations became increasingly systematized toward the end of the Johnson Administration. They were tending to become elaborate instruments of incremental adjustment rather than catalytic agents of change. A leadership technique designed to produce policy innovation worked so well initially that overuse was rendering it counterproductive. It also appears that the substantive innovations resulting from the task forces may have been less than their advocates claimed. As a Bureau of the Budget official acknowledged, "They tended to pull together existing things instead of coming up with new ideas."

To the extent that task forces were made representative through their membership, tendencies toward innovation may have been mitigated. This appears likely since consensus was the fundamental decision-making rule and final agreement tended to represent compromise rather than creative thinking. However, the fact that task forces may not have been as inventive as their proponents claimed does not mean that essentially the same courses of action would be followed without them. The ideas which they promoted may not have been entirely new, but they were not yet embodied in the presidential policy agenda, nor, in most cases, were they supported by the bureaucracy.

Although the task force device provided a substantial advantage to an innovation-minded President, it also entailed sizeable costs in the form of resentments engendered in the bureaucracy and among powerful clientele groups. But whatever its costs and benefits, the Johnson task force operation helped the President to dominate national policy formulation in education. Its failure to survive in the Nixon Administration reflects the different leadership style and policy objectives of Johnson's successor and not the insignificance of the task forces as they functioned between 1964 and 1969.

THE PRESIDENCY AND POLICY CONTROL

Policy formulation in the education policy system centered, then, in the presidency. The key participants were the President, the White House staff members, and Budget Bureau officials. Acting in response to explicit presidential directives or in accordance with their interpretations of more general presidential objectives, the central decision-makers set education policy priorities within the parameters imposed by budgetary constraints and other external considerations. Also included among the central decision-makers were the Commissioner of Education and selected HEW officials. Their involvement, while frequent and often intensive, was regulated by the presidency. They were necessarily included as leaders and representatives of the bureaucracy, and they wielded substantial influence in consequence of their positions. Additional influence and involvement was based on their standing with members of the institutionalized presidency. Both Commissioner Howe and Secretary Gardner were held in high regard and exerted considerable influence on personal rather than positional grounds.

Of equal significance in this analysis of educational policy formulation, were the kinds of participants who were not included. Not surprisingly, in contrast to the direct participation of congressional leaders in policy formulation in 1964 and 1965, there was little involvement during the 90th Congress (1967–1969). Congressional leaders were informed of the content of the legislative program before it was made final, but they were not consulted during its development. The major legislative innovations of the 89th Congress were not repeated in the 90th, although the Administration continued the search for new ideas and attempted to give the appearance of creativity in its legislative proposals by authorizing small programs which could later be expanded. There was no need for early or sustained congressional involvement in what was basically a noninnovating period. Loyal administration spokesmen on Capitol Hill could be relied on to push the ESEA, HEA, and Vocational Education extension bills through along with the eye-catching but minor new programs and, most importantly, to ward off opposition attempts to redirect the basic legislation. Congressional considerations under such conditions would be effectively incorporated during the adoption of legislation. The education establishment groups were accorded access to the formulation stage through their White House contact, Douglass Cater. Noneducation groups, including labor, civil rights, and other black organizations, were conspicuous by their absence during the formulative stage (Wolman & Thomas, 1970).

TABLE 1

Perceptions of Power Distribution in Policy System by Policy Role

Role	*Generally Satisfied*	*Generally Dissat.*	*BOB/W. House Too Powerful*	*Foundations Too Powerful*	*Own Group Requires More Power*
Bureaucrat	2	2	5	1	3
Legislator			1	1	
Leg. Staff	1		3		1
Lobbyist		3	3	3	1
Expert	2	1			
Total	5	6	12	5	5

N = 33

Although priorities were determined and the policy agenda set by a group of central decision-makers operating in the presidency, there were effective limits to the scope of their action. For example, in spite of a strong preference in the presidency for imaginative programs that would change American education, some highly innovative proposals, such as the Educational Opportunity Bank (EOB), were kept off the policy agenda by strong opposition from certain higher education groups and from key members of Congress. The prospect of conflict with some major supporters of the administration's education policies prevented the EOB from receiving serious consideration. Anticipated reaction accorded strategic interests a veto without a fight. Once the Land Grant College Association attacked it publicly, the EOB was a dead letter.

Much of the decision-making regarding the policy agenda did not take place in public, however. Task force reports and, to a large extent agency submissions, were the subject of debate and negotiation inside the presidency. Direct congressional and interest group input was readily available, but generally it was obtained indirectly through brokers. The principal brokers in the education policy system were HEW's legislative liaison officials, Ralph Huitt and Samuel Halperin. Both were highly regarded by the establishment associations and both had the confidence and support of top HEW officials.

In spite of the constraints imposed through anticipated congressional and interest group reactions and indirect external influence exerted through brokers, the formulation stage of the policy process remained under the effective control of the institutionalized presidency. The effectiveness of the presidency in establishing priorities and setting the agenda for action is reflected in the hostility that several respondents expressed to the Bureau of the Budget and the White House staff. Of 33 responses to a question which asked if the major elements involved in making and implementing education policy ought to be more or less powerful, 12 called for a reduction in the power of the Budget Bureau or the White House staff. (See Table 1.) Although these data cannot be regarded as accurate reflections of the participants' perception of the conversion process, they do indicate the presence of extensive dissatisfaction with the perceived balance of power in the system. The Bureau of the Budget was the focus of much of that dissatisfaction. Bureaucrats, legislative staff members, and lobbyists particularly tended to regard it as too powerful. Their complaints were directed toward the Bureau's role in developing legislative proposals and establishing basic policy goals rather than its budgetary function. A recurring theme was the Bureau's lack of expertise in education. Typical of the Bureau's negative image among other policy system members were the comments of a bureaucrat:

> The Budget Bureau strikes me as moving a bit too far into content questions which they aren't competent to carry through. Here and there, because of the frantic pace, many thoughtful program people are at the mercy of the Budget Bureau people who don't know what is in the black book.

A legislator:

> The Budget Bureau is far too powerful. It is much too influential in setting national priorities. More so than any other element in the process. This is especially disturbing since the Budget Bureau people have no special competence or expertise in education. They are generalists who have no knowledge of the real needs and problems.

A legislative staff member:

> The Budget Bureau is exercising too much control. It plays two roles. Before OE and HEW can come up with legislative proposals, the Budget Bureau must approve. I don't know where they get the competence to do it. . . . Secondly, when appropriation requests are being made I have less quarrel.

And, a lobbyist:

> The Bureau of the Budget ought to be de-emphasized. They don't know enough about education. They have a transitory staff and the directors are laymen.

Objections to the foundations and expressions of general discontent were much less explicit.

For a significant portion of the members of the education policy system, then, too much control over policy was lodged in the institutionalized presidency. The problem as they perceived it was not so much that the President, with the help of his supportive staff aides and units defined goals, established priorities, and set the agenda, but that access to that critical stage of formulation was limited and tightly controlled. As the NEA's principal lobbyist, Dr. John Lumley, remarked in discussing the Bureau of the Budget, "It is the one place in the system which is closed to us. Other than trouble getting access to the Budget Bureau, we have our day in court everywhere else." Yet, it was that very lack of open access to congressional, clientele, bureaucratic, and other interests that enabled the Bureau to serve the President so effectively and which led presidents since Roosevelt to rely so heavily on its judgment. The absence of professional experts in the Bureau and on the White House staff was no handicap to a President whose primary goal for federal educational programs was to promote change. Furthermore, the lack of education professionals in the presidency was partially compensated for by the inclusion of Commissioner Howe among the central decision-makers, the ready availability of input from external interests, and the acquired expertise of Bureau of the Budget personnel. Had President Johnson not been so disposed to promote change through Federal programs, the Bureau's influence would probably have been considerably less. Even so, if one notes only casually the visible effects or outcomes of the education policy "innovations" of the Johnson Administration it is apparent that the Bureau's impact was somewhat exaggerated. The education programs of the Administration contributed more to the maintenance of existing educational systems than to the promotion of fundamental changes. Programs with potential for breakthrough change, e.g., ESEA Title III, were brought under control of the establishment by the end of 1967 despite the protests of the presidency, the reports of task forces, and the arguments of intellectuals and experts in universities and foundations.

CONCLUSION

One of the hallmarks of President Johnson's Great Society was a strong commitment to education with a heavy emphasis on innovation. He wanted the federal role in education to produce qualitative improvements and he wished to be remembered as a President who accomplished a great deal for education. Even as budgetary pressures forced a reduction of the ambitious funding levels visualized in the legislation of 1964 and

1965, he maintained the aspirations which underlay his commitment to education.

By the start of the 90th Congress in January, 1967, a new equilibrium involving the presidency, USOE, its clientele groups, and the congressional subcommittee with jurisdiction over its authorizing legislations and its appropriations had been established. The dominance of the presidency in policy formulation in that equilibrium cannot be denied, but it must be noted that the system lacked resources to sustain additional major policy innovations, and it needed time to absorb fully and evaluate the effects of ESEA and the other breakthroughs of the mid-1960's. Therefore, too much significance should not be attached to the Rube Goldbergian process developed in the Johnson Administration to formulate policy. Much of that machinery has since been dismantled. The Johnson educational policies and the programs that implement them, although still in effect, are under attack by the Nixon Administration as it moves to institute the New Federalism, and the task force reports peacefully accumulate dust in the LBJ Library.

However, when and if some future President decides that the time has arrived for a new round of innovations in federal education policy, those reports may have some utility and the Johnson Administration's policy formulation procedures may be of value as a strategy for circumventing, if only temporarily, the federal bureaucracy and its congressional and clientele group supporters.

REFERENCES

Cronin, T. E., The presidency and legislation, *Phi Delta Kappan,* 1968, 49, 295–299.

Gergen, K. J. Assessing the leverage points in the process of policy formation in R. A. Bauer & K. J. Gergen (eds.). *The study of policy formation.* New York: The Free Press, 1968. Pp. 182–203.

Leuchtenberg, W. E. The genesis of the Great Society, *The Reporter,* April 21, 1966, 36–39.

Neustadt, R. E. The presidency and legislation: The growth of central clearance, *American Political Science Review,* 1954, 48, 641–670.

Neustadt, R. E. The presidency and legislation: Planning the president's program, *American Political Science Review,* 1955, 49, 980–1018.

Thomas, N. C. & Wolman, H. L. The presidency and policy formulation: The task force device, *Public Administration Review,* 1969, 29, 459–471.

Wolman, H. L. & Thomas, N. C. Black interests, black groups, and black influence in the federal policy process: The cases of housing and education, *Journal of Politics,* 1970, 32, 875–897.

Yarmolinsky, A. Ideas into programs, *The Public Interest,* 1966, 2, 70–79.

EPILOGUE

Watergate and the Presidency: A Preliminary Assessment

In the year following the second inauguration of Richard Nixon the complexion of American politics was sharply altered as a consequence of the Watergate affair. In a few months the thirty-seventh president of the United States found himself cast from the crest of twin triumphs, a landslide reelection victory and the long-awaited settlement of the Vietnam war, to the depths of suspicion and scandal. A major crisis of confidence in the president and the government had developed that was not resolved until after President Nixon resigned from office on August 9, 1974.

The extent and scope of the crisis were revealed in public opinion polls. According to the Gallup Poll, President Nixon's popularity index (i.e., the percentage of survey respondents who approved his performance) dropped from 68 percent in January, 1973, the highest point recorded since he assumed office, to 24 percent by July, 1974, the lowest point recorded prior to his resignation. A Roper survey conducted in November, 1973, reported that 79 percent of the respondents felt that the president was guilty of one or more of the charges made against him. In a national survey completed on August 6, three days prior to Nixon's resignation, 64 percent of the respondents were reported in favor of impeachment by the House of Representatives, and 55 percent advocated his removal from office. According to the polls, the president's loss of support was greatest among Democrats and the least well-educated, but it was substantial in all groups including Republicans.

It is not my purpose in this essay to recount the tangled chain of events that led to the break-in and bugging of Democratic National Committee Headquarters in late May and again on June 17, 1972, or to recount the subsequent conspiracy to conceal the involvement of members of the White House staff. Those activities have been widely reported in the news media, and several books detailing the affair are in print or in preparation. I assume that my readers either have a working knowledge of the basic facts or that they can readily obtain them.

CAUSES

Time magazine described the Watergate affair as "probably the most pervasive instance of top-level misconduct in the nation's history," and *Newsweek* called it "the most damaging scandal since Teapot Dome." Although the morality of the men running America is a central issue in all political scandals, Watergate differed sharply from past instances of major misconduct in that avarice and personal financial gain were not the primary motivating factors. The illegal activities in the Watergate affair were undertaken in pursuit of political power for its own sake. In spite of the large sums of cash that figured so prominently in the break-in and the subsequent cover-up, none of the principal participants appear to have utilized the numerous opportunities to enrich themselves,[1] or did so only incidentally. The principals were, in the terms of Harold Lasswell and Arnold Rogow, acting as "game" rather than "gain" politicians.[2]

The fact that power rather than venality was the driving force behind Watergate makes the search for probable causes and explanations more difficult. A further complication is added when one takes into account that by the time of the break-in, the President's reelection was

---

[1] John Dean's financing of his honeymoon trip and other personal expenses with $4,800 of "borrowed" campaign funds under his control is a possible exception. Dean claimed he did not hide his use of the money and that he had resources to repay it. The dubious financial dealings of Florida banker Charles "Bebe" Rebozo, President Nixon's closest personal friend, undoubtedly helped to turn public opinion against the former president, but they did not directly enter in the House Judiciary Committee's adoption of three articles of impeachment. Rebozo used campaign funds to purchase gifts for members of the Nixon family.

[2] Arnold A. Rogow and Harold D. Lasswell, *Power, Corruption, and Rectitude* (Englewood Cliffs, N.J.: Prentice-Hall, 1963).

virtually a certainty. Why, then, was it necessary? What could have led to the clumsy and devious conspiracy to prevent a full investigation and disclosure following the arrests? How could a skilled campaigner and politician like President Nixon allow himself to become tainted by such nefarious activity undertaken on his behalf?

Analysts will undoubtedly be offering and rejecting answers to these questions and others for a long time to come. At this point, the various explanations put forward are highly tentative. They tend to focus on President Nixon's personality and goals, on the nature of the modern presidency, and on the prevailing atmosphere in the White House and in national politics. Most explanations combine more than one of these elements and some conflict with others. Among the major causes suggested are the isolation of the president in the presidency and his dependency on a staff of loyal zealots who were also political amateurs, presidential detachment from partisan politics in order to pursue national security policy objectives, a conviction concerning the rectitude of presidential policy goals and an amoral willingness to use any available means to achieve those goals, an atmosphere of hostility toward and suspicion of political opponents, and a constitutional imbalance in favor of the presidency that was strengthened by a contempt for Congress and the democratic process on the part of the president and his staff. Although the precise pattern of causation cannot be established, evidence is available to support all of these hypothesized causes of the Watergate affair.

Since the Eisenhower administration, presidential isolation has been regarded as a serious consequence of the development of the institutionalized presidency. Some of President Eisenhower's most difficult and embarrassing moments (e.g., the Dixon-Yates affair) occurred in part because he established a staffing pattern in the White House that restricted access and limited the flow of information to him. President Nixon, a man with a strong preference for working alone, isolated himself more than any recent occupant of the presidency by limiting contacts with cabinet members, congressional leaders, party leaders, and the press by physically absenting himself from Washington much of the time in his retreats at Camp David, Key Biscayne, and San Clemente. This self-imposed isolation made him dangerously dependent on the judgment of key aides such as H. R. Haldeman and John Ehrlichman. The loyalty of Haldeman and Ehrlichman and their assistants, and the president's dependence on them, were widely noted in analyses of his first term. Whether they were zealots and political amateurs is a matter of opinion. It is quite clear, however, that their conduct in the Watergate affair did not serve the president's interests. But presidential isolation and overdependence on subordinates does not by itself explain Watergate, nor does it afford a viable excuse for it.

Closely related to the phenomenon of isolation and a partial cause of it was President Nixon's deliberate detachment from partisan politics in order to devote his energy to the national security policy goals of peace in Vietnam and détente with China and the Soviet Union. This preoccupation with foreign affairs left little time for the reelection campaign or for domestic policy matters. Consequently, the reelection effort was placed in the hands of a special organization headed by the president's closest political adviser, former Attorney General John N. Mitchell. Domestic policy matters were the province of John Ehrlichman, chairman of the Domestic Council. H. R. Haldeman acted as the president's chief of staff and controlled access to him. These delegations of responsibility placed the president in a highly vulnerable position.

In the eyes of the president's aides and associates, the reelection of President Nixon would insure the continuity of his foreign policy and provide the basis for new domestic policy initiatives as well as protect the nation from the "radic-lib" forces that were behind the McGovern candidacy. The larger the margin of victory and the more complete the defeat of the opposition, the better off the nation and the president would be. Because their ends were so manifestly noble (in their view), they willingly used any means that seemed appropriate to obtain them, however ignoble those means might have been. Furthermore, they apparently believed they had presidential authorization for their goals. This explanation is perhaps best illustrated in the testimony of Jeb Stuart Magruder, deputy director of the Committee to Reelect the President, before the Ervin committee. When asked by Senator Howard Baker (R–Tennessee) whether in the days immediately after the June 17 break-in he or any of his associates had ever considered telling the truth, Magruder replied that their only thought was to cover-up any traces of White House involvement. They feared, Magruder stated, that honesty might lead to the president's defeat.

Closely related to the philosophy of ruthless pragmatism that prevailed throughout the president's political entourage was an atmosphere of suspicion and hostility toward all opponents and critics. This paranoia was reflected in attacks on the news media, in the formation of the "plumbers" group, and in the "political enemies" list. In such a climate, the employment for domestic political purposes of the techniques of espionage and intelligence developed in the area of national security policy under the pressures of the cold war was a natural development. The president, being an old "cold warrior" with a long history of antagonism toward the press and having a somewhat reclusive and suspicious personality, encouraged the development of an atmosphere in which the break-in and the cover-up were perfectly normal events. The testimony of several witnesses before the Ervin committee, particularly that of John Dean, indicated the presence of a pattern of surreptitious domestic political activity born of fear, suspicion, and arrogance.

Finally, it is argued that Watergate was made possible by a dangerous constitutional imbalance in which power had become increasingly concentrated in the presidency. Although this imbalance had been developing since the administration of Franklin Roosevelt, it had been restrained by the political pragmatism of succeeding presidents and their staffs and by a healthy respect for the constitutional separation of powers. Under President Nixon, these restraints were largely "inoperative." According to this explanation, the president and his advisers regarded Congress with hostility and contempt and the courts as malleable instruments for the pursuit of political objectives. The systematic transfer of power to the presidency from the executive departments and agencies, the extensive use of the impoundment of funds to circumvent congressional intent, and the assertion of a sweeping doctrine of executive privilege all provide evidence of such an imbalance. It is charged that the imbalance led the president and his key advisers to place themselves above the law. Although the imbalance did not cause the Watergate affair, it provided the institutional environment—the imperial presidency and the accompanying commitment to the supremacy of presidential power—within which it occurred.

These explanations place much of the blame for Watergate on President Nixon. According to them, he is held accountable for having failed to establish and maintain standards of conduct—including respect for the law and a high regard for the truth—for members of his staff and the reelection committee. He is charged further with having had an operational commitment to expediency rather than to principle in major matters of policy and politics. Having established such an atmosphere in his administration, he made Watergate possible.

The political climate of the nation, however, is primarily not the president's responsibility. This too may have facilitated the occurrence of Watergate. The seeming acceptance by the public during the 1972 campaign of the use of extralegal methods and the widespread belief that such practices pervade the political system undoubtedly contributed to their employment. The cold war and the domestic political tensions wrought by strife over Vietnam also contributed to the general political climate. The cold war helped make the public and its leaders less sensitive to considerations of due process of law. As a result, tactics that were developed to deal with enemies of the nation could be turned on domestic political opponents without seriously offending public sensibilities. The controversy over Vietnam polarized Americans more than any event since the Civil War. In these circumstances, there were large numbers of threatening political opponents, such as Daniel Ellsberg, against whom the techniques of intelligence and espionage could be applied.

Another contributing factor lodged in explanations of the Watergate affair is that of the strong presidency itself. The growth of the presidential institution and presidential powers is a long-run secular phenomenon that cannot be laid at President Nixon's doorstep. However, it proceeded much further under his stewardship than ever before. More claims were advanced on behalf of the presidency and its powers under President Nixon than in any previous peacetime administration. The centralization of authority over the operations of the bureaucracy was more complete than in the past, and conflict between Congress and the presidency intensified. And the establishment of a substantial domestic political intelligence and espionage operation (i.e., the plumbers unit), the attempted use of the FBI and the CIA in White House political activity, and the political enemies project provide evidence of new and frightening uses that could be made of the presidency.

CONSEQUENCES

An early consequence of Watergate was its impact on President Nixon's ability to assert policy leadership. He began his second term with a series of initiatives in domestic policy that appeared designed to produce changes as revolutionary as those he implemented in foreign policy during his first four years in office. He set out to decentralize the administration of federal domestic policy by replacing the categorical grant-in-aid programs that had been the cornerstone of federal activity since the New Deal with special revenue-sharing legislation. Under Nixon's New Federalism, agencies of the federal government were to become in the main conduits for the transfer of funds to state and local governments. Determination of the specific purposes of domestic policy within broad areas (e.g., health, education, housing, welfare, etc.) of federal expenditure was to be made primarily at state and local levels. No longer would the national government undertake to deal directly with problems that the states and cities were unable or unwilling to confront. The shift from national to state and local establishment of spending priorities was justified as an appropriate response to the 1972 election mandate that the president interpreted as being strongly opposed to big, centralized government and to new federal spending programs.

The Nixon administration's conservative counterrevolution in domestic policy was partially dependent on congressional approval of the special revenue-sharing bills, but by March, 1973, it had been sent off to a flying start through a series of executive and administrative actions. An acting director was well on the way to dismantling the Office of Economic Opportunity without congressional authorization and was prevented from completing his task only by a ruling of the U.S. Circuit Court of Appeals that the administration did not contest. Impoundments of funds were directed at major programs such as water pollution control and threatened in a number of other areas. Much of the subsidized housing and urban renewal activity of the Department of Housing and Urban Development was suspended by an executive order. The resignations of several cabinet and subcabinet officials were accepted, in part because their loyalty to the administration was in question. Presidential control over the bureaucracy was to be strengthened by the establishment of "supercabinet" positions. The secretaries of agriculture, health, education and welfare, and the treasury received concurrent appointments as presidential counselors and were given responsibility for coordinating policies across several departments and agencies for the areas of natural resources, human resources, and economic affairs. This attempt to tighten presidential control of policy implementation was abandoned after the Watergate scandal broke.

The Nixon administration's domestic policy counterrevolution suffered a sharp setback with the explosion of the Watergate affair. Congressional opposition to impoundment was reflected in anti-impoundment provisions in authorization and appropriation bills; legislation to implement special revenue sharing was never reported from committee in either house of Congress; several grant-in-aid programs marked for extinction acquired renewed vigor; and attempts to further centralize control over the federal bureaucracy were abandoned or postponed. Instead of aggressively pushing substantive and procedural innovations in domestic policy areas, the Nixon administration was forced to assume a defensive posture against increasing congressional opposition. The impact of Watergate on the president's foreign policy leadership was much less apparent. However, commentators have argued that he was weakened in dealings with the USSR in seeking détente in the form of mutual arms limitation and expanded trade, with China in attempting to bring about stability in Southeast Asia, and with Western Europe in meeting the energy crisis and stabilizing international trade and finance. His critics challenged his handling of the Arab-Israeli war in October, 1973, as being motivated by an attempt to divert public attention from his Watergate problems. Finally, some observers believed that the Cyprus crisis of July, 1974, occurred because first Greece and then Turkey were emboldened by a weakened American administration preoccupied with the president's troubles.

Further consequences of Watergate include the attention it focused on the quality and character of the presidential staff, on the president's employment of his staff, and on the accessibility of the president within the presidency. It also raised doubts about the integrity of the institution. Revelations of the existence of a domestic political intelligence unit within the presidency, the involvement of the CIA and the FBI in White House political activity, the attempt to shift the blame for Watergate to the CIA, plans and threats to use the Internal Revenue Service to increase the president's political muscle, and the presence of a conspiracy at the highest levels of the presidency—all of these have called the "imperial presidency" into question. The fact that these things occurred reveals that the presidency can be used for malign as well as benign purposes. Hopefully the public and its leaders henceforth will tend to regard the presidency with less awe, more suspicion, and more concern for the ends to which it is being directed. In turn, this should impose higher standards of conduct on the president and his entourage, make it more difficult for him to acquire additional power and resources for the presidency, and limit his ability to conceal the operations of the presidency under a cloak of secrecy.

The presence of clandestine illegal or ethically questionable activities within the presidency has resulted in charges of constitutional imbalance and demands for corrective measures. Efforts of President Nixon and his aides to justify these activities on the basis of national security and to claim executive privilege when threatened with exposure have been withstood. The prospect of an American police state developing under the aegis of the presidency has caused liberals as well as conservatives to question the seemingly inexorable twentieth-century trend toward increased presidential power. Thus, the dogmatic belief of the liberal establishment in a strong presidency has suffered a serious blow. A more realistic awareness of the potential uses of the presidency could be a healthy aftermath of Watergate. Indeed, President Ford's conduct during his first weeks in office was characterized by repeated expressions of his commitment to an open presidency, intentions of easy accessibility to members of Congress and the press, express disavowal of the tactics of electronic espionage, a reorganization of the presidency that reduced sharply the president's dependence on a few key advisers, and a pledge to full cooperation with Congress in making public policy.

Although the legitimacy crisis centering on the presidency that resulted from Watergate has abated, it could recur unless its causes are clearly recognized and understood. The imperial presidency is a phenomenon that has been developing for some time and has multiple origins in previous administrations. The aggrandizement of the presidency and the belief in the benign character of presidential power go back to Wilson and the two Roosevelts. In the last three decades, cold war pressures and fears led to extensive secret operations and the use of a wide range of ethically questionable tactics on the part of the presidency. This extended pursuit of national security by dubious means laid the basis for development of an ends-justifies-the-means attitude in domestic politics. The traumatic polarizations of the 1960s arising from the antiwar movement and the increased militancy of disadvantaged minorities provided multiple targets toward which intelligence and espionage activities were directed. Polarization also increased the alienation of a sizable number of citizens who were convinced that the political process was responsive only to the corporate elites who constituted the establishment. In this context, the events surrounding Watergate and the exposure of clandestine domestic political activities within the presidency have heightened the crisis of confidence in the political process.

Hopefully, the much closer scrutiny of the presidency and the president's behavior in office resulting from Watergate will bring about an end, at least for the time being, of the long period of expansion of presidential power and growth of the presidential office, and a redress of the constitutional balance between the three branches of the national government will be effected. If nothing else impeachment has been revived as a viable constitutional device. Nevertheless, it is not yet possible to predict how far the balance will swing away from the presidency, nor is it apparent how Congress will react to the opportunity to reassert itself or how long the partial eclipse of the presidency will last.

A note of caution is in order at this point. Any worthwhile post-Nixon reform of the presidency must be undertaken with full awareness that the combination of constitutional requirements and the exigencies of life in a complex industrial society leave the nation highly dependent on viable presidential leadership. The redressing of the balance between the presidency and Congress must occur within the framework of the Constitution. It would be easy to impose constraints on the presidency that would seriously tip the balance too far in the congressional direction and leave the nation dangerously ill-equipped to cope with unforeseen future problems. The task of reforming the presidency is a delicate one that must, above all, find means of strengthening wisdom and virtue in the conduct of the office.

More careful scrutiny of the internal operations of the presidency and greater skepticism concerning requests for additional presidential powers are long overdue and are a probable positive consequence of Watergate. It is not at all clear, however, whether Congress will utilize the opportunity to exert more forceful and positive policy leadership. Nor can we predict how long increased congressional surveillance of the presidency will last. There is a real challenge to Congress in the Watergate aftermath to reassert its authority vis-à-vis the president. If it should fail to do so, then governmental stalemate and stagnation, or a reassertion of presidential power, are probable long-term alternatives. Claims that the exposure of Watergate and the resignation of President Nixon have demonstrated the viability of the constitutional system may be valid, but they have yet to be substantiated over time. Such a result may be one that will have to be judged in the long run by future historians.

The possibility that the full exposure of Watergate will have arrested a dangerous reactionary, if not fascistic, trend in America is of more immediate importance. The value of a free press and an independent judiciary to the maintenance of individual liberty and the preservation of integrity in public life has been demonstrated more clearly than ever before. At the same time, the disclosures should increase awareness of the potential to curb freedom that is inherent in all governments. If Watergate has prevented the development of an American police state, it will have been well worth its costs. Of course, the vigilance it has sparked will have to be maintained lest future abuses of power occur.

Finally, as expected, more stringent campaign finance legislation has been enacted as a result of Watergate. If a thoroughgoing reform of campaign financing and the conduct of campaigns for federal office ensues, the nation will benefit. There is a real danger, however, that enthusiasm for reform will wane once the shock of Watergate and the resignation of a president have subsided. Some improvements are almost certain to occur, but their extent may be limited by congressional inertia and compromise.

This analysis of the Watergate affair is highly tentative, speculative, and incomplete. The totality of its political effects is only beginning to become apparent. What is clear is that the nation has experienced the worst scandal in the history of American politics, that the Constitution has survived its most serious challenge since the Civil War, and that Watergate will affect the future of the presidency and the course of American political life for some time to come.

POSTSCRIPT: THE PRESIDENTIAL PARDON

It is a mark of the unexpected nature and high drama that have characterized Watergate that I find it necessary to append a postscript to an epilogue devoted to the subject. When President Nixon resigned on August 9, 1974, and for the month thereafter, it seemed as if closure could finally be written on that momentous affair. The new president promised an open administration the hallmark of which would be candor, and he stated that the ethical standard for the administration would be set by his own example. He suggested to a Watergate-weary public that it turn its attention to neglected substantive problems, primarily inflation. With an almost audible sigh of relief the nation did so.

In August the euphoric atmosphere of a presidential-congressional honeymoon pervaded Washington. President Ford met with members of the congressional Black Caucus who found him receptive to their concerns, if not in sympathy with their policy prescriptions. Pundits spoke of Ford as a "Republican Truman," and his fellow partisans looked forward to the congressional elections in November with more optimism than they had felt since the scandal first broke in April, 1973. In his first presidential popularity poll, Ford scored a strong 71 percent approval rating (3 points higher than his predecessor's best showing) with only 3 percent expressing disapproval.

The only cloud that darkened the pleasant skies of Ford's first month in office was the unanswered question of what, if anything, would be done about the former president. Ford set minds at rest when in late August at his first formal press conference he told reporters that while he reserved the option of exercising his power to pardon, he would deal with the matter in due course after the special prosecutor and the courts had acted.

Ford's honeymoon with Congress and the nation came to an abrupt end on Sunday, September 8. He announced to television cameras and a handful of newsmen that he was granting former president Nixon a full and unconditional pardon for all offenses that he had "committed or may have committed or taken part in" during his term of office. In accepting the pardon, Mr. Nixon issued a statement acknowledging "mistakes" and "errors in judgment," but admitting no guilt.

The response to Ford's action was, with the exception of that of Republican stalwarts, overwhelmingly negative and highly critical. Among other things, Ford's critics charged him with abusing his powers, with subverting the integrity of the judicial process by establishing a dual standard of justice, and with having been a party to a deal that continued the cover-up of Watergate. Ford gave as the major reasons for his action a desire to put Watergate behind the nation without the agony of a protracted trial of Mr. Nixon and a deep feeling of compassion for the former president and his family. Ford insisted at his next news conference that no deals had been struck and that he was moved only by a strong desire to make a clean break with Watergate and the issue of Nixon's complicity in it.

At this writing there appears to be a strong conviction that President Ford acted precipitously and without adequate advice, consultation, or consideration of the consequences. His critics have tended more to fault his timing, his judgment, and the limited study given to the action than the pardon itself. Many critics expected that Nixon eventually would be pardoned.

Regardless of their positions on the pardon, the timing, or the manner in which the decision was reached, most Washington observers and politicians agreed that Ford had damaged his credibility and expended a substantial portion of his political capital by his action. A Gallup poll taken shortly after the pardon revealed a sharp 22 percent drop in the public's approval of his performance (to 49 percent). Democrats again looked forward to an election campaign in which Watergate and Mr. Nixon were the principal issues. President Ford and his staff found themselves on the defensive in Congress and in much of the press.

The full story of the pardon remains to be told to the satisfaction of this writer, and I will not attempt to review the available information here. It does seem, however, that some of the themes and ideas expressed in the selections and my prior comments in this book offer a basis for placing the pardon in perspective.

It is important to bear in mind furthermore that the transition from the Nixon to the Ford administration occurred in a few days' time, whereas a normal presidential transition takes two and one-half months. This meant that at the time of the pardon, Ford was still operating with a staff largely selected by Nixon and according to procedures designed to accommodate his predecessor. He had not had the opportunity to shape and staff the presidency to suit his needs and style. The few staff aides whom he brought to the White House with him were longtime personal or political associates unaccustomed to the pressures of presidential politics or to thinking in terms of the full, macro-level impact of presidential decisions. Abrupt changes of administration cannot be avoided, but they carry with them a high risk of flawed judgment and erroneous decisions. Even normal transitions are not immune to serious mistakes, as the Bay of Pigs fiasco demonstrated in 1961. It will become apparent only over time whether the reaction to the pardon will lead to shakedown in the White House staff and in presidential decision-making procedures that produce a presidency more suited to Ford's particular abilities and talents.

Ford's pardon of the former president also stopped or at least slowed the process of "regalization" that was in full swing by the end of his first month in office. The pardon action made it apparent to both his supporters and his opponents that he was not a miracle worker, but rather a fundamentally conservative, midwestern congressman who had rather suddenly found himself in the White House through circumstances largely not of his own design or execution. The pardon served to scale down to more realistic levels the lofty expectations generated for Ford in his first month in office. It also placed Congress on notice that the problem of constitutional imbalance and the need for more forceful and aggressive congressional leadership had not passed with Mr. Nixon's departure.

Finally, some found in Ford's action evidence that he was not afraid to make a difficult decision and stick with it. Some commentators had expressed concern that Ford's geniality would lead him to avoid hard choices and to seek refuge in equivocation and inaction.

Whether one opposes or supports the pardon, it marked a turning point in the new Ford administration and it affected the subsequent course of the Watergate affair. Former President Nixon was not subject to indictment for any actions taken during his tenure in office. This fact overshadowed the trial of his former top aides, H. R. Haldeman and John D. Erlichman, his closest political adviser, former Attorney General John N. Mitchell, and two lesser figures, attorneys Robert C. Mardian and Kenneth

W. Parkinson, in the Fall of 1974 on charges stemming from their involvement in the break-in and/or cover-up. (In their defense, some of Nixon's former associates advanced the argument that they were acting under his orders.)

Judge John J. Sirica, in charging the jury, pointed out that as a matter of law the pardon had no effect on the responsibility of the defendants for any crimes they committed. On January 1, 1975, the jury found the three principal defendants guilty of conspiracy, obstruction of justice, and perjury. (Mardian was convicted of conspiracy and Parkinson was acquitted).

The trial was significant because the bulk of the government's evidence, the now-famous tapes of Mr. Nixon's Oval Office conversations with several of the Watergate principals, clearly established his complicity. They revealed more fully than previous information, the extent to which the former president and his chief aides had attempted to subvert the democratic process. Notwithstanding the results of any appeals (on grounds primarily of the nonappearance of Mr. Nixon as a defense witness by reason of physical disability), the trial served to reaffirm the principle of the rule of law and its corollary that individual officials, however highly placed, are responsible for their actions.

As a final footnote, a week following the convictions of Haldeman, Erlichman, and Mitchell, Judge Sirica reduced the prison sentences of three other major Watergate figures, John Dean, Jeb Stuart Magruder, and Herbert Kalmbach to time already served. Each had pleaded guilty to single charges and had cooperated with the Ervin committee and the special prosecutor. Their release from confinement, closely coupled with the conviction of their former associates, reemphasized the enormity of the Watergate crimes and the fact that the individual primarily responsible, former President Nixon, would never be called to account. The sense of displeasure and injustice born of these phenomena cast a heavy shadow on the presidency of Gerald Ford as he confronted such problems as the nation's most serious economic crisis since the 1930's, the possibility of renewed warfare in the Middle East, world financial upheavals, resulting from the pricing policies of the oil producers' cartel, and declining public trust in government and in his leadership performance.

Selected Bibliography

PART ONE. THE CONSTITUTIONAL CONTEXT

The reader who wishes to explore the general literature on the presidency will find a rich body of works available for consideration. The traditional legal approach explores the historical development of the presidential office and its powers through constitutional interpretation, statutory enactment, and presidential practice. It is best exemplified in the late Edward S. Corwin, *The President: Office and Powers,* 4th ed. (1957); Joseph P. Kallenbach, *The American Chief Executive* (1966); and Louis Fisher, *President and Congress* (1972). A useful collection of documents and commentary that reflects this approach is Robert S. Hirschfield, ed., *The Power of the Presidency* (1968). The early development of the presidency is brilliantly depicted in James S. Young, *The Washington Community 1800–1828* (1966).

The most comprehensive textual treatment is Louis Koenig, *The Chief Executive,* revised ed. (1968). Somewhat dated but still popular is the late Clinton Rossiter's *The American Presidency,* revised ed. (1960). More recent short texts include Grant McConnell, *The Modern Presidency* (1967); Dorothy Buckton James, *The Contemporary Presidency* (1969); Dale Vineyard, *The Presidency* (1971); and Philippa Strum, *Presidential Power and American Democracy* (1972). A valuable comprehensive general anthology is Aaron Wildavsky, ed., *The Presidency* (1968). Two major and widely cited analytical discussions are Richard E. Neustadt, *Presidential Power* (1960); and James M. Burns, *Presidential Government* (1965). An orthodox and somewhat romantic but highly useful recent analysis is Emmet John Hughes, *The Living Presidency* (1973).

PART TWO. THE POLITICAL CONTEXT

A voluminous body of literature surrounds the many aspects of presidential politics. An excellent overview and a good guide to the literature is Nelson W. Polsby and Aaron B. Wildavsky, *Presidential Elections,* 3rd ed. (1972).

Voting in presidential elections has been the subject of systematic analysis by many scholars. Among the most useful and informative works are *The American Voter* (1960) and *Elections and the Political Order* (1966) by Angus Campbell, Philip E. Converse, Warren E. Miller, and Donald E. Stokes. Somewhat different treatments are accorded the subject by Walter Dean Burnham in *Critical Elections and the Mainsprings of American Politics* (1970) and by the late V. O. Key, Jr., in *The Responsible Electorate* (1966).

Presidential nominations and campaigns also attract wide attention. The key reference works are Gerald Pomper, *Nominating the President,* 2nd ed. (1966); James W. Davis, *Presidential Primaries* (1967); and James David Barber, ed., *Choosing the President* (1974). Presidential campaigns have been chronicled in a multitude of books, among the most popular of which are Theodore H. White's accounts of the 1960, 1964, 1968, and 1972 election contests entitled *The Making of the President.* An informative but somewhat cynical view of Richard Nixon's 1968 campaign is Joe McGinnis, *The Selling of the President* (1969). The formal process for electing the president, the electoral college, is analyzed in Neal Pearce, *The People's President* (1968).

Some clues to the shape of presidential politics in the future may be gleaned from the writings of analysts who venture into the misty realm of speculation and prediction. Among the more recent efforts of this type are Kevin Phillips, *The Emerging Republican Majority* (1969); Richard Scammon and Ben Wattenberg, *The Real Majority* (1970); and Samuel Lubell, *The Hidden Crisis in American Politics* (1970) and *The Future While It Happened* (1973).

The president's relationship with public opinion is examined in Elmer E. Cornwell, Jr., *Presidential Leadership of Public Opinion* (1965), and John E. Mueller, *War, Presidents, and Public Opinion* (1972). The press and the president have not attracted much recent attention except for the Twentieth Century Fund study *Presidential Television* (1973) by Newton N. Minow, John B. Martin, and Lee M. Mitchell.

PART THREE. THE GOVERNMENTAL CONTEXT

There are a number of perspectives from which to approach the dynamics of the workings of the presidency. The means through which the president receives advice and information are a vital aspect of the presidency. Among the most notable books in this area are Thomas E. Cronin, *The State of the Presidency* (1975); Cronin's anthology edited with Sanford Greenberg, *The Presidential Advisory System* (1969); and Richard E. Fenno, *The President's Cabinet* (1958), which remains the definitive treatment of the subject. The development and operation of a major presidential advisory body are analyzed in Edward S. Flash, Jr., *Economic Advice and Presidential Leadership: The Council of Economic Advisers* (1965). The White House staff receives consideration in Louis Koenig, *The Invisible Presidency* (1960), and in Patrick Anderson, *The President's Men* (1968). Harold Seidman provides a comprehensive overview of the president's role in the federal executive branch in *Politics, Position and Power* (1970).

Presidential relations with Congress receive consideration in Nelson Polsby, *Congress and the Presidency,* 2nd ed. (1971), and Abraham Holtzman, *Legislative Liaison: Executive Leadership in Congress* (1970). Studies of presidential leadership were pioneered in Pendleton Herring, *Presidential Leadership* (1940). The most recent major study of presidential leadership behavior is James David Barber, *Presidential Character* (1972). Other useful studies include Thomas A. Bailey, *Presidential Greatness* (1966), and Erwin C. Hargrove, *Presidential Leadership: Personality and Political Style* (1966).

The memoirs of former White House staff members are a revealing source of information on the workings of the presidency. Insights into the Kennedy administration can be found in Theodore Sorensen, *Decision-Making in the White House* (1963) and *Kennedy* (1965), and in Arthur Schlesinger, Jr., *A Thousand Days* (1965). McGeorge Bundy's *The Strength of Government* (1968) contains reflections and observations based on service that spanned the Kennedy and Johnson administrations. Former press secretaries provide the most intimate views of the Johnson presidency, especially George Reedy, *The Twilight of the Presidency* (1970) and *The Presidency in Flux* (1973), and George Christian, *The President Steps Down* (1970). Daniel P. Moynihan's *The Politics of a Guaranteed National Income* (1972) is perhaps the best portrayal of the Nixon administration's internal operations.

Washington-based journalists are particularly skilled at describing and interpreting the actions of presidents during or shortly after their terms of office. The most notable works of this variety include Henry Fairlie, *The Kennedy Promise: The Politics of Expectation* (1972); Hugh Sidey, *John F. Kennedy, President* (1963); Rowland Evans and Robert Novak, *Lyndon B. Johnson: The Exercise of Power* (1966) and *Nixon in the White House: The Frustration of Power* (1971); Tom Wicker, *JFK and LBJ: The Influence of Personality upon Politics* (1968); and Gary Wills, *Nixon Agonistes* (1970).

PART FOUR. THE POLICY CONTEXT

The president's role in making national security policy has been the focus of careful scholarly attention in recent years. The major general treatments include Sidney Warren, *The President as World Leader* (1965); Roger Hilsman, *To Move a Nation* (1967) and *The Politics of Policy-Making in Defense and Foreign Affairs* (1971); Keith Clark and Lawrence Legere, eds., *The President and the Management of National Security* (1968); and I.M. Destler, *Presidents, Bureaucrats and Foreign Policy: The Politics of Organizational Reform* (1972).

Case studies of major national security policy decisions written from a theoretical standpoint provide valuable insights and alternative analytical frameworks. Most important are Graham T. Allison, *The Essence of Decision* (1971), and Richard E. Neustadt, *Alliance Politics* (1970). A participant's view of the Cuban missile crisis is the late Robert F. Kennedy's *Thirteen Days* (1969).

The Vietnam war has been the occasion for some sharp criticism of national security policy making. Among the more notable books are Townsend

Hoopes, *The Limits of Intervention* (1969); David Halberstam, *The Best and the Brightest* (1972); and Daniel Ellsberg, *Papers on the War* (1972). The same conflict also has brought forth demands to curtail presidential war-making powers as reflected in Jacob K. Javits, *Who Makes War: The President Versus Congress* (1973), and Arthur M. Schlesinger, Jr., *The Imperial Presidency* (1973).

Presidential leadership and participation in domestic policy areas also receive scholarly attention, but they are not so widely noted by the attentive public. Among the most informative works are Daniel P. Moynihan, *Maximum Feasible Misunderstanding* (1969) and *The Politics of a Guaranteed Income* (1972); James L. Sundquist, *Politics and Policy: The Eisenhower, Kennedy, and Johnson Years* (1968); and Harold L. Wolman, *The Politics of Federal Housing* (1971).

The flow of materials on Watergate is increasing and threatens to become a flood. The principal publications to date include Bob Woodward and Carl Bernstein, *All the President's Men* (1974); Congressional Quarterly Service, *Watergate: Chronology of a Crisis,* Vol. 1 (1973) and Vol. II (1974); the *New York Times* staff, *The Watergate Hearings: Break-in and Cover-up* (1973); and David C. Saffell, ed., *Watergate: Its Effects on the American Political System* (1974). Two works related to Watergate issues but not dealing directly with it are Raoul Berger, *Impeachment: The Constitutional Problems* (1973), and David Wise, *The Politics of Lying* (1973).

The presidency and the actions of the president are frequently the subject of articles and essays in periodicals and scholarly journals. The reader intent on following the subject closely should keep abreast of the *Washington Monthly, Commentary, Atlantic,* and the *New York Times Magazine.* Journals which upon occasion contain analytical discussions include *The Public Administration Review, The American Political Science Review, Foreign Affairs,* and *Foreign Policy.*

The United States Government Printing Office publishes a *Weekly Compilation of Presidential Documents,* and the National Archives publishes an annual volume entitled the *Public Papers of the President.* Executive orders and regulations of administrative agencies are published five times weekly in the *Federal Register* by the National Archives and Record Service. All government publications are listed in the *Monthly Catalog of Government Publications.*

This collection of materials on the presidency (all selections first published since 1969) represents a turning away from the concept of the strong presidency that dominated the political science thinking of the last decade. The emphasis is behavioral and scientific with close examination of presidential power and leadership. The editor contributes substantial and well-written introductions.

Norman Thomas (Ph.D., Princeton University) has taught at the University of Michigan and at Duke University. He is presently Professor and Head of the Political Science Department at the University of Cincinnati.

DODD, MEAD & COMPANY, INC.
79 Madison Avenue
New York, New York 10016